BORDER AS METHOD, OR, THE MULTIPLICATION OF LABOR

SOCIAL TEXT BOOKS

———

Edited for the collective by
Brent Edwards, Randy Martin,
Andrew Ross, and Ella Shohat

BORDER
AS METHOD,

OR, THE
MULTIPLICATION
OF LABOR

SANDRO MEZZADRA
AND BRETT NEILSON

Duke University Press
Durham and London
2013

© 2013 Duke University Press

All rights reserved

Printed in the United States of America on acid-free paper ∞

Designed by Heather Hensley

Typeset in Warnock Pro by Keystone

Library of Congress Cataloging-in-Publication Data

Mezzadra, Sandro.

Border as method, or, the multiplication of labor /
Sandro Mezzadra and Brett Neilson.

p. cm. — (Social text books)

Includes bibliographical references and index.

ISBN 978-0-8223-5487-1 (cloth : alk. paper)

ISBN 978-0-8223-5503-8 (pbk. : alk. paper)

1. Boundaries. 2. Borderlands. I. Neilson, Brett. II. Title.

JC323.M49 2013

320.1'2—dc23   2013010105

CONTENTS

Fog and dirt, violence and magic have surrounded the tracing and institution of borders since late antiquity. Sources from around the world tell us wonderful and frightening stories about the tracing of demarcation lines between the sacred and the profane, good and evil, private and public, inside and outside. From the liminal experiences of ritual societies to the delimitation of land as private property, from the fratricide of Remus by Romulus at the mythological foundation of Rome to the expansion of the imperial *limes*, these stories speak of the *productive* power of the border—of the strategic role it plays in the fabrication of the world. They also convey, in a glimpse, an idea of the deep heterogeneity of the semantic field of the border, of its complex symbolic and material implications. The modern cartographical representation and institutional arrangement of the border as a line—first in Europe and then globalized through the whirlwind of colonialism, imperialism, and anticolonial struggles—has somehow obscured this complexity and led us to consider the border as literally marginal. Today, we are witnessing a deep change in this regard. As many scholars have noted, the border has inscribed itself at the center of contemporary experience. We are confronted not only with a multiplication of different types of borders but also with the reemergence of the deep heterogeneity of the semantic field of the border. Symbolic, linguistic, cultural, and urban boundaries are no longer articulated in fixed ways by the geopolitical border. Rather, they overlap, connect, and disconnect in often unpredictable ways, contributing to shaping new forms of domination and exploitation.

Violence undeniably shapes lives and relations that are played out on and across borders worldwide. Think of the often unreported deaths of migrants challenging borders in the deserts between Mexico and the United States or in the choppy waters of the Mediterranean Sea. New and old forms of war continue to target vast borderlands. Think of Waziristan, Kashmir, Palestine. This book was born out of indignation and struggles, particularly migrants' struggles, against such violence and war at the border. As our research and writing proceeded, we also learned (once again, particularly from migrants) to valorize the capacities, skills, and experiences of border crossing, of organizing life across borders. Literal and metaphorical practices of translation have come to be more associated in our minds with the proliferation of borders and border struggles in the contemporary world. Although this proliferation of borders, as we have stressed, is deeply implicated in the operation of old and new devices of dispossession and exploitation, we contend that it is precisely from this point of view that struggles revolving around borders and practices of translation crisscrossing them can play a key role in fostering the debate on the politics of the common. This book can be partially read as a contribution to this debate, in which we see some of the most promising conditions for the reinvention of a project of liberation in the global present.

In the past few years, we have become increasingly uncomfortable with the fixation in many critical border studies as well as activist circles on the image of the wall. This does not mean we do not recognize the importance of the worldwide spread of walls just a few decades after the celebration of the fall of the Berlin wall. But independent of the fact that many walls are far less rigid than they pretend to be, taking the wall as the paradigmatic icon of contemporary borders leads to a unilateral focus on the border's capacity to exclude. This can paradoxically reinforce the spectacle of the border, which is to say the ritualized display of violence and expulsion that characterizes many border interventions. The image of the wall can also entrench the idea of a clear-cut division between the inside and the outside as well as the desire for a perfect integration of the inside. As we show in this book, taking the border not only as a research "object" but also as an "epistemic" angle (this is basically what we mean by "border as method") provides productive insights on the tensions and conflicts that blur the line between inclusion and exclusion, as well as on the profoundly changing code of social inclusion in the present. At the same time, when we speak of the importance of border crossing, we are aware that this moment in the operation of borders is important not just from the point of view of subjects in transit. The same is true for states, global political actors, agencies of governance, and capital. Sorting and filtering flows, commodities, labor, and information that happens at borders are crucial for the operation of these actors. Again, taking the border as an epistemic angle opens up new and particularly productive perspectives on the transformations currently reshaping power and capital —for instance, shedding light on the intermingling of sovereignty and governmentality and on the logistical operations underlying global circuits of accumulation.

Our work on borders is to be read in this sense as a contribution to the critical investigation of actually existing global processes. Gone are the days in which a book like *The Borderless World*, published in 1990 by Japanese management guru Kenichi Ōmae, could set the agenda for the discussion on globalization and borders. The idea presented there of a zero-sum game between globalization and borders (insofar as globalization progresses, the relevance of borders will be diminished) has been very influential but has been rapidly displaced by evidence of the increasing presence of borders in our present. Although our work charts this process of multiplication of borders, our argument is not that the nation-state has been untouched by globalization. We concur with many thinkers who have argued that the nation-state has been reorganized and reformatted in the contemporary world. This leads us to focus not only on traditional international borders but also on other lines of social, cultural, political, and economic demarcation. For instance, we investigate the boundaries circumscribing the "special economic zones" that proliferate within formally united political spaces in many parts of the world.

To repeat, one of our central theses is that borders, far from serving merely to block or obstruct global passages of people, money, or objects, have become central devices for their articulation. Borders play a key role in the production of the heterogeneous time and space of contemporary global and postcolonial capitalism. This focus on the deep heterogeneity of the global is one of the distinguishing points we make, in a constant dialogue with many anthropological and ethnographic works as well as with social and political thinkers. Subjects in motion and their experiences of the border provide a kind of thread that runs through the nine chapters of the volume. We analyze the evolving shape of border and migration regimes in different parts of the world, looking at the way these regimes concur in the production of labor power as a commodity. At the same time we focus on the long-term problem of relations between the expanding frontiers of capital and territorial demarcations within the history of modern capitalism, conceived of as a world system since its inception. We are convinced that in the current global transition, under the pressure of capital's financialization, there is a need to test some of the most cherished notions and theoretical paradigms produced by political economy and social sciences to come to grips with that problem—from the international division of labor to center and periphery. Again, taking the point of view of the border, we propose a new concept—the multiplication of labor—and we attempt to map the very geographical disruption that lies at the core of capitalist globalization. *Border as Method* can therefore also be read as an attempt to contribute to the ongoing discussion on the evolving shape of the world order and disorder.

Our emphasis on heterogeneity is also important for the analysis of what we call with Karl Marx the composition of contemporary living labor, which is more and more crisscrossed, divided, and multiplied by practices of mobility and the operation of borders. To gain an analytical purchase on these processes we interlace multiple gazes and voices, crossing and challenging the North–South divide. While we stress the relevance of migration experiences and control regimes from the point of view of the transformations of labor in the Euro-Atlantic world, intervening in the discussion on care and affective labor as well as precarity, we also focus, to make a couple of examples, on the *hukou* system of household registration in contemporary China and the complex systems of bordering that internally divide the Indian labor market. We are aware of many differences that must be taken into account in doing this. We do not propose a comparative analysis of these and other instances. We are interested in another kind of knowledge production, one that starts from concepts and works on the (often unexpected) resonances and dissonances produced by the encounters and clashes between these concepts and a materiality that can be very distant from the one within which they were originally formulated. This is part and parcel of what we call border as method. In the case of the composition of living labor, it points to the strategic relevance of heterogeneity (of, for example, figures, skills, legal and social statuses) across diverse geographical scales. Nowadays, multiplicity is the necessary point of departure for any investigation of the composition of labor, and *Border as Method* attempts to provide some tools for identifying the points of more intense conflict and friction where such an investigation can focus. Although multiplicity and heterogeneity are cut and divided by devices of control and hierarchization, it is no less true today that unity is strength (to use words that marked an epoch in the history of class struggle). But the conditions of this unity have to be fully reimagined against the background of a multiplicity and heterogeneity that must be turned from an element of weakness into an element of strength.

It will not be surprising that our work on borders leads us to engage in a discussion with some of the most influential elaborations on the topic of political subjectivity circulating in current critical debates. Borders in modernity have played a constitutive role in the modes of production and organization of political subjectivity. Citizenship is probably the best example of this, and it is only necessary to reflect on the important connection between citizenship and labor in the twentieth century to grasp the ways the movements of the dyadic figure of the citizen-worker have been inscribed within the national confines of the state. Working through citizenship studies, labor studies, as well as more philosophical debates on political subjectivity, we map the tensions and ruptures that crisscross the contemporary figures of both the citizen and the worker. The borders circumscribing these figures have become blurred and unstable, and, to reference a slogan of Latinos in the United States ("we did not cross the border, the border crossed us"), they are themselves increasingly crossed and cut, more than circumscribed, by borders. Around these borders, although often far away from the literal border, some of the most crucial struggles of the present are fought. Liberating political imagination from the burden of the citizen-worker and the state is particularly urgent to open up spaces within which the organization of new forms of political subjectivity becomes possible. Here, again, our work on borders encounters current debates on translation and the common.

ACKNOWLEDGMENTS

This book has been a long time in gestation, and there are too many people to thank for their questions, support, provocations, and readings. The distance at which we live has been a productive factor in our approach to borders and in our desire to write a book that was truly global in scope. Practically, however, the experience of collaboration and research has required travel, and for supporting this we acknowledge a number of sources: the University of Western Sydney Professional Development Scheme, the University of Western Sydney Eminent Visitor Scheme, and the Australian Research Council Discovery Project Scheme (DP0988547).

Along the way we have presented our work to many audiences. The feedback on these occasions has been vital to the development of our thinking. In particular, we are thankful for invitations to speak at the Franklin Humanities Institute, Duke University; the Collège International de Philosophie, Paris; the Centre for the Study of Invention and Social Process, Goldsmiths College, London; the Institut für Soziologie, University of Hamburg; the Department of Media, Culture and Creative Industries, King's College London; the School of Culture and Communication, University of Melbourne; the Research Institute of Comparative History and Culture, Hanyang University, Seoul; the European Institute for Progressive Cultural Policy, Vienna; the Calcutta Research Group, Kolkata; the Refugee Studies Centre, Oxford University; the Universidad Nacional de San Martín, Buenos Aires; the Tate Modern Gallery, London; the Universidade Nova de Lisboa, Lisbon; the Institute of International Visual Arts (Rivington Place), London; the Haute École d'Art et de Design, Geneva; and the Centro de Estudios Sobre la Identidad Colectiva, Universidad del País Vasco, Bilbao.

These invitations have been balanced by an intense engagement with migrant and activist groups, among them the Frassanito Network, the Cross-border Collective, the Uninomade Network, and Colectivo Situaciones.

Arguments herein have been foreshadowed in articles published in the journals *Transversal* and *Theory, Culture & Society*. A book chapter in *Borders of Justice* (edited by Étienne Balibar, Ranabir Samaddar, and Sandro Mezzadra, Temple University Press, 2011) anticipates some of the arguments presented in chapters 5, 6, and 8. Sections of chapters 2 and 3 have been published in a slightly altered version in the journal *Scapegoat: Architecture/Landscape/Political Economy*. Earlier versions of parts of chapter 6 appeared in the journal *Global/Local: Identity, Community, Security*. Thanks to the editors and reviewers on all occasions.

In writing this book we have drawn on many works unavailable in the English language. Translations from these texts are ours. We have also used quotation marks when using the term "illegal" to describe migrants. We have followed this practice for terms such as "boat people" and "people smugglers." This is part of an effort to denaturalize these widespread categorizations as well as the anxieties and phobias that frequently accompany their use.

We owe a special thanks to Anja Kanngieser for her research assistance, bibliographic work, and deep understanding of the argument and politics that animate this book. Other friends and colleagues we want to thank are Rutvica Andrijasevic, Étienne Balibar, Paula Banerjee, Vando Borghi, Ida Dominijanni, Verónica Gago, Rosalind Gill, Giorgio Grappi, Michael Hardt, Stefano Harney, Katie Hepworth, Rada Iveković, Randy Martin, Angela Mitropoulos, Toni Negri, Federico Rahola, Fabio Raimondi, Maurizio Ricciardi, Gigi Roggero, Ned Rossiter, Devi Sacchetto, Naoki Sakai, Ranabir Samaddar, Jon Solomon, William Walters, Jessica Whyte, Vassilis Tsianos, and Adelino Zanini. Thanks also to Courtney Berger at Duke University Press for her editorial work, two anonymous reviewers for their comments, and the Social Text Collective.

Finally, we thank those who have remained close to us during the writing of this book: Giovanna, Lisa, Luce, Marcello, and Mila.

Chapter One

THE PROLIFERATION OF BORDERS

The World Seen from a Cab

Anyone who has used the taxi system in New York City over the past decade will know the vast diversity that exists within the labor force that drives the city's yellow cabs. Fewer people will know what it takes to organize a strike among these predominantly migrant workers who speak more than eighty different languages. In *Taxi! Cabs and Capitalism in New York City* (2005), Biju Mathew, himself an organizer of the grassroots New York Taxi Workers Alliance (NYTWA), documents the history of the many strikes that led to the historic fare rise victory for the city's cab drivers in March 2004. Mathew's book is in many ways a story about borders—not only the linguistic borders that separate these workers but also the urban borders they routinely cross as part of their working lives, the international borders they cross to reach New York City, and the social borders that divide them from their clients and the owners from whom they lease the cabs. Investigating the restructuring of the NYC cab industry and its links to the wider shifts of capitalism in a global era, *Taxi!* illustrates how these many borders figure in the composition, struggles, and organizational forms of the labor force in this sector.

It is no secret that many NYC cab drivers are highly qualified individuals, whose presence in such a job is often a kind of transit station or waiting room for further labor mobility. Indeed, as has also been noted in a recent study of Indian techno-migrants in Silicon Valley (Ong 2006, 163–65), it is frequently the case that the "illegal" juridical status of these workers produces another border that criss-crosses and multiplies the already existing diversity of this workforce. More-over, the wounds of history resurface in the composition of the labor force. This is particularly the case with migrant workers coming from South Asia, for whom the memory and actual legacy of the subcontinent's partition is an ongoing experience. It is thus all the more remarkable that, as Mathew recalls, Pakistani and Indian drivers acted side by side during the 1998 New York taxi strike when some 24,000 yellow cab drivers took their cars off the road to protest new safety measures that subjected them to higher fines, mandatory drug testing, higher liability insurance requirements, and a pro-hibitive means of attaching penalty points to their licenses. Just one week after their home countries tested nuclear weapons in an environment of escalating nationalist tensions, these drivers acted together in two day-long strikes that brought the city to a halt.

Mathew bases his research on a particular image of globalization and neoliberalism as well as a critique of multiculturalism and postcolonialism as a set of state- and market-friendly discourses that protect established class positions. At times this seems to us too rigid. More interesting, in our view, is the way *Taxi!* can be read as a chronicle of the proliferation of borders in the world today and the multiscalar roles they play in the current reorganization of working lives. Although Mathew's study focuses on a single city, the increasing heterogeneity of global space is evident in the stories he tells about negotiating the metropolis. Issues of territory, jurisdic-tion, division of labor, governance, sovereignty, and translation all collapse into the urban spaces that these drivers traverse. This is not merely because the city in question is New York, where migrant labor has played a key role in the reshaping of the metropolitan economy and the development of social struggles in the past fifteen years (Ness 2005). As we show in the chapters that follow, the proliferation of borders in other parts of the world (whether on the "external frontiers" of Europe, the sovereign territory of China, or the Australian sphere of influence in the Pacific) displays tenden-cies common to those discussed by Mathew.

Our interest is in changing border and migration regimes in a world in which national borders are no longer the only or necessarily the most rele-vant ones for dividing and restricting labor mobilities. The nation-state still provides an important political reference from the point of view of power configurations and their articulation with capital–labor relations. Never-theless, we are convinced that contemporary power dynamics and struggles cannot be contained by national borders or the international system of states they putatively establish. This is an important point of departure for our work. Though we emphasize the strategic importance of borders in the contemporary world, we do not intend to join the chorus that in recent years and from many different points of view has celebrated the return of the nation-state on the world stage, dismissing the debates on globalization as mere ideological distortion. To the contrary, one of our central theses is that borders, far from serving simply to block or obstruct global flows, have become essential devices for their articulation. In so doing, borders have not just proliferated. They are also undergoing complex transformations that correspond to what Saskia Sassen (2007, 214) has called "the actual and heuristic disaggregation of 'the border.'" The multiple (legal and cultural, social and economic) components of the concept and institution of the border tend to tear apart from the magnetic line corresponding to the geopolitical line of separation between nation-states. To grasp this process, we take a critical distance from the prevalent interest in geopolitical borders in many critical approaches to the border, and we speak not only of a proliferation but also of a heterogenization of borders.

The traditional image of borders is still inscribed onto maps in which discrete sovereign territories are separated by lines and marked by different colors. This image has been produced by the modern history of the state, and we must always be aware of its complexities. Just to make an example, migration control has only quite recently become a prominent function of political borders. At the same time, historicizing the development of linear borders means to be aware of the risks of a naturalization of a specific image of the border. Such naturalization does not assist in understanding the most salient transformations we are facing in the contemporary world. Today borders are not merely geographical margins or territorial edges. They are complex social institutions, which are marked by tensions between practices of border reinforcement and border crossing. This definition of what makes up a border, proposed by Pablo Vila (2000) in an attempt to critically take stock of the development of studies on the U.S.–Mexican borderlands since the late 1980s, points to the tensions and conflicts constitutive of any border.

We are convinced that this constituent moment surfaces with particular intensity today, along specific geopolitical borders and the many other boundaries that cross cities, regions, and continents. Borders, on one hand, are becoming finely tuned instruments for managing, calibrating, and governing global passages of people, money, and things. On the other hand, they are spaces in which the transformations of sovereign power and the ambivalent nexus of politics and violence are never far from view. To observe these dual tendencies is not merely to make the banal but necessary point that borders always have two sides, or that they connect as well as divide. Borders also play a key role in producing the times and spaces of global capitalism. Furthermore, they shape the struggles that rise up within and against these times and spaces—struggles that often allude problematically, but in rich and determinate ways, to the abolition of borders themselves. In this regard, borders have become in recent years an important concern of research and political and artistic practice. They are sites in which the turbulence and conflictual intensity of global capitalist dynamics are particularly apparent. As such they provide strategic grounds for the analysis and contestation of actually existing globalization.

What Is a Border?

In an influential essay titled "What Is a Border?," Étienne Balibar writes of the "polysemy" and "heterogeneity" of borders, noting that their "multiplicity, their hypothetical and fictive nature" does "not make them any less real" (2002, 76). Not only are there different kinds of borders that individuals belonging to different social groups experience in different ways, but borders also simultaneously perform "several functions of demarcation and territorialization—between distinct social exchanges or flows, between distinct rights, and so forth" (79). Moreover, borders are always *overdetermined*, meaning that "no political border is ever the mere boundary between two states" but is always "sanctioned, reduplicated and relativized by other geopolitical divisions" (79). "Without the *world-configuring function* they perform," Balibar writes, "there would be no borders—or no lasting borders" (79). His argument recalls, in a very different theoretical context, that developed in 1950 by Carl Schmitt in *The* Nomos *of the Earth* (2003), a text that maintains that the tracing of borders within modern Europe went hand in hand with political and legal arrangements that were designed to organize an *already global* space. These arrangements, including different kinds of "global lines" and geographical divisions, provided a blueprint for the colonial partitioning of the world and the regulation of relations between Europe and its outsides. To put it briefly, the articulation between these global lines of colonial and imperialist expansion and the drawing of linear boundaries between European and Western states has constituted for several centuries the dominant motif of the global geography organized by capital and state. Obviously, this history was neither peaceful nor linear.

The history of the twentieth century, which was characterized by the turmoil of decolonization and the globalization of the nation-state and its linear borders in the wake of two world wars, witnessed an explosion of this political geography. Europe was displaced from the center of the map. The U.S. global hegemony, which seemed uncontested at the end of the Cold War, is rapidly giving way, not least through the economic crisis that marks the passage from the first to the second decade of the twenty-first century. On the horizon is a more variegated and unstable landscape of global power, which can no longer be fully described with such concepts as unilateralism and multilateralism (Haass 2008). New continental spaces emerge as sites of uneasy integration, regional interpenetration, and political, cultural, and social mobility. Although this is a long and doubtlessly unfinished process, we can identify several factors at play in its unfolding. Devastating wars, anticolonial upheavals, changing patterns of communication and transport, geopolitical shifts, financial bubbles and busts—all have contributed to re-drawing the world picture. Furthermore, under the pressure of class strug-gles and interrelated contestations of race and gender, the capitalist mode of production continues to undergo momentous and uneven transformations. A crucial aspect of these changes is the realignment of relations between the state and capital—sometimes seen to work in tandem, at other times under-stood to exist in logical contradiction—but always implicated in shifting regimes of exploitation, dispossession, and domination.

If the political map of the world and the global cartography of capitalism were never entirely coincidental, they could once be easily read off one another. In the post–Cold War world, the superposition of these maps has become increasingly illegible. A combination of processes of "denational-ization" (Sassen 2006) has invested both the state and capital with varying degrees of intensity and an uneven geometry of progression. In particular, the national denomination of capital has become an increasingly less signifi-cant index for the analysis of contemporary capitalism. In this book, we tackle this problem, elaborating the concept of "frontiers of capital" and investigating the relations between their constant expansion since the ori-gin of modern capitalism and territorial boundaries. Although there has always been a constitutive tension between these relations, the develop-ment of capitalism as a world system has given shape to successive forms of articulation between the demarcations generated by economic processes and the borders of the state. One of our central points is that contemporary capital, characterized by processes of financialization and the combination of heterogeneous labor and accumulation regimes, negotiates the expan-sion of its frontiers with much more complex assemblages of power and law, which include but also transcend nation-states. Looking at the expansion of capital's frontiers and considering the proliferation of political and legal boundaries, we are thus confronted with a geographical disruption and a continuous process of rescaling. A deeply heterogeneous global space corresponds to this process, and the border provides a particularly effective angle from which to investigate its making.

Meanwhile, the crisis of cartographical reason (Farinelli 2003), which has been at the center of debate between geographers since the early 1990s, has raised epistemological questions that are of great relevance for the study of the material transformation of borders. The increasing complexity of the relation between capital and state (as well as between their respective spatial representations and productions) is one of the factors at play in this crisis. This has given rise to a certain anxiety surrounding the figure and institution of borders, questioning their capacity to provide stable reference points and metaphors with which to geometrically order and frame the world (Gregory 1994; Krishna 1994; Painter 2008).

Borders today still perform a "world-configuring function," but they are often subject to shifting and unpredictable patterns of mobility and overlapping, appearing and disappearing as well as sometimes crystallizing in the form of threatening walls that break up and reorder political spaces that were once formally unified. They cross the lives of millions of men and women who are on the move, or, remaining sedentary, have borders cross them. In places like the Mediterranean or the deserts between Mexico and the United States, they violently break the passage of many migrants. At the same time, borders superimpose themselves over other kinds of limits and technologies of division. These processes are no less overdetermined than those of the modern world order, but the ways in which they configure the globe has dramatically changed. Rather than organizing a stable map of the world, the processes of proliferation and transformation of borders we analyze in this book aim at managing the creative destruction and constant recombining of spaces and times that lie at the heart of contemporary capitalist globalization. In this book we do not aim to discern the shape of a future world order. Rather, we investigate the present disorder of the world and try to explain why it is highly unrealistic to think of the future in terms of a return to some version of Westphalian order.

We know that the border is not a comfortable place to live. "Hatred, anger and exploitation," wrote Gloria Anzaldúa over twenty years ago in describing the background for the emergence of what she called the "new Mestiza," "are the prominent features of this landscape" (1987, 19). Walls, grating, and barbed wire are the usual images that come to mind when we think about borders, whether that between Mexico and the United States, those in the occupied Palestinian territories, the "fence of death" constructed around the Spanish enclave of Ceuta in north Africa, or the many gated communities that have sprung up all over the world to protect the privileged and shut out the poor. We are prone to see borders as physical walls and metaphorical walls, such as those evoked by the image of Fortress Europe. This seems even more the case after the events of September 11, 2001, when borders became crucial sites of "securitarian" investment within political rhetoric as much as the actual politics of control. We are painfully aware of all of this. Yet we are convinced that the image of the border as a wall, or as a device that serves first and foremost to *exclude*, as widespread as it has been in recent critical studies, is misleading in the end. Isolating a single function of the border does not allow us to grasp the flexibility of this institution. Nor does it facilitate an understanding of the diffusion of practices and techniques of border control within territorially bound spaces of citizenship and their associated labor markets. We claim that borders are equally devices of inclusion that select and filter people and different forms of circulation in ways no less violent than those deployed in exclusionary measures. Our argument thus takes a critical approach to inclusion, which in most accounts is treated as an unalloyed social good. By showing how borders establish multiple points of control along key lines and geographies of wealth and power, we see inclusion existing in a continuum with exclusion, rather than in opposition to it. In other words, we focus on the hierarchizing and stratifying capacity of borders, examining their articulation to capital and political power whether they coincide with the territorial limits of states or exist within or beyond them. To analyze the pervasive character of the border's operations—let alone the marked violence that accompanies them—we need a more complex and dynamic conceptual language than that which sustains images of walls and exclusion.

Border as Method introduces a range of concepts that seek to grasp the mutations of labor, space, time, law, power, and citizenship that accompany the proliferation of borders in today's world. Among these are the multiplication of labor, differential inclusion, temporal borders, the sovereign machine of governmentality, and border struggles. Taken together, these concepts provide a grid within which to fathom the deep transformations of the social, economic, juridical, and political relations of our planet. They point to the radically equivocal character of borders and their growing inability to trace a firm line between the inside and outside of territorial states.

The political theorist Wendy Brown (2010) has illustrated how the proliferation of walls and barriers in the contemporary world is more a symptom of the crisis and transformation of state sovereignty than a sign of its reaffirmation. Particularly important, in our view, is Brown's thesis that "even the most physically intimidating of these new walls serves to regulate rather than exclude legal and illegal migrant labor," producing a zone of indistinction "between law and non-law of which flexible production has need" (Brown 2008, 16–17). Our argument goes beyond Brown's by considering how borders regulate and structure the relations between capital, labor, law, subjects, and political power even in instances where they are not lined by walls or other fortifications. The distinctiveness of our approach lies in its attempt to separate the border from the wall, showing how the regulatory functions and symbolic power of the border test the barrier between sovereignty and more flexible forms of global governance in ways that provide a prism through which to track the transformations of capital and the struggles that mount within and against them.

The most acute architects and urbanists who have studied one of the most physically intimidating walls the world currently knows—the one that runs through the occupied Palestinian territories in Israel—have shown how it produces an elusive and mobile geography, which is continually reshaped by Israel's military strategies. Far from marking the linear border of Israel's sovereignty, the wall functions as "a membrane that lets certain flows pass and blocks others," transforming the entire Palestinian territory into a "frontier zone" (Petti 2007, 97). According to Eyal Weizman: "The frontiers of the Occupied Territories are not rigid and fixed at all; rather they are elastic, and in constant formation. The linear border, a cartographic imaginary inherited from the military and political spatiality of the nation state has splintered into a multitude of temporary, transportable, deployable and removable border-synonyms—'separation walls,' 'barriers,' 'blockades,' 'closures,' 'road blocks,' 'checkpoints,' 'sterile areas,' 'special security zones,' 'closed military areas' and 'killing zones'" (2007, 6). Shortly we return to the distinction between the border and the frontier. For now, we want to note the emphasis Weizman places on the elasticity of the territory and the mobility of techniques for controlling the limit between inside and outside in a situation dominated by what should represent the most static crystallization of the linear border: a wall, no less. Clearly the situation in the occupied Palestinian territories needs to be examined in its specificity. But what Weizman calls the elasticity of territory is also a feature that can be observed in relation to the operation of many other borders across the world. Attentiveness to the historical and geographical significance of individual borders does not disqualify an approach that isolates particular aspects of a situation and lets them resonate with what takes place in very different spatial and temporal zones. This is what we propose to do in the following chapters, which explore not only how individual borders connect and divide but also the patterns of connection and division that invest the relations between radically heterogeneous *borderscapes*.

In the Borderscape

Our aim is to bring into view a series of problems, processes, and concepts that allow us to elaborate a new theoretical approach to the border. In so doing, we take distance from arguments that center on the image of the wall or the theme of security. We also depart from the classical paradigm of border studies (Kolossov 2005; Newman 2006), which tends to proceed by the comparison of discrete case studies, assuming clear and distinct differences between the various situations and contexts under investigation. The instances of bordering that we analyze in the following chapters are selected according to the intensity with which the relation between the two poles of border reinforcement and border crossing manifests itself in border struggles. We are of course aware of the radical difference between the elusive borders that circumscribe special economic zones in China and the external frontiers of the European Union, to mention an example. But our primary interest is not in comparing different instances or techniques of bordering. Rather, we want to interlace, juxtapose, superimpose, and let resonate the practices, techniques, and sites in question, highlighting their mutual implications and consonances as well as their differences and dissonances, their commonalities, and their singularities. The result is a different means of knowledge production, one that necessarily involves practices of translation, although more in a conceptual than a linguistic sense. Later in the book we elaborate on this question drawing on Antonio Gramsci's reflections on the translatability of scientific and philosophical languages, which is constructed on the structural friction between concepts and heterogeneous specific concrete situations. Border as method is an attempt to make this friction productive both from a theoretical point of view and for the understanding of diverse empirical borderscapes.

To do this, we draw on a great wealth of ethnographic writings and materials without ever limiting our analysis to a single ethnographic focus. By engaging with ethnographic works, alongside writings from fields such as geography, history, and jurisprudence, we hope to provide an empirical

foil to test our conceptual propositions. We also aim to conceptually question and revise the assumptions and methods that typically lie behind the
construction of the ethnographic object: assumptions about the relations
between time and space, methods of reflexivity, approaches to translation,
and so on. Our concentration on connections and disconnections, both
conceptual and material, is thus highly indebted to the careful work of
ethnographers but also seeks to move beyond even the most complex multi-
site studies, which remain tethered to the ethics of "do-ability" and the
imperative of "being there" that are the hallmarks of ethnographic practice
(Berg 2008). It is not that we necessarily agree with sage figures like George
Marcus, who in discussing anthropology's "professional culture of method"
suggests that recent ethnography has produced "no new ideas" (2008, 3–4).
More simply, we believe that efforts to theorize globalization must account
for "indirect social relations" that can be mediated through "abstract third
agents," such as logistical calculations, legal orders, economic forces, or
humanitarian narratives. These orders and processes channel movements
of capital, goods, and labor in ways that are not immediately accessible to
"an ethnographic data set obtained primarily through direct sensory experience" (Feldman 2011, 375). Moreover, the sites and instances we discuss are
not always ones that it has been possible for us to visit, for reasons of both
time and resources. Although we occasionally draw on our own experiences
and observations, we question the limiting perspective imposed by the view
that the breadth of research compromises its depth and rigor. Rather, we
proceed with the commitment that breadth can produce depth, or better,
produce a new kind of conceptual depth, "new ideas." Our study is thus
deliberately wide-ranging. What we seek to develop is a relational approach
to the study of borders, one that remains politically responsive to the experiences of border crossing and border reinforcement and also adequate to the
equivocations of definition, space, and function that mark the concept of
the border itself.

For both of us, the theoretical engagement with issues of borders, labor,
and migration is rooted in a history of travel, intellectual engagement, and
political activism that, in very different geographical and symbolic contexts,
has molded patterns of friendship and relationships that have deeply influenced our work and lives. As it happens, 1993 was an important threshold in
these political histories. In that year, Mezzadra was living in the Italian city
of Genoa, where what was labeled the country's first "race riots" unfolded
during the summer. Violent street tussles broke out as migrants were com-

pelled to defend themselves from attacks by local youths. The attempt to build up a kind of antiracist front in Genoa following these events proved crucial to Mezzadra's intellectual and political trajectory, profoundly skewing his activity toward the articulation of migration politics at the European level. It was also the year of Neilson's return to Australia after a period in the United States, where he had participated in actions against the interception and return of Haitian migrants (via Guantánamo Bay) who had sought to flee after the military overthrowing of the Aristide government in 1991. The violation of UN conventions implicit in the policy of President George H. W. Bush—which was continued by President Bill Clinton—had provided the trigger for Australia's introduction of mandatory detention in 1992 and subsequent practices of migrant interception. This less-than-fortuitous connection between border regimes convinced Neilson (1996) that the struggle against detention camps in Australia, which was often articulated exclusively at the national level, urgently needed to be linked to border struggles in other parts of the world.

A decade later, we met and began to carry out our first dialogues (Mezzadra and Neilson 2003). By that time the border regimes in Europe and Australia had considerably mutated and, in many respects, in similar ways. Following the *Tampa* incident of 2001, when Australia refused to accept some 438 migrants who had been rescued by a Norwegian tanker and arranged their incarceration on the Pacific island of Nauru, the processes of "externalization" of migrant detention and border control were fully under way. Similar arrangements were already in place with the involvement of third countries in the border control practices and technologies of the European Union. Moreover, there were similarities of activist experience in Australia and Italy. For instance, the actions at the Woomera detention camp for "illegal" migrants in the south Australian desert in April 2002 and at the Bari-Palese camp in Puglia in July 2003 were occasions when protest activities allowed detainees to escape. From the polemics and debates that followed these important and to some extent politically confusing incidents, in which the borders that separate migration activists from detained migrants were temporarily removed by the physical dismantling of fences, we learned the perils of too insistently correlating the activist desire to challenge or democratize borders with the risk assumed by migrants who actually transgress these borders. As tempting and as politically effective as slogans like "*Siamo tutti clandestini*" (We are all illegal migrants) may be, there are important differences of ethics and experience at hand here. These are differences that we attempt to keep in mind, both theoretically and politically, as we draw on our experiences to inform the arguments and concepts that populate the following chapters.

Although our experiences of migration activism have unfolded in contexts where there has been attention to global connections, they are by necessity limited. Over the years we have had the opportunity to participate in research projects, both academic and activist, that have taken us to sites where many of the questions and challenges posed by this book come into dramatic relief: production zones in China, new towns in India, La Salada informal market in Buenos Aires, and the fortified borderzones on both sides of the Strait of Gibraltar, just to name a few. These are all situations we write about. We also seek to make connections between them and other instances of bordering in ways that intertwine ethnographic observation and political analysis. In this way, we reach beyond existing debates on borders, migration, and labor to add to the literature on global power and governance, the mutations of capital and sovereignty, and their implications for subjects and struggles across different configurations of space and time. This research process attempts to filter both theoretical and ethnographic materials, whatever their provenance, through our own political experiences, which are, as is always the case in collaborative work, diffuse and inconsistent. Although this filtering may not always be foregrounded on the surface of our text, it has remained a crucial part of our writing practice—a kind of political pivot and editorial razor. This technique, we like to believe, gives our writing the possibility to range across radically diverse borderscapes in different parts of the world.

We take the term *borderscape* from the work of Suvendrini Perera (2007, 2009). In her analysis of the shifting and elusive borders that circumscribe Australia's territory from the Pacific zone, Perera highlights—using terms analogous to those Weizman deployed to describe the occupied Palestinian territories—the simultaneous expansion and contraction of political spaces and the "multiple resistances, challenges, and counterclaims" to which they give rise. Her work is closely engaged with the regime of border control known as the Pacific Solution, which was introduced following the *Tampa* incident in 2001. This involved the establishment of offshore detention camps for migrants attempting to reach Australia by boat and the excision of remote Australian territories from the country's migration zone, making it impossible to claim asylum on outlying islands that are key destinations on maritime migration routes. Placing these developments in the context of the longer *durée* of mobilities and exchanges across the "maritime highways of the Indian and Pacific Oceans," Perera points to the formation of a "shifting and conflictual" zone in which "different temporalities and overlapping emplacements as well as emergent spatial organizations" take shape (2007, 206–7).

Independently from these developments in the Pacific zone, the concept of the borderscape nicely captures many of the important conflicts and transformations that have been at stake in border studies debates in the past two decades, whether in fields such as political geography (Newman and Paasi 1998) or international relations (Bigo 2006), to name only two. The concept suggests the dynamic character of the border, which is now widely understood as a set of "practices and discourses that 'spread' into the whole of society" (Paasi 1999, 670). At the same time, it registers the necessity to analyze the border not only in its spatial but also in its temporal dimensions. Mobilizing the concept of the borderscape allows us to highlight the conflictual determination of the border, the tensions and struggles that play a decisive role in its constitution. Our approach is very different from arguments that stress the "normative" illegitimacy of the exclusion effected by borders (see, for example, Cole 2000 and Carens 2010) and issue in various calls for their opening or abolition (Harris 2002; Hayter 2004). Readers will not find recipes for a future borderless world in the following pages. We agree in this regard with Chandra Mohanty (2003, 2) when she writes of a need to acknowledge "the fault lines, conflicts, differences, fear, and containment that borders represent." Extending and radicalizing Perera's line of thought, we try to move one step further by focusing on *border struggles* or those struggles that take shape around the ever more unstable line between the "inside" and "outside," between inclusion and exclusion.

Writing of border struggles is for us a way of placing an emphasis on the production of political subjectivity. We are not interested only in movements that openly contest borders and their discriminatory effects, such as those in which undocumented migrants have emerged as protagonists (Suárez-Naval et al. 2008). We want the notion of border struggles to refer also to the set of everyday practices by which migrants continually come to terms with the pervasive effects of the border, subtracting themselves from them or negotiating them through the construction of networks and transnational social spaces (Rodríguez 1996). Moreover, we want to register how border struggles—which always involve specific subjective positions and figures—invest more generally the field of political subjectivity, testing its intrinsic limits and reorganizing its internal divisions. In this way, border struggles open a new continent of political possibilities, a space within which new kinds of political subjects, which abide neither the logics of citizenship nor established methods of radical political organization and action, can trace their movements and multiply their powers. The exploration of this continent, beginning with the material conditions that generate the tensions of which border struggles are the sign, seems to us more promising—and more politically urgent—than the simple denunciation of the capacity of borders to exclude or the wish for a world "without borders."

Border as Method

More than once we have recalled Balibar's notion of the polysemy of the border, a concept that corresponds with the multiplicity of terms that, in many languages, refer to the semantic area of the border (just think, in English, of the words *boundary* and *frontier*). It is no accident that today the metaphoric use of these terms is widespread (Newman and Paasi 1998). This is evident not only in everyday language (e.g., the "frontiers of scientific research") but also in the specialist language of the social sciences, where phrases such as "boundary work" and "boundary object" have entered into common use (Lemont and Molnár 2002). Aside from its geographical, political, and juridical dimensions, the concept of the border has an important symbolic dimension, which has come to the fore today with the multiplication of the tensions that invest the classically modern configuration of the border as a separating line between sovereign state territories (Cella 2006; Zanini 1997). Both sociology, beginning with the work of Georg Simmel (2009), and anthropology, beginning with an important essay by Fredrik Barth (1979), have made fundamental contributions toward understanding this symbolic dimension of the border, including its role in distinguishing social forms and organizing cultural difference. In the following chapters, particularly when we discuss internal borders, we keep these notions of social and cultural borders in play. At the same time, we explore the complex modes of articulation (and also the tensions and the gaps) between different dimensions of the border. In doing this, we use with a certain degree of freedom the words *border* and *boundary* as interchangeable, while we make a clear-cut distinction between *border* and *frontier*.

The geometrical abstraction of exclusive territoriality and linear borders, while it has exerted an extremely important influence on the way in which politics has been conceived and executed in the modern era, was only ever a convention (Cuttitta 2006, 2007; Galli 2010, 36–53). It would certainly be worthwhile to reconstruct the complex and nonlinear processes that led in Europe to the decline of the medieval marches and the rise of modern borders between states (Febvre 1962). More relevant for our study, however, is to highlight how the history of the modern system of states unfolded under the horizon of global space from its very beginning. To fully understand this history, and the linear conception of the border that informs it, we argue that it is necessary to account for the *constitutive* role of the *colonial frontier*.

The frontier, as is evident from the narrative around which one of the foundation myths of U.S. identity is constructed (Turner 1920), is by definition a space open to expansion, a mobile "front" in continuous formation. When we write of the colonial frontier, we refer, on one hand and in very general terms, to the qualitative distinction between European space, in which the linear border evolved, and those extra-European spaces, which were by definition open to conquest. This distinction is certainly an essential aspect of the modern juridical and political organization of space, as encoded, for instance, in works such as Emerich de Vattel's 1758 treatise *The Law of Nations* (1916). On the other hand, we refer to the fact that in actual colonial situations, the reality of frontier, with its characteristics of opening and indetermination, was often present. In these contexts, the frontier tended to superimpose itself over other divisions (most obviously that between colonists and natives, but also lines of territorial demarcation that cut through formally unified domains), rendering colonial space and its cartographic projection much more complex than its metropolitan counterpart (Banerjee 2010).

It is important to remember that mapping was a key tool of colonial domination. The tensions and clashes between cartographic tools constructed on the model of the sovereign state with its firm boundaries and specific "indigenous" geographies gave rise to wars and shaped the "geo-bodies" of postcolonial states (Winichakul 1994). They also influenced the configuration of vast border areas such as the Indian northeast (Kumar and Zou 2011). It is also worth remembering that in the colonized parts of the world, a whole series of spatial innovations was forged, from the camp to the protectorate, the unincorporated territory to the dependency, the concession to the treaty port (Stoler 2006). Later in this book we map the metamorphosis and continuous development of such indeterminate and ambiguous spaces in the contemporary world. The analysis of bordering technologies within emerging postdevelopmental geographies in Asia and Latin America is an important feature of our work. We try to analyze these geographies by letting our investigations of them resonate with what we have learned from other borderscapes. Though critical border studies are often focused on specifically Western contexts, such as the U.S.–Mexican borderlands or the "external frontiers" of the European Union, border as method allows us to cross disciplinary and geographical divides and take a truly global and postcolonial angle.

The distinction between the border and the frontier is undoubtedly important (see Prescott 1987). The former has typically been considered a line, whereas the latter has been constructed as an open and expansive space. In many contemporary contexts, however, this distinction seems to dissolve. The borders of the current European space, for example, take on aspects of the indetermination that has historically characterized the frontier, expanding into surrounding territories and constructing spaces according to a variable geometry articulated on multiple geographical scales (Cuttitta 2007). *Border as Method* deals with such instances of tricky conceptual overlapping and confusion through the punctual analysis of concrete borderscapes. In any case, as should be clear from the title of this book, for us the border is something more than a research object that can be subject to various methodological approaches or a semantic field whose multiple dimensions it is necessary to explore. Insofar as it serves at once to make divisions and establish connections, the border is an epistemological device, which is at work whenever a distinction between subject and object is established. Once again, Balibar most precisely describes this aspect of the border, noting the difficulty inherent in defining the concept itself:

> The idea of a simple definition of what constitutes a border is, by definition, absurd: to mark out a border is precisely, to define a territory, to delimit it, and so to register the identity of that territory, or confer one upon it. Conversely, however, to define or identify in general is nothing other than to trace a border, to assign boundaries or borders (in Greek, *horos*; in Latin, *finis* or *terminus*; in German, *Grenze*; in French, *borne*). The theorist who attempts to define what a border is is in danger of going round in circles, as the very representation of the border is the precondition for any definition. (2002, 76)

Borders, then, are essential to cognitive processes, because they allow both the establishment of taxonomies and conceptual hierarchies that structure the movement of thought. Furthermore, they establish the scientific division of labor associated with the sectioning of knowledge into different disciplinary zones. Cognitive borders, in this sense, often intertwine with geographical borders, as occurs for example in comparative literature or in so-called area studies, with which we concern ourselves in chapter 2. In any case, it should be clear that cognitive borders have great philosophical relevance, since they describe a general—perhaps one could even say a universal —dimension of human thought.

A thinker who has for many years studied the violence and border conflicts in regions such as the Balkans and the Indian subcontinent, Rada Iveković (2010), has recently proposed to rethink the "politics of philosophy" in relation to what she calls *la partage de la raison*. The French term *partage*, which combines the sense of both division and connection, has no straightforward English translation. Nominating at once the act of division and the act of connection, the two actions constitutive of the border, *la partage de la raison*, in Iveković's formulation, highlights the crucial role of translation as a social, cultural, and political practice that enables the elaboration of a new concept of the common. We return to this point in the final chapter of the book. Here, the reference to Iveković's work allows us to clarify the sense in which we write of border as method. On one hand, we refer to a process of producing knowledge that holds open the tension between empirical research and the invention of concepts that orient it. On the other hand, to approach the border as a method means to suspend, to recall a phenomenological category, the set of disciplinary practices that present the objects of knowledge as already constituted and investigate instead the processes by which these objects are constituted. It is by rescuing and reactivating the constituent moment of the border that we try to make productive the vicious circle Balibar identifies.

Just as we want to question the vision of the border as a neutral line, then, we also question the notion that method is a set of pregiven, neutral techniques that can be applied to diverse objects without fundamentally altering the ways in which they are constructed and understood. At stake in border as method is something more than the "performativity of method" (Law 2004, 149) or even the intriguing idea of "analytic borderlands" (Sassen 2006, 379–86). That is, while we accept that methods tend to produce (often in contradictory and unexpected ways) the worlds they claim to describe, for us the question of border as method is something more than methodological. It is above all a question of politics, about the kinds of social worlds and subjectivities produced at the border and the ways that thought and knowledge can intervene in these processes of production. To put this differently, we can say that method for us is as much about acting on the world as it is about knowing it. More accurately, it is about the relation of action to knowledge in a situation where many different knowledge regimes and practices come into conflict. Border as method involves negotiating the boundaries between the different kinds of knowledge that come to bear on the border and, in so doing, aims to throw light on the subjectivities that come into being through such conflicts.

For all of these reasons, the border is for us not so much a research object as an epistemological viewpoint that allows an acute critical analysis not only of how relations of domination, dispossession, and exploitation are being redefined presently but also of the struggles that take shape around these changing relations. The border can be a method precisely insofar as it is conceived of as a site of struggle. As we have already stressed, it is the intensity of the struggles fought on borders around the world that prompts our research and theoretical elaborations. Once we investigate the multifarious practices with which migrants challenge borders on a daily basis, it becomes clear that border struggles are all too often matters of life and death. Although we elaborate a wider concept of border struggles, which corresponds to what we have called the proliferation and heterogenization of borders in the contemporary world, we never forget this materiality. This focus on struggles also ensures the punctuality of border as method. It guides us not only in the selection of the relevant empirical settings for our investigations but also in the very construction of the "objects" to be studied.

Our perspective is thus very close to several projects of militant investigation that are currently developed by critical scholars and activists in many parts of the world. It also builds on many developments that have taken place in the field of postcolonial studies over the past twenty years. Walter Mignolo, in particular, has elaborated a comprehensive rereading of the history of modernity in the light of what he calls "colonial difference," proposing a new theoretical paradigm that he labels *border thinking*. In many respects, Mignolo provides a crucial reference point for the development of our approach, particularly regarding the "displacement" of Europe that he advocates alongside other postcolonial critics and his questioning of the use of categories such as "center," "periphery," and "semi-periphery" within world systems theory. Insofar as these categories crystallize and mark the epistemology that orients research, they effectively reproduce the marginality (or the peripheral status) of the histories, spaces, and subjects of the colonial frontier of modernity. At the same time, Mignolo's border thinking also seems to paradoxically reinscribe the consistency (and hence the borders) of Europe and the West when he writes of an "epistemology of the exteriority" (Mignolo and Tlostanova 2006, 206). By contrast, it is precisely the problematic nature of the distinction between interior and exterior that the approach we call border as method seeks to highlight.

In any case, at the center of our analysis are specific landscapes, practices, and border technologies. The method we pursue emerges from a continual confrontation with the materiality of the tensions and conflicts that constitute the border as an institution and set of social relations. Even when we confront apparently abstract themes, such as translation, we seek to keep this materiality present. In the particular case of translation, our reflections turn on experiences such as those of the taxi drivers analyzed by Mathew, with which we opened our discussion. In this instance, the processes of translation between dozens of languages, along with the affective investments and misunderstandings that accompanied them, were one of the essential elements in the development of struggles and organizational forms among a specific transnational component of labor power in New York City.

Containing Labor Power

We have just mentioned another concept that, in the specific determination it assumes within Marxian theory, orients our research. Central to any consideration of current global processes is the fact that the world has become more open to flows of goods and capital but more closed to the circulation of human bodies. There is, however, one kind of commodity that is inseparable from the human body, and the absolute peculiarity of this commodity provides a key to understanding and unraveling the seemingly paradoxical situation mentioned above. We have in mind the commodity of labor power, which at once describes a capacity of human bodies and exists as a good traded in markets at various geographical scales. Not only is labor power a commodity unlike any other (the only possible term of comparison being money), but the markets in which it is exchanged are peculiar. This is also because the role of borders in shaping labor markets is particularly pronounced. The processes of filtering and differentiation that occur at the border increasingly unfold within these markets, influencing the composition of what, to use another Marxian category, we call living labor.

There is also a peculiar tension within the abstract commodity form inherent to labor power that derives from the fact that it is inseparable from *living* bodies. Unlike the case of a table, for instance, the border between the commodity form of labor power and its "container" must continuously be reaffirmed and retraced. This is why the political and legal constitution of labor markets necessarily involves shifting regimes for the investment of power in life, which also correspond to different forms of the production of subjectivity. The concept of labor power, in its Marxian elaboration, acquires its most profound sense in light of a reflection on subjectivity and its relation to power. In the same moment as Karl Marx affirms the "property of the self" as the essential character that has delimited the basis of modern subjectivity at least since Locke (Mezzadra 2004), he also introduces a radical scission into this field: labor power marks one of the poles of this scission and the other is marked by money, which Marx describes as the "social power" that the individual carries "in his pocket" (1973, 157). This scission changes the way the "property of the self" is lived by two different classes of individuals: one of which acquires experience through the *power* of money and the other of which is continuously and necessarily restricted, to organize its relation with the world and its own reproduction, to labor power, defined by Marx as a generally human *potentiality*, as "the aggregate of those mental and physical capabilities existing in the physical form, the living personality, of a human being" (1977, 270).

In general terms, this scission in the field of subjectivity provides a fundamental criterion for the analysis of contemporary global capitalism. This remains true even in the presence of transformations that allow, through the use of information and communication technologies, the organization within sectors such as software programming and business processing of what has been called the "virtual migration" of workers (Aneesh 2006). At the same time, it is important to note that the "generically human" potentiality of labor power, to recall Marx's formulation, is always incarnated in sexed bodies that are socially constructed within multiple systems of domination, not least among them racism. To put it simply: the modalities through which "bearers" (another crucial term employed by Marx) of labor power access their "potency" are structurally and originally (that means, not secondarily!) marked by race, nation, geographical origin, and gender.

We seek to bring together a perspective on the border marked by a concern with labor power with our interest in border struggles and the production of subjectivity. Our analysis thus focuses on the tense and conflictual ways in which borders shape the lives and experiences of subjects who, due to the functioning of the border itself, are configured as bearers of labor power. The production of the subjectivity of these subjects constitutes an essential moment within the more general processes of the production of labor power as a commodity. Once seen from this perspective, both the techniques of power that invest the border and the social practices and struggles that unfold around it must be analyzed with regard to multiple and unstable configurations of gender and race, the production and reproduction of which are themselves greatly influenced by the border. To affirm that the border plays a decisive role in the production of labor power as a commodity is also to contend that the ways migratory movements are controlled, filtered, and blocked by border regimes have more general effects on the political and juridical constitution of labor markets, and thus on the experiences of living labor in general. We show that the struggles that develop around these experiences, whether centrally organized or autonomous, always imply a confrontation with the question of the border. Furthermore, we argue that in this context translation can play a key role in the invention of new forms of organization and new social institutions.

It is precisely the relation between labor power, translation, and political struggle that links the situation of the NYC taxi drivers to the other instances of border reinforcing and border crossing that we analyze. This is not to imply that we deal with a stable or linear set of relations between labor forces, borders, and political processes in the various subjective and objective situations that our analysis brings together. To the contrary, we seek to mark the constant and unpredictable mutations in these arrangements by introducing the concept of the *multiplication of labor*. We elaborate this notion as part of an ongoing engagement with various attempts to materially ground a new theory of political subjectivity, whether through the concept of the multitude (Hardt and Negri 2000; Virno 2003), or the ongoing debates surrounding the transformations of citizenship (Balibar 2003a; Isin 2002) and the category of the people (Laclau 2005). The multiplication of labor in this regard is a conceptual tool for investigating the composition of living labor in a situation characterized by a high degree of heterogeneity. In part it refers to the intensification of labor processes and the tendency for work to colonize the time of life. It also attempts to grasp the subjective implications of the diversification and heterogenization of workforces that are the other side of the growing relevance of social cooperation in contemporary capitalism. The concept of the multiplication of labor is therefore meant to accompany as well as supplement the more familiar concept of the division of labor, be it technical, social, or international.

By inverting this classical notion from political economy, we want above all to question the orthodoxy that categorizes the global spectrum of labor according to international divisions or stable configurations such as the three worlds model or those elaborated around binaries such as center/periphery or North/South. We also seek to rethink the categories by which the hierarchization of labor is specified within labor markets, however they may be defined or bordered. Our discussion of old and new theories of the international division of labor from the point of view of the Marxian analysis of the world market in chapter 3 shows that the geographical disruption lying at the heart of contemporary global processes needs to be analyzed not just in terms of division. More important, we argue, is the multiplication of scales, zones, and channels that undermines the stability of global space. Speaking of a multiplication of labor provides an angle from which these dynamics can be analyzed in terms of their consequences for the subjective composition of living labor. This requires a careful investigation of the processes of legal and political constitution of labor markets, within which migrant labor plays a crucial role today.

In particular, we critically discuss the notion that skill is the predominant factor that divides workers from each other. The multiplication of labor certainly points to the multiplication of elements of division and hierarchy. For instance, the shift from quota to points systems for the selection and management of labor migration by many countries (Shachar 2006, 2009) indicates that skill is only one criterion among many—including cultural factors such as religion and language—that contribute to the shaping of national labor markets. Moreover, the fact that many workers who perform supposedly unskilled tasks, such as taxi driving, possess high qualifications and skills points to other factors, in this case primarily juridical status, that are at stake in the production of laboring subjects. In a world where market rights are increasingly independent of the territorial configuration of power, the processes constituting labor markets are themselves increasingly de-linked from the nation-state. In this sense, the multiplication of labor acquires a political meaning. Though it is necessary to remember that multiplication is a process of division, it is also important to consider how the contemporary multiplication of labor can produce political subjects who do not fit into established categories of political belonging and expression, such as those associated with citizenship, trade unions, political parties, non-governmental organizations, or even activism. This is no more so than at the border, where the struggles of those who challenge some of the most stringent and sophisticated techniques of discipline and control open possibilities for articulating labor to politics in powerful ways.

"If *labor* supplies the crucial theoretical key that opens up the practical linkage between the antithetical poles of bare life and sovereign (state) power," writes Nicholas De Genova, "the literal and also conceptual terrain that necessarily conjoins them, nevertheless, is *space*" (2010, 50). Likewise, the literal and conceptual terrain on which we explore the multiplication of labor is the heterogeneous domain of global space as it is continuously divided and redivided by the proliferation of borders. This entails a necessarily wide-ranging analysis in the geographical sense but a tightly integrated conceptual and theoretical line of argument. On one hand, we explore the het-erogenization of global space and the way it forces seemingly discrete ter-ritories and actors into unexpected connections that facilitate processes of production, dispossession, and exploitation. On the other hand, we draw attention to the axiomatic workings of capital, which permeate the encoun-ters and processes of negotiation, mixing, conflict, and translation that such heterogenization necessitates and allows. Working between these poles, we investigate how the unity of contemporary capital is fractured through a multiplicity of particular, fragmented, and material operations while also asking how border struggles remake the political subjectivity of labor in ways that provide contested grounds for building a politics of the common.

Chapter 2 engages the spatial dimension of borders and asks why geo-graphical and in particular territorial borders have come to dominate under-standings of the border in general. Working between the history of cartogra-phy and the history of capital, we trace the intertwining of geographical with cognitive borders and the role of civilizational divides in making the modern state and capitalism, European imperialism, the rise of area studies, and the emergence of contemporary world regionalism. This focus on the making of the world, or what we call *fabrica mundi*, underlies a critical investigation in chapter 3 of the political economic concept of the international division of labor. Investigating the historical origins of this term and surveying the political, economic, and analytical uses to which it has been put, we argue that heterogenization of global space throws into question any understand-ing of the division of labor that reflects a mapping of the world as a series of discrete territories. The concept of the multiplication of labor is proposed from within an analysis of the contemporary "transitions of capital." Focus-ing on how the current patterning of the world corresponds to a deep heter-ogeneity in the composition of living labor, chapter 4 explores the borders that connect and divide two particularly significant subjective figures of contemporary labor, namely, the care worker and the financial trader. This leads us not only to provide a specific angle on the widely discussed topics of the feminization of labor (as well as migration) and the financialization of capitalism but also to question the taken-for-granted nature of the division between skilled and unskilled labor and in particular the role it plays in migration studies and policies.

Chapter 5 continues this line of questioning, placing an emphasis on the temporal aspects of methods of border policing and labor control. Here we introduce the concept of differential inclusion and draw parallels between more and less disciplinary ways of filtering and governing labor mobilities.

These include the strategies of delay and withdrawal used to force up the price of labor in the body shop system for the transnational mobility of Indian IT workers (Xiang 2006) and the more violent forms of temporal bordering enforced in migrant detention centers, such as those on the external frontiers of the EU or on Australia's remote islands and desert territories. Reading the history of migrant detention in the context of border struggles brings us to a critical discussion of the way detention has been widely interpreted by critical scholars following Giorgio Agamben's analysis of the camp and "bare life." Chapter 6 places this analysis in a wider frame of governmental approaches to the border, systems of migration management, and the concerted efforts to integrate humanitarian interventions into the work of border control. In the end, we argue that neither the category of governmentality nor that of sovereignty as developed by Agamben and others can fully account for the complexities of the system of differential inclusion that characterizes current migration regimes. The concept of a sovereign machine of governmentality is proposed as more adequate to grasping emerging assemblages of power in the global age. This concept is tested in chapter 7 through a consideration of the graduated sovereignties that shape labor practices in special economic zones and the different kinds of corridors, enclaves, and new towns that facilitate contemporary processes of accumulation. Investigating the internal borders that construct these spaces, particularly in China and India, we argue that they are paradigmatic sites that render visible complex connections between patterns of dispossession and exploitation and show how contemporary capital works the boundaries between different accumulation regimes.

The concluding chapters of the book recast the question of political subjectivity from the epistemic viewpoint of the border. Chapter 8 investigates the decline of the figure of the citizen-worker. This involves a consideration of how the mobility and proliferation of borders adds an unprecedented intensity and diffusion to the divisions and hierarchies that characterize the organization of labor under capitalism. Taking this into account, we also grapple with the critical discussion on the issue of translation that has developed in recent years through the boundaries of a number of disciplines, from cultural and postcolonial studies to political theory and philosophy. We stress the materiality (the "labor") of translation to derive a concept of translation adequate to the production of a political subject that can meet the challenge of the bordering processes that cut and cross the contemporary world. Chapter 9 extends this discussion by relating this concept of translation to practices of struggle, in particular to the problem of how a new conception of the common might be forged by practices of translation between different struggles. Critically discussing theories of articulation and universalism, we attribute a special role to the encounter with the untranslatable in tearing established political subjectivities away from themselves and opening new horizons for the production of the common. This leads to an emphasis, throughout our argument, on the contestation of the border practiced daily by subjects in transit.

Chapter Two

FABRICA MUNDI

Shadow Lines

"A place does not merely exist," muses the young Indian narrator of Amitav Ghosh's novel *The Shadow Lines* (1988), "it has to be invented in one's imagination." With this thought, Ghosh's narrator criticizes his family friend for taking space, place, and geography too much for granted. We might make the same claim about borders. Invented and instituted through often violent historical processes, borders are sites of confrontation, contact, blocking, and passage. Their inscription within our perception of space shapes what Martin W. Lewis and Kären E. Wigen call "metageography": "the set of spatial structures through which people order their knowledge of the world: the often unconscious frameworks that organize studies of history, sociology, anthropology, economics, political science, or even natural history" (1997, ix).

Ghosh's novel is a testimony to such processes of bordering. Centrally concerned with the 1947 Partition of the South Asian subcontinent and the communal riots that preceded the East Pakistan Liberation War, which led to the creation of Bangladesh in 1971, *The Shadow Lines* also explores another series of borders that divide people from others and themselves. These include the borders separating colonizer from colonized, present from past, memory from reality, identity from image, and, last but not least, the cognitive and generic borders that mark different territories of knowledge and writing. This proliferation of borders, both conceptual and material, is part of what we call border as method. One of our primary concerns in this book is to trace and analyze the relations between different kinds of borders, as well as the struggles and knowledge conflicts that arise along them. With this approach comes the need to negotiate the sense in which borders are typically understood as predominantly geographical constructs. We do not want to fully disavow this view. Before probing the relations between different kinds of borders, we find it necessary to explain how and why geographical borders are usually the first ones to spring to mind. We confront this task in this chapter, along the way grappling with issues such as the role of cartography, the rise of area studies, and the intertwining of geographical and cognitive borders.

Consider the following episode from *The Shadow Lines*. A family argument occurs when the narrator's grandmother, who grew up in Dhaka, decides she will travel there to visit family after many years in Calcutta. The year is 1964, and the narrator recalls the old woman's anxiety about the trip: "For instance, one evening when we were sitting out in the garden she wanted to know whether she would be able to see the border between India and East Pakistan from the plane. When my father laughed and said, why, did she really think the border was a long black line with green on one side and scarlet on the other, like it was in a school atlas, she was not so much offended as puzzled" (Ghosh 1998, 185). Explaining herself, the old lady asks if she might be able to see trenches, soldiers, or barren strips of land. If the border has no defining features, she surmises, people would not know it is there, and all the violence of Partition would have been in vain. Her son replies by explaining that the trip to Dhaka is not like flying over the Himalayas into China. The border "isn't on the frontier," he says, "it's right inside the airport" (186).

Apart from highlighting family tensions, this scene raises serious issues about borders, territory, maps, and history. The exchange between mother and son registers how mapping practices and technologies have contributed to how we dwell historically and geographically on Earth. To put it in more technical language, the conversation shows how maps are involved with "encoding" rather than "decoding" the world (Pickles 2004, 52). Ghosh manages to deliver a sense of how maps create territory while simultaneously undermining any form of cartographic determinism. At stake in the family's negotiation of the geographical border that has transformed their lives is another border: the epistemological border between reality and representation. By exploring the relation between these borders, *The Shadow Lines* evokes what Derek Gregory (1994) calls "cartographic anxiety"—the sense that maps are powerful devices for creating knowledge and trapping people in their grid lines on one hand, and, on the other hand, the awareness that they are mere representations with uncertain capacity to reflect or control historical, political, or geographical processes.

This sense of cartographic anxiety, or "crisis" as some commentators (Farinelli 2009; Pickles 2004) call it, permeates the contemporary discussion on borders. To be sure, it is a pronounced feature of work that investigates what Étienne Balibar describes as the "vacillating" quality of borders—their tendency to be "multiplied and reduced in their localization and their function," to be "thinned out and doubled," to form "*zones, regions*, or *countries*" (Balibar 2002, 91–92). The perception that the border is "no longer *at the border*, an institutional site that can be materialized on the ground and inscribed on the map" (89) has significant consequences for theories and practices of mapping. Such claims are no longer made just by thinkers who seek to radically rethink the political by questioning the view of borders as "territorial markers of the limits of sovereign political authority and jurisdiction" (Vaughan-Williams 2009, 1). The call to heed the "equivocal character" of borders has also seeped into the work of mainstream political geographers such as John Agnew who maintain a "normative commitment" to the capacity of borders to "enhance or restrict the pursuit of a decent life" (Agnew 2008, 176, 183). Even in work that retains a strong sense of borders as territorial edges between sovereign states, the question of the reliability and influence of cartographic representation has become unavoidable.

In their discussion of the evidentiary role of maps in international boundary disputes, John Robert Victor Prescott and Gillian D. Triggs recount the varied and shifting approaches that international tribunals have taken to "the probity of maps" (Prescott and Triggs 2008, 193). Although the general principle is that maps should be secondary to other kinds of evidence, tribunals have taken distinct approaches in different cases. Maps have been admitted as evidence of state practices and intentions, as independent documents with the function of illustrating legal texts, and as annexes to legal instruments, such as treaties. To establish the sense in which they may provide only secondary evidence, Prescott and Triggs cite the Guatemalan countercase submitted to the Tribunal of the Guatemalan-Honduras Boundary Arbitration, which delivered its decision in January 1933:

> A map is primarily a statement of geographical facts, designed in theory to present visually the unvarnished truth. Its purpose is to bring home that truth to the mind through the eye. . . . But the map-maker does not stop at this point. He commonly undertakes to do much more—to state the political as well as geo-

graphical facts. Here again his duty in such a case is to reveal the truth, relative to national pretensions or accepted limits and known boundaries. The sources of his information simply differ, however, from those concerning the purely geographical facts. The tests of his accuracy are not in the decrees of Nature, but in those of states. (quoted in Prescott and Triggs 2008, 196)

Although this submission operates entirely in terms of the modern geopolitical imaginary that approaches borders as territorial boundaries between sovereign states, the sense of cartographic anxiety is palpable. As much as the spatial border between Guatemala and Honduras is at stake, so are the epistemological and political borders between "geographical facts" and "national pretensions." Recognizing this as an element of even the most traditional border disputes, however, does not exhaust the sense in which we write of border as method. Since the early 1970s, critical geographers have criticized the intertwining of knowledge and power in mapping practices, investigating, for instance, the intersection between mapping and war (Lacoste 1976), empire (Edney 1999), or nation-building (Winichakul 1994). In the contemporary discussion, however, the focus is on the specific deficit of representation that troubles attempts to map the spatial disruptions that lie at the core of capitalist globalization. For us, it is not enough to imagine a border politics that remains caught in the regression between epistemology and boundary drawing. Also crucial is the ontological sense in which borders are involved in making or creating worlds—their role in the scene of *fabrica mundi,* to pick up an expression circulating among Renaissance philosophers such as Pico della Mirandola and Giordano Bruno. The concept of *fabrica mundi* resonates with the celebrated image of the *homo faber fortunae suae* ("man as master and creator of his own destiny"), employed by these thinkers to designate the liberation of "man" from the subjugation to natural and transcendent forces. It is salutary to keep in mind that Gerardus Mercator, the first "scientific" cartographer, also mobilized this concept in the title of his *Atlas sive cosmographicae meditationes de fabrica mundi et fabricati figura* (1595). Only by heeding the world-making capacity of borders, we believe, is it possible to discern their role in the processes of accumulation and exploitation that arose with mapping the modern world.

The Primitive Accumulation of Modern Cartography

The emergence of the cartographic gaze has been investigated from a wide variety of angles. For instance, the aforementioned studies by John Pickles (2004) and Franco Farinelli (2009) explore its links with the spatialization of matter in mechanistic philosophy, with the geometrical representation of space provided by René Descartes, and with the invention of perspective in early modern painting. Less explored are the implications of the use of the expression *fabrica mundi* in the title of Mercator's *Atlas*, as well as in the works of other early modern geographers. Twenty years before Mercator, Giovanni Lorenzo d'Anania, a Calabrian scholar who specialized in geography and demonology, called his geographical treatise *L'universale fabrica del Mondo overo cosmografia* (1573). *Geographia naturalis, sive, Fabrica mundi sublvnaris ab artifice et avthore saturæ inventa et elaborata* was the title of a work by Heinrich Scherer (1703). In these works, particularly in Mercator's *Atlas*, the term *fabrica mundi* comes to denote the "proportion," the "order," or "texture" of the world the map is supposed to represent. Early modern cartographers participate in a process of abstracting the meanings of the word *fabrica* that can be traced in medicine, astronomy, and architecture between the sixteenth and seventeenth centuries. During this period, *fabrica* comes to describe the fabricated work itself, rather than the process of its fabrication. The original theological meaning of *fabrica mundi* (as present, for instance, in the work of the early Christian writer Victorinus of Pettau) is thus transposed into the image of the perfection of the object under investigation (from Vesalius's human body to Palladio's buildings to Mercator's world). What is lost in this transposition is precisely the act or the process of *creation*, which was at the core of the reinvention of materialism in the humanist thought of the Renaissance. One has only to think of Giordano Bruno's theory of the infinity and potency of matter and the continuity of creation to get a sense of the radical and powerful nature of this reinvention of materialism, which struck out against theological orthodoxy and transcendental, deified visions of life and cosmology (Raimondi 1999).

The birth of modern cartography therefore must be located within the broader process of the appropriation and neutralization of the humanist and materialist challenges of Renaissance thought. This led to the emergence of modern science and philosophy, in which Descartes played a crucial role (Negri 2007a). What Michel Foucault famously argued about *Don Quixote* in *The Order of Things* can be said also of modern cartography. Emerging out of the crisis of the cosmographical notion of *imago mundi* (Lestringant 1991), modern cartography is also "a negative of the Renaissance world" (Foucault 1989, 53). Along with writing, as Foucault suggests, mapping "has ceased to be the prose of the world; resemblances and signs have dissolved their former alliance" (53). One could venture that the use of the expression *fabrica mundi* signals, in the form of a slippage, the cartographer's awareness of the fact that representing the world on a map also means *producing* it. This recalls Martin Heidegger's notion of "representing production" (Heidegger 2002, 71), which also resonates in Foucault's analysis of "representation" in *The Order of Things*. But such awareness assumes the form of a disavowal, because the abstraction of the word *fabrica*—its transposition to denote the produced work, its perfection, proportion, and inner order—obscures the very process of production.

While modern cartography was emerging in Europe, new lines were being traced, on both European land (in the forms of the enclosures of the commons that marked what Karl Marx called the so-called primitive accumulation of capital) and the new maps of the Americas, to legally organize the colonial conquest and expansion of European powers. Tracing these lines, which Gavin Walker (2011) invites us to consider together in an essay on Marx and Carl Schmitt, anticipated and made possible the establishment of linear borders among European nation-states in the wake of the Peace of Westphalia. Once we consider this entanglement of lines, another meaning of the word *fabrica* comes to the fore. In *Totius latinitatis lexicon* (1771), the eighteenth-century scholar Egidio Forcellini informs us that *fabrica* properly denotes the *fabri oficina* ("the smith's workshop") or *ergasterion*. This meaning prevails in the words derived from *fabrica* in many European languages, such as Italian and German. *Ergasterion*, the Greek word Forcellini used, refers to a type of workshop found in ancient Greece, the Hellenistic East, the eastern provinces of the Roman Empire, and Byzantium, which as a rule employed slave labor. Long before the Industrial Revolution took off in England, this type of workshop reemerged on a mass scale in the Caribbean, where the sugarcane plantation anticipated the industrial organization of (slave) labor (Mintz 1985, 50). It was also present in the mines around the city of Potosí in present-day Bolivia, where the extraction of silver was predicated on the forced labor system known as the *mita*, established by the Spanish viceroy Francisco de Toledo in 1573 (Bakewell 1984).

The role of Potosí as a global city in the development of the capitalist world system between the sixteenth and the seventeenth centuries has been highlighted by an impressive exhibition held in Madrid, Berlin, and La Paz, *Das Potosí-Prinzip* (2010). Cartography, which has become an important site of artistic practices, figured prominently in this exhibition. The work titled "*WORLD* map," produced by the Austrian artist Anna Artaker, redraws a world map that was published in Siena in 1600 by Arnoldo di Arnoldi. The relation between the birth of modern cartography and primitive accumulation is explicitly at stake in this work. Artaker uses rubbings from a historical silver coin minted in Potosí at the end of the sixteenth century to superimpose on her copy of the original map "the sea routes on which the silver traveled eastward [toward Europe] and westward [through Manila toward China] from Potosí around the world" (Artaker 2010, 232). The global channels of the new trade and monetary circuits of capital are thus inscribed on the map, and so is the materiality underlying the emergence of the first global currency, made possible by the extraction of silver from the mines of the Cerro Rico (the "Rich Mountain") of Potosí. Artaker's map sheds light on the logistics underlying the abstract power of money (the channels of silver circulation, the galleons carrying it, and the new global geography opened up in the Pacific by the Spanish conquest of Manila in 1571). At the same time, its location in the exhibition unearths the "secret" of its production: the "tens of thousands of Indios working in forced labor under deadly conditions" (Artaker 2010, 232).

This global scene of the primitive accumulation of capital provides another point of view on the birth of modern cartography. The connection between map making and modern colonialism has been often noted and critically investigated, stressing, for instance, the role played by atlases in illustrating collections of travel reports between the end of the sixteenth and the beginning of the seventeenth century. As Frank Lestringant writes, the "open form" of the space resulting from the combination of maps, tales, and juridical documents in these collections, its "theoretically unlimited growth," served to "prepare colonial expansion" (Lestringant 1991, 256). The space of modern cartography was definitely "open." But to open up this space (to open it up at the same time to the primitive accumulation of capital and to colonial expansion), tracing boundary lines (of the enclosures famously analyzed by Marx in the final chapter of *Capital*, volume 1, as well as of the "global lines" of the *jus publicum Europaeum* reconstructed by Schmitt in *The* Nomos *of the Earth*) played an absolutely crucial role.

Marx was well aware of the global geography of so-called primitive accumulation. "The discovery of gold and silver in America," he famously writes, "the extirpation, enslavement and entombment in mines of the aboriginal population, the beginning of the conquest and looting of the East Indies, the turning of Africa into a warren for the commercial hunting of black skins, signalized the rosy dawn of capitalist production. These idyllic proceedings are the chief moments of primitive accumulation" (Marx 1977, 739). Gavin Walker invites us to pay particular attention to Marx's mention of Africa as a "warren" ("a bounded, fenced, captured territory ideal for cultivation, breeding, and experimentation, in short, for reproduction"). It is worth quoting Walker's comment at length.

> Marx points to the formation of "area" or "civilization" as a political technology of control, the effect of bordering (which can be understood as the ideational mapping of primitive accumulation on a global scale) whose primary function is to constantly reproduce the naturalizing and grounding of difference in a phenomenal-material form, thereby legitimizing and sustaining it. This reproduction is essential, because while it is ostensibly intended to signal the reproduction of Africa, it is also simultaneously and unavoidably a figuration also of the "West," as something differentiated from this "other" space. (Walker 2011, 390)

What Walker describes in this passage is the simultaneous emergence (and structural intertwining) of geographic and cognitive borders in the scene of primitive accumulation. Cartographic proportion reshapes the world according to its measure and thus inscribes this structural intertwining in the very "metageography" underlying modern maps. It is precisely at this metageographical level that borders begin to crisscross the cartographic imagination from early modernity, collapsing geographical and "civilizational" divides. As Jerry Brotton shows in *Trading Territories* (1998), the orientation underlying Mercator's projection was "arguably more complex than simply instating the centrality of Europe." His world map established "a distinction between a geopolitical East and West which reflected their growing polarization in line with the territorial and commercial interests of the sixteenth-century imperial powers." It also contributed to the creation of the epistemic conditions "for the discursive deployment of the idea of the 'Orient' within European travel accounts and geographical discourse of the seventeenth and eighteenth centuries, which implicitly framed descriptions of an exotic, indolent and mysterious 'East' in relation to a dynamic and enlightened 'West'" (Brotton 1998, 168). This is consistent with Walter Mignolo's investigation of the role of cartography in the colonization of the Americas, which stresses that the process of putting this part of the world on the map from the European perspective in the sixteenth century was a decisive step toward the birth of "Occidentalism" (Mignolo 1995, 325).

Long before the nationalization of territory and state that determined the generalization of the linear border within European space (the opening up of frontier spaces remained for many years characteristic of colonial expansion outside of Europe), early modern maps had already anticipated the connection between boundary lines, the territorialization of identity, and even civilizational thought. They established a cognitive border that anticipated later divides between the "West and the Rest." The operation of this border (as well as of borders in general) cannot be simply described in terms of exclusion. Here we can relate the rise of modern cartographic reason to the discussion of Foucault's interpretation of Descartes in *Madness and Civilization* provided by Jacques Derrida in 1963. Challenging any easy binary opposition between reason and madness, Derrida stressed the importance of shedding light on the "hyperbolical moment when [the *Cogito*] pits itself against madness, or rather lets itself be pitted against madness" (Derrida 1978, 72). This overlapping of reason and madness, this "hyperbolical" moment of clash between the Self and the Other, is characteristic of every border, already apparent in the commonsense truth according to which a border separates as much as it connects. To be produced as the Rest (and to be constructed and excluded as its other), the non-Western world already had to be included in the West itself, in the hyperbolical moment in which both the West and the Rest (as well as the world itself) are produced. This hyperbolical moment—the ontological moment of the production of the world—is what we must read off modern maps.

"As a sign," Thongchai Winichakul writes in *Siam Mapped*, "a map appropriates a spatial object by its own method of abstraction into a new sign system" (Winichakul 1994, 55). The appropriation of space that lies at the core of modern mapping replicates the appropriation of the commons that establishes private property as well as the colonial conquest with its global geography of genocide and extraction. In all these gestures of spatial appropriation, tracing boundary lines played a crucial role: no private property without enclosure, one could say with Marx or for that matter with Jean-Jacques Rousseau: "the first man, who, having enclosed a piece of ground, to whom it occurred to say *this is mine*, and found people sufficiently simple to believe him, was the true founder of civil society" (Rousseau 1997, 161). No colonial conquest without the global lines that legally construct non-European spaces as open to conquest, one could say with Schmitt. No modern map, we can now add, without the geographical and cognitive borders that articulate the cartographic production, the *fabrication* of the world. What we want to stress is precisely this ontological moment of production connected with tracing borders. Just as classical political economy removed from the historical horizon of capitalism the "original sin" and violence of primitive accumulation, naturalizing the "laws" of capitalist accumulation, so modern cartography congealed the ontological moment of the fabrication of the world, constructing its epistemology on the idea of a natural proportion and measure of the world, an abstracted *fabrica mundi* to be projected onto maps. The naturalization of geographical and cognitive borders was the necessary outcome of this epistemological move. At stake in border as method is an attempt to rescue this ontological moment congealed in modern mapping, to open up a space in which a different imagination and production of the world becomes possible.

Farinelli notes the elective affinity between cartographic symbols and money in capitalist societies. Whereas the first work on the map and the second works in the market, they both perform the role of "general equivalents," making space and commodities commensurable (Farinelli 2009, 29). This means that the logic of exchange value permeates modern cartographic reason from the time of its emergence in the same way it constitutes the conceptual skeleton of the "phantomlike objectivity" of the world made by commodity fetishism (Marx 1977, 128). As Société Réaliste, a Paris-based cooperative created by artists Ferenc Gróf and Jean-Baptiste Naudy, writes in the introduction to the catalog of an exhibition in which cartography features prominently among the topics of artistic intervention, "Gerardus Mercator may be the Latin translation of the Flemish name Gerhard de Kremer, but the fact remains that *mercator* means 'the merchant'" (Société Réaliste 2011, 13). We know that Mercator was a good merchant. We are well informed about his "ability to combine geographical skill with an astute management of the commercial and political implications of his work," converting his products, at the dawn of "print-capitalism," into "some of the most sought after in sixteenth-century Europe" (Brotton 1998, 160). But the very space produced by the modern cartographic gaze is what transposed onto maps the sovereignty of the commodity form.

Many authors have investigated the development of the link between modern geography, maps, and commodity fetishism, following, for instance, the analysis of the economy of display and mass consumption in urban life provided by Walter Benjamin in *The Arcades Project* (Gregory 1994, 214–56). Our intention has been to work from within the conceptual and material space established by this link, bringing to light the ontological moment that produces it and illuminating the function of the intertwined action of cognitive and geographical borders in what we call *the primitive accumulation of modern cartography*.

Once this intertwined action was established and inscribed onto the map, the world was ready to host different continents, tribes, civilizations, cultures, peoples, nations, and languages. Naoki Sakai and Jon Solomon grasp an important point when they write about the way "nationalization" reshapes knowledge, bodies, and life: "the archive, the language, the culture and the history—in short, the modern fetishization of 'communicable experience'—are as much sites of primitive accumulation for the construction of majoritarian subjects of domination as are the modes of production and labor for Capital" (Sakai and Solomon 2006, 20). These "epistemic" sites are reflected as well as produced by maps, as Winichakul (1994) shows in his remarkable history of the "geo-body" of Siam/Thailand. The emergence of homogeneous, discrete, and bounded national languages is part and parcel of this process of what Sakai and Solomon call the "primitive accumulation for the construction of majoritarian subjects and domination."

A crucial site for the further investigation of the intertwining of geographic and cognitive borders would be the concept of world literature forged by Johann Wolfgang von Goethe and the later emergence of the study of comparative literature (Damrosch 2003). Likewise, an investigation of the history of linguistics between the eighteenth and nineteenth centuries sheds light on overlapping linguistic and racial taxonomies (Poliakov 1974). In the majestic tale of world history told by Hegel at the beginning of the nineteenth century, this intersection of geographic and cognitive borders governs the recomposition of time and space within the progression of the Spirit (and its material bearer, the state), organizing its hierarchies both in the temporal and spatial dimensions. As Ranajit Guha (2002) observes, Hegel's providential vision establishes borders between history and prehistory, between different "stages" of development, and between continents and civilizations, languages, races, and nations. Finally and importantly, the mutual implication of geographical and cognitive borders continues to invest the metageographical patterns that traverse the contemporary world, fashioning areas, blocs, zones, ecumenes, networks, matrices, and regions. Considering the processes of bordering, accumulation, and production that invest these spatial (and temporal) structures is vital to discerning the connections, concatenations, and movements that make what we call fabrica mundi.

The Pattern of the World

Let us return to *The Shadow Lines*. At a certain point after the killing of his relative amid the 1964 communal riots in Dhaka, Ghosh's protagonist draws a circle on a map. Centering his compass on Khulna, the East Pakistani city where the violence first erupted, and placing the other point on Srinigar, where the incident that catalyzed the unrest occurred, he is astounded by the reach of the curve.

I was struck with wonder that there had really been a time, not so long ago, when people, sensible people, of good intention, had thought that all maps were the same, that there was a special enchantment in lines; I had to remind myself that they were not to be blamed for believing that there was something admirable in moving violence to the borders and dealing with it through science and factories, for that was the pattern of the world. They had drawn their borders, believing in that pattern, in the enchantment of lines, hoping perhaps that once they had etched their borders upon the map, the two bits of land would sail away from each other like the shifting tectonic plates of the prehistoric Gondwanaland. (Ghosh 1988, 285–86)

Ghosh evokes the geological process of continental drift to register the popular belief in the "enchantment of lines" and the official approach to borders as instruments of separation. His narrator goes on to muse that "there had never been a moment in the 4000-year-old history of that map when the places we know as Dhaka and Calcutta were more closely bound to each other than after they had drawn their lines" (286). The passage shows that the two-sided nature of borders—their capacity to both connect and divide—cannot be thought in isolation from their world-making capabilities. Nor can the pattern of the world be reduced to a jigsaw puzzle of sharply bounded territorial units with no overlap and no unclaimed spaces. Mapping is not merely a matter of proportion and scale. Rather, it intersects with powerful processes that move "violence to the borders" and deal with it "through science and factories"—that is, through the production of knowledge and the harnessing of labor. At least this is the vision of Ghosh's narrator in the wake of Partition in the Indian subcontinent—an event that was crucial to establishing the metageographical construct of South Asia, which came into being only after this moment of division.

In this section, we investigate the genealogy and preconditions of the pattern of the world that emerged with the mid-twentieth-century institution of area studies. What interests us are the intertwining cognitive and geographical borders at stake in this division of the world into different macroregions or areas. There are strong precedents for such patterning in "the ancient and ubiquitous division of the earth into Europe, Asia and Africa (with the Americas as a latter addition)" (Lewis and Wigen 1997, 29). In the nineteenth century, when the modern discipline of geography was taking shape, this continental scheme was formalized and naturalized. Figures such as the German geographer Carl Ritter argued that each continent was "planned and formed as to have its own special function in the progress of human culture" (Ritter 1864, 183). It is difficult to underestimate the influence of this image of continents as "geographic individuals," especially when one notes that Hegel, a colleague of Ritter's at the University of Berlin, adapted it to establish his understanding of the geographic foundations of world history and above all his theory of "national spirits" (*Volksgeiste*) as "moments" of the deployment of the "world spirit" (see Rossi 1975, 24–33). The nineteenth century was characterized by the nationalization of the state in Europe. But this process, which corresponded to the inscription of linear borders (between "national spirits") onto the European map, took place within a wider metageographic pattern (the world spirit, to use Hegel's jargon) whose global scope had been established since the inception of modern history (and cartography).

The development of political geography as a discipline was shaped after Ritter by the intertwining of these heterogeneous boundary lines. On one hand, it had to work within a mobile cartography, fostered by the "becoming national" of European states and by the tracing of borders. To use the words of Friedrich Ratzel, these processes marked the edge of the "diffusion of a form of life" (1899, 259), circumscribing the state as a "piece of humanity and a piece of land" (1923, 2) and producing it as an object for the scientific work of "national" geographers. On the other hand, geographers were also following (and often anticipating) the imperialist movement of the expansion of European powers in the colonial world. The integrity of domestic borders, Lord George Curzon wrote a couple of years after concluding his service as viceroy of India, is "the condition of existence of the state." Although this condition seemed guaranteed in Europe, Curzon was very much concerned about the continuous reproduction of disputes and conflicts between "the Great Powers" along the colonial frontier.

> As the vacant spaces of the earth are filled up, the competition for the residue is temporarily more keen. Fortunately, the process is drawing towards a natural termination. When all the voids are filled up, and every Frontier is defined, the problem will assume a different form. The older and more powerful nations will still dispute about their Frontiers with each other; they will still encroach upon and annex the territories of their weaker neighbours; Frontier wars will not, in the nature of things, disappear. But the scramble for new lands, or for the heritage of decaying States, will become less acute as there is less territory to be absorbed and less chance of doing it with impunity, or as the feebler units are either neutralized, or divided, or fall within the undisputed Protectorate of a stronger Power. We are at present passing through a transitional phase, of which less

disturbed conditions should be the sequel, falling more and more within the ordered domain of International Law. (Curzon 1908, 7)

It was 1908. World War I did not turn out to be the demonstration of Curzon's prophetic vision. Moreover, the war's conclusion, which spelled the end of four multinational empires in Europe, laid the foundations for an attempt (accomplished in Versailles under the decisive pressure of Woodrow Wilson) to accomplish redrawing the European map under the sign of the national. In some memorable pages, Hannah Arendt (1951) showed how the dream of nationalism turned into a nightmare for linguistic, national, and religious minorities in the historically heterogeneous territories of Central and Eastern Europe. Arendt's analysis can be retold from the perspective of the attempt to trace linear borders dividing territories that had long been considered "marches" or *krajina* (to mention a word that figures in the very name of Ukraine and was bound to become associated with ethnic cleansing in the 1990s during the wars in the Balkans).

It was not by accident that the heyday of imperialism in the age of the "scramble for Africa" and its culmination in World War I witnessed the emergence of a new spatial "discipline" (and a new political rhetoric) that reframed the understanding of borders according to the crisis of a specific "pattern of the world." Toward the end of the century, the Swedish scholar Rudolf Kjellén seems to have been the first to have coined the term *geopolitics* (Chiaruzzi 2011). This word's rapid circulation among German, British, and North American geographers and its popularity at the level of public discourse in the age of the world wars suggest that geopolitics was catching something relevant in the "spirit of the age." The conflict between imperial powers that culminated in World War I marked the crisis of the conception of geographical space that evolved through the nationalization of the state in Europe *and* through the European imperial adventure, particularly that of the British Empire. The age of Britain as hegemonic global power was coming to an end, and this corresponded to the crisis of what we discuss in the next chapter as a specific balance between "territorialism" and capitalism (between land and sea, to put it with Schmitt).

The rise of geopolitics was a symptom of the crisis of that pattern of the world. It also nurtured numerous attempts to overcome this crisis. Infamous as it has become, the concept of *Lebensraum* (even in its criminal use by the national socialist project of bringing Central and Eastern Europe under a form of colonial domination) was itself an expression of a widespread awareness in the age of world wars of the collapse of the international order centered on the nation-state in Europe and European imperialism on a world scale. The name Karl Haushofer is particularly redolent here, partly due to publications such as *Life* magazine painting this figure as the hidden mastermind of Nazi geopolitics in the period before the United States entered World War II (Ó Tuathail 1996, 115–31).

Indeed, it is possible to trace the influence of the concept of Lebensraum on U.S. geopolitical thought as it evolved during and after the war. Part of this story involves the role played by Central European émigrés like Hans Weigert and Robert Strausz-Hupé, who moved to the United States and developed the concept in a different direction than the one followed by national socialism. In the hands of Isaiah Bowman, a leading political geographer in the United States from the 1920s, the concept was remade to emphasize economic (rather than territorial) expansion and influence. In early 1940, Bowman, in his role as the founding director of the Council of Foreign Relations, declared that the answer to German territorial Lebensraum should be "an American *Lebensraum*, a global *Lebensraum*, and an economic *Lebensraum*" (quoted in Smith 2003, 250). In a later article, "Geography vs. Geopolitics" (1942), Bowman explicitly disavowed the concept of geopolitics, excluding it from the scientific boundaries of the discipline of geography and promoting his vision of U.S. economic expansion that was at once rooted in earlier Wilsonian doctrines and looked toward a future of globalization. What interests us is not only the aspect of depoliticization that marks this moment but also its subsequent intertwining with the parallel depoliticization of the discourse of development, which tended more and more to be presented in a kind of objective and technical way within the metageographical pattern of the Cold War.

The notion of world regions, defined less by geography than by historical and cultural factors, emerged in the mid-twentieth century to displace some of the teleological and taxonomic assumptions that informed earlier continental visions. The abstraction of such metageographical units, although fundamental and perhaps unavoidable for understanding how the world is put together, is not independent from changing configurations of power— whether military, economic, or political—across the twentieth century. That the region of South Asia emerged only in the wake of Partition is only one register of this.

As usually told, the emergence of the geographical schema of world regions accompanies the rise of the United States as a global power during and after World War II. This is despite the fact that figures such as José Martí, W. E. B. Du Bois, and Rabindrinath Tagore articulated culturally complex and politically charged visions of regionalism in the early twentieth century. The appearance in the United States of area studies as a fully fledged and funded academic pursuit can be understood as a neutralization of these earlier visions, as is particularly clear in the case of the remapping of Africa predicated on the erasure of the great tradition of African American radical anticolonialism (Von Eschen 1997). The rise of area studies also involved an effort to bestow a sense of scientific authority and objectivity on the division of the world into more or less boundable areas, supposedly united by social and cultural features and understood as comparable and thus separable entities. Although there was always debate and uncertainty around the exact arrangement of world regions, by the time of the Cold War, an intellectual consensus and institutional infrastructure had loosely formed around the following geographical units: North America, Latin America, Western Europe, Eastern Europe and the Soviet Union, the Middle East, Sub-Saharan Africa, South Asia, East Asia, Southeast Asia, and Australia and New Zealand.

The emergence of this geographical framework in the sights of U.S. military interests is perhaps most clearly and dramatically articulated by Rey Chow, who links area studies and the evolution of "comparative work" more generally with a "world that has come to be grasped and conceived as a target—to be destroyed as soon as it can be made visible" (Chow 2006, 12). The "age of the world as target," as she calls it, paraphrasing the title of a famous essay by Heidegger we already mentioned, is characterized by a profound "militarization of thinking" in the age of the atomic bomb. Though we share Chow's concern with the militarization of thinking (it is important to recall her emphasis on the fact that comparative literature also arose out of an age of unprecedented war in Europe at the turn of the nineteenth century), we suggest that the birth of area studies after World War II was far from limited to focusing on "targets" to be immediately destroyed. Rather, area studies played a crucial role in a new *production* of the world, a new fabrica mundi, or the invention of what we have called a new pattern of the world. Framing the planet in such a way meant that tracing new (literal as well as metageographic and cognitive) borders produced new maps of domination and exploitation for capitalist development in the long decades of the Cold War, inscribing the specter of European hegemony within a new geographic imagination. We use the word *specter* with reference both to Dipesh Chakrabarty's critique of persistent influence of the "imaginary figure" of Europe (2000, 4) and to the fact that the world wars and the emergence of U.S. global power concretely coincided with the displacement of Europe from the center of the map.

Neil Smith (2007) and David Nugent (2007, 2010) trace in historical detail the emergence of area studies through the building of collaborative relations between philanthropic foundations, government, universities, the military, and intelligence agencies. Responding to the need for knowledge to administer the growing number of populations falling under the U.S. sphere of influence, these alliances enabled the "institutionalization of a new geography of knowledge and power" (Nugent 2010, 19). Central to this enterprise was the formation of "new centers of intellectual activity, policy analysis and career possibility" (22). Organizations such as the Social Science Research Council and the American Council of Learned Societies had key roles to play. In 1943, the former issued an influential document titled "World Regions in the Social Sciences" (Hamilton 1943). This report prescribed the kind of intelligence that should be gathered about world regions, provided a rationale for ranking them according to geopolitical significance, and suggested techniques for training experts to produce the desired knowledge about these entities. This is not the occasion to fully explore the historical and institutional processes that made area studies a dominant perspective in the U.S. social sciences, although we can mention an organization that led the creation of this new "knowledge geography": the Ford Foundation.

Accounts of the Ford Foundation's role in the establishment of area studies are legion. Writings by Edward Berman (1983), George Rosen (1985), David Szanton (2004), Timothy Mitchell (2004), and Nugent (2010) detail the funding of new infrastructures of training, research, and publication that resulted in the building of interdisciplinary, advanced degree–granting area studies institutes at thirty-four major U.S. universities by 1966. Less examined is the relation between this extraordinary effort and the system of large-scale industrial production that Antonio Gramsci was among the first to name Fordism. Although it is important to trace the influence of military and intelligence agencies on the rise of area studies, there are elements of the Ford Foundation's involvement that cannot fully be captured by the concept of the world target (Chow 2006). Nor are these aspects of Ford's involvement fully explained by the notion of the so-called military-industrial complex, which refers to policy and monetary relationships between legislators, armed forces, and the industrial sector. Taking Fordism as a crucial point of reference sheds new light on the pattern of the world that was emerging with the rise of area studies and the activities of players such as the Ford Foundation.

The Trained Gorilla and the Holy Cow

We do not mention Gramsci by accident. The analysis of Fordism that he provided in his *Prison Notebooks* focused on the fact that the rationalization of labor and production linked to Fordism was not merely a technical process. It was rather to be understood as a reshaping of the whole fabric of society, which "has determined the need to elaborate a new type of man" (Gramsci 1971, 286). Questions of sexuality, the family, moral coercion, consumerism, and state action were all at stake in this effort to create a new kind of worker "suited to the new type of work and production process" (286). As feminist thinkers have pointed out, the Fordist manufacturing of a "new type of man" was partly accomplished by the relegation of women to the home and the sphere of domestic labor through the introduction of the "family wage" (Lewchuk 1993; May 1982). If today we consider such a process to involve the production of subjectivity, it is worth remembering that Gramsci foreshadowed the invention of this concept in a famous passage that discusses the place of Fordism in the history of "industrialism." "The history of industrialism has always been a continuing struggle (which today takes an even more marked and vigorous form) against the element of 'animality' in man. It has been an uninterrupted, often painful and bloody process of subjugating natural (i.e., animal and primitive) instincts to new, more complex and rigid norms and habits of order, exactitude and precision which make possible the increasingly complex forms of collective life which are the necessary consequence of industrial development" (Gramsci 1971, 298). Obviously, it was particularly the working class that needed to be reshaped according to the new scope of this "continuing struggle" of industrialism in the field of human nature. We are far away here from the "animalization" of the worker referred to by Frederick Taylor at the beginning of the twentieth century. "American industrialists," Gramsci added, "have understood that 'trained gorilla' is just a phrase, that 'unfortunately' the worker remains a man and even that during his work he thinks more, or at least has greater opportunities for thinking. . . . And not only does the worker think, but the fact that he gets no immediate satisfaction from his work and realizes that they are trying to reduce him to a trained gorilla, can lead him into a train of thought that is far from conformist" (310).

Such a nonconformist train of thought sheds light on the fact that the Ford Foundation was actively involved in funding research that sought to discern the condition of the working classes across different global settings. This was understood as a means of influencing labor movements and securing a coherent U.S. strategy for the production of "harmonious" industrial relations on a worldwide scale, along lines that had already been experimented on with the Marshall Plan and the creation of the new area of Western Europe soon after the war (Maier 1991). Central to this effort was a team of researchers lead by Clark Kerr, who later emerged as a key academic administrator at the University of California. Kerr led a project called the Inter-University Study of Labor Problems in Economic Development, which spanned over two decades, involved more than ninety researchers from more than two dozen countries, and attracted over $1 million of funding from the Ford Foundation and later the Carnegie Corporation. In the initial proposal, submitted to the Ford Foundation in 1951, Kerr wrote that "the development of an effective American worldwide strategy demands a profound understanding of the position of the working class in a variety of societies" (cited in Cochrane 1979, 61).

Although Kerr's application was initially unsuccessful, a second proposal submitted the next year was judged by a Ford Foundation official as important "for the purpose of influencing the development of the labour movement in other parts of the world and of encouraging the development of free rather than communist-controlled labour unions" (59). Kerr was funded to pursue research that used the International Labor Organization as a hub for its activities and produced about forty books and more than fifty papers. Central to this research was a vision of industrialism characterized by "an open and mobile society, an educated and technocratic workforce, a pluralistic set of organized interest groups, a reduced level of industrial conflict, and increasing government regulation of the labour market" (Kaufman 2004, 259). In a key publication that appeared in 1960, *Industrialism and Industrial Man*, Kerr and his colleagues argued that the prime factor shaping the evolution of industrial society is not labor movements or class conflicts but the strategies and values of managers and other elites. They thus turned "from concentration on protest to providing a structure for the managers and the managed" (Kerr et al. 1960, 8). Overall the project sought to provide strategies for defusing industrial conflict and channeling it into systems of arbitration that could be adapted to different contexts.

Thus it becomes possible to discern how the new "knowledge geography" of area studies was linked institutionally and methodologically to attempts to deactivate and depoliticize labor movements around the world. The supposed emergence of "industrial society" cannot be extricated from the management of labor conflicts in the frame of a neutralized and technocratic view of development. Many authors have noted how area studies are implicated in the rise of post–World War II discourses and practices of development, replete with built-in temporal and spatial assumptions about progress and difference (Sanyal 2007). The very form of the state, its legitimacy in the wake of decolonization, as well as its attempts to accomplish a full "national" citizenship through the generalization of wage labor (and what Gramsci called industrialism) were shaped outside of the West by these discourses and practices. It was the age of the "developmental state."

Through the work of critical scholars such as Arturo Escobar and Wolfgang Sachs we are now well informed about the role played by the discourse of development in U.S. global politics since the formulation in 1947 of what came to be known as the Truman doctrine. It was an attempt to "colonize anti-colonialism" (Esteva 2010, 6–8), which means an attempt to establish a new Western and capitalist hegemony under the conditions created by successful anticolonial uprisings and struggles. This implied a reformulation of theories of economic stages of development that had shaped colonial discourses and governmentality since the early nineteenth century. The discipline of economics was directly involved in tracing a new form of intersection between temporal and spatial borders within the new pattern of the world emerging with the rise of area studies. *The Stages of Economic Growth* by Walt Whitman Rostow, the "noncommunist manifesto" published in 1960, is probably the best example of this. Although it is important to trace the colonial genealogy of "development" (the British Development Act of 1929 was, for instance, crucial in fostering a transformation of the verb *develop* from the intransitive into the transitive form in the colonial context), it is equally relevant to stress the discontinuity produced by decolonization. It was only in the 1950s, Kalyan Sanyal writes, that development came to be "perceived as a systemic change that was to be brought about by purposeful, rational action, a task to be performed, a goal to be achieved and a mission to be carried out" (Sanyal 2007, 108–9). "Planning" ceased to be only a "socialist" concept. It became a magic word of the Cold War decades (Escobar 2010a). In areas of the world that were constructed as "underdeveloped," the concept of planning pointed to a societal process, in which the state was a key actor but which also involved domestic and international agencies such as the Ford Foundation.

Clearly the Ford Foundation was not the only agency to operate in the nexus of area studies and development, but its role as a key grant maker and its relations to the Ford Motor Company make it an important example to examine. As Simon Clarke writes, Kerr's theory of industrial society offered "an altogether more humanistic and optimistic Fordist project, which it was expected would sell better on world markets than Henry Ford's earlier offer of hard work and puritanical self-discipline" (Clarke 1990, 13). Nonetheless, Kerr hypothesized an ideal type of industrial society that faced many barriers to realization. Although the task of social science research was to remove these barriers, they eventually proved too difficult to overcome. The theory of industrial society exercised "surprisingly modest influence on the intellectual (science-building) side of the industrial relations field" (Kaufman 2004, 261), while the edifice of area studies itself moved into crisis.

One need only mention Beverly Silver's (2003) study of twentieth-century labor conflicts—not least those that crossed the auto industry—to register how labor struggles in the so-called developing world intensified each time management shifted sites of production, transformed production processes, or withdrew money from production for investment in financial channels. Similarly, it is important to remember that the emergence of the paradigm of development as the key concept for the governance of the "third world" from the point of view of the U.S.-led West was matched by the ethos of the Bandung Conference of 1955, which brought together leaders from the recently decolonized countries in Africa and Asia (Young 2001, 191–92). As complex and ambiguous as the relation between the moment of Bandung, the technologies and rhetoric of development, and the multifarious struggles of decolonization that reached a peak with the Vietnam War may be, the conceptual frameworks that link these historical phenomena cannot be easily accommodated within theories of industrial society or the geography of area studies.

To understand these discontinuities from the point of view of border as method means probing the significance of the various military, industrial, economic, and political developments that resulted in the dominance of area studies by the height of the Cold War. Indeed, we can say that at stake in the approach of border as method is precisely what remains occluded in area studies: that is, what might be designated the "area form," as well as the processes of bordering at stake in the materiality of its constitution. What we propose is a move close to that made by Ranabir Samaddar in his analysis of South Asian nationalisms. Samaddar highlights that in the past decade, a growing number of critical scholars have come to focus on "the analysis of forms by studying the conflicts that constitute the form, its margins, the interrelations between forms, etc." The study of nationalism has been consequently supplemented by studies of the "national form." Samaddar explains: "Borders, boundaries, fault lines, ethnicities, geopolitics and national structures—which were ignored in studies of nationalism—have now made possible critical inquiries into the nation form." Investigations of the nation form must therefore be opened up toward the interplay of "internalities" and "externalities" that constitutes it, conveying a sense of their "juxtapositions, coherence, and contradiction" (Samaddar 2007a, 7).

Samaddar thus links his ongoing engagement with the nation form to a critical concern with the definition of a particular area, that is, "South Asia." Especially in *The Marginal Nation* (1999), his important work on the Bengali borderland, he stresses that it was "the carving up of South Asia at the end of the colonial period into a number of nation states" that laid the basis for the prevalence in this same borderland of ongoing violence against migrants and refugees. Samaddar's focus on practices of mobility against the background of the double process of bordering that inscribed both new nation-states and a new area onto the map is what makes his work particularly important from the point of view of border as method. Describing postcolonial nationalism in the wake of the India–Pakistan partition as a "reflexive nationalism" (a nationalism defined against neighboring nations) and as a "gross caricature of its predecessor: anti-colonial nationalism," he also points to the necessity of going beyond the nation-state to address the above-mentioned problems in a regional perspective (Samaddar 1999, 28, 43). In Samaddar's analysis, both the material tensions and conflicts that shaped and continue to shape nation and area formation in South Asia and the possibility of a radically different definition of that area come to light. His analysis of South Asia from the point of view of the Bengali borderland and transborder migration offers an approach to the notion of the area that allows us to better highlight the tensions and conflicts at stake in the production of the area form.

Samaddar's emphasis on the material constitution of the area form offers a different perspective on the question of the area than that which arises from earlier forms of comparative history and civilizational thought (Oswald Spengler and Arnold Toynbee are crucial twentieth-century references here) and the particular geopolitical inflections they received during the Cold War. His approach allows us to retrieve a sense of the political importance of the myriad struggles and even dreams that surrounded the moment of anticolonial nationalism. By mapping the unfolding trajectory of these struggles and dreams, it becomes possible to track how they continually exceed the borders of the nation and the nation form, giving rise to particular forms of regionalism and even transcontinentalism (Anderson 2005; Samaddar 2007b). At the same time, focusing on the area form means reactivating within the depoliticized geography of development and area studies the material production of space that is connected with the tracing of borders. The violence of Partition—its shadow lines, to recall Ghosh's novel—resurface at the very center of the area form of South Asia as investigated by Samaddar: its "reality" as well as its "memory" has "continued to be associated with population movements both at the point of origin and resettlement" (Samaddar 1999, 70).

Once this violent history of bordering is recognized as crucial to the production of the area that has come to be known as South Asia, the national borders that traverse it can be seen in a different light. They appear as elements of an overdetermined system of demarcation that makes the very existence of a subcontinental region possible. Taking stock of his fieldwork and experiences in border towns such as Malda, Bongaon, Hasnabad, or the "zero line towns like Hili," Samaddar observes, "The *inside* and the *outside* along the borders were being incessantly produced and they revealed the physical, but even more, the psychological and epistemic violence that accompanies the enterprise of nation-building" (1999, 108). This perspective also gives rise to a new way of studying movements and struggles of migration across the region. Samaddar explains that in the 1990s, parallel to the growth of the Hindu right (Bharatiya Janata Party) in India, migration came to be closely associated with "the issue of power, security and the destiny of a state." This aggressively nationalist politicization of migration and border control can only be understood if one takes into account that for the migrant herself, mobility is charged with political meanings that crisscross and often exceed economic motivations. "The immigrant's flight," Samaddar writes, "is his/her form of resistance" (150). Border fencing as well as issuing photo identity cards to villagers close to the border (the main control techniques deployed by the Indian state) confront a transborder mobility that "contradicts the absoluteness of political borders and boundaries" and challenges "the 'holiness of the cow' that citizenship is" (77).

The resulting cartographic anxiety signals a temporal as well as spatial suspension, where both the gap between the "former colony" and the "not yet nation" and the demarcation between the inside and outside are blurred (Samaddar 1999, 107–9). It also sheds light on a conflict between practices of mobility and border reinforcement that has to be understood as a conflict between different modalities of the production of space at the "local," "national," and "regional" levels. The migrants' space is indeed beyond that organized by the national partition of the South Asian area. Obviously, stating this does not correspond to any simplistic apology for migrants' nomadism. On one hand, migration has to be analyzed against the backdrop of the rise of an integrated regional market, however imperfect, in goods and services, particularly labor services. On the other hand, the persistence of violence, exploitation, and trafficking (with a gender specificity that becomes particularly clear in the way HIV has been transformed into a "border disease" in the whole Indian northeast) would make such an apology offensive from the point of view of migrants who move from Bangladesh to West Bengal (Banerjee 2010).

As in many other borderscapes across the world, "illegal migration" in the Bengali borderland has become the cornerstone of "a mode of political and economic management which exploits the difference between the legal and the illegal." Migrant labor, Samaddar adds, becomes "one of the principal forms of the investment of national boundaries with power," and this needs to be understood within the framework of the radical restructuring of capitalist production that since the early 1980s has produced waves of "deindustrialization" and dismantling of strongholds of labor power in India as well as in many other places in the "global South" (Samaddar 1994). A recognition of the political tensions and subjective claims that crisscross migration paves the way for the imagination of political practices that aim at combining the "granting of rights," the exercise of "counterpower," and a new way of inhabiting the area in the global present. A new political perspective emerges from Samaddar's investigation of processes of bordering and movements of migration, wherein the granting of rights must be in "direct proportion to exercise of power, a critique of nationalist chauvinism," and the "recognition of South Asia as an interlinked region from within" (Samaddar 1999, 44).

In sounding the importance of borders and boundaries as well as practices and struggles of migration to Samaddar's approach, it is important to distinguish it from perspectives that question the legacy of area studies without engaging in political arguments about labor, migration, and border struggles. Nugent notes how the same organizations that funded the rise of area studies began to withdraw support in the 1970s and then in the 1990s to direct "research away from areas and toward the changing configuration of global and regional space under late capitalism" (Nugent 2010, 26). A Ford Foundation report titled *Crossing Borders* from the late 1990s states: "The notion, for example, that the world can be divided into knowable, self-contained 'areas' has come into question as more attention has been paid to movements between areas. Demographic shifts, diasporas, labor migrations, the movements of global capital and media, and processes of cultural circulation and hybridization have encouraged a more subtle and sensitive reading of areas' identity and composition" (Ford Foundation 1999, ix).

We have no fundamental disagreement with this argument, which we understand as an important symptom of the crisis and transformations of the pattern of the world within which area studies emerged. Our difference is rather one of emphasis. Though we recognize the analytical usefulness, even necessity, of identifying world regions in debates about mobilities, globalization, and labor, we suggest that attention to borders, in their conceptual and material aspects, is even more analytically useful than attention to "movements between areas" at the present time. This difference in emphasis not only is analytical but also points to a difference in political perspective. Taking the border as a methodological point of view, as well as investigating concrete borders and borderscapes, we can bring to light the intense tensions and conflicts that crisscross and change the material constitution of "areas" as far as their current shape and insertion in global circuits of capitalist accumulation, governance, and even culture is concerned. Obviously, these tensions and conflicts are visible not just "at" borders; they also inscribe themselves within each "area." But it is precisely from the border that the very shape and constitution of areas appear in a different light. The area itself, as we showed through Samaddar's investigation of the Bengali borderland, becomes open to forms of political imagination and practices that lead to a more nuanced approach to its "identity and composition" and also make clear the continuous processes of remaking and remarking that are crucial features of current processes of capitalist creation and destruction.

Continental Drift

If today the Cold War construction of area studies has entered into crisis, it is not so much because of the erasure or overcoming of borders as their proliferation. To understand why this is so, it is necessary to recognize how the continentalist schema of area studies intersected the tricontinentalist scheme of three worlds: first, second, and third. Michael Denning suggests that perceived discontinuities between the three worlds prevented the emergence of a vision that could mediate "between the philosophically oriented 'critical theory' of the First World, the dissident formations of the Second World, and the peasant and guerilla Marxisms of the Third World" (Denning 2004, 9). Even the intellectual tradition of the Cold War era that most rigorously tried to think the world as one—world systems or dependency theory—devised a typology of center, periphery, and semi-periphery that echoed the tricontinentalist scheme. According to Denning, "not until the three worlds dissolved into one" could the affinities between these earlier projects be fully explored (9). The globalizing tendencies that gave rise to interests in hybridity, flows, and transnationalism were themselves susceptible to new forms of fracture, differentiation, and bordering. Economic regions, graduated sovereignties, export processing zones, and offshore spaces are just a few of the new kinds of heterogeneous global spaces that come to the fore with the emergence of so-called postdevelopmental geographies (Sidaway 2007). Thinkers like Daniel J. Elazar (1998), Ulrich Beck (2000), and Carlo Galli (2010) highlight the reorganization of political space that accompanied the transformations of state sovereignty and capital's global expansion. What needs to be noted is how this expansion of capital was thus met by a countermovement that led to the establishment of continental blocs, the pursuit of nationalist projects, securitization, and harsh controls on labor mobility.

The concept of continental drift has been employed by many thinkers and writers concerned with borders and globalization, including Amitav Ghosh, whose evocation of "shifting tectonic plates" we already discussed. By evoking this concept, we also want to recall the Continental Drift seminar series that ran from 2005 to 2008 under the organization of 16Beaver group in New York City. The introduction to this experimental seminar series begins: "Continental integration refers to the constitution of enormous production blocs—and particularly, to NAFTA and the EU (while awaiting the emergence of a full-fledged Asian bloc around Japan and China). But continental drift means you find Morocco in Finland, Caracas in Washington, 'the West' in 'the East'—and so on in every direction. That's the metamorphic paradox of contemporary power" (16Beaver 2005).

This concurrent sense of integration and scrambling, regionalization and drift, captures well the complex machinations of power and production in the contemporary world. Obviously, the perspective of fabrica mundi, which emphasizes the ontological dimension of producing the current global conjuncture, lends this dynamic a significance that is not immediately evident in the familiar Deleuzian claim that processes of deterritorialization are always accompanied by those of reterritorialization. At stake is not only a new kind of intermingling of geographical and cognitive borders but also shifts in labor regimes that have led on one hand to the increased productivity of social cooperation and, on the other hand, to the diffusion of nonwage forms of labor and, more generally, labor insecurity and precarization. This intermingling and these shifts must stay in view as we balance claims for "disorganized capitalism" (Lash and Urry 1987) or the "new global disorder" (Joxe 2002) against the observed tendency for economy and culture to organize themselves in vast regional units such as the European Union, the North American Free Trade Agreement (NAFTA), the Association of Southeast Asian Nations (ASEAN), the Asia-Pacific Economic Cooperation (APEC), Mercado Común del Sur (MERCOSUR), the Organization of American States, the Arab League, and so on.

There is indeed a sense in which continental blocs—which often replicate or closely parallel the geographical units established by area studies— are beginning to function as governmental apparatuses one scale up from the nation-state. These regional units are provisional assemblages of markets and states that represent specific attempts to articulate and manage the vast constructive and destructive energies that have been unleashed by the development of global capitalism over the past four decades. They exhibit varying degrees of political formalization or constitutionalization, functioning in some instances by means of complex forms of multilevel or heterogeneous governance such as the EU's Open Method of Coordination (Beck and Grande 2007). Yet they can also emerge as stubborn civilizational constructs, as the debate about "Asian values" that erupted in the 1990s in countries such as China, Malaysia, Singapore, Indonesia, and Japan illustrates (Barr 2002). We are all familiar with Western variants of this civilizational approach, ranging from Samuel Huntington's (1996) advocacy of a clash of civilizations to fundamentalist defenses of white and Christian values against the challenges of multiculturalism.

Indeed, these dual and sometimes conflicting aspects of global regions often intersect in their approach to border control and migration management. Thus we find governmental measures such as the introduction of the EU Schengen Agreement or the formation of the Frontex agency (which coordinates the border control efforts of EU states) to unevenly and sometimes uneasily articulate with civilizational views or new forms of "racism without race" (Balibar 1991, 23) that politically and culturally reinforce efforts of migration control. Regional arrangements can also intensify border policing within economic blocs, as the example of the U.S.–Mexico border as well as attempts to establish regional frameworks of border control in Central America (Kron 2010) show in the case of NAFTA. The important point is that the contemporary formation of continental blocs, which is a contested and incomplete process, cannot be understood in isolation from precisely the kind of migratory movements, labor mobilities, and border struggles that are central to the approach of border as method.

It is possible to trace a continuity between the legacy of area studies and the newer forms of global regionalism. But contemporary migratory movements are also one of the most important forms of continental drift responsible for the scrambling and displacement of the civilizational divides between East and West as well as the economic divides between North and South. The presence of Morocco in Finland, Caracas in Washington, or Hyderabad in Melbourne is largely, although not exclusively, accomplished through the transnational movement of people. There is an increasing urgency to read these metropolitan presences in a frame that exceeds the debates about cultural diversity, identity, multiculturalism, and cosmopolitanism. In the case of Samaddar's analysis of the South Asian area form, we obtain a new perspective on regionalism by asking how border and labor struggles, which are increasingly carried out in urban spaces far from territory's edge, imply ways of making the world—fabrica mundi—that are socially and politically remote from the dominant continentalist visions. Again, it is a question of how the *production of subjectivity* intersects the *production of space*. To quote 16Beaver:

> World regional blocs are developing not only a functioning set of institutions, but also a dominant form of subjectivity, adapted to the new scale. This form of subjectivity is offered to or imposed upon all those who still live only at the national level, or on the multiple edges or internal peripheries of the bloc, so as to integrate them. At the same time it serves to rationalize—or to mask—the concomitant processes of exploitation, alienation, exclusion and ecological devastation. In what different ways does this integration of individual and cultural desire take place? How is it resisted or opposed? How to imagine an excess over the normative figures of continentalization? Where are the escape hatches, the lines of flight, the alternatives to bloc subjectivity? And what types of effects could these exert on the constituted systems? (2005)

To understand migration, border, and labor struggles as producing "alternatives to bloc subjectivity" does not imply a romanticization of migration. Rather, it means working through the ambivalences that characterize practices of mobility: the forms of domination, dispossession, and exploitation forged within them as well as the desires for liberty and equality they often express. Obviously, the geography of migrant mobilities is crucial to the ways and the extent to which they may exceed "the normative figures of continentalization." The migrant from a new member state of the EU (such as Romania) who works without a permit in Italy faces a different set of circumstances than a "clandestine" worker from northern Africa in the same country (although those circumstances can be even harder if the migrant from Romania is a Rom). The internal Chinese migrant who flouts the country's household registration system challenges migration controls in a different way than an Indian who works more than the twenty-hours-a-week time limit imposed by an Australian student visa. Bolivian migrants in Buenos Aires enjoy freedom of movement under a fairly liberal migration law adopted by the country in a continental perspective, but they often live in urban ghettos (*villas miseria*) within internal borders reinforced by virulent forms of racism and are exploited in textile sweat shops run according to ethnic logics. Yet all are agents whose mobility embodies desires, habits, and forms of life that rewrite the normative scripts of national as well as continental belonging. In later chapters we explore more fully the myriad ways this excess crosses capital's attempts to simultaneously valorize and contain labor mobility. For now, it is important to note that such mobility plays a role in remaking and reconfiguring both the external and internal borders of contemporary world regions. In contrast to their official constitution as tightly bounded entities, migratory movements throw into question the possibility of identifying an inside and outside to such continental spaces. They also tend to harden and soften their internal boundaries, depending on the pressures exerted on them by migratory flows and the composition of the populations traversing them. These tendencies are themselves important examples of continental drift, and they need to be analyzed in relation to the longer history of cartographic anxiety and metageographic uncertainty that this chapter unfolds.

Although continental integration and the formation of production and trading blocs such as the EU and NAFTA are features of contemporary globalization, the hatching of new cultural visions, political projects, and anti-identitarian regionalisms within continentalist frames is by no means a recent phenomenon. Indeed much work in so-called critical regionalism harks back to an earlier era of continentalist thinking and movement that was effectively effaced by the rise of area studies after World War II. For instance, Paul Gilroy's *The Black Atlantic* (1993) finds its impulse in W. E. B. Du Bois's notion of "double consciousness" and bases its radical reassessment of the African diaspora on the latter's hemispheric and pan-African visions of racial politics. Jeffrey Belnap and Raul Fernández (1998) return to José Martí's essay "Nuestra America" (1892) to "negotiate comparatively the tension between national and transnational forces at work in the Americas" (Belnap and Fernández 1998, 4; see also Saldívar 2012). Shakespeare's Caliban continues to spur radical cultural and political imagination across the Caribbean and Latin America, since this character from *The Tempest* was proposed as a symbol for decolonizing struggles in 1969 by the Cuban writer Roberto Fernández Retamar and by Aimé Césaire. Gayatri Spivak's *Other Asias* (2008) evokes Du Bois and Martí alongside figures such as Rabindrinath Tagore in a series of ponderings on "how to be a continentalist." Rustom Bharucha's *Another Asia* (2009) sets the background for contemporary inter-Asian cultural politics with an exploration of the entangled biographies of Tagore and the Japanese art historian and curator Okakura Tenshin.

The earlier continental visions that inspire these interventions go beyond foreshadowing today's interest in critical regionalism or alternative modernities (Gaonkar 2001). If read critically, they display how the perspective of alternative modernities tends to congeal the dimension of culture, isolating it from the material forces that shape societal modernization and producing the appearance of their neutrality. Du Bois's emphasis on race, slavery, and citizenship, for instance, places a strong focus on the harnessing and valorization of labor. As such, it displaces the vision of Marx and classical political economy by which "free" wage labor is presented as a capitalist norm. Later we show that recent research in the field of postcolonial and "global labor history" has taken up and further fostered this displacement. This strain of work demonstrates that rather than being seen as archaisms or transitory adjustments destined to be wiped out by modernization, "unfree" labor regimes such as slavery or indenture are integral to capitalist development and arise precisely from the attempt to control the worker's flight. A radical rewriting of the manifold modalities of subsumption and capture of labor in historical capitalism has resulted from this research. Although these works challenge the idea of a structural and necessary link between modern capitalism and "free" wage labor, they have also displaced the geographical coordinates of its history. Du Bois and other "black Marxists" such as C. L. R. James anticipated this spatial shift in their own way (Robinson 2000). They point to the constitutive relevance of slavery and primitive accumulation not only for the origin but also for the structure of modern capitalism, which continues to be haunted by the specters of Caliban and enslaved laborers in the silver mines of Potosí. This tradition of radical political thought displaced the spatial coordinates that inform mainstream histories of capitalism and also located the beginning of labor struggles for emancipation outside of Europe. "The slave revolts," Du Bois wrote in 1946 in *The World and Africa*, "were the beginning of the revolutionary struggle for the uplift of the laboring masses in the modern world" (Du Bois 1992, 60).

From this viewpoint, we can trace a line between Du Bois's concern with the hemispheric dimensions of the slave trade and the corresponding new geography of struggles and the perspective of border as method. Du Bois's thinking was shaped from the early 1890s by an acute awareness of the global dimension of modern politics, particularly of what he famously described as the "color line." This led him to continually blur and overturn the very boundary between "inside and outside, home and abroad" (Kaplan 2002, 172) in both his scholarly work and his activism in the African American, pan-African, and anticolonial movements. He gave memorable anticipations of what we call continental drift. He writes in his 1928 novel *Dark Princess*: "Here in Virginia you are at the edge of a black world. The black belt of the Congo, the Nile, and the Ganges reaches by way of Guyana, Haiti, and Jamaica, like a red arrow, up into the heart of White America" (Du Bois 1995, 286).

This mixing up of spatial coordinates and scales opened Du Bois's political imagination toward an identification with "Africa" that soon broke the borders of that continent, making the establishment of new transcontinental geographies of struggle for liberation possible. Trying to make sense of his tie with Africa, "a tie which I can feel better than I can explain," he wrote in *Dusk of Dawn* (1940): "The real essence of this kinship is its social heritage of slavery; the discrimination and insult; and this heritage binds together not simply the children of Africa, but extends through yellow Asia and into the South Seas" (Du Bois 2002, 116–17).

Du Bois's lifelong interest in "yellow Asia," culminating in his visit to communist China in 1959, is particularly important from the point of view of contemporary discussions of continental drift and critical regionalism (Du Bois 2005). His contribution to the African American encounter with Japan and China (Gallicchio 2000) and to the rise of a specific form of internationalist Afro-Orientalism in the 1920s has been obscured by his infamous endorsement of the Japanese occupation of China. There is no way to rescue Du Bois from his blindness in front of the violence and ferocity of Japanese imperialism. Nevertheless, as Naoki Sakai explains in an interview with Richard Calichman and John Namjun Kim, Du Bois's interest in Japan was fostered by the search for a different kind of universalism, one liberated from the burden of racism. Sakai notes how U.S. intellectuals engaged in "ideological warfare" during World War II were particularly concerned about the possibility that because of American "racial problems," Japan might come "to occupy the position of universalism against America, though it was supposed to occupy the position of particularism." He adds that "one of the missions of area studies, which was established during and after the war, was to disavow this crisis of ideological warfare for the United States and create the myth that the United States had constantly occupied the position of universalism" (Calichman and Kim 2010, 225).

This myth assumed the material and political form of the Allied occupation of Japan following the war. In her book *Borderline Japan*, Tessa Morris-Suzuki recounts how U.S. forces and their families freely came and went from Japan under the occupation and continue to be exempt from Japanese migration controls and alien registration to the present day under an agreement signed in 1952. This contrasts strongly with the fate of Koreans and Taiwanese in Japan who, at this same point in time, lost the Japanese nationality they held during the imperial era and the U.S. occupation. Morris-Suzuki's account of the notorious Ōmura Detention Center, where Japan detained many Koreans whom South Korea refused to accept, is particularly redolent. The fact that many of the detainees held political sympathies with North Korea made the situation tense and led to their separation from those loyal to South Korea. As Morris-Suzuki writes, Ōmura was a place "in which three conflicts became concentrated and magnified: first, the conflict between the Japanese state and its Korean former colonial subjects; second, the conflict between Japan and the Republic of Korea (ROK—South Korea); and third, the conflict between the two sides of the divided Korean peninsula—North and South" (2010, 49). It is significant that such a multiplication and intensification of borders could underscore the myth of universalism established by the extraterritoriality enjoyed by the United States in Japan and the rise of area studies. But such conflicts are precisely what matters from the point of view of border as method. Whether they collapse continental tensions into confined and oppressive spaces like Ōmura, which remained Japan's largest detention center until 2008, or range across the globe like Du Bois's hemispheric visions of political resistance is less important than their capacity to generate geographies-in-the-making. Border as method points to that elusive moment when new spaces emerge from violent clashes and struggles that simultaneously challenge and disassociate established geographical and cognitive borders.

Such a production of new spaces gets lost easily in debates on alternative modernities. Far from leading to the formation of regions and continents as given and bounded containers of alternative modernities, continental drifts and struggles around borders and mobility are central to the constitution of these spaces as sites of capitalist accumulation as well as the emergence of new territories of "altermodernity" (Hardt and Negri 2009). Border as method thus gives rise to a critical regionalism that understands attempts to control migrants' mobility as essential to the workings of capitalism and contemporary border policing and technologies as part of a long line of administrative mechanisms that work to this end. It implies a stress on the intertwining of cognitive and geographical borders. It also requires an attention to the axiomatic workings of capitalism, which are inherent to modernity and permeate the encounters, processes of negotiation, mixing, and translation within which plural processes of social modernization take place.

This means we have a slightly different perspective on what we are calling continental drift than a thinker like Kuan-Hsing Chen, who in his important book *Asia as Method*, argues that the West asserts cultural influence in East Asia through "bits and fragments that intervene in local social formations in a systematic, but never totalizing way" (Chen 2010, 223). Although we feel very close to Chen's idea of inter-referencing as a way of imagining Asia, we suggest that the "bits and fragments" that appear as Western for Chen are, rather, part and parcel of the capitalist axiomatic of modernity, which manifests itself in spatially heterogeneous ways. In this sense, we see the global dominance of capital as more and more disentangled from a world order centered on the primacy of Europe or the West (as the current forms of capitalist development in East Asia surely attest). By the same token, we see migration, border, and labor struggles as forms of social conflict that challenge capitalist ways of being precisely by contesting the "pattern of the world" that establishes the conditions for capital's flourishing and regular crises. Border as method is thus a proposition that extends far beyond the domain of human geography. It also demands a fundamental rethinking of one of the most time-honored and entrenched concepts of political economy: the international division of labor. This is a task we reserve for the next chapter.

——— Chapter Three ———

FRONTIERS OF CAPITAL

The Heterogeneity of Global Space

It was only a year after 1989—the year of the fall of the Berlin Wall, the Tiananmen protests, and the incipient collapse of the Soviet Union—that Japanese artist Yukinori Yanagi produced his famous work "World Flag Ant Farm." Yanagi filled a series of interconnected transparent boxes with colored sand so that each represented a national flag. He then built plastic channels between these boxes and released into the lattice a bevy of ants. As the ants transported food and sand throughout the system, their "border crossings" slowly degraded the integrity of each flag, creating a complex mélange of colors and patterns. In his book *La globalización imaginada*, Néstor García Canclini takes Yanagi's work as a paradigm of the cross-cultural and cross-border hybridization he sees as a prominent feature of globalization. Borders, in this perspective, appear to García Canclini as "laboratories of the global" (1999, 34). This phrase captures nicely for us the sense in which borders sit at the center of a number of global processes of transition, which are as much economic as cultural, social as political.

The early 1990s was a period in which there was a rich and preliminary production of images and concepts to describe the shape that contemporary globalizing processes would take. Flows, hybridization, smooth space, flatland, the global/local nexus, and postnationalism were some of the key words that circulated at this time, in both mainstream and critical idioms. Many were convinced of a movement toward a borderless world. The work of

Japanese management guru Kenichi Ōmae, *The Borderless World* (1990), is only the most famous of these pronouncements. The market economy seemed to be breaking free from the constraints of territory, and some were convinced that class struggle was dissipating in an "end of history." García Canclini's image of the border as the laboratory of the global, although the fruit of an analysis that in our opinion stresses cultural hybridization at the expense of economic and political processes, provides an effective counterpoint to these tendencies and foreshadows what was to come.

One of the central claims of *Border as Method* is that the globalizing processes of the past twenty years have led not to the diminution of borders but to their proliferation. We are not the only ones to make this point. Criticisms of "gated globalism" and "global apartheid" were already widespread in the 1990s. Étienne Balibar, with his book *Les frontières de la démocratie* (1992a), began to develop a rigorous analysis of the role of borders in modern history, political theory, and contemporary processes of globalization. At the same time, new forms of activism against the violence implicit in the existence and policing of borders were developing. To take one example, at the *Documenta* exhibition in Kassel in 1997, there was an important crossing of the art and activist worlds that led to the campaign *Kein Mensch ist illegal* ("No one is illegal"), a high-profile effort of border and migration activism that resonated well beyond Western Europe. How are we to make sense of such developments in the context of claims for postnationalism and predictions of a borderless world?

García Canclini's work provides a strategic point of reference precisely because of the paradoxes that haunt his dealings with the question of the border. Writing of Yanagi's "World Flag Ant Farm," he suggests that "massive migrations and globalization will transform the current world into a system of flows and interactivity, where differences among nations will disappear" (1999, 53). We do not want to enter the tireless debate about globalization as a process in which, as Arjun Appadurai puts it, sameness and difference attempt "to cannibalize one another" (Appadurai 1996, 43). Rather, we want to note the implications of García Canclini's emphasis on the "differences between nations" for debates concerning the constitution of global space. García Canclini's vision at once suggests that borders are salient sites for understanding the workings of globalization and that the nation-state is the primary unit of transformation under this process. But it is less interesting to criticize him (or Yanagi for that matter) for focusing his analysis on the "differences between nations" than to note that his description of global space, like most, is negative, specifying what globalization displaces rather than what it creates. We have more sophisticated approaches that describe, for instance, how processes of "denationalization" (Sassen 2006) are initiated from within the nation-state as well as effected from its outside, as the movement of Yanagi's ants suggests. It is not that the modern space of the nation-state has disappeared or been rendered irrelevant by global processes. Rather, it has been placed under stress, altered, and made to coexist with a variety of other spatial formations that have transformed it, recalibrated it, and made the borders that cross and exceed it as crucial as those that define its territorial and symbolic limits.

We are convinced that one of the key characteristics of current globalizing processes lies in the continuous reshaping of different geographical scales, which can no longer be taken for granted in their stability. It is not just a matter of the coexistence of multiple scales that shape the unfolding of events and processes, for this has always been a feature of the world's spatial constitution. Nor is it simply an issue of interscalar relations that relay events and processes across the boundaries that separate geographical scales. Also at stake is the tendency for scale to become at once more volatile and determining—the intensification of its contradictory capacities to contain social activity and to shift and mutate as a result of social activity. *Border as Method* addresses this paradoxical process of intensification and seeks to make sense of it in relation to the proliferation of borders that characterizes the current remaking of global space. In so doing, it engages the different kinds of mobilities that traverse and intersect different scales and spaces, making the very concept of space increasingly complicated and heterogeneous in its constitution.

The contemporary configuration of global space cannot rightly be mapped as a series of discrete territories. This is because it comprises a series of overlaps, continuities, ruptures, and commonalities, which trouble not only the mapping of the world as a set of contiguous territories but also the large scale civilizational (East–West) and economic divides (North–South) that have structured systematic approaches to world history and commerce. The East–West divide is a relic of Eurocentric spatial and cultural constructions that persisted and mutated through the classical, medieval, and modern (imperial) periods (Groh 1961). By contrast, the North–South divide provides a means of distinguishing wealthy from poor regions with origins in the narratives of social modernization and economic development that arose (and acquired an increasingly technocratic elaboration) in the wake of World War II (Brandt Commission 1980). Both of these divisions have been seriously questioned by analytical approaches that complicate their binary heuristic, which in any case could never be given a definitive geographical representation. Whether by means of the three-worlds model of first, second, and third worlds, which entered an irreversible crisis with the collapse of the Soviet Union, or the division of the world into core and periphery in world systems theory, which eventually made recourse to the unstable category of the semi-periphery (Wallerstein 1974), these binary divisions were already under pressure before the analytical stress on transnationalism and hybridization assumed its present dominance in the 1990s. Nonetheless, they still structure many serious debates in international relations and development economics (see, for instance, Reuveny and Thompson 2010). It is possible that material changes to the constitution of global space alone will not be sufficient to shift the reliance on these binary categorizations. In the long run, however, the refusal to heed the turbulent and structurally unstable transformations of the contemporary world can only lead to analytical disorientation and political confusion.

Already in mainstream international relations there are voices that question the monopoly role of states as the exclusive protagonists of world politics. Writing in *Foreign Affairs*, Richard Haass points to a "tectonic shift" that effects the movement to a "nonpolar world" dominated "neither by one or two, nor by a certain number of states, but instead by dozens of actors possessing and exercising different kinds of power" (Haass 2008, 44). Regional and global organizations, militias, nongovernmental organizations, corporations, electronic networks, and global cities, according to Haass, profoundly complicate the international system of states, making the world a "difficult and dangerous" place where efforts of "global integration" are paramount (56). Likewise, in the field of economic geography, we find visions of complexity, randomness, and fragmentation that make it difficult to interpret global processes using rigid, fixed categories such as North and South or center and periphery (Vertova 2006). The hierarchical relations between the different spaces that articulate the global circuits of capitalist accumulation have ceased to connect relatively homogeneous areas according to the classical modalities of imperialism, uneven development, and dependence. Poor countries, like rich ones, are increasingly differentiated not only from each other but also from within. In marginalized metropolitan areas of the world's wealthiest nations, "third-world" conditions often apply. At the same time, in former so-called third-world countries those areas and sectors that are integrated into global networks tend to exist alongside other areas and sectors that experience extreme privation and dispossession. It thus becomes useful to hypothesize a hybrid constitution of global economic and social space in which what matters is the proportion between different functions, all of which are tendentially present at the same time.

In the previous chapter we emphasized the production of global space as a densely heterogeneous field in which borders and differences are always made rather than given. This implied an emphasis on *fabrica mundi* that showed how ontological questions of world-making are neither prior nor anterior to social, political, and economic processes of spatial transformation but, indeed, historically and temporally coeval with them. In this chapter, we switch our attention to the global constitution of economic space, keeping in view the ontological complexities we previously explored and their implications for the production of subjectivity. In particular, we hold up to critical interrogation one of the most cherished notions of classical political economy, which has influenced not only debates about the globalization of economic space but also discussions of labor history, labor politics, and labor processes: the concept of the international division of labor. The current chapter revisits the history of this concept and examines the practical uses to which it has been put. Moreover, we contend that the viewpoint of border as method allows us to grasp the heterogeneity of the emerging global space of capital and power, throwing the concept of the international division of labor into deep question. To confront these difficulties, we extend and supplement the concept of the international division of labor by introducing a new concept adequate to the proliferation of borders in today's world: the global multiplication of labor. Conceived not as a replacement but as a strengthening of the classical concept, the aim is to understand how emerging global modes of production work by exploiting the continuities and the gaps—the *borders*—between different labor regimes.

Implicit in this investigation is an attempt to bring García Canclini's vision of borders as laboratories of the global into line with a sophisticated empirical and theoretical understanding of the transitions and workings of contemporary capitalism. Gone are the days when, as Carlo Galli put it in an important book on political space first published in 2001, the view of globalization as "a particular phase in the development of the system of capital" could be characterized as a "monocausal reading," as opposed to the "multicausal" approach preferred by sociologists who emphasize "elements of discontinuity or differentiation" (Galli 2010, 102). This is because the hybridizing processes explored by figures like García Canclini at least partly inform the dynamics of commodity consumption and strategies of marketing. Capitalist production processes are organized in hybrid and flexible networks that extend across increasingly differentiated global terrains. From this point of view, arguments about the international division of labor must focus not only on differentials of class and wealth but also on the borders established by differences of gender and race. *Border as Method* seeks to critically discern these modes of differentiation and assess their relevance for border struggles and the various forms of political subjectivity to which they give rise. This involves an investigation of the intertwining of the economic space of capitalism with political and legal spaces, which are no longer fully conjoined in the territorial form of the state. It also requires a reconsideration of the kinds of global mobility that are typically understood to have undone this conjuncture.

Modern Capitalism and the World Market

The global space of modern capitalism has already loomed in the analysis we offered in the previous chapter. It was fundamental in our description of the intertwining of the so-called primitive accumulation of capital and the birth of modern cartography against the background of the fabrication of a new world (made possible by the material and cognitive tracing of a series of new lines of enclosure, separation, and partition). Our aim here is to provide a more focused conceptual analysis of the world space of capital from the point of view of border as method. If one looks at the history of economic thought from the early modern age, it is easy to trace a genealogy of the concept of "foreign" and "international" trade, starting with bullionist and mercantilist theories of the balance of trade in the seventeenth century and culminating in the theory of comparative advantages elaborated by David Ricardo in chapter 7 ("On Foreign Trade") of his seminal work *On the Principles of Political Economy and Taxation* (1821) (see, for instance, Viner 1965). Far more interesting for us, at this stage of the book, is to emphasize the conceptual rupture that was produced within this genealogy by the *critique* of political economy articulated by Karl Marx. A crucial aspect of border as method is the analysis of the articulation and disarticulation of heterogeneous borders and boundaries: first the tense balance and dramatic unbalance between political borders (which means primarily, in the modern age, the borders of states) and what we call the *frontiers of capital*, traced not only by capital's expansionist drive but also by its need to organize space according to multiple hierarchical criteria.

In the famous pages of the *Communist Manifesto*, which have been recently rediscovered and praised as "prophetic" even by neoliberal authors and gazettes, Marx and Friedrich Engels insisted on the "cosmopolitan character" given to "production and consumption in every country" by the bourgeoisie "through its exploitation of the world market" (Marx and Engels 2002, 223). Precisely this emphasis on the *world market*, which is something different from "foreign" or "international" trade, is what matters to us. In one of the several plans Marx made for his critique of political economy, he explicitly distinguishes the world market from the "international relation," stressing that the former "forms the presupposition of the whole as well as its substratum" (Marx 1973, 227; see Ferrari Bravo 1975). Though the international relation is predicated on the previous moment distinguished in Marx's plan (the concentration of production in the state), the world market refers to a spatiality of capital that structurally exceeds the topographic space of the state and its related system of "international" relations. From this point of view, the tension (as well as the necessary articulation) between the frontiers of capital and political borders emerges.

There are at least three aspects of Marx's concern with the world market (a concern that we do not find with such intensity in any classical political economist) that need to be highlighted. First, and this explains our use of the phrase "frontiers of capital," Marx's concern with the world market is crucial to forging an analytical framework for the critique of the capitalist mode of production. This critique is entirely built on capital's structural need to continuously expand itself. Marx writes in the *Grundrisse*: "The tendency to create the *world market* is directly given in the concept of capital itself. Every limit (*Grenze*) appears as a barrier to be overcome" (Marx 1973, 408; emphasis in original). It is interesting to note that the German word *Grenze* used by Marx is the same one usually employed to denote a political border. The passage of the *Grundrisse* from which we take this quote is also important from the point of view of the parallel (and once again the articulation) between the analysis of capital's creation of "absolute surplus value" and "production of relative value"—that is, the "production of surplus value based on the increase and development of the productive forces" (408). Although the first requires an *extensive* growth of the spaces subjugated by capital, the second requires an *intensive* reshaping of the whole social life submitted to the imperative of capital's accumulation. "The production of new consumption" (which also means the "production of *new* needs and discovery and creation of new use values") is crucial in this respect. What is needed, Marx writes, is "that the surplus labour gained does not remain a merely quantitative surplus, but rather constantly increases the circle of qualitative differences within labour (hence of surplus labour), makes it more diverse, more internally differentiated" (Marx 1973, 408).

Although the constitution of the world market is directly posited as the tendency corresponding to the first "extensive" axis of capital's expansion, it also sets the rule (the "substratum" in Marx's terms) for the second one, which we call "intensive" expansion. Capital's production of space is characterized from the beginning by the intertwining of these two axes, which leads to the second aspect of Marx's analysis of the world market that we would like to stress. In a way that is entirely consistent with his method and philosophical approach, the most abstract level of analysis (the world market itself) has direct consequences for the determination of the most concrete aspects of the everyday life of any individual who has entered the reign of capital. The intricate and weird relationship between "home and the world" is already apparent from an economic viewpoint, especially with respect to the "money market." The world market "is not only the internal market in relation to all foreign markets existing outside it, but at the same time the internal market of all foreign markets as, in turn, components of the home market" (Marx 1973, 280). The reference to money (famously analyzed in the *Grundrisse* as a "social relation") is crucial. In fact, he considers the world market as the highest level of representation (and as the last practical guarantee) of both "the connection of the *individual with all*" and the "*independence of this connection from the individual*" (161; emphasis in original)—that is, according to Marx, of the very material conditions for the possibility of individuals in their modern capitalist shape.

In the middle of the nineteenth century, the world market and the frontiers of capital came to play a crucial role, according to Marx's analysis, in producing the "spatial coordinates" of the everyday experience of individuals. This was in a time during which these same individuals in most European countries were quite far from having completed their transformation into citizens determined (in the spatial coordinates of their legal and political existence) by the linear borders of the modern state. Quite an exceptional example of multiscalar geographical materialist analysis of the production of subjectivity, indeed!

Once the absolutely concrete nature of the world market has been emphasized, its abstract character also needs to be briefly highlighted. This is the third analytical element we want to pick up from Marx. The world market is not just the scale on which each "industrial capitalist" is compelled to operate, comparing as we read in *Capital*, volume 3, "his own prices not only with domestic market prices, but with those of the whole world" (Marx 1981, 455). It also becomes more and more—with the progressive "socialization" of capital and its reproduction "on an expanded scale"—the scene of the "turnover" of capital and the "autonomization of value as a mere abstraction," which is to be considered as "abstraction in action." We are confronted here, as Marx emphasizes in *Capital*, volume 2, with a movement that is initiated by individual capitalists but always tends to revolve against them, especially in times of crisis: "The more acute and frequent these revolutions in value become, the more the movement of the independent value, acting with the force of an elemental natural process, prevails over the foresight and calculation of the individual capitalist, the more the course of normal production is subject to abnormal speculation, and the greater becomes the danger to the existence of the individual capitals" (Marx 1978, 185).

The "autonomization of value," which gives rise and consistency to a "total capital" that operates independently and often against "individual capitals," occurs necessarily within the horizon of the "world market." This is because of the privileged relation it has with finance and credit, which means with money: and "real money is always world-market money, and credit money always depends on this world-market money" (Marx 1981, 670). Even from the point of view of the conditions prevailing in his time, when capitalism had yet to fully become industrial, Marx provides us with quite an effective framework for the analysis of current developments in financial capitalism. More important, for us, his approach offers the possibility of grasping the tendency of capital itself, more and more evident (we want to repeat it) with the progress of its socialization (or to recall the terms used already, its extensive and intensive expansion), to produce an abstract and global space for its movement—for its *abstraction in action*. The "autonomization of value" that takes place within this space nowadays tends to impose its law against "individual capitals" as well as whole "nations" and "peoples," enormously complicating the relations between the frontiers of capital and political, legal, and cultural borders and boundaries.

The abstract character of value as the new criterion through which social relations were increasingly organized (through the "objective" mediation of money), as well as its representation in the new spatiality of the world market, was part and parcel of what was perceived as a radical challenge to "traditional" notions of social order by a whole generation of European (and more and more U.S. American) scholars at the end of the nineteenth century. Such people as Max Weber, Ferdinand Tönnies, Herbert Spencer, Thorstein Veblen, and Emile Durkheim come to mind here as representatives of the great season of "classical sociology." The very concept of capitalism evolved from an attempt to come to grips with the above-mentioned challenge. Reacting to the threat of socialism, embodied in a vivid way by the

Paris Commune of 1871, these thinkers sought to move beyond the paradigm of classical political economy (Hilger and Hölscher 1972; Ricciardi 2010). It is well known that the concept of capitalism, as Marc Bloch wrote in *The Historian's Craft*, is "altogether young" (Marx still spoke of the "capitalist mode of production"): "its ending," he added, "shows its origin— *Kapitalismus*" (Bloch 1953, 170).

The debate on capitalism at the end of the nineteenth century was fostered by increasing tensions between the world scale of capital accumulation and processes of valorization as they unfolded within national borders. This is evident in the writings of the young Max Weber on the conditions of agricultural workers in the eastern provinces of Prussia (Ferraresi and Mezzadra 2005; Tribe 1983). At stake in Weber's writings were, among other issues, the pressures of the world market for grain that led the Prussian Junkers to employ an increasing number of Polish migrant workers on their farms. In so doing, according to Weber, the Junkers acted as a "de-nationalizing" force within territories that were characterized by a deeply heterogeneous demographic composition due to the "partitions" of Poland in the eighteenth and nineteenth centuries. Weber struggled his entire life to carve out new criteria of legitimation for social and political power before what he perceived as the radical challenge posited by capitalism to the stability of social relations (Ferraresi 2003). At the same time, he kept looking for a balance between the growth of the German nation-state (with its political borders) and the world scale of "advanced capitalism" (*Hochkapitalismus*)—that is, the increasingly global scope of the expanding frontiers of capital (Mommsen 1984). A few decades later, Carl Schmitt, in his 1942 text *Land and Sea* (1997), reinterprets against this background a sentence from Hegel's *Elements of the Philosophy of Right*: "Just as the earth, the firm and *solid ground*, is a precondition of the principle of family life, so is the sea the natural element for industry, whose relations with the external world it enlivens" (Hegel 1991, 268; emphasis in original). Schmitt's goal was to inscribe within a world historic framework the antagonism between Germany and sea powers such as the United Kingdom and the United States. Independently of this political goal, his reading of this paragraph from Hegel (which is very close to the Marxian reading of the paragraphs on "civil society," as he perfidiously added in a preface written in 1981) nicely foreshadows what is currently discussed in world systems theory as the tense relationship between "territorialism" and capitalism (see, for instance, Arrighi 2007, 211–49) or what we have reframed as the relationship between political borders and frontiers of capital.

Obviously, a crucial site for the elaboration of this relationship was the great debate on imperialism that involved Marxists, liberal intellectuals, and political militants around the years of World War I. Although this is not the place for reconstructing this debate, it is worth emphasizing its importance from the point of view of border as method. The concept of imperialism brings the world scale of capital accumulation and valorization back into the analysis. It also provides another perspective on the crisis of political geography constructed on linear borders between nation-states in Europe and colonial frontiers beyond Europe that we discussed in the previous chapter. Although imperialism seemed to reconcile the global frontiers of capitalism and territorialism, it was precisely the growing relevance of the abstract dimension of the world market so carefully analyzed by Marx that destabilized imperialist projects from their inception. Eventually it led, as we anticipated through our analysis of the writings of Isaiah Bowman, to the end of the territorial bias of imperialism—if not, as we tend to agree with Michael Hardt and Antonio Negri (2000), to the end of imperialism as such. What needs to be added to this picture is the role played by anti-imperialist struggles, which found after the Soviet revolution and particularly after the 1920 Baku "congress of the peoples of the East" a transnational forum for political discussion and coordination (Young 2001, 127–39). New geographies of struggle began to emerge, reshuffling spatial coordinates and mixing up the heterogeneous scales on which modern history had developed under the constraints of political borders between European states, colonial frontiers, and the capitalist world market. A book such as *Darkwater* (1920) by W. E. B. Du Bois, who made a notable contribution to the debate on imperialism with his 1915 essay "The African Roots of War," warrants further critical investigation here (see Kaplan 2002).

Though the organization of the world scale of capital accumulation and valorization was at stake in the debates on imperialism, the limits of the project of superimposing capital's logic and the territorial expansion of imperialist states (which in a way erased the tensions between political borders and the frontiers of capital) were apparent. An important work that has been recently rediscovered in debates on the topicality of "the so-called primitive accumulation" (Mezzadra 2011a), "new imperialism," and "accumulation by dispossession" (Harvey 2005) is Rosa Luxemburg's 1913 book on the accumulation of capital. Luxemburg connected imperialism with capitalism's need for "an environment of non-capitalist forms of production" (Luxemburg 2003, 348)—for an *outside* that capital metaphorically colonizes while literal colonization opens up spaces for the penetration of capital within new territories. Though this analytical framework is definitely interesting, an overly rigid and literal interpretation of the expansive drive lying at the heart of capital led Luxemburg to identify in imperialism "the final phase of capitalism," precisely because it was rapidly leading to the exhaustion of any "outside" to capitalism. She writes: "With the high development of the capitalist countries and their increasingly severe competition in acquiring non-capitalist areas, imperialism grows in lawlessness and violence, both in aggression against the non-capitalist world and in ever more serious conflicts among the competing capitalist countries. But the more violently, ruthlessly and thoroughly imperialism brings about the decline of non-capitalist civilizations, the more rapidly it cuts the very ground from under the feet of capitalist accumulation" (427).

Though Luxemburg's emphasis on the role played by a "constitutive outside" in capitalist development remains important (Mezzadra 2011b), the literal understanding of this outside in territorial terms did not allow her to grasp the exceptional elasticity of Marx's theoretical framework. The combination of "absolute" and "relative surplus value" in understanding the (extensive and intensive) expansion of capital's frontiers opens up a new perspective on the continuous *production* of this constitutive outside (through the "production of *new* needs and the discovery and creation of new use values") that can continue well beyond the point when territories literally lying outside the domination of capital no longer exist. Far from becoming only intensive (through the creation of relative surplus value and what Marx calls the real subsumption of labor under capital), this process continuously redefines the meaning of space—opening up the possibility of a new extensive expansion of capital's frontiers (which corresponds, again in Marx's terms, to the continuity of the movement of formal subsumption).

The concept of "spatial fixes" introduced by David Harvey (1989) to trace capital's movements of geographical relocation in search of profitability, control, and the resolution of crises nicely captures this mobility of the frontiers of capital. Combining this concept with the notions of "product," "technological," and "financial fixes," Beverly Silver (2003) provides an effective framework for jointly analyzing what we call the extensive and intensive dimensions of this mobility. The concept of the world market, understood by Marx as both the presupposition and result of capitalist production, points to the abstract space within which these fixes take place, producing heterogeneous geographies of capitalist production, valorization, and accumulation. Within these geographies, the expanding frontiers of capital enter into complex territorial assemblages, in which they intertwine with political borders and produce shifting relations between capital and state. They also establish their own lines of connection and disconnection, always in excess over political boundaries. In an encyclopedia entry on economic space written in the early 1980s, Immanuel Wallerstein emphasizes this point, introducing the concept of the "spatial and temporal boundary" of an economic system and pointing to the impossibility of superimposing it over the linear border of the state. To make such a superimposition, he argues, would be to consider the state border as the natural "container" of economic activities, a supposition continuously challenged by historical transformations and dynamism over the time and space of economic systems (Wallerstein 1985, 94–95). This argument is even more valid for world systems and particularly for the modern capitalist world system, which has produced a complex network of relationships of interdependency and dependency stretched over the whole planet.

Wallerstein makes a path-breaking contribution to the analysis of the shifting global geographies of capitalism. Elaborating on the results of critical theories of uneven exchange, underdevelopment, and dependency, whose history is closely connected with the rising tide of anticolonial and anti-imperialist movements and struggles after World War II, he forges a sophisticated theoretical framework to map the relationships between core and periphery. In the first volume of *The Modern World-System* (1974), he introduces the concept of semi-periphery as "a necessary structural element in a world-economy" (349). This works as a kind of compensation chamber that articulates and mediates the more brutal relationships of domination and dependency between core and periphery. Wallerstein's triple scheme of interpretation of the global geography of capitalism (and the boundaries traced by the expansion of its frontiers) has been very influential. It was crucial for the elaboration of Giovanni Arrighi's important theory of hegemonic cycles, developed in *The Long Twentieth Century* (1994). What we find important in Wallerstein's work is the attempt, for instance in his 1991 dialogue with Balibar, to connect his analysis of the spatial hierarchies of capitalism to the critique of the ideological tensions underlying modern universalism. Crucially, these ideological tensions have a structural relationship with other sets of boundaries, such as the ones established by racism and sexism. It is indeed very important to keep in mind that modern racism and sexism always need to be critically investigated with regard to their intermingling with political borders and the expanding frontiers of capital. This leads Wallerstein to a statement, which is very close to our idea of differential inclusion (see chapter 5): "as racism is meant to keep people inside the work system, not eject them from it, so sexism intends the same" (Wallerstein 1991, 34). With the proviso that this is not true for every form of racism (just think of genocidal Nazi anti-Semitism), these words shed light on the working of racism and sexism within the constitution and shifting arrangements of labor markets.

Nevertheless, a certain rigidity in the way the concepts of core and periphery are elaborated and used looms very clearly in the pages of Wallerstein and other world system theorists. We agree with the critical point made by Latin American scholars such as Anibal Quijano (1997) and Walter Mignolo, according to whom "colonial difference" is not sufficiently acknowledged by Wallerstein and his colleagues, who effectively "understand the modern world-system from the point of view of its own imaginary, but not from the angle of the conflictive imaginary arising with and from colonial difference" (Mignolo 2000, 57). The concept of periphery becomes problematic in this perspective, whereas the one of semi-periphery continues to appear to us too close to Christian Purgatory, sharing its elusiveness. More generally such concepts as core, semi-periphery, and periphery seem to overemphasize (even from a historical point of view) the stability of the global geographies produced by the expansion of capital's frontiers on a world scale. We do not deny that they are useful analytical tools. But a too rigid understanding of them leads to an overemphasis on the objective and structural nature of capital's accumulation, as if the "enigma of capital" (to quote the title of a recent book by Harvey, which presents similar problems to us) could be deciphered by discovering a kind of eternal law of its accumulation. This problem is relevant for understanding the current global transition of capitalism, which confronts us with a set of radical transformations that produce new articulations and disconnections between the world market, regions, and states. New assemblages of the frontiers of capital, boundaries, and borders are in the making, and we need to investigate them with attention to empirical detail. Before tackling this task, we turn to an analysis of the concept of international division of labor, which is also crucial for Wallerstein. In fact, he writes:

> We have defined a world-system as one in which there is extensive division of labor. This division is not merely functional—that is, occupational—but geographical. That is to say, the range of economic tasks is not evenly distributed throughout the world-system. In part this is the consequence of ecological considerations, to be sure. But for the most part, it is a function of the social organization of work, one which magnifies and legitimizes the ability of some groups

within the system to exploit the labor of others, that is, to receive a larger share of the surplus. (Wallerstein 1974, 349)

Genealogy of the International Division of Labor

There are many ancient precedents for the concept of the division of labor. In the writings of Xenophon and Plato, we find insights that anticipate the work of the classical political economists: the notion of increasing returns to labor specialization, for instance, or the limitation of the division of labor by the extent of the market. Xenophon explored the sexual division of labor within and beyond the household. Plato, and Aristotle after him, emphasized how the growth of the city and barter between households led to a professional merchant class and the emergence of the institution of money. The writings of the medieval Islamic scholar Ibn Khaldûn, who is sometimes credited with anticipating the labor theory of value, contain discussions of how the division of labor facilitated by a larger market leads to cheaper products and higher productivity. Thus, even before the historical rise of capitalist production and its theorization in the works and tables of physiocrats and mercantilists, there was a strong appreciation of how the division of labor links to the expansion of markets and the creation of a greater capacity for generating wealth (Guang-Zehn 2005).

In the important historical account of Fernand Braudel (1979), such market expansion involves a gradual scaling up of economic activities from the small market town to regional, provincial, and eventually national markets such as that which emerged in England during the eighteenth century. But the national market was not easily achieved. It was "a network of irregular weave, often constructed against all odds: against the over-powerful cities with their own policies, against the provinces which resisted centralization, against foreign intervention which breached frontiers, not to mention the divergent interests of production and exchange" (Braudel 1979, 287). To this must be added the factor of long-distance trade, which was most often the business of powerful cities (sometimes connected in wide-ranging networks, as in the case of the Hanseatic League), and the international markets to which it gave rise. Braudel goes so far as to speculate that as a rule, "a measure of expansion in foreign trade *preceded* the laborious unification of the national market" (277). Indeed, the interplay between national and international markets, which was essential to the emergence of the world market that we already traced, proved central to the evolution of the concept of the division of labor in the works of classical political economy. At the risk of oversimplification, we can say that the evolution of this concept across the seventeenth and eighteenth centuries involved recognizing that the division of labor not only is limited by the extent of the market but is also a key factor in determining the market's expanse. This realization, which accompanied and prompted the industrial organization of labor and its technical division for the purposes of manufacture, is most clearly articulated by Adam Smith in the late eighteenth century (Zanini 2008). We need to travel a century back in time, to the interventions of William Petty, to trace how this revolution in understanding the division of labor was linked to the rise of capitalism, the conquest of foreign markets, and the gradual emergence of a world market for the commodity of labor power.

Although Bernard Mandeville is generally credited with being the first to use the phrase "division of labor," it was in fact Petty who anticipated "all the essentials of what Adam Smith was to say about it, including its dependence upon the size of markets" (Schumpeter 1986, 207). The author of *Political Arithmetick* (written in 1676) emphasized even more than Smith the spatial dimension of division of labor, which is particularly important from the point of view of a genealogy of the "international division of labor." Appointed as a physician to Oliver Cromwell's army in Ireland, Petty made a name for himself "surveying Ireland" in the mid-1650s (McCormick 2009). In the *Political Anatomy of Ireland*, he tried to calculate the economic prices of the massacres and deportations during rebellion and war using his theory of the value of populations. He also gave an early and vivid example of the role played by the invention of the "white race" (Allen 1994–97)—the racial boundary in our terms—in the emerging intertwining of political borders and the expanding frontiers of capital: Englishmen, he calculated, were worth £70 apiece, whereas Irish laborers he estimated "as Slaves and Negroes are usually rated, viz. at about £15 one with another" (quoted in McCormick 2009, 189). We cannot dwell on Petty's "alchemical" proposal for a "transmutation" of Irish into English. Suffice it to say that it was developed with a general concern for a more rational administration of the English empire and the optimal disposition of its population. The competition with Holland for the world hegemony of the seas spurred both his work on Ireland and the formulation of the "essentials" of a theory of the division of labor. In *Political Arithmetick*, he writes: "Those who predominate in *Shipping* and *Fishing* have more occasions than others to frequent all parts of the World, and to observe what is *wanting* or *redundant* every Where; and what each People can do, and what they desire; and consequently to be the *Factors* and *Carriers*, for the whole World of Trade. Upon which ground they bring all Native Commodities to be Manufactured at home; and carry the same back, even to that Country in which they grew" (Petty 1690, 15; emphasis in original).

We find in this passage the original formulation of what was later called the international division of labor. It is important to note that Petty established a close relationship between the "benefits" of having "command of the sea trade" and the technical division of labor. Just "as cloth must be cheaper made, when one cards, another spins, another weaves, another draws, another dresses, another presses and packs; than when all the operations above-mentioned, were clumsily performed by the same hand," so world-scale hegemony on the sea allows diversification in the building of ships and vessels, accelerating and making cheaper the transportation of commodities. According to Petty, this is "the chief of several Reasons, why the *Hollanders* can go at less Freight than their Neighbours, *viz.* because they can afford a particular sort of Vessels for each particular Trade" (19–20). Translating Petty's analysis into our terminology, we can say that the establishment of capitalist relations of production at "home" (with their related technical and social divisions of labor) is made dependent on a specific alliance between capital and a political power capable of holding "command" of the sea trade—that is, on the expansion of capital's frontiers on a world scale. The Calico Act (1721), banning the importation of cheap cotton from India, made it clear that a mix of free trade and protectionism would become the rule once Britain succeeded Holland, in accordance with Petty's hopes, as the hegemonic power in the sea trade and more generally in the capitalist world system. The international division of labor has never been the "natural" outcome of free trade (even considering the role of cannon balls and wars in imposing it).

Obviously, although Petty's *Political Arithmetick* shows an early awareness of the necessary mediation between what Marx called the "world market" and the emerging capitalist social formation within bounded territories, he did not employ the term *international*. This is simply because the world was not conceived of within an "international" framework in the seventeenth century. The process that led to drawing linear borders between territorial nations in Europe after the Treaty of Westphalia ran parallel to the emergence of British hegemony on a world scale and only slowly gave rise to alliances between states and capital. It was not before the nineteenth century that these borders and states became nationalized, laying the foundations for the rise of national markets (above all for labor power) and the steady formation of "fractions" of capital denominated as national. Imperialism was, among other things, an expression of the processes by which the world became international. While new assemblages of political borders played a role in prompting the expansion of capital's frontiers, the old phrase "divide and rule" enjoyed a renaissance in pushing forward the colonial frontier and in establishing new sets of boundaries in "domestic" spaces. After the publication of Smith's *Wealth of Nations* (1776), the "division of labor" became both a theoretical tool to decipher the growth of productivity within the factory and a practical weapon used to impose capitalist discipline on living labor. Age, gender, geographical location, "ethnic" provenance, and "skill" worked as criteria for the establishment of new boundaries, while capitalist development disrupted and reshaped old geographical lines of demarcation such as the one between city and country.

Although Smith's pin factory became the epitome of the technical and social division of labor, English cloth and Portuguese wine became closely associated with the theory of comparative advantages developed by David Ricardo as the basis of "foreign trade," geographical division, and specialization of production. Even though cloth could be produced in Portugal "with less labor than in England," he famously contended, the more remarkable difference in the labor needed for the production of wine would make it advantageous to Portugal to employ her capital in this branch, exporting wine and importing cloth (Ricardo 1821, 141). We do not need to elaborate on the complicated conditions under which, according to Ricardo, these exchanges would give rise to what today is called a win-win game. The complex processes that led England and Portugal to exist as bounded national spaces that could be taken as analytical units for an investigation of "foreign trade," as well as their relatively different positions within the world market, did not figure as prominent topics in Ricardo's writings or in classical political economy as a whole. It is again in the writings of Karl Marx that one can find one of the earliest uses of the phrase "international division of labor," in close connection with his analysis of the world market. "Before the invention of machinery," Marx writes in *The Poverty of Philosophy* (1847), "the industry of a country was exercised principally on the raw material which was the product of its soil." But "thanks to the machine the spinner can live in England while the weaver dwells in India." Industry becomes detached from the national soil and "depends only on the markets of the world, on international exchanges, and on an international division of labor" (Marx 2008, 152).

Already before the revolutions of 1848, Marx conceived of an international division of labor in relation to a world market and a global scope of proletarian struggles. Although the world was still becoming "international," the concept of international division of labor provided him a theoretical lens for understanding the world scale of capitalist production as well as a material basis for politically anticipating its disruption through the theory and practice of proletarian internationalism. Though this extraordinary political invention was bound to prompt an ambivalent history, made of struggles that changed the shape (and boundaries) of the world as well as of catastrophic backlashes of "national interests" (in 1914 no less than in the age of Stalin), the theory of competitive advantages went through a series of complex refinements that laid the foundations for describing the division of the world into discrete labor markets delineated on one hand by the borders of nation-states and on the other by the separation between core and periphery. In 1937, Jacob Viner summed up the development of such debates when he wrote: "in the analysis of gain from trade, attention was definitely centered upon particular boundaries, enclosing areas of community of interest, and these areas were also generally countries or nations" (Viner 1965, 599). The deepening of the meaning of the core–periphery divide for the international division of labor was left in the following decades to (mainstream and critical) debates on development, underdevelopment, uneven exchange, and dependency. In the shadow of stable borders between nations and a clear-cut separation between core and periphery, labor was considered to be spatially divided into homogeneous units and concentrated according to processes of functional specialization of production. The prevalence of industrial production signified "development," while "primary production" was considered an unmistakable sign of "underdevelopment."

Transitions of Capitalism

To ask whether the international division of labor is an analytical concept that reflected the shape of capital's global operations for a certain period or a heuristic that informed attempts to manipulate aggregate economic forces so as to mold these operations in the image of the nation-state is to enter a vicious circle. International divisions never coincided perfectly with what we call the frontiers of capital. The extended historical episode of imperialism at once established, reinforced, and undermined the role of national boundaries in containing and organizing the relations of capital to labor. Crucial to establishing the links between imperialism and the global patterning of labor were theories of monopoly, organized, or finance capitalism that emerged at the beginning of the twentieth century. In important but differing ways, both Rudolf Hilferding (1981) and Vladimir Ilich Lenin (1975) argued that the role of banking and investment in the creation of national trusts and monopolies (they primarily had Central European economies in view) was inseparable from the internationalization of capital. Lenin famously contended that "the characteristic feature of imperialism is not industrial but finance capital" (1975, 109). He linked the growing prevalence of finance capital to the production of what he called "the *actual* division of the world" (79). This involved not just the capitalist annexation of agrarian or noncapitalist areas but expansion into areas where capitalist industry was already established. Importantly, Lenin contrasted the "*actual* division" of the world, which is established "in proportion to capital," to the way that "capital exporting countries have divided the world among themselves in the figurative sense of the term" (79)—that is, territorially. While his writings on imperialism grappled centrally with the struggle between the European imperial powers that culminated in World War I, he maintained an important analytical distinction between the economic and territorial division of the world: "The epoch of the latest stage of capitalism shows us that certain relations between capitalist combines grow up, based on the economic division of the world, while parallel and in connection with it, certain relations grow up between political combines, between states, on the basis of the territorial division of the world, of the struggle for colonies, of the 'struggle for economic territory'" (Lenin 1975, 89).

In this distinction between the economic and territorial division of the world we find a strong precedent for the distinction between the expansion of the frontiers of capital and the proliferation of political, legal, and social borders that informs the approach of border as method. In an important sense, Lenin's conviction that these two divisions grow up in "parallel and in connection" remains accurate, although in the contemporary world these relations have acquired a high degree of complexity and unpredictability. Parallelism is not necessarily (and certainly no longer) a superposition that stitches economic divisions into the political borders of an international world. Tracing the evolution of this complexity and its implications for the gradual and incomplete separation of the global patterning of labor from international territorial divisions is a crucial task. But Lenin's observations about the role of finance capital in the division and redivision of labor remain a fundamental guide, because it is often on the basis of changes to the operations of finance that the more general transformations of capitalism, beginning in the 1970s, are explained.

Disorganized capitalism (Lash and Urry 1987), flexible accumulation (Harvey 1989), late capitalism (Mandel 1975), the knowledge economy (Drucker 1969), post-Fordism (Aglietta 1979; Lipietz 1992), cognitive capitalism (Moulier Boutang 2011; Vercellone 2006), neoliberalism (Harvey 2005; Touraine 2001), Empire (Hardt and Negri 2000)—these are some of the many terms that circulate to describe the transitions to capitalism that began to unfold in the early 1970s. Each carries particular empirical and theoretical implications, some pointing to the emergence of a historically novel form of capitalism and others tracing lines of continuity with the past. The historical and political propositions attached to any one of these terms are not necessarily compatible with those attached to the others—for example, the emphasis on regulation that often accompanies arguments about post-Fordism does not sit easily with claims for disorganization or theories about the forms of deregulation that accompany liberalization. Nonetheless, the proliferation of these terms suggests that some kind of transition is at hand. Even this, however, is a controversial statement. Thinkers who point to the historical coexistence of different varieties of capitalism suggest that a period of transition can become "too long to have any real meaning as a transition" (Chalcraft 2005, 16). Conversely, those who emphasize "dynamic process over static property" argue that "a truly historical perspective" can inform us about "the *commonalities* of capitalism" (Streeck 2009, 226, 1). In seeking to discern the relevance of these claims for debates about the international division of labor, it is necessary to keep both the systematic and differentiating capacities of capitalism in view. The notion of an "axiomatic of capital" developed by Gilles Deleuze and Félix Guattari (1983) is useful in this regard because it explains how capital can establish an isomorphism between situations and scenarios that are in fact quite heterogeneous in kind. As we shall see later in the book, this is crucial for understanding the variation among different historical forms of capitalism, particularly outside of Europe, and the significance of laboring subjects who do not conform to the role of the "free" wage laborer privileged by Marx.

A feature that many approaches to the transition of capitalism hold in common, regardless of the nomenclature they adopt, is an emphasis on processes of financialization in the world economy. The declaration of the inconvertibility of the U.S. dollar, which inaugurated the regime of flexible currency exchange in 1971, is frequently cited as a key event. But the growth of the systemic power of finance and financial engineering is by no means a phenomenon that can be restricted to the latest wave of capitalist transformation. World systems theory has taught us that financial expansion has been a characteristic phase of historical cycles of accumulation. Arrighi (2007), for instance, identifies financialization as a relatively brief process of speculative expansion that marks the end of an economic cycle and presages a shift of geo-economic power. The role of finance in the current transmutations of capitalism, however, cannot be isolated in this way. Christian Marazzi (2010, 28) convincingly argues that the "financial economy today is pervasive, that is, it spreads across the entire economic cycle, co-existing with it, so to speak, from start to finish." Citing examples such as the use of credit cards in supermarket shopping or the dependency of a large industrial manufacturer like General Motors on credit mechanisms such as leasing and installments, Marazzi proposes that finance has become "*cosubstantial* to the very production of goods and services" (29). This should not be taken to imply that the industrial production of goods and services is somehow in decline. To the contrary, such productive activity is on the rise across a range of territories, pockets, corridors, and enclaves around the world. What differs is the role of finance in articulating and commanding such production and the division of labor necessary to it in ways that are partly discontinuous with the processes of accumulation and valorization that applied at the height of industrial capitalism. Marazzi identifies this shift with the turn to financial markets of companies that were "no longer able to 'suck' surplus-value from living working labor" (31). The results are well known: "reduction in the cost of labor, attacks on syndicates, automatization and robotization of entire labor processes, delocalization in countries with low wages, precarization of work, and diversification of consumption models" (31).

Of these, the shift of production processes to take advantage of low wages has dominated the discussion about the international division of labor. The notion of a "new international division of labor" is among the most influential to have circulated in debates about the transitions of capitalism under the pressures of pervasive finance. Originally proposed by Folker Fröbel, Jürgen Henrichs, and Otto Kreye (1980), the concept has spread into many fields, including cultural studies, where Toby Miller and colleagues propose the emergence of a "new international division of cultural labor" (Miller et al. 2001). As originally elaborated, the concept describes the shift of international production from developed to less developed countries as the result of a fragmentation of production in which different phases of production are undertaken in different countries, often by the same firm. Facilitated by changes in transport and communications technology, the implications of this new international division of labor are an increase of manufacturing in less developed countries, the deindustrialization of developed nations, the decentralization of production and centralization of control, and intensified competition in product and labor markets. In many ways, the notion of a new international division of labor is a continuation of dependency theory because it posits that the partial development of export-oriented manufacturing in less developed countries will keep them dependent on the wealthier parts of the world. The theory thus not only assumes the superposition of the frontiers of capital and international borders, it also maintains a strong commitment to an analysis that works through core–periphery binaries. Perhaps this became clearest with the extension of the concept to discuss "peripheral Fordism" (Lipietz 1986), a proposition that implies the core has actually shed its former methods of production and exported them to developing countries.

Notable about this approach is not only its maintenance of stable international spatial divisions but its related implications for debates about the division of labor. Whereas classical political economy tended to focus on the specialization of labor tasks within the firm and between firms, the new international division of labor thesis suggests that the most important contemporary trend is the division and distribution of different processes in the production of commodities within a network of firms. In this respect, it shares the concern of a related approach that focuses on the formation of global commodity chains (Gereffi and Korzeniewicz 1994). Although we will discuss the notion of commodity chains later in the book, it is worth noting at this stage that, like the theory of the new international division of labor, it tends "to consider labor forces as an *a priori* factor in the spatial disbursement of productive processes" (Taylor 2008, 18). There is little attention to the creation and reproduction of labor forces, which is to say that these approaches tend to elide precisely what border as method seeks to highlight and politically explain: the production of subjectivity.

To be sure, there are analyses of the new international division of labor that give due attention to the question of labor forces. An important book by feminist scholar Maria Mies, *Patriarchy and Accumulation on a World Scale* (1998), investigates the intertwining of the new international division of labor with the sexual division of labor. Mies argues that women have become the "optimal labor force for capitalist accumulation on the worldwide scale" because "their work, whether in commodity production or use value, is obscured, does not appear as 'free wage labour,' is defined as an 'income generating *activity*,' and hence can be bought at a much cheaper price than male labour" (1998, 116). This is certainly a compelling account of the global feminization of labor and an effective critique of efforts to integrate women into development. From the point of view of the analysis we are developing here, it shows how the expanding frontiers of capital are able to reactivate and to resignify the meaning of a specific and fundamental boundary—the sexual boundary. Nevertheless, more recent accounts of the feminization of labor allow us to go beyond the analytical framework proposed by Mies and question the division between productive and reproductive labor, say, in the migration of domestic care workers (Akalin 2007; Anderson 2000). What is urgently needed is an emphasis on the tense and contradictory experiences of subjectivity that can accompany the feminization of labor. A good example here is Pun Ngai's (2005) account of how the integration of young female rural-urban migrants into the exploitive environment of China's coastal factories can also involve a liberating escape from the patriarchal world of the peasant household.

What often remains unmentioned in discussions of the new international division of labor is how the developments it describes were responses to powerful and dispersed workers' struggles that disrupted factory discipline in the core and challenged the economic nationalism that was the hallmark of the Fordist era. As we recalled in the previous chapter, Beverly Silver has effectively shown that delocalization of manufacturing to the periphery, particularly in the motor industry, generally implied the reproduction of these workers' struggles and refusal strategies in the periphery itself—from Brazil to South Korea (Silver 2003). The root difficulty with the new international division of labor approach is that it is primarily a theory of capital mobility, rather than a theory of how labor divisions, processes, mobilities, and struggles relate to the transitions of capitalism under pervasive financialization and the accompanying deep heterogenization of global space. As Robin Cohen explains, theorists of the new international division of labor "use measures of the migration of capital to measure changes in the division of labour." A better approach would be "measurements of the movement of labour to indicate changes in the division of labour" (Cohen 1987, 230).

These comments are consonant with the perspective of border as method, which sees labor mobilities (and the border struggles and production of subjectivity that accompany them) as central to understanding the division of labor in the contemporary globalizing world. It is nonetheless important to recognize that the movement of labor cannot be assessed without paying attention to the movement of capital. This is because labor in capitalism is always abstract as well as social, since in its concrete manifestations it is always one moment of the social division of labor that is mediated through the exchange of commodities. As Mario Tronti (1966) famously argued, productive labor exists not only in relation to capital but also in relation to capitalists as a class, which is where in fact the element of subjectivity becomes important. But if, for Tronti, the subjective face of labor remained that of the industrial mass worker, it is necessary for us to take the struggles and movements of a much more heterogeneous array of subjective figures into account. As we discuss in the next chapter, following the work of global labor historians such as Marcel van der Linden, the very idea that free wage labor represents a kind of standard in capitalism has to be radically challenged with regard to history and the present. Practices of mobility are part and parcel of the resulting heterogeneity of living labor commanded and exploited by capital. The deepening of this heterogeneity must be grasped if we are to successfully explain the proliferation of boundaries and borders that characterizes our global present.

This deepening of the heterogeneity of labor and this proliferation of boundaries and borders cut and cross the map of the world. They destabilize the very possibility of taking such grand divides as core and periphery for granted, while also questioning the capacity of national borders to circumscribe homogeneous economic spaces. This is not to claim that the concept of an international division of labor has become useless. Rather, it is to suggest that this concept no longer organizes a stable fabric of the world or possesses an ontological consistency and force sufficient to undergird an act of *fabrica mundi*. Obviously, we do not live in a "smooth" world, where geography no longer matters and the gap between capital's command (and frontiers) and political sovereignty (and borders) is vanishing. This gap continues to exist but is articulated within shifting assemblages of territory and power, which operate according to a logic that is much more fragmented and elusive than it was in the classical age of the nation-state.

If we take Lenin's analysis of the relation between the territorial and economic division of the world as a point of reference, the contemporary situation looks quite paradoxical. On one hand, the expanding frontiers of capital seem to have crystallized in the world market some of the main political functions that have long been monopolized by the state. Just think of a memorable definition of the state provided by Marx in the chapter of *Capital*, volume 1, on "so-called primitive accumulation": "the concentrated and organized force of society" (Marx 1977, 915). This is a quite accurate description of contemporary global finance, which is able to dictate policies to whole countries, profoundly shaping the rationality of governance and citizenship across diverse territorial scales. On the other hand, processes of territorial fragmentation, the heterogeneity of labor and social cooperation, and the multiplication of borders and boundaries correspond to the ways those policies and rationality are implemented.

Going back to the concept of an axiomatic of capital that we picked up from Deleuze and Guattari, we can say that its tendency to produce an isomorphy has never been so real as today. But, as the authors of *A Thousand Plateaus* remind us, "it would be wrong to confuse isomorphy with homogeneity"; instead, it allows, "even incites," a great deal of social, temporal, and spatial heterogeneity (Deleuze and Guattari 1987, 436). The highest degree of isomorphy seems to coexist in contemporary capitalism with the highest degree of heterogeneity. Although the concept of the international division of labor remains useful for tracing specific commodity chains as well as the territorial specialization of production in certain areas, it does not explain these polarities of isomorphy and heterogeneity whose tension is constitutive of life under capitalism these days.

In preceding ages of capitalism, it was possible to identify a single leading product cycle (textile or automobile production) and map its spatial distribution to get a cartographic representation of the general geography of capitalism. Today this seems much more difficult. "One striking characteristic of contemporary capitalism," Silver writes, "is its eclecticism and flexibility, visible in the dizzying array of choices in consumer goods and the rapid emergence of new commodities and new ways of consuming old commodities" (Silver 2003, 104). This leads Silver to identify at least four emerging industries as candidates to pick up the role of the automobile in leading a product cycle: the semiconductor industry, producer services, the education industry, and personal services. Each of these sectors clearly produces its own economic space on a world scale, with peculiar geographic imbalances and hierarchies. The resulting frames of spatial organization far from coincide. Nonetheless (and this is even more important), a specific combination of these four sectors characterizes, although in very different proportions, contemporary capitalism across diverse geographic scales and well beyond any divide between core and periphery.

If one takes another possible candidate to figure as the leading economic sector today—that is, "biocapital," "postgenomic" drugs, and medicine—it is again both possible and necessary to map its spatial hierarchies and divides. In his pathbreaking multisited ethnographical analysis of biocapital, Kaushik Sunder Rajan has effectively excavated the ways in which, in a kind of repetition of "the so-called primitive accumulation" described by Marx, the creation in Parel (Mumbai) of "a new population of subjects who are created as sites of experimental therapeutic intervention" was a necessary condition to satisfy the needs of consumers living on the U.S. West Coast (Rajan 2006, 97). But this boundary between Mumbai and California, which "reflects an old story of colonial expropriation of Third World resources" (281), begins to blur when Rajan deepens his analysis of the entangled imaginaries, of the practices of mobility and labor that make the development of biocapital possible: "The relationship of India to the United States as I'm trying to configure it, is *not* the relation of an outside to an inside . . . but the story of the outside that is always already within the hegemonic inside—but within it in ways that make the inside uncomfortable, distend it, but never turn it 'inside out'" (83). To make sense of these processes and transformations, connections and disconnections, and entanglements and disentanglements, we find it useful to introduce, as a kind of supplement to the international division of labor, the concept of a multiplication of labor.

The Multiplication of Labor

One could say that multiplication was always at stake in debates about (and practical translations of) the division of labor. Division has always had multiplication (of productivity, of scale, of wealth, etc.) as its goal. For instance, Adam Smith writes: "It is the great multiplication of the productions of all the different arts, in consequence of the division of labor, which occasions, in a well-governed society, that universal opulence which extends itself to the lowest ranks of the people" (Smith 1976, 22).

Behind this statement we can discern the problem of the relation (and the potential tensions) between social cooperation and specialization of social functions that was effectively formulated by David Hume. "By the conjunction of forces," Hume writes in his *Treatise of Human Nature*, "our power is augmented; by the partition of employments, our ability encreases; and by mutual succour, we are less exposed to fortune and accidents" (Hume 1994, 8). In his analysis of machinery and large-scale industry, Marx speaks of an "absolute contradiction" between the revolutionary tendency of industry itself to continually transform "not only the technical basis of production but also the functions of the worker and the social combinations of the labor process" and the capitalist's need to reproduce "the old division of labor with its ossified particularities." He adds that "large-scale industry, by its very nature, necessitates variation of labor, fluidity of functions, and mobility of the worker in all directions," while capital is compelled to continuously limit, harness, and block these processes (Marx 1977, 617).

The crisis of Taylorism and Fordism, which was widely discussed in the 1980s, can be understood along these lines, although one has to note that first, workers' claims and practices of "variation, fluidity, and mobility" accelerated this crisis (Boltanski and Chiapello 2005). The discussion, above all within the corporate world and in management literature, was dominated by the need to go beyond any technical rigidity in the organization of labor. "Total quality," "the Japanese model," and "Toyotism" were the slogans of the day, and *The End of the Division of Labor?* was the title of a celebrated and influential book by the German sociologists Horst Kern and Michael Schumann (1984). What interests us here is not so much criticizing the ideological moment in these discourses and practices: it would be easy to show how quickly new forms of rigidity reproduced themselves in "total quality" factories and other labor environments. Instead, we focus on how the "absolute contradiction" highlighted by Marx was effectively acknowledged and managed by capital after the general crisis of the 1970s. From this angle, the concept of multiplication of labor seems useful to us. Although financialization, according to the analysis of Marazzi we quoted, opened up new continents for the valorization of capital in front of the limits posed by the working class within the factory walls, capital itself smashed these walls, outsourcing labor not only geographically but also to the whole society.

Labor was multiplied through these processes in at least three important ways. It was first *intensified*, in the sense that its tendency to colonize the entire life of laboring subjects became even more pronounced than before. Second, it was internally *diversified*, according to a process already identified by Marx in his analysis of the creation of relative surplus value in the *Grundrisse*, which continuously pushes capital beyond the division of labor and toward "the development of a constantly expanding and more comprehensive system of different kinds of labour, different kinds of production, to which a constantly expanding and constantly enriched system of needs corresponds" (Marx 1973, 409). Third, it was *heterogenized* as far as legal and social regimes of its organization are concerned.

Once again it is at the level of the world market, following Marx's analysis, that the unity of the two dimensions of capitalist transformations we identify (finance and labor) can be fully grasped. As we read in a passage of his *Theories of Surplus Value*, money becomes "world money" indeed only with the development of the world market, which is in turn the stage where "abstract labor" becomes "social labor." The world market, in other words, is the site of representation and continuous reproduction of capital's "axiomatic," the last guarantee of its command over the "totality of different modes of labor embracing the world market" (Marx 1971, 253).

To understand how labor has been intensified with the general crisis of the 1970s, it is useful to contrast contemporary labor regimes with those described by Marx. In chapter 17 of the first volume of *Capital*, Marx distinguishes three major factors influencing the extraction of surplus value: the length of the working day, the rate of productivity, and the intensity of labor. Although it is possible for all three of these factors to vary at the same time, there is a limit to which the working day can be extended while the intensity of labor is increased. This limit is imposed by the very corporeality of the worker's body, the living matter that "contains" the abstract quantity of labor power. It is a mark of what the body can stand before breaking down or introducing inefficiencies that result from exhaustion, illness, or the inability of labor to reproduce itself on a daily basis. From this limit, against which capital constantly pushes, stem certain arrangements in the technical division of labor—the institution of shift work, for example. As Marx puts it, "a point must be inevitably reached where the extension of the working day and intensification of labor become mutually exclusive so that the lengthening of the working day becomes compatible only with a lower degree of intensity, and inversely, a higher degree of intensity only with a shortening of the working day" (Marx 1977, 533).

One way of characterizing the intensification of labor in an era when the financialization of capital has opened new channels of valorization is to say that this limit and the inverse relationship it creates between the intensity and extensity of labor has been unbalanced. This is not to deny the continued existence of many scenes of manufacture and production—from the sweat shop to the cube farm—where a tightening of this inverse relation between the extensive and intensive magnitude of labor places workers' bodies and lives under increasing duress. But along with this tightening, which has accompanied the technical coordination of production across global assembly chains, have come new demands for the flexibilization and socialization of labor. What we earlier described as capital's smashing of the factory walls also involves severing labor from the measure of socially necessary labor time. At stake is less a lengthening of the working day than the tendency for work to occupy more of life. Whether it involves the encroachment of work into the domestic sphere or the more general putting to work of the individual's capacity for communication and sociality, the propensity of work to colonize more of life is a factor observed by many critics and commentators (see, for instance, Fumagalli 2007; Hardt and Negri 2004; Hochschild 1983; Virno 2003; Weeks 2007).

These developments do not necessarily entail a diminution in the intensity of labor. The relation of inverse proportionality between the extensity and intensity of labor described by Marx has become more elastic and negotiable. The production of absolute and relative surplus value, the allocation of paid and unpaid work, as well as the growing intertwining of productive and reproductive labor are all at stake. The factory regime tended to balance the demands of extensive and intensive labor at precisely that point where the worker's body began to break. In the Fordist era, a whole series of social institutions evolved to support the bodily integrity of the workforce. As we emphasized in the previous chapter, the sexual division of labor between the household and the workplace was central to this arrangement, the first being the feminized domain of unpaid reproductive labor and the second being the masculine domain of paid work. With the onset of financialization, the household itself emerges as a site of capitalist calculation. As Dick Bryan, Randy Martin, and Mike Rafferty (2009, 462) argue, the household is increasingly "seen as a set of financial exposures to be self-managed." Health insurance, education expenses, mortgages, and retirement investment are just some of the financial issues for which households assume responsibility. The upshot is that the reproduction of labor power tends to begin with credit, rather than the consumption of commodities, and thus becomes a source of surplus value (in the form of rent) through the payment of interest. As became evident in the subprime-induced global economic crisis of 2007–8, the inability of labor to meet credit commitments can have a dramatic effect on financial volatility.

Corollary to these processes of financialization, which liquefy formerly fixed forms of capital through the introduction of devices such as derivatives, is an intensification of labor. As capital is driven to deliver higher productivity and profitability, labor not only assumes increased degrees of risk but is also subject to demands for increased productivity, more flexible hours, and the payment of lower real wages. The condition known as precarity (or the movement away from "standard" full-time, continuous working arrangements with a single employer) unbalances the inverse proportionality of labor's extensive and intensive moments (Neilson and Rossiter 2008; Ross 2009; Standing 2011). A growing number of precarious workers are unable to support a household, and under these circumstances, the capacity of labor to reproduce itself becomes uncertain. Labor is thus increasingly divided between those who maintain a household and those whose ability to earn a living wage is unknown or subject to highly volatile conditions of demand. In either case there is a multiplication of labor, whether it entails the work of managing the financialized household (including the upkeep of the body through exercise and activities that might mitigate exposure to risk) or juggling positions in the precarious labor market. As Marazzi observes, "fixed capital, if it disappears in its material and fixed form, reappears in the mobile and fluid form of the living" (Marazzi 2005, 111).

The intensification of labor described here runs parallel in so-called Western advanced capitalist societies to processes of *diversification* that challenged the hegemony of a specifically homogeneous figure—that is, the industrial worker—over the entirety of dependent labor. While labor is taking on more and more social characteristics, due to the intensification of cooperation and to the role increasingly played by "common" powers such as knowledge and language as basis of production, subjective labor positions are multiplied both from the point of view of tasks and skills and from the point of view of legal conditions and statuses. No longer is it possible to claim, as Émile Durkheim so influentially argued in the late nineteenth century, that the division of labor increases solidarity and the cohesion of human groups into social unities. As labor is increasingly socialized, relations of social solidarity have themselves become more fluid. Rather than assuming that society is a whole that labor divides, it is necessary to track the differences, inconsistencies, and multiplicities that invest the field of labor and in turn fragment the organic notion of society. Such a heterogenization of labor is also mirrored and fostered by the flexibilization of labor law, particularly by the explosion of contractual arrangements corresponding to the decline of collective bargaining (Salento 2003; Supiot 1994, 2001). It is also registered by the proliferation of corporate codes and charters pertaining to labor standards and conditions, particularly in situations where capital's globalizing search for low-cost labor leaves it vulnerable to political criticism and consumer actions. Such codes and standards are clearly performative, but they can also display strong normative tendencies that fragment the field of global law and begin to separate jurisdiction from territory.

One can obviously interpret this situation as a further deepening of the division of labor now combining its technical and social dimension and producing a new set of boundaries across the composition of living labor. We do not deny this. Emphasizing the element of multiplication over the one of division, we want to point first to the disproportion between the intensified social dimension of contemporary labor ("the conjunction of forces" in the terms employed by Hume) and the deepening of the social and technical division of labor ("the partition of employments," to put it again with Hume). Although "multiplication" points to these elements of structural excess (the contemporary manifestation of the "absolute contradiction" identified by Marx in his analysis of large-scale industry), it also indicates the parallel operation of the three tendencies—intensification, diversification, and heterogenization of labor—that are increasingly reshaping labor experiences and conditions. The biopolitical mobilization of life, resulting from the combination of these tendencies, provides a key to the interpretation of the shifting composition of living labor under contemporary capitalism independently of the great divides between global North and global South, core and periphery, and so on. One could even say that the periphery strikes back, in a classical postcolonial move, because the radical heterogeneity of labor relations that was long a characteristic of the colonial world increasingly invests the former metropolitan territories as a result of the processes we have sketched here.

Once again, this is not to say that space and territory no longer play a significant role in the composition (as well as the division) of labor. What we wrote about the four emerging industries identified by Silver is valid also here. Processes of intensification, diversification, and heterogenization are reshaping laboring lives and conditions across the diverse spaces and scales of capital's global operations, but they produce very different concrete assemblages of employment and unemployment, misery, subsistence and exploitation, flight, refusal, and struggles. It is certainly still possible to speak of a global division of labor connecting (as well as dividing) workers employed within specific productive cycles and commodity chains. But the concept of an *international* division of labor is becoming less relevant due to processes of heterogenization that single out "regions" more than nations as significant economic units. This means that too insistent an emphasis on the element of division can easily obscure the multiplication of labor that we have described so far, as well as the subjective tensions, movements, and struggles that crisscross it.

While the expanding frontiers of capital have pushed the "world market" onto the new dimension of global financial markets representing and implementing what Deleuze and Guattari term the "axiomatic of capital," abstract labor has been violently imposed as the standard to which life is subdued across the planet. Even the subsistence economy on which the reproduction of large masses depends, for instance in the "planet of slums" described by Mike Davis (2006), is increasingly included in financial circuits. The arrangements of microcredit are one means by which the entire life of these masses is coded as "human capital" that should not be wasted (although it is often wasted) but rather compelled to generate value according to the logic of abstract labor. But the generalization of abstract labor does not delete the gap that separates it from living labor (Chakrabarty 2000; Mezzadra 2011c).

On the one hand, this gap widens in the actual processes and form of labor, and, in this sense, its multiplication plays the role of "divide and rule." On the other hand, living labor has still the chance to refuse to subordinate itself to the norm of abstract labor—or at least to negotiate its subordination. It is from this point of view that multiplication can become an incalculable element in the relations between capital and labor, giving rise to unforeseeable tensions, movements, and struggles. As we shall see in the next chapter, practices of mobility play a key role in these tensions, movements and struggles (as they do generally in contemporary processes of multiplication of labor). The control of labor mobility is also one of the key sites where the expanding frontiers of capital continue to intertwine with political and legal borders. Here the production of labor power as a commodity is a key issue.

—— Chapter Four ——

FIGURES OF LABOR

Workers of the World

"The proletarians have nothing to lose but their chains. They have a world to win. Working men of all countries, unite!" These are among the most famous words written by Karl Marx and Friedrich Engels (2002, 258), and in an important sense, their validity has never faded. It is difficult for us not to write in the spirit of this rallying cry. Yet the key concepts we elaborate in this book—border as method and the multiplication of labor—suggest the need to interrogate the metaphors of unity and chains that animate this memorable statement. At the root of our investigation is the perennial question of the many and the one. The notion of unity, for instance, implies overcoming divisions and diverse parties acting in concert. Similarly the notion of the chain, though it carries a sense of ligature or bondage that should not be discounted or diminished, suggests the linkage or articulation of multiple units into a single linear system. Central to our approach and argument is the contention that the proliferation of borders in the contemporary world means the political organization of labor must be carried out in an irreducibly multiple sense. No longer is it a matter of overcoming divisions through international solidarity or appeals to the human condition. Only by analyzing the heterogeneous constitution of global space and the complex ways it crisscrosses the production and reproduction of labor power as a commodity is it possible to begin the work of translating between subjects and struggles.

In this chapter we confront some of the difficulties encountered in this task. We seek to trace the production of borders and hierarchies within and between labor markets by considering the relations between two very different fields of work that are given to high degrees of labor mobility: care work and financial trading. Our analysis of carers and financial traders emphasizes the specificity of the positions and subjective experiences of these figures. It is also shaped by more general debates on the feminization of labor and migration, on one hand, and on the financialization of capitalism on the other hand. In writing about carers and traders, we try to flesh out some characteristics that are relevant for an investigation of contemporary living labor well beyond these peculiar figures. Such topics as affective and emotional labor, the role played by borders in the production of labor power as a commodity, the mimetic rationality implied in the financialization of abstract labor, and capital's command through the logic of debt are particularly important in this regard. From the point of view of border as method, there is also a need to emphasize that carers and traders occupy crucial positions in the contemporary proliferation of borders, revealing the intensity of the tensions that surround them. This means investigating how currently globalizing systems of production complicate not only constructs like the international division of labor but also other means of dividing the field of labor, such as the notion of a split between manual and mental labor. At what point, we ask, does the concept of global labor come into being, and what are its political and analytical uses? Is there a tension or even a gap between global labor and international solidarity? What has happened to the political project of internationalism we referred to in the previous chapter?

It would be a fantasy to pretend that questions of solidarity, alliance, coalition, and even organization have been pushed aside by the inclusive figure of the global. Many of the traditional problems of international solidarity now pose themselves within the confines of nation-states due to the increasing heterogenization of populations and workforces. At the same time, movements of migration and practices of mobility have acquired relevance beyond the statistical weight of their present growth. What is distinctive about these movements, write Stephen Castles and Mark Miller, is "their global scope, the centrality to domestic and international politics and their enormous economic and social consequences" (Castles and Miller 2003, 2). The emergence of transnational social spaces (Faist 2000; Gutiérrez and Hondagneu-Sotelo 2008; Rouse 1991; Smith 2001) and new forms of regionalism points to patterns of connection and disconnection that can no longer necessarily be analyzed using the classical model of migration chains

(Reyneri 1979). It has also muddled the geographies of proximity and distance that were always at stake in projects of international solidarity. This has opened new channels of communication, circulation, and exchange, for instance, through the use of digital networks. New boundaries of identity and communalism have established themselves within these circuits. The rise of international organizations (from intergovernmental organizations to nongovernmental organizations) has further led to the formation of new kinds of bureaucracy that have saturated these spaces. In this situation, it is important to see the limits as well as the potentialities furnished for the present day by even the most radical and original past experiences in organizing mobile workforces. The early-twentieth-century experience of the International Workers of the World, the revolutionary "one big union" that was extraordinarily open to migrants, minorities, experiences of labor mobility, and nonhierarchical forms of organization, comes to mind here.

In a concrete sense, we can suggest that it was more difficult for Marx than it is for us to imagine the workers of the world, as Michael Denning puts it, "constituting an interconnected global labor force sharing a common situation" (Denning 2007, 126). In fact, the concept of abstract labor, which implies capital's indifference to the concrete social circumstances under which labor is performed, allowed Marx to hazard the political figure of an international working class. Although the abstraction of labor remains an important part of the workings of global capitalism, what we have been calling the multiplication of labor shows how complicated the process of translating the abstract into the concrete has become. The switch between the abstract and the concrete does not necessarily produce the homogenizing effects that give rise to what Marx saw as a revolutionary working-class subject. This is the origin of the problem of heterogeneity that we discuss from the point of view of global space and time and from the point of view of the composition of global labor. It is clear that globalizing processes have not put an end to the operation of aggregate economic forces and the consequent fracturing and competition between national and regional working classes. The arguments that attribute the current economic crisis to the roles of the U.S. American working class as a "consumer of last resort" and Chinese workers as "cheap" producers illustrate this fact. By the same token, the challenges that trade unions face in many parts of the world when confronted with migration and outsourcing on one hand and new forms of work and "precarity" on the other hand are an effective illustration of a different set of problems posed by the increasing heterogeneity of labor.

Negotiating these problems does not mean abandoning Marx and Engel's call for the world's workers to unite, but it presents us with one of the most important and challenging tasks of political organization in the present.

One revealing symptom of this predicament is the expansion of debates and the testing of the relevance of the concept of class. Notwithstanding the continued proliferation of positions that deny that social class is a useful analytical and descriptive tool, this concept clearly has always attracted multiple definitions. What is peculiar about the current moment in these debates is that these different definitions have expanded and drifted apart from each other almost to the point where the concept of class itself seems unable to contain them. As Fredric Jameson comments, "social class is at one and the same time a sociological idea, a political concept, a historical conjunction, an activist slogan, yet a definition in terms of any one of these perspectives alone is bound to be unsatisfactory" (Jameson 2011, 7). Regardless of this diffusion of meanings, one has only to consider Stanley Aronowitz's criticism of the cartographic uses of social class to map social stratification in contemporary sociology to register the underlying relevance of an older tension. His emphasis on the constitutive role of struggles, power relations, and historical differences in processes of class formation points to the subjective dimension that has always animated the concept of class in contradistinction to the weight of objective and structural forces (Aronowitz 2003). Marx himself struggled throughout his writings with this tension, which he was never able to resolve satisfactorily. Famously, in the final and abruptly unfinished chapter of *Capital*, volume 3, he grapples with this conundrum. "At first sight," he observes, "classes seem to correspond with objective sources of income: profit, rent and wages." Nevertheless, he experiences a kind of dizziness in front of "the infinite fragmentation of interests and positions" that social classes entail, reopening the specter of class's subjectivity in the last page of his manuscript and leaving the question "what makes a class?" in suspension (Marx 1981, 1026). Those social scientists who continue to map class in a clearly neutral and objectivist manner would do well to remember Marx's disorientation at this moment.

We are interested in exploring the implications of this moment of disorientation, emphasizing the subjective, which is to say, the political dimension of the concept of class. Our investigation of labor, migration, and borders thus joins a long line of inquiries that seek to work through the gap between what the young Marx called class "in itself" and class "for itself." Vladimir Ilich Lenin and Georg Lukács, Theodor Adorno and Herbert Marcuse, E. P. Thompson's *The Making of the English Working Class* (1963), and the panoply of Italian *operaismo* are some of the milestones here. Within these debates there were differences and dissonances pertaining to how the subjective element of class should be handled. To simplify, the notion of class consciousness, which implies a whole political anthropology of deception and revelation, was contested and displaced from a number of perspectives, including psychoanalytical, structuralist, and sociological approaches.

Among the challenges to the concept of class consciousness, the one we find most innovative and politically useful is the *operaista* notion of class composition, which suggests a complex play of social forces, experiences, and behaviors in the making of class. Emphasizing a continuous process of adaptation by which labor repositions itself within and against the social relation of capital, this notion was always double-sided, because it centered on the tension between its technical and its political dimensions. The technical composition of the working class was understood as the expression of the structural organization of labor power in the production process, as well as the conditions for the reproduction of labor power. By contrast, the concept of political composition attempted to grasp the subjective element of class, particularly as manifest in practices of struggle and experiences of labor organization. In the *operaista* elaboration, this subjective element of class was considered a key driver of the development of capital, which was continuously compelled to mutate its forms and dynamics by the challenge and threat of workers' struggles and sabotage. Importantly, this meant that traces of the political composition of class were inscribed in its technical dimension and that an element of subjectivity had to be taken into account to analyze the apparently most "neutral" changes in the organization of labor at the point of production. As initially developed within Italian *operaismo*, the concept of class composition was associated with an extremist and unilateral emphasis on the Fordist factory and industrial "mass worker." However, the flexibility built into this same concept also allowed *operaisti* thinkers and practitioners to anticipate the breaking of the factory gates and the emergence of new constellations of labor beyond the exclusive reference to the industrial worker that has dominated Western Marxism (Negri 2007b; Wright 2002).

Although our work derives important lessons from the experience of *operaismo*, we are also aware of the deeper questioning of this emphasis on the industrial worker by anticolonial thinkers and practitioners such as W. E. B. Du Bois and Frantz Fanon (Renault 2011; Robinson 2000), global labor historians (Lucassen 2006; van der Linden 2008), and postcolonial and subaltern theorists (Chakrabarty 1989; Guha 1983; Young 2001). Likewise,

feminist arguments and struggles that have exploded the line between productive and reproductive labor have been crucial to challenging the mas-
culinist bias in the representation of the industrial working class (Dalla
Costa and James 1972; Federici 2004; Pateman 1988; Weeks 2011). The
combined implications of these historical, anticolonial, and feminist reflections are important for our inquiry because forms and experiences of labor
mobility, both historically and in the present day, are repeatedly linked with
processes of heterogenization of the workforce. A crucial contribution of
these theoretical and political elaborations has been to show how such a
differentiation of labor is the historical and geographical norm, rather than
the exception of capital writ large. The boundaries between free and unfree
labor have been blurred, throwing into deep crisis the Marxian no less than
the liberal emphasis on the freely concluded labor contract as judicially
constitutive of the relations between capital and labor. As Yann Moulier
Boutang (1998) convincingly argues, the terms and stakes of labor mobility
have always been a crucial field of struggle because one of the principal
means by which capital exercises control over labor is by attempting to
harness and channel its movement and flight. This is true for the slave, the
indentured coolie, or the labor migrant who negotiates today's fractured
borderscapes as much as for the industrial worker chained to the factory.

The resulting widening of the concept of the working class has overrid-
den without entirely eliminating a variety of internal boundaries that cross
the field of living labor, including those between productive, "unproductive,"
and reproductive labor, "free" and unfree labor, and formal and informal
labor. It has also occasioned controversy about the constitution of the external borders of the working class and the ways different national denominations of this class have come into existence. Even such an innovative and
groundbreaking study as Thompson's *The Making of the English Working
Class* makes a series of assumptions in this regard. For Thompson, it is
precisely the *English* working class that is made. As historians Peter Linebaugh and Marcus Rediker suggest in *The Many-Headed Hydra*, their account of the making of Atlantic capitalism in the seventeenth and eighteenth centuries, this leads to a removal of an entire epoch in the history of
capitalism and class struggles. The "motley crew" of sailors, slaves, and
commoners who crossed the Atlantic in this period was not divided into
"national and partial" fractions (Linebaugh and Rediker 2000, 286). Like the
moment in which industrial workers figured as the working class tout court,
so the emergence of national working-class formations is historically (and
geographically) contingent.

The national and industrial moments of working-class formation are clearly mutually implicated, even if the terms of their relation shift decisively across time and space (just think, for instance, of the difference between Thompson's account of the English case and the Nehruvian plans of nation building and industrialization in India or the Peronist program of nationalist development in mid-twentieth-century Argentina). In those countries that underwent an industrial revolution in the nineteenth or early twentieth century, the legal and political constitution of a national labor market run parallel to forging the figure of the free laborer. As Robert J. Steinfeld (1991, 2001) argues for the Anglo-American world, it was not market dynamics but the struggles of industrial workers that compelled capital to adapt to a homogeneous legal framework guaranteed by the state. The relative stability that resulted from this arrangement eventually benefited capital and provided a grid within which labor movements became increasingly nationalized. Such nationalization also had its international dimensions, which, it is important to remember, were partly created through imperial adventuring and expansion as well as through the rise of a web of regulations, treaties, and agencies that led to an emerging formal internationalism. This implied a hardening of international borders and the creation of a kind of seal around the nation-state, its community of citizens, and its labor market. Not accidentally, the institution of technologies of border and migration control was an important part of this process (Sassen 1996; Torpey 2000). Migrants assumed a supplemental role in this international conjuncture. They were at once needed to staff national labor markets but were also seen as threatening outsiders who challenged the system's relative stability.

In the industrial and nationalist moment of the history of capitalism, it is possible to trace the emergence of a series of problems and techniques associated with migration and its control that became constitutive of the experience of Western countries for several decades. These practices contributed to the creation of various mappings of the world and the patterning of global divisions that would issue in schemes such as the three-worlds model and eventually the economic divide of North and South. More generally, as Harald Bauder shows in *Labor Movement* (2006), migration plays a crucial role in the regulation of labor markets. By policing their borders, nation-states engage in a continual process of politically and legally making and remaking their labor markets. Considered in this national frame, migration is pivotal to the encounter between labor and capital. If considered from a critical and theoretical angle, however, migration also displays the inherent limits of the concept of the national labor market. If the very idea of a market presupposes the existence of independent actors of exchange and a tendency toward equilibrium which seem problematic in the case of labor markets (Althauser and Kalleberg 1981), the figure of the migrant creates an unbalancing element. This, we suggest, is not simply a matter of the question of freedom, although migrant workers are frequently subject to specific forms of coercion and take on a special status that limits their choices and opportunities in comparison to domestic workers (Moulier Boutang 1998). More important, it is a matter of the production of the commodity of labor power and the peculiar status of this commodity among others.

Because the commodity of labor power cannot be separated from its bearer, the living body of the worker, its production necessarily crosses the systems of discipline and control to which this body is subject. In the industrial and nationalist moment of capitalism, there was a wide assumption that the labor power furnished by the domestic worker was already produced. The problem was its reproduction—hence the Fordist innovation of the family wage, the Keynesian institutions of welfare, and the sexual division of labor within the nation-state. The labor power of the migrant worker, by contrast, was seen as an import that could be filtered and chosen through recruitment schemes and border controls that came to play a role in the production of this commodity. The corporeal aspects of this commodity, such as sex, age, or race, were approached as raw materials and criteria for selection in ways that did not apply to the existing stock of the domestic workforce, whose reproduction and discipline occurred through different social channels and institutions, including the family, school, and army. The labor power furnished by migrant workers was managed in many different ways during the industrial and national moment in the history of capitalism. But basically the attempt was made to treat it as a kind of supplement to the stock of labor power present within the bounded space of the national labor market, to meet the needs of capital in its industrial formation without disturbing the reproduction of the national workforce. From the quota system and its successive amendments in the United States to the guest worker regimes in West Germany, from colonial and postcolonial migration schemes in France and the United Kingdom to the "white Australia" policy, these efforts were marked by racism and exploitation, struggles and resistance, and the governmental forging of programs of integration and multiculturalism (Bojadzijev 2008; De Genova 2005, 221–36; Gilroy 1987; Hage 1998; Sayad 2004).

Far from merely existing as a supplement to an already constituted national labor market, migratory movements and the labor power they mobilized became a kind of turbulent excess to these attempts to contain, channel, and integrate them (Papastergiadis 2000). That this occurred at the same time as a series of other pressures began to unsettle the national order of labor markets and the international order of nation-states is a matter of historical record. The emergence of multiple and more porous borders within and between labor markets, the growing prevalence of lateral zones of labor mobility and exchange, the desperate search for new flexible and just-in-time migration schemes, the efforts of capital to play off the unequal opportunities for labor mobility within different regions against each other —all of these, to which we return in later chapters, are part and parcel of the repositioning and reorganization of labor markets. What interests us here is an extension of our previous arguments regarding the multiplication of labor with particular regard to the forms of subjectivity produced by migrant mobilities in this global framework. This is why we turn our attention to two emblematic figures of current living labor that are often positioned at opposite ends of the spectrum, both with respect to earnings and the relative balance of mental and manual effort involved in their activities: the care worker and the financial trader.

Taking Care

Female experiences of labor migration intersect some of the most tumultuous moments of contemporary capitalist development. Gone are the days, however, when it was possible to represent the experience of migrant labor as revolving around a single iconic figure, as happened with the celebrated photographic book by John Berger and Jean Mohr, *A Seventh Man* (1975). The migrant workers they portrayed in several European countries were male factory workers in the heyday of Fordism. They were caught at the sunset of an age in which mass production was setting the rule for the recruitment of migrants and their struggles made them an important subject in political and even iconic representations of the "multinational worker" in Europe (Serafini 1974). Representing the experience of migrant labor today means taking into account the processes of multiplication that we analyzed in the previous chapter. It implies focusing on a multiplicity of figures as well as on the shifting boundaries between them. But between the construction worker and the janitor, the street vendor and the taxi driver (just to mention a couple of examples), there is a figure that definitely figures in a prominent way in this representation, regardless of its geographical scale: the female domestic and care worker.

Labor has been feminized over the past few decades. This is not just because there has been an explosion in the number of women that work outside the household on the world scale. At stake is a remarkable transformation that has to be critically understood both as an outcome of women's struggles for emancipation and as an effect of a more general diversification and heterogenization of the workforce. Concurrently, as has often been underscored in debates on the changing nature of labor in contemporary capitalism (Marazzi 2011; Morini 2010), a whole set of qualities and competences historically constructed as female under patriarchal regimes of the sexual division of labor have come to define standard performances required from workers in a wide variety of occupations. This is not just true for the ability to negotiate the shifting boundaries between employment and unemployment, labor time and the time of life, which are associated with increasingly precarious conditions of work. It also applies to a whole range of relational, linguistic, and emotional competences that are of key relevance in the expanding service economy. The concepts of affective and emotional labor are often employed to grasp these specific forms of investment, valorization and exploitation of the subjectivity of the workers, for instance, in the health care industry (Ducey, Gautney, and Wetzel 2003) or in such diverse cases as McDonald's workers or life insurance sales agents (Leidner 1999). These concepts have a long history in feminism, where they have been "part and parcel of the struggle to expand the category of labor to include more of its gendered forms" (Weeks 2007, 233). The important book by Arlie Hochschild, *The Managed Heart* (1983), is a landmark work in this regard. Focusing on the emotional labor of "pink-collar" workers, of which the flight attendant provides a paradigmatic example, Hochschild analyzes the management of emotions at the very heart of daily laboring processes. As Kathi Weeks comments, this produced an important shift in discussions of labor. The emotional work analyzed by Hochschild, she writes, "requires not just the use but the production of subjectivity" (Weeks 2007, 241).

Parallel to these processes, the gender composition of migration has also undergone dramatic changes in the last three decades, leading many scholars to speak of a "feminization of migration" (Castles and Miller 2003, 9). It is important to note that women have always migrated, and not necessarily as wives and mothers. The exclusive focus of mainstream research on the figure of the male migrant worker has been contested by feminist scholars, who have pointed out the relevance of subjective motives for women's migration such as negotiating difficult marital relations or overcoming gendered hierarchies within their home country (Morokvasic 1984 and 1993; Kofman et al. 2000). Gender has thus become a crucial lens for investigating the subjective dimension and the stakes of migration, challenging the rigidity of theoretical models constructed on the interplay of economic (or for that matter demographic) push and pull factors (Mezzadra 2011d). This has important consequences for historical studies of migration; what we are interested in here is its relevance for analyzing the contemporary landscape of migration and its connection with more general transformations of labor.

At stake in the feminization of migration is something more than the mere fact that almost 50 percent of migrants in today's world are women (International Labour Organization 2010). Even more relevant are the conflict-ridden and tense processes of crisis and transformation of gender relations and the sexual division of labor that lie behind this huge increase of women's participation in migratory movements. Negotiations and contestations within the household in particular shape the experience of women who migrate "alone." Although it is important to analyze this in the context of the laboring process, there is also a need to emphasize that these struggles over gender relations and hierarchies crisscross the whole migratory experience of women. They are a constituent element of the production of labor power as a commodity, showing the impossibility of considering the bearers of labor power as neutral subjects who exist independently of the power relationships of gender, ethnicity, and race that are inscribed onto their bodies.

Female domestic care workers embody both the feminization of labor and the feminization of migration. These figures bear the material as well as affective and emotional weight of reproducing what Hochschild (2000, 131) calls "global care chains." Their labor is a prism that allows the analysis of the monetization and commoditization of a wide array of tasks that used to be performed within the household as part of women's domestic work and whose female character, notwithstanding important challenges, tends to remain "naturalized." Dismantling welfare systems and the explosion of the Keynesian family wage associated in many Western countries with neoliberal policies and reforms since the 1980s have contributed to this trend. Complex affective economies are at play here, involving relations with elder relatives in aging societies, face-to-face encounters between women of different class and ethnicity within the private space of the home, and long-distance caring for children within transnational families. The boundaries between proximity and distance appear intertwined and blurred. On one hand, strangers deal with some of the most intimate aspects of the life of a household (pain, sickness, aging, and shitting). On the other hand, migrants often work with another family in mind and maintain distant relatives and even communities through their remittances, often a considerable part of the gross domestic products of their own countries. The case of the Philippines, where the export of labor became a key element of economic policy in the 1970s under the rule of Ferdinand Marcos, is often mentioned in this regard but is far from being unique (Castles and Miller 2003, 168–69).

A distinctive feature of the work performed by (mainly) female migrants within households is its tendency to go beyond the traditional definition of domestic work and involve a wide range of activities that require an extensive interpretation of the concept of care. Physical tasks such as cooking, cleaning, and ironing are increasingly combined with services rendered for ill, disabled, elderly, and young people (Yeates 2004, 371). These services continue to imply bodily exertion on the part of the worker. But at stake here are also affects, emotions, and concerns that come to define the kind of competences required from the worker. Soft skills and characteristics, such as language, culture, and religion, play an important role in the recruitment process. These elusive and shifting qualities lie at the heart of the definition of care labor. They show the continuities between the experiences of "nannies, maids and sex workers," the three figures constitutive of what Barbara Ehrenreich and Arlie Hochschild call global woman in their book of the same title (2003). It would be worth exploring these continuities beyond the mainstream rhetoric on trafficking, keeping in mind the complex interplay of coercion and autonomy that often shape migrant women's experiences in the sex industry (Andrijasevic 2010a) and the carcereal modes of existence of many nannies and maids. A consideration of the foreign bride market in many parts of the world would disclose further facets of the contemporary global woman in migration, shedding light on what Bonnie Honig describes as processes of commoditization and eroticization of feminine "powerlessness," often used by women to pursue their own exit strategies (Honig 2001, 89–90). What interests us more is how the affective and emotional nature of many tasks and activities required from migrant domestic workers point to the absolute peculiarity of the relationship between them and their employers. One should add here that because they both tend to be women, notions of sisterhood have been employed and tested in feminist debates to interpret and reform this relationship (Anderson 2003, 113). An important feature of these debates is their questioning of the notion of "universal sisterhood," which has been criticized by postcolonial feminists, such as Chandra Mohanty, who focus on the "material and ideological differences within and among groups of women" (Mohanty 2003, 116).

In her book on migrant Filipina domestic workers in Los Angeles and

Rome, Rhacel Salazar Parreñas describes "four key dislocations" associated with the migratory experience of these laborers: "partial citizenship, the pain of family separation, contradictory class mobility, and non-belonging" (Parreñas 2001, 23). It is important to keep in mind the relevance of these dislocations, because they (particularly the first and fourth) provide a key to the analysis of the processes of ethnicization that organize the domestic and care labor markets. At the same time, it is important to emphasize the transnationalism of migrant domestic workers, noting that their daily lives and practices are predicated on multiple, constant interconnections across borders (28–29). The transnational spaces of mobility inhabited by these women are indeed spaces of circulation of affect (through the daily communication with children, families and friends "at home") and money (through remittances). They are also spaces within which patriarchal relations are contested, negotiated, and reconfigured in the face of the challenge of the material affirmation of women's freedom through migration. There is a deep intertwining between these more positive elements and the negative dislocations already mentioned. Indeed, precisely this kind of intertwining contributes to the high stakes and intensity of the battles fought across borders in the contemporary world. Though there is a need to reflect on the implications for feminist and more general debates on globalization of what Ehrenreich and Hochschild call "the transfer of the services associated with a wife's traditional role . . . from poor countries to rich ones" (Ehrenreich and Hochschild 2003, 4), it is even more relevant to recall that the demand for migrant domestic and care labor is booming well beyond the traditional boundaries of the so-called first world. This "transfer of services" is far from being smooth because it occurs within transnational spaces that are also spaces of struggle and resistance.

What we want to stress in the analysis of migrant domestic and care workers is how the molding of their activities within the employment relation implies blurring the boundaries between the production and reproduction of labor power that occurs across transnational spaces. Research on migrant domestic workers from Eastern Europe in Germany and Italy has shown how migration has often meant for these women a "widening of the horizon of action" (Vianello 2009, 160). At the same time, it has explained how migration provides a way to negotiate the crisis of gender roles and masculinity connected to the transition from socialist to market economies in their home countries. It is particularly important to analyze the way migratory policies—in this case in the European Union—confront these elements of agency and autonomy. Transnational forms of life and mobility take shape through this encounter (Hess 2007, 239), which also produces the conditions within which a multitude of middlemen and brokers operate to channel the mobility of these women. Training centers and agencies intervene within this process in many parts of the world, for instance, in Indonesia (Anggraeni 2006). As far as Europe is concerned, one only has to follow the routes of the hundreds of buses and vans that every day connect the cities where migrant women work as care laborers with their home-towns in Ukraine, Romania, Slovakia, or Belarus, to grasp another impor-tant aspect of these transnational spaces. Due to the relative geographic proximity, as Sabine Hess shows, migrant women, often traveling under illegal conditions, are able to physically disconnect the social reproduction of their labor power from the places where they work. Although this process of production and continuous reproduction of a "globalized and flexible labor power" clearly corresponds to the needs of the contemporary regime of capital accumulation, there is also a need to analyze the proletarian sub-sistence economies and the density of migratory networks that arise from these patterns of circular mobility and from the social practices that sustain them (Hess 2007, 244).

It should be clear by now that the subjective stakes and tensions that invest the transnational spaces and experiences of female migrants em-ployed as care and domestic workers open up a crucial angle on what we have discussed as the production of labor power as a commodity. A multi-plicity of borders and boundaries as well as multifarious tensions between practices of border crossing and border reinforcement concur to establish "global care chains" and to make possible the encounter between the de-mand and supply of care labor. The shadow of these borders and border experiences continues to hang over domestic work also in so-called coun-tries of destination, be it in the form of the processes of ethnicization that fragment and divide this particular labor market or in the reality of segrega-tion and confinement in households of many domestic workers, especially if they lack the proper papers. Independently of the most extreme forms of live-in domestic and au pair work, direct abuse and the insistence that a worker perform degrading tasks as well as the affective dimension that often becomes a source of blackmailing shape the normality of domestic and care labor.

As Bridget Anderson writes, the affective dimension of care work ex-poses "the relationship between worker and employer as something other than a straightforward contractual one," even in the case in which a contract has been signed (Anderson 2003, 111). An element of personal subordina-tion is always implied and regulated by each labor contract, as it has been often underscored by Marxism as well as feminism. Parallels between slavery, serfdom, and the condition of women within the family as regulated by marriage characterized early feminist theories and movements in the nineteenth century in the United States and Europe. Domestic labor was always at stake in these developments, which forged an acute understanding of the reality of the worker's personal dependency and the command over her body established by labor contracts (Pateman 1988, 116–53). Summing up her research into the living and working conditions of migrant domestic workers in five European cities (Athens, Barcelona, Bologna, Madrid, and Paris) and her experiences as a member of Kalayaan, a U.K.-based group campaigning for the rights of migrant domestic workers, Bridget Anderson makes an important contribution to this feminist critique of the labor contract. Playing an indispensable role in "the physical, cultural and ideological reproduction of human beings," migrant domestic workers occupy a peculiar position on the labor market. Though they usually attempt to frame their employment relationship in terms of their "sale" of labor power, "employers want more than labor power." "They often openly stipulate," Anderson writes, "that they want a particular type of person justifying this demand on the grounds that they will be working in the home." It is "the power to command, not the property in the person, but the whole person" of the worker that employers are buying (Anderson 2000, 113–14).

Arbitrariness and abuse thus appear as structurally linked with the condition of migrant domestic and care workers. Nevertheless, keeping in mind the elusive and shifting nature of care as well as Kathi Weeks's emphasis on the production of subjectivity in emotional and affective labor, it is possible to go a step further in the analysis of the relationship between employers and employees in this particular case. In her research on live-in migrant caregivers in Turkey, Ayşe Akalyn focuses precisely on these aspects. She emphasizes the flexibility and adaptability, what she calls the ability to *become* the right person, required by employers of migrant domestic and care workers. Their demand, Akalyn writes, is "for a 'genderly' capacity . . . that can then be shaped and reformed, based on the needs of the employers. The services that they buy from their migrant domestics are not their personalities as fixed entities, but the capacity to mould them" (Akalyn 2007, 222). This point is particularly important to us because the "genderly" capacity described by Akalyn seems to be a *potential* attitude "contained" in the living body of the worker. This is consistent with the Marxian definition of labor power that we discussed in chapter 1. However, the experience of migrant domestic and care workers analyzed in this section allow us to complicate and enrich that definition. On one hand, as we have already pointed out, there is a need to stress that the qualities of the container of labor power—that is, the body in its sexualized and racialized materiality—matter both in the production of labor power as a commodity across borders and in the conditions of its "consumption." On the other hand, through an analysis of the specific figure of the care worker we have focused on the limits of the construction of the labor contract in terms of buying and selling labor power. We know that this construction was central to the foundation of the idea of free wage labor as the standard labor relation under capitalism in Marx's critique of political economy. Though we have discussed the critique of this idea developed by global labor historians, it is important to note that the legal construction of the labor contract through which the commodity labor power is sold and bought is also problematic from a conceptual point of view. If we keep in mind that Marx defines labor power as inseparable from the living body of the proletarian, it is clear that the alienation of this specific good, which is legally required in each act of selling, appears problematic here. It seems more appropriate to speak of leasing, hiring, or renting labor power, but it is worth remembering that the body of the worker is always at stake in these operations, which are often facilitated by the array of legal, informal, and illegal middlemen and agencies that we have mentioned regarding migrant care workers (Kuczynski 2009; Mezzadra 2011c).

This critical observation emphasizes even more the peculiarity of the commodity labor power at the center of Marx's theory. It goes beyond the exclusive legal framework of free wage labor and deepens the analysis of the multifarious arrangements through which labor is subsumed under capital. Feminist and gender analysis brings to the fore the bodily and even biopolitical aspects of the production of subjectivity always implied by these arrangements. This is particularly apparent in the role played by borders in the production of the labor power of migrants as a commodity. "Living labor," a concept fully developed by Marx in the *Grundrisse*, where he uses it to distinguish "labor as subjectivity" from the "past" and "dead" labor that is objectified in machines (Marx 1973, 272), nicely captures the complexity of this subjective situation. It also highlights, as Dipesh Chakrabarty has shown, the multiplicity and heterogeneity constitutive of a labor that, as *living*, can never be fully reduced to the code of "abstract labor" employed by capital to measure and "translate" it into the language of value (Chakrabarty 2000, 60). These tensions and gaps between living and abstract labor have never been as intense and wide as under contemporary capitalism. Migrant domestic and care workers embody these tensions and gaps in a specific and nevertheless paradigmatic way. While the entire spectrum of their physical, affective, emotional attitudes is put to work, they experience the abstract nature of their labor only when they get paid. The tens of thousands of Indonesian and Filipina domestic workers who gather in and around Victoria Park, Hong Kong, during their day off may not think of the relation between their living labor and the iconography of capital's power surrounding them, for example, in the form of the HBSC Building under which they frequently assemble (Constable 2007). In an age of financialization of capitalism, the reproduction of abstract labor as a universal societal norm is more and more predicated on the working and reproduction of financial circuits, to which we now turn.

Financial Traders

Financial traders sit at the pinnacle of a global system that exercises a sovereign control over contemporary ways of life and mobility. Yet they are no less subject to the whims and forces of the markets they work to make than are other contemporary figures of labor, from the carer to the cleaner, the professor to the programmer. The expansion of global financial markets, despite the crashes and defaults that have crossed them in recent years, has been prolific since the first signs of the crumbling of the Fordist production system in the 1970s. To remember one often-quoted statistic, the total value of the wealth generated by the world's financial markets is now eight times greater than that produced in real terms through industry, agriculture, and services (Office of the Comptroller of the Currency 2011). Finance now permeates all sectors of the global economy and all phases of the economic cycle (Marazzi 2011). This expansion of finance has partly shifted strategies of capitalist valorization and accumulation away from industry, agriculture, and services and toward more immaterial and relational forms of productive activity. Along with this has come an increasing exploitation of mental or intellectual labor alongside the manual labor whose exploitation remains an important part of the global economy.

There can be no doubt that financial traders are prominent and even privileged figures in the world's cognitive workforce. Though their earnings can be staggering, so is their exposure to risk and stress. The global and 24/7 nature of financial markets and the increased use of electronic communications mean that a trader's work is never done. Likewise, the volatility and expansion of these markets have meant increased competition and a faster pace of work. When the stakes are high and the potential for earnings and losses never remote, the bodies and brains that stoke the world's financial system are pushed to ever higher degrees of exertion. This has implications not only for traders but also for those who exist in close relation to them. In a study involving traders with children, Mary Blair-Loy and Jerry A. Jacobs (2003) link the seemingly endless hours put in by these workers and their frequently "workaholic" tendencies to a "care deficit" within their families. Indeed, most of the traders surveyed in this study indicated that they experience more stress in the presence of their families than when they are at work. Not only does this deficit entrench gender asymmetries, encouraging a traditional domestic division of labor in which women take on most of the work and men position themselves as bread winners. It also increases the demand for paid domestic work, fueling the conditions that lead to the expansion of migrant care labor in cities where financial markets provide the pulse of economic activity. If the image of Indonesian and Filipina women gathered beneath the HBSC Bank building in Hong Kong signals the possibility of the emergence of new forms of sociality and organization among such migrant care workers, so it also registers their economic, spatial, and emotional connection with workers in the financial sector. These two groups of workers—carers and traders—occupy seemingly opposite ends of the world labor spectrum in terms of gender, earnings, and the relative assignment of bodily and cognitive tasks. But they are materially and symbolically linked within the global multiplication of labor.

The typical image of the financial trader is male, brash, and cynical. It is hard to forget figures such as Gordon Gekko in Oliver Stone's film *Wall Street* (1987) or Patrick Bateman, the violent sociopath and investment banker who narrates Bret Easton Ellis's novel *American Psycho* (1991). With their self-serving ideologies, misogyny, and operations on the dark side of the law, Gekko and Bateman join a long line of fictional characters who find their literary precedent in Frank Cowperwood, the protagonist of Theodore Dreiser's novel *The Financier* (1912). This exaggerated male stereotype, which itself signals a kind of crisis of masculinity, certainly has its real-life versions. Financial trading remains a male-dominated profession. It is not rare to encounter news stories that report the dalliances of traders with prostitutes and strippers (Schecter, Schwartz, and Ross 2009). One study even purports to demonstrate that traders with higher testosterone levels perform more effectively in the marketplace (Coates and Herbert 2008). But for every study suggesting that hormones, machismo, or other extremes of masculine behavior promote more lucrative market performance, another makes a counterclaim. Brad M. Barber and Terrance Odean (2001) claim to have discovered that women make better financial investors than men do because they pursue a less overconfident trading style and thus cut transaction costs. Although it is certainly necessary to question the methodological individualism that informs studies that correlate particular fixed gender or personality traits with successful financial trading, it is also true that the financial workforce is becoming more diverse by both race and gender.

In *Out of the Pits*, an ethnographic study of trading on Chicago and London futures markets, Caitlin Zaloom describes how London financial firms in the first years of the twenty-first century sought to make their operations prosper by recruiting "professionalized traders" within a "multiculturalist paradigm." They "hired Asians, blacks, and women, all of them educated, to bring in different views of the market. According to this logic, the categorical differences of each trader would lead him or her to interpret the market differently, providing a range of insights into the market's actions" (Zaloom 2006, 91). Furthermore, these workers should preferably be single because "they should not be worried about such 'extraneous' matters as whether [they] will be able to pay for" their partner's car "or the family vacation" (84). Zaloom's observations register how financial traders have become part of an elite and highly mobile cognitive workforce in high demand across the world's global cities. As Andrew M. Jones explains, "there exists a global pool of labour which is concentrated in a limited number of key financial centres in Europe, North America, and Asia" (Jones 2008, 6). Employers therefore "recruit from an (increasingly) global labour market with little difference between national labor markets in terms of the characteristics of this specialised pool" (6). It is crucial to register here the way the differences between national labor markets have become negligible when it comes to recruiting financial traders. This kind of reorganization of the borders within and between labor markets, as much as the multiplicity and diversity that now makes up labor forces, is a key feature of what we call the global multiplication of labor. One implication in terms of hiring practices in the financial sector is the increased use of international agencies to fill high-end vacancies. According to Jones, there is also "strong evidence that international mobility is an explicitly desirable characteristic of employee experience in many of these occupations, and that there are complex patterns of short-term migration as a consequence of international secondment practices within transnational financial service firms" (7).

Traders have become the objects of what Ayelet Shachar (2006) calls the "race for talent" or the competition among wealthier nations to attract highly skilled migrants. Often involving preferential paths to permanent residency and eventually citizenship, this competition has led to the international diffusion of migration schemes that carefully measure the degree of skill and the potential wealth-generating capability that migrants can bring to a national economy. Such regimes also have mirror effects in migrant-sending countries, which increasingly encourage dual citizenship, investments in the national economy, and return migration. Just as much as border control technologies that function through strategies of interception, detention, and illegalization, these methods of border control and filtering, which actually serve to articulate and encourage global mobility, function through processes of discrimination and selection. We investigate such differential inclusion further in the next chapter. For now it is important to note that a growing proportion of the world's high-order financial positions are filled by migrants. Jones (2008) estimates a 10–15 percent presence of migrants in the top end of London's financial workforce. Although this is nowhere near as high as the percentage of migrants that compose the global care workforce, it is now impossible to study financial traders and trading, theoretically or empirically, without taking such transnational mobility into account.

What, then, are the subjective aspects, the capacities, or potentialities contained in the brains and bodies of financial traders, particularly migrants, which lead to their appointments and successful operations in making global markets? The literature that seeks to identify and enumerate these attributes is prodigious. To take one example, Thomas Oberlechner (2004, 23) conducts an analysis of ratings given by professional traders at leading European banks to identify eight characteristics that are perceived to be important for a successful trader: "disciplined cooperation, tackling decisions, market meaning making, emotional stability, information processing, interested integrity, autonomous organization, and handling information." Such research, which almost always focuses on individual personality factors that are considered to be fully formed before the trader comes to market, is often conducted with the pretense of improving hiring decisions. It is tempting to observe that such behavioral studies of work and personality did little to bias hiring decisions in ways that might have prevented the global economic crisis of 2007–8. Perhaps, however, it was precisely the efficient wealth-generating behavior of traders that triggered the economic meltdown, with disastrous results for working people around the world.

To repeat ourselves, traders are an extremely privileged category of workers. They are the masters of the global capitalist system, whose seemingly immaterial manipulation of esoteric instruments and devices has undeniably material consequences. Because the financial world is constantly and unpredictably shifting, it is difficult for the contracts under which traders are hired to specify how their terms of employment (wages, conditions for breaking the contract, etc.) will evolve in response to future events. As Olivier Godechot explains, "there is no pre-existing, stabilized nomenclature for the set of the employee's future states at the time the contract is signed." In most cases, this means "the job is not assigned by the contract but assigned gradually as employees become integrated into the work group" (Godechot 2008, 10). Like the migrant care workers Akalyn studied, traders sell not a predefined set of personality traits but their ability or potential to *become* the right person, the one required by their employers (or by the market) as circumstances change. There is, however, an important difference between traders and carers. Traders can (and usually do) acquire control over transferable assets and can thus threaten to leave or inflict damage on an employer who refuses to accept a contract renegotiation. This is the reason for the payment of huge bonuses to traders, particularly those who lead offices and teams—a practice that attracted outrage from politicians and the media in the onset of the current economic crisis.

Because the legal device of the contract is unable to set the terms under which labor power is bought and sold, companies must pay out huge sums to ensure the trader's loyalty. Many commentators focus on how these bonuses induce reckless risk-taking that lowers shareholder value and creates financial instability (see, for instance, Crotty 2011). Steering away from the moralism that typifies much discussion of this topic, we want to make a more general point about the conditions of labor, freedom to move, and contract that cross the multiplicity of working lives and are particularly pronounced in the case of migrants. The implicit threat of blackmail or even sabotage that haunts the payment of traders' bonuses is a reverse image of the reality of coercion produced by the combination of labor regulation, border, and visa regimes that apply to care workers and other less skilled migrants. Labor markets, far from being smoothly governed statistical constructs, are characterized by practices of manipulation, violence, and preference that intervene in the precarious balance of mobility and harnessing that invests the bordering of labor relations and processes today. The various forms of obligation, limitation, and intimidation that cross the general field of labor are a reminder of the specific conditions and experiences negotiated in different ways by the variegated and multiple array of contemporary laboring subjects. At the same time, the differentiation of juridical statuses within the boundaries of formally unified "labor markets" stretches and tangles the chains that bind workers to employers and to the capital relation. Whether this takes the form of the traditional wage relation or involves other mechanisms or enticements (the bonuses paid to traders, the affects that invest relations between care workers and their employers, or visa conditions that bind migrants to labor contracts), the "free exchange" between money and labor power appears ever more entwined in complex situations where the production of subjectivity is immediately at stake.

Keeping in mind the absolute specificity of the financial traders' position in the more general composition of relations between labor and capital, we see a series of paradoxes come into view. The trader is a particular kind of worker whose labor produces a subjectivity that is forever becoming a capitalist. This peculiar production of labor power seems to be not only fully included within the space of capital but also actively engaged in the expansion of this space and its continuing colonization of resources, time, and lives. Nevertheless, it also involves a kind of constituent excess that shows the labor contract for what it is: a piece of paper that is insufficient to regulate the labor relation in the absence of a deep embeddedness within specific workplace and market dynamics. Moreover, the living labor of financial traders embodies a series of features that from the point of view of a traditional economic analysis could be considered as a form of fixed capital. This is what makes up their strength in the relation with their employers (Marazzi 2005, 117–18). The threat to quit is particularly potent in their case, so much so that it does not need always to be made explicit. This is because, as Godechot explains, if traders go, "they leave with information, knowledge, know-how. They leave with teams. They leave with clients." From this perspective, the labor market for financial traders appears as "fundamentally dual: a market of persons and a market for what those persons carry away." The value of the transfers made by traders "lies more in the assets transferred than in the intrinsic skills of the persons who bear those assets" (Godechot 2008, 21).

From this perspective, the approach of financial behaviorism that links the trader's performance to a series of fixed personality traits encounters severe difficulties. If the trader is a figure whose work of becoming a capitalist is never done, he or she is not merely or not only *homo economicus*. We do not want to join the chorus of studies that emphasize the role of the individual's emotional dispositions in financial decision-making activities (see, for instance, Seo and Barrett 2007). Clearly financial trading is not simply a rational exercise but a specifically embedded social and spatial practice that involves particular modes of bodily communication and affective expression. As Zaloom observes, the "processes that produce abstract information in financial markets are not themselves abstract." Managers and designers "integrate people, technologies, places and aesthetics into a zone of autonomous economic action" (Zaloom 2006, 117). A growing body of work emphasizes the social and affective dimensions of financial trading. Markets are sites where people are mutually susceptible and engage in patterns of imitation (MacKenzie 2004; Orléan 1999). Moreover, such activity is economically consequential. Christian Marazzi writes that "financialization depends on a *mimetic rationality*, a kind of herd behavior based on the information deficit of individual investors" (Marazzi 2008, 21). In contemporary trading scenarios, such collective action is mediated by electronic technologies and receives a complex graphic representation on the computer terminal. Nested before the screen, the trader gains the impression that the market comes to life (Zwick and Dhokalia 2006). The market thus emerges as a kind of "epistemic object" with an ontologically open and unfolding structure (Cetina 1997). Nonetheless, it moves, morphs, and changes only with the input of multiple transactions, which interact and aggregate to acquire the characteristics of a social force.

Despite the recent emphasis on the role of affect in market dynamics, there is clearly a continued role for rational calculation and behavior. Indeed, market actions can be both affective and rational at the same time. It is important that Marazzi, in the quote we just cited, characterizes mimetic or imitative behavior in financial markets as a form of rationality. In the current moment of financial capitalism, this kind of mimetic rationality displaces the dominant processes of capital in its industrial form that Marx described with the famous formula M-C-M'. For Marx, this process directed and shaped the logic of investments in both constant and variable capital. But the tendency within financial markets for money to beget money (M-M') has acquired a new quality and intensity with the multiplication and extension of sources and agents of what Marx analyzed in *Capital*, volume 3, as "interest-bearing capital" (Marazzi 2011). This positions labor very differently than how it appears in the wage relation that dominated under industrial capitalism. If the carer engages in the social reproduction of human beings, the labor of traders also has social reproduction as its target, but in this case what is reproduced is the very social relation of capital.

Financialization is the technical name given to the social effects of the particular form of reproduction that the trader performs. Although we have discussed this concept in the previous chapter, our analysis of the relations between carers and traders allows us to add something more. At stake in the expansion of finance over daily life (Martin 2002) is not simply the devolution of financial logic and calculations to the management of households—that is, to the domestic domain where caring and many other reproductive activities are carried out. There has also been a globalization and peculiar form of distancing that has invested this expansion of financial activity to the domestic sphere, for instance, through the circuits of remittances sent by many migrant workers to attend to the needs, both material and affective, of families and individuals afar. Furthermore, these processes of financialization impose the discipline of debt on populations across the world and thus contribute to the conditions that encourage migration in the first place. In an important sense, which is even more pronounced in current times of economic crisis, debt differentiation and distribution have become means for governing the entire life of populations (Lazzarato 2012). From public to sovereign debt, household to personal debt, student to health care debt, the specter of debt has spread across contemporary societies. More and more, the standard or norm of abstract labor—which compels individuals and whole populations to measure their activities in terms of the production of monetary value—is entangled with the logic of debt and its colonization of life. The tasks of hedging risk and securitizing value, which are so much the work of the trader in the era of "capitalism with derivatives" (Bryan and Rafferty 2006), far from being merely technical operations, have become central moments of political command. The increasing interpenetration of finance and war, markets and militaries, is an important sign of these changes in the deployment of political power (Martin 2009). The boundaries between sovereignty and governance have been blurred, leaving figures of labor such as carers and financial traders to negotiate their productive and reproductive roles in the labyrinths of a global system that seems increasingly without a stable center.

Chains that Bind, Chains that Link

Migrant domestic and care workers and financial traders often cross paths in physical and emblematic ways. This can involve direct employment relations as well as more indirect forms of connection, as for instance those that come into being when migrants' remittances become the objects of financial speculation and risk-management strategies. Moreover, the urban environment and style of life of many contemporary cities, not just those that Saskia Sassen (1991) identifies as "global cities," are characterized by the coeval presence of and encounter between these two figures. How do we make sense of such relations of connection, reliance, and indifference, which, it is important to remember, are invested by the social relation that is capital itself? What are the terms and conditions that enable these linkages across vast stretches of physical and virtual space? How do material processes of division invest the multiplication of labor in which these two figures are enmeshed?

Let us return to the metaphor of the chain, which was never just a means of describing the ties that bind the worker to capital but also a way of figuring the various links and stages in processes of assembly and production. Lenin seems to have had both these connotations in mind when he advocated that capitalism should be fought at the weakest link of the chain, a strategic ideal of political action that has since been displaced and used in contexts far from those in which it was initially elaborated. In more recent usage of the concept of the chain, the emphasis is more on the multifarious ways in which chains link or articulate different elements in the productive process (Bair 2009). Currently one of the most influential ways of conceptualizing how various instantiations of labor and productive activity connect with and detach from each other is by means of the notion of the global commodity chain. Introduced by world system theorists (Chase-Dunn 1989; Gereffi and Korzeniewicz 1994; Hopkins and Wallerstein 1986), global commodity chain analysis traces how transnational labor and production processes materially connect economies, firms, workers, and households in the contemporary world economy. Focusing not only on the emergence and consequences of a global manufacturing system but also on the elaboration of global care chains, this approach stresses the inputs and outputs that occur along each link in the sequence. At the same time, it sheds light on the patterns of geographical dispersion and structures of governance that determine the allocation of material, financial, and human resources throughout the chain as a whole. Although such analysis is highly sensitive to the multiple ways of organizing the production and distribution of commodities in a globalized economy, it needs to be supplemented by an approach that focuses on the kinds of questions we have asked about to carers and traders.

The global commodity chain approach, like the debates about the new international division of labor we explored in the previous chapter, tends to assume stable geographical divides that cross the world of labor and production. Our hesitancy before this approach derives precisely from the kinds of activities carried out by figures such as financial traders, who constantly pursue strategies that cut and blur such geographical divides, fragmenting and redeploying these barriers by collecting and aggregating assets into tranches of risk that are divided by newer and more abstract kinds of borders. Conversely, global care chains have mutated in recent years well beyond the old divisions of first and third world, global North and global South, to include patterns of movement and transaction that stretch to Dubai as much as New York, Mumbai as much as Paris, Rio de Janeiro as well as Shanghai. The model of the chain can undoubtedly account for these new locations quite easily, although the rapidity and unpredictability of these fluctuations also challenge the idea of stability conveyed by this image. Furthermore the subjective and relational elements that are so important to the care encounter are obscured by this approach, along with the episodes of upheaval and displacement that frequently characterize migratory experiences. In the case of financial traders, it is no accident that the world they live in and help make has been increasingly described with metaphors of turbulence and liquidation (Ho 2009). These also have very different implications to the image of the chain, with its solid and linear links.

What concerns us about the global commodity chain approach is not just the linear and teleological process of linkage implied by the metaphor of the chain. Critics have already pointed to the need for more attention to iterative feedback, networks, clusters, and webs to better conceptualize contemporary processes of production (Dicken et al. 2001; Pratt 2008; Raikes, Jensen, and Ponte 2000). Anna Tsing's analysis of "supply chain capitalism," for instance, stresses how commodity chains have evolved in ways that need to be "understood in relation to contingency, experimentation, negotiation, and unstable commitments." She extends this point in a way consistent with our discussion of labor forces and commodity chains by noting that it is not only "internal governance standards" but also social and cultural conditions that exist outside the chain that contribute to the production and disciplining of workforces (Tsing 2009, 150–51). Global commodity chain analysts tend to consider the stock of labor forces to be already given in and distributed across the bounded spaces that are joined up by the productive processes that occur along the chain. Although they often analyze the impact of changes in interfirm linkages on labor forces, especially regarding wages and technological upgrading, they tend to sideline questions about subjectivity and power in the production and reproduction of labor power. Thus, they give scant attention to labor mobilities and labor struggles, let alone the connection between the two.

Commodity chain approaches offer minimal analysis of the concrete conditions in which labor forces are constructed and embedded: practices of state regulation; hiring and labor control strategies of employers; patterns of inclusion and exclusion based on social origin, sex, ethnicity, age, and so on;

or relationships within families that influence decisions about who enters the workforce. They also pay little attention to the abstract social relations generated by every act of production and manifest in the measurement of abstract labor that, as we argued before, represents the regulatory nexus of global capitalism and exists in tension with the multiplicity constitutive of living labor. Without due attention to the mutual constitution of the embedded and abstracted elements of production, global commodity chain analysis cannot fully come to grips with the conflict-ridden processes by which various social actors, including migrants, respond to the abstract demands of the market by attempting to change the concrete relationships in which the social tissues of labor, even the labor of abstracting, come to life.

Crucial to our analysis of carers and traders in this chapter has been an emphasis on the production of subjectivity specific to these forms of labor. We have also tried to deliver a sense of how the contours of living labor discerned through an investigation of carers and traders extend into other fields of employment as well as into the more general domain where capital's command and production of space are shaped by its encounter with heterogeneous working subjects. In these investigations borders have a special role to play. Female migrants' practices of mobility across borders, crucial to the reproduction of global care chains as well as domestic care labor markets, are crisscrossed by a search for freedom from and a contestation of patriarchal patterns of sexual division of labor. In the case of traders, their activities foster the expansion of the frontiers of capital in a financial domain that is increasingly disconnected from the space of territorial borders. The tension between the political logics of financial command and territoriality that traders help produce also has important consequences for any consideration of the changing nature of borders in the present. This tension and this disconnection lie at the heart of contemporary global capitalism, and they fracture its spaces in ways that are not adequately reflected by the image of commodity chains. Nevertheless, the notion of the commodity chain is not easily dispensed with because it describes the material terms of connection and linkage that gird a world so easily seduced by the fetishism of the product and image.

Our approach to commodity chains is informed by the conviction that they cannot be properly understood, even in the most technical aspects of their formation and maintenance, without due attention to another sense of the chain: that mentioned by Marx and Engels when they entreat the workers of the world to free themselves of their chains. Our discussion of carers and traders draws attention to the very different kinds of chains that bind these figures to the labor relation. In the case of carers, these are primarily the ligatures of affect and the judicial mechanisms, embodied in the form of migration papers, which they negotiate with their employers, middlemen, and the bureaucratic agencies of the states they leave, traverse, and work in. For traders, who work the differences between the frontiers of capital and territorial borders, chains can be highly remunerative as well as binding devices. The payment of bonuses and all sorts of other incentives and fringe benefits serve as a bridle that harnesses these masters of capital to firms and specific market locations. This is true despite the fact that financial fluctuations and turbulences also provide an additional ligature that binds traders to the very form of command that they work to reproduce.

Drawing attention to chains that bind allows us to rethink the connecting function of the chains that link up the global capitalist world from the point of view of the frictions, discords, and struggles that cross the field of labor and contribute to the production and reproduction of labor forces. These tensions are often played out in the personality of the worker. Think of the carer who acquires affection for the person she tends to but hates the employer who pays her to do this work. Or imagine the trader who continually displaces his own capitalist instincts and desires onto supposedly objective market forces and the way they command him to act. Carers and traders are not the only ones who have their personalities shaped in this way. There is a multitude of other instances. Think of the industrial worker who engages in actions against labor market reforms that aim to quantitatively ease the markets on which her pension funds accumulate. Or consider the displaced peasant in India who is compelled to perform service work for the same populations that inhabited his former farmlands. It is necessary to take this multiplicity into account if the workers of the world are to collectively reimagine and materially construct their unity. This means renegotiating a whole series of splits and divisions that cross the bodies and souls of individual workers and invest the traditional separation between skilled and unskilled labor, manual and mental labor, and the processes of ethnicization and illegalization that contribute to the composition of living labor. Shaking free from the chains of capital today requires an explicit act of refusal. It cannot be achieved by merely rearranging the ways commodity chains link up the world. In other words, a politics of articulation is not enough. What is required is a constituent politics that can come to terms with what we call the multiplication of labor, with the heterogeneous array of subjects that constitute the workers of the world.

Whose Unity?

Perhaps today we are too suspicious of the concept of unity. It is hard to deny the political and rhetorical utility that calls for unity have had in many labor struggles and throughout the whole history of labor movements. Nevertheless, the traditional languages of unity and the organizational practices of acting in union have been challenged both by struggles and insurgencies around gender and race and by the increasing fragmentation of the workforce in the face of recent transformations of capitalism. This has led on one hand to a proliferation of separatist positions, whether identitarian or "micropolitical," as well as to the spread of single-interest political campaigns and movements. A new salience has been acquired by jacqueries and riots, which are often sparked by quotidian and even minor acts of injustice but in their levels of antagonism come to symbolize much wider issues of subordination, precariousness, and desolation (Hardt and Negri 2009, 236–38). Although many of these positions and events do not immediately present themselves as labor struggles, they can be symptomatically read against the background of the mutations of labor and capital that we analyze in this chapter. These changes trouble the easy invocation of unity and suggest why it risks being reduced to mere rhetoric. They foster a proliferation of borders and boundaries that cut across the composition of living labor, graduating and diffusing its subordination to capital in a wide variety of forms and to different degrees. They also intensify the relevance of social cooperation in the production of the subjective qualities and excesses that invest contemporary experiences of work and life. The concept of the multiplication of labor attempts to grasp the two sides of this process, fragmentation and excess, and points to the crucial relevance of the gap between them for rethinking unity in a theoretical as well as a political perspective.

Getting beyond the dilemmas that the concept of unity now presents means recognizing that systems of labor control and disciplining have become ever more sophisticated and finely calibrated since Marx and Engels encouraged the workers of the world to lose their chains. But it also implies an analysis of the convoluted ways in which capital produces its own unity that is at the same time its global command. A provocative way of addressing this fundamental aspect of capital can be found in the important book by Alfred Sohn-Rethel, *Intellectual and Manual Labour* (1978), which offered some quite counterintuitive approaches to the highly contested question of the role of knowledge and cognitive capacities in the development of twentieth-century capitalism.

To deal with the question of the changing significance of the relations between intellectual and manual labor across a wide historical vista, Sohn-Rethel introduces the concept of "social synthesis," which he defines in a very general way as "the network of relations by which society forms a coherent whole." He explains that as "social forms develop and change, so also does the synthesis which holds together the multiplicity of links operating between them according to the division of labour" (1978, 4). Although the invocation of synthesis in this context carries for us a whole series of unnecessary connotations (linked to Sohn-Rethel's training in German critical and idealist philosophy), this approach suggests a means of grappling with the ways in which various patterns of labor's multiplication and division mutate under the pressure of social and historical forces. Working the tension between what Sohn-Rethel calls a "network of relations" or "multiplicity of links" and the processes that he understands to hold society together is also a useful way of confronting the question of unity in the face of current social theories that draw centrally on notions such as the network or assemblage (Castells 1996; DeLanda 2006; Latour 2005). The way these theories criticize the organicism that underlies much sociological thought implies an emphasis on how society itself comes together (or falls apart) that tends to deny the systemic properties and logic of capital. Sohn-Rethel launches a scathing critique of such organicism, highlighting what he calls the processes of "societisation" that compose the links and divisions that shape society (1978, 139). His juggling of the categories of multiplicity and unity points to shifting and varying strategies of social organization, which at the beginning of the modern period begin to converge around "monetary exchange activated by money being used as capital" (139). Like contemporary network and assemblage theorists, Sohn-Rethel draws attention to the ways that categories like society and capital are constructed. Unlike many of these thinkers, however, he does not deny the validity and analytical utility of these concepts for a wide variety of purposes, including most prominently the investigation of changing configurations of intellectual and manual labor. The relevance of this approach is clear if one considers the controversies surrounding the evolution of these configurations since the crisis of Fordism in the 1970s.

Consider the concept of immaterial labor, which has attracted much debate since it was first introduced in the early 1990s by Italian operaisti thinkers exiled in Paris as part of an attempt to rethink the political conditions of antagonism and subversion under post-Fordist conditions (Lazzarato 1996; Negri and Lazzarato 1991). Importantly, this concept, which describes "labor that produces an immaterial good, such as a service, a cultural product, knowledge, or communication" (Hardt and Negri 2000, 290), implies the existence and production of a complex "network of relations," whether it arises from communication and linguistic exchanges or from affective and emotional "labor in the bodily mode" (Smith 1987, 78–88). The elaboration and controversies surrounding immaterial labor were always traversed by an oscillation between the two poles of the concept. On one hand, it wanted to register the growing importance of knowledge work and the field that Robert Reich (1991) famously designated as "symbolic analytical services." It also emphasized the prominence of relational activities in other sectors of employment, such as informationalized manufacturing, the creative industries, and care work. On the other hand, the concept of immaterial labor implied a claim about the hegemony of these kinds of laboring activity and the way they were supposed to drive capitalism's development in its global phase. Most criticism tended to center around this second point, worrying that claims for immaterial labor's hegemony obscured both social and spatial hierarchies that invest and structure the field of labor (Caffentzis 2005; Holmes 2005; Wright 2005). To be fair, this was a problem that the initial elaborators of the concept had already struggled to take into account, and it is also true that the debate has moved on. Immaterial labor must now be approached as a historical concept that opened a new field of research and debate on labor after the crisis of Fordism but has been superseded more by material circumstances than theoretical criticisms.

Even figures such as Michael Hardt and Antonio Negri (2009) tend not to use the concept of immaterial labor in their recent works, preferring to speak about the "forms of labor that produce . . . immaterial goods," or more colloquially, "labor of the head and heart" (132). What we call the multiplication of labor and the related proliferation of borders signal the shift registered by this change of nomenclature. Focusing on the heterogenization that today characterizes the spectrum of labor positions requires a slower and more patient process of mapping the "multiplicity of links" (to recall Sohn-Rethel's phrase) that connect and divide various figures of labor. Rather than assuming that the concept of immaterial labor can hold together experiences as different as those of carers and traders, it is necessary to piece together fragments and follow leads to discern the processes of societization that generate both divisions and linkages between and beyond them. In this regard, the work we undertake in chapter 7 of tracing how the connections and separations between different laboring figures are constantly shuffled and recombined and how these assemblages move or stretch across global or "lateral" spaces (Ong 2006) is an important supplement to the current discussion. For the time being, it is necessary to return to the boundary between intellectual and manual labor.

One of the most pressing questions with regard to the boundary between intellectual and manual labor concerns how it has been reorganized and recoded in new ways since the incorporation of knowledge into machines instituted a formal division between the standardization of manual labor and the forms of intellectual work that established capital's control of the productive process. In the account of Sohn-Rethel (1978, 66), what divides mental from manual labor is its use of abstractions that find their origin in commodity exchange. For him, such abstractions are drawn not from "the primary nature of physical reality but the second, purely social nature which, in the epochs of commodity production, constitutes a vital part of that 'social being of men which determines their consciousness'" (74). We cannot dwell here on the sophisticated rethinking of the peculiarity of historical materialism provided by Sohn-Rethel. What interests us, rather, is his rooting of mental or intellectual labor in an analysis of the "commodity form," which means in the sphere of exchange and the market. Sohn-Rethel emphasizes the tension between this sphere and the sphere of production, where manual labor is located. He characterizes the "social synthesis" corresponding to early phases of capitalism as an assemblage that reproduces the subordination of manual to intellectual labor on the basis of their autonomy with respect to each other. Since the end of the nineteenth century, however, this autonomy has come to be challenged by the development of capitalism.

In his analysis of the "Taylor system" and its related "flow methods of production," Sohn-Rethel points to the fact that now "it is labor itself that forms the starting-point" of the capitalist social formation (1978, 140–41). We are confronted here with an analysis of Taylorism that is quite different from the influential one provided by Harry Braverman (1974), which focuses on the "degradation" of both mental and manual work. Sohn-Rethel sees flow and mass production as the highest moment of the "socialization of labor" under the domination of capital (Sohn-Rethel 1978, 165). The dramatic increase in the incorporation of science in production processes displaces the position of intellectual labor toward the domain within which manual labor had previously been located in an exclusive way. For Sohn-Rethel this is the origin of a destabilization of intellectual labor's autonomy from its manual twin. At the root of the problem for him is the relation between cognition and abstraction. Sohn-Rethel questions the "age-old idea that abstraction is the exclusive privilege of thought" (7), fashioning the concept of "real abstraction" by emphasizing those elements of Marx's thought that locate the abstractions of labor and money at the heart of the social mediation of the commodity form. This concept implies an undermining and restriction of the domain of thought and intellectual labor, which Sohn-Rethel traces in his reconstruction of the adventures of the notion of an "independent intellect" in the face of the steady intertwining between science and capital in modernity (67–79). This process enters a new stage with the rationalization and socialization of labor associated with "flow production" and capitalism in its "monopoly" form. A new principle of societization, directly emerging out of the labor process, threatens to explode the "social synthesis" constructed on the commodity form, market exchange, and the private appropriation of the products of labor. In the face of this "dual economics" of "monopoly capitalism" (163–65), Sohn-Rethel points to structural transformations of intellectual labor itself, which come to be increasingly shaped by the new principle of societization. He claims that these transformations provide a chance for a revolutionary transition that would overcome the division between manual and intellectual labor.

Other thinkers supplied parallel accounts of this integration of mental labor into productive processes, emphasizing its political consequences. Already in the early 1960s, Italian operaisti thinkers such as Romano Alquati and Mario Tronti discussed the expanded scope of the socialization of labor and sought to describe it in a way that established the theoretical necessity for workers' struggles to move beyond the office and the factory. Though this insight inspired several strains and more than one generation of political thinkers and organizers, one of its most interesting elaborations regarding the manual/mental labor division comes from Hans-Jürgen Krahl, the German student leader and apostate of Adorno who died in a car accident in 1970. In a series of essays and philosophical fragments, Krahl (1971) argued that the analytical separation between the sphere of production and the sphere of consciousness, which remains valid when productive labor is structurally separated from mental labor, loses its meaning when intellectual work becomes a constitutive element of the production process. With the progressive intellectualization of the production cycle, emotional, linguistic, and creative energies become involved in the production of value. Consequently, the organizational modalities and political project of the workers' movement had to change. No longer could they be based on the supposition that the worker knows his or her job without having an awareness of the system of knowledge that structures society. Intellectual workers develop a specific knowledge and perception—no matter how fragmentary and tormented—of the social system of knowledge that traverses the productive cycle. As a result, they are increasingly unable to tolerate the objectified form of work imposed by capital, and their sociality develops in a direction that can be organized toward autonomy and refusal.

There is a need to investigate the ways capital was able to displace the revolutionary chance identified by Sohn-Rethel, Tronti, Krahl, and others, which crystallized in the social turmoil and historical rupture of the "world Sixties" (Connery 2007). This not only resulted in capital's formation of what Sohn-Rethel would have described as a new social synthesis. It also involved the tumultuous forms of spatial reorganization and heterogenization that we investigated in previous chapters. This is the point at which global labor comes into being and processes of heterogenization and multiplication join new techniques of extracting value from labor, often based around notions of flexibility and innovation. Luc Boltanski and Eve Chiapello (2005) trace, for instance, how workers' demands for flexibility and the reduction of working hours, which at the beginning of the 1970s were perceived as a refusal of capital's command, precipitated capital's own development of practices and ideologies of flexibility. These changes profoundly influenced "the organization of work and the techniques employed (multitasking, self-control, development of autonomy, etc.)," giving rise to strategies of lean production and subcontracting that created a workforce "malleable in terms of employment (casual jobs, temping, self-employed workers), working hours, or the duration of work (part-timers, variable hours)" (218). While innovation and the accumulation of knowledge assets became key economic features, a recombination of intellectual and manual tasks and activities fostered a profound transformation of the composition of living labor and challenged established notions of working-class unity. A new conceptual armature was forged by neoliberal economists and social scientists who sought to rethink the workings of the whole social fabric according to the generalization of the logics of investment and risk management. The notion of "human capital" (Becker 1962), famously discussed by Michel Foucault (2008, 215–33), exemplifies this tendency.

The globalization of financial markets that entered a new stage after U.S. President Richard Nixon's decision to delink the dollar from gold in 1971 provided the framework for an unprecedented expansion of risk management across many spheres of life. At the same time, it came to supplement a fundamental function played according to Sohn-Rethel (as well as Marx) by commodity exchange: the reproduction of the "social nexus" that "operates the commensuration of labour" (Sohn-Rethel 1978, 169). This commensuration is precisely what we have analyzed in terms of abstract labor. Stressing the tension between the regulatory function that the abstraction of labor continues to have even in the current era of seemingly unharnessed financialization and the multiplicity that invests living labor, we have explored the growing unpredictability and dispersion of attempts to translate between the abstract and the concrete. In this chapter we analyzed the discrepancies that invest this work of translation for female care workers and for financial traders—two figures whose subjective positions result in very different negotiations of the nexus of abstract and living labor. In particular, we argued that such efforts of translation do not generate a homogeneous class subject. Rather, they give rise to a wide array of contemporary figures of labor whose subjective dimensions and capacities can only be organized across a highly differentiated field in which alliances and solidarities often take on odd and unexpected forms. This is as much a matter of spatial as social positioning, as again we have shown in the cases of carers and traders. Any application of Sohn-Rethel's notion of societization in the current global context must account for a proliferation of borders and reorganization of space that radically question the inevitability of networks of social relations converging on a "coherent whole," particularly when that whole is associated with the bounded space of the modern state. It must also explain how global processes and financialization pertain to the ways capital itself represents the unity of labor, which means to the criteria and the devices through which capital accomplishes the commensuration of labor and its translation into the code of value.

The analysis of financial traders provided in this chapter aims to grasp some of the characteristics of the labor implied in the making of global financial markets and shed light on the mimetic rationality that pervades them. This is not the only complicating element that must be taken into account when rethinking the spatial and social dimensions of labor in the contemporary world. The stretching and crossing of global commodity chains connect in unanticipated and sometimes bewildering ways laboring subjects across scales and spaces, while they fracture and disconnect other fractions of labor. New problems of material and symbolic relation arise from these processes, which are quite different from the traditional questions of solidarity and coherence that derive from classical sociology, for instance, from the writings of Émile Durkheim. At the same time, new patterns of the combination and distribution of intellectual and manual tasks emerge. In the production of the heterogeneous spaces of global capital, which are far less stable than most studies of global commodity chains assume, borders and boundaries acquire a new salience. Our analysis of female migrant domestic and care workers points to the relevance of these borders and boundaries through practices of mobility and migration that increasingly shape the composition of living labor. The mobilization of affects and emotions—that is, of intensities that cut through the divide between intellectual and manual labor as well as through the partitions between cognition, abstraction, and physical efforts—is an important element of contemporary border struggles. From the point of view of border as method, an analysis and deepening of the meaning of these struggles must figure prominently in any attempt to rethink the concepts of unity and class within and against the strategies of commensuration produced by capital in its global age. This is an urgent task if we are to overcome our suspicion of calls for unity to invent new methods of organization, translation, and alliance that can arouse and embolden the workers of the world in all their heterogeneity and multiplicity.

Chapter Five

IN THE SPACE OF TEMPORAL BORDERS

From the Tea Shop to the Bench

The work hours are long in the row of makeshift tea shops and eateries that has sprung up opposite the Unitech Special Economic Zone, one of the primary developments for information technology (IT) services in the New Town area on Kolkata's northeast fringes. These establishments, run and staffed by former peasants displaced from the land on which the IT development sits, stay open into the early hours of the morning to cater to young, English-speaking professionals whose work hours follow the rhythms of a different time zone. Part of the army of so-called virtual migrants (Aneesh 2006) who stoke the mills of India's call centers and IT-enabled services, the requirement for these well-educated youngsters to keep work hours that match the patterns and pace of daily life on other continents has a knock-on effect for those older and less privileged workers who supply them with snacks and the obligatory caffeine. In the previous chapter, the growing heterogeneity of global space, the proliferation of borders, and the multiplication of labor provided an angle to discern some of the limits of the commodity chain approach to the study of global production and labor. As this instance shows, such spatial arrangements always have temporal dimensions as well. This chapter grapples with the relevance of time, temporality, and temporalizing processes in the workings of border regimes, migration schemes, and the technologies of differential inclusion that have come to invest them.

India's virtual migrants are by no means the only figures subject to shifting parameters of time and space in their working lives. Alongside them in this chapter we also encounter detained migrants, asylum seekers, *banlieusards*, international students, and IT workers who leave India. What these figures have in common are experiences of passing through and living in borderscapes where the compression, elongation, and partitioning of time exerts effects of control, filtering, and selectivity. Beginning with a consideration of skilled migration schemes, we argue that they produce discrepant temporalities of waiting, withdrawal, and delay by compelling subjects to negotiate their way among different administrative and labor market statuses. This leads us to question the heuristic value of the distinction between skilled and unskilled migration, which we also find tested by the growing pressure on the distinction between the asylum seeker and the economic migrant. The chapter then moves on to examine how the legal production of illegal and deportable subjects has evolved with the reorganization of labor markets to accommodate processes of informalization and flexibilization. We argue that the growth of migration detention facilities across the globe serves less as a means of excluding migrants than of regulating the time and speed of their movements into labor markets. This perspective delivers a very different understanding of the detention camp than what derives from the philosopher Giorgio Agamben's discussion of such spaces as sites of sovereign exception. It also allows us to draw continuities between the temporality of detention and the ongoing experiences of migrants and migrant communities in metropolitan areas. Examining the conditions that prompted the 2005 riots among youngsters with a migrant background in the *banlieues* of Paris and other French cities, we ask how long migrants remain migrants—that is, how long they remain objects of difference and targets of integration. The chapter closes with a discussion of the politics of differential inclusion and its relevance for debates about the nation-state, multiculturalism, and the multiplicity of times and temporalizing practices that cross migratory experiences in the contemporary world.

This focus on time and temporality deliberately supplements the emphasis on space that has thus far characterized our discussions of the primitive accumulation of modern cartography and the multiplication of labor. Time and again we encounter analyses of capitalist development suggesting that it attempts to overcome the limits of space and geography through temporal shifts and arrangements. Karl Marx's analysis of the formation of the world market, for instance, points to capital's expansion of "the spatial orbit of its circulation" and its simultaneous striving for the progressive "annihilation of space by time" (1973, 539). More recently, geographers like

David Harvey (1989) have drawn out the implications of this tendency for the latest wave of capitalist development, pointing to processes of "time-space compression" as a means of capturing the velocity, acceleration, and new kinds of propinquity that accompany capital's global expansion. The important claim that "space matters" and that concerns of locality, territory, and scale provide a privileged angle for understanding capital in the era of globalization has been a distinctive feature of the so-called spatial turn in humanities and social sciences (Massey 1984; Soja 1989; Thrift 1996). This widespread intellectual movement, which took on several twists and variations, supplied a powerful counternarrative to the dominant image of the globe as a "smooth space" that had circulated since the 1970s. Our discussion of figures such as detainees, banlieusards, and workers in the Indian "body shopping" system at once extends and questions this approach to contemporary capitalism. Exploring the life trajectories and quotidian experiences of these figures implies an emphasis on mobilities and temporal variations that not only occur in space but actively structure and constitute it. The chapter thus confirms Michel de Certeau's claim that "a space exists when one takes into consideration vectors of direction, velocities, and time variables." Space, in this perspective, "is composed of intersections of mobile elements. It is in a sense actuated by the ensemble of movements deployed within it" (de Certeau 1984, 118).

The idea of the border as a spatial arrangement or device is a powerful one that reflects concerns of cartography, territoriality, and jurisdiction, especially as they were configured in the Westphalian patterning of the world. Nevertheless, when the subjective dimension of border crossings and struggles is introduced, the border acquires a temporal thickness and diversity that is not fully discernible within an analysis that systematically privileges spatial qualities. As we show in this chapter, border regimes themselves increasingly use technologies of temporal management, whether they seek to speed border-crossing processes by using biometrics and chipped passports or to slow and even block border passages through such techniques as detention, interceptions, or "preemptive *refoulement*." The concept of temporal borders attempts to grasp these diverse temporal processes and strategies. It also seeks to detect the ways these processes and strategies interact with subjective experiences and practices to create dissonances, interferences, and interruptions that resonate well beyond the moment of border crossing.

By writing of temporal borders, we seek to demonstrate how subjective experiences of border crossing and border struggles have temporalizing effects that cannot be contained by chronological forms of measure or progressive models of history. In his "Theses on the Philosophy of History," Walter Benjamin (1969, 263) famously characterizes the time of historical progress as "homogenous, empty time." This model of time as "measured by clock and calendar" has subsequently assumed a prominent role in debates about nationalism. In *Imagined Communities*, Benedict Anderson writes that the "idea of a sociological mechanism moving calendrically through homogenous, empty time is a precise analogue of the idea of the nation" (1991, 26). Exploring the heterogeneous temporalities of migration provides a means of showing how border crossings and struggles elude this analogical model of nationalism. It also supplies a way of highlighting the temporal dimensions of labor. Migratory experiences of temporariness and transit not only leave their traces on the bounded spaces of the state. They also confront another homogeneous and empty temporality—the abstract time of capital's measure. In this perspective, the border appears as a regulative device that attempts to manage the fractious processes arising from the encounter between abstract and living labor. The temporal aspects of this encounter become clear if one contrasts the chronological measure of labor time that underlies capital's efforts to economize on labor with Marx's description of living labor as "form-giving fire," "the transitoriness of things, their temporality," and "their formation by living time" (Marx 1973, 361). For the figures we deal with in this chapter, the tensions and conflicts between these diverse temporalities are played out across the many borders that cross their biographies, often in ways that question the easy chronology of future and past. Echoes of the past and uncertainty about the future invade a present in which experiences of life and techniques of measure at once overlap and clash.

In the previous chapter we discussed the relationship between the construction of national labor markets and processes of bordering. It is important to remember that the temporal measurement of labor was at stake in the establishment of this relationship. The concept of socially necessary labor time, introduced by Marx, describes that portion of the working day during which the worker reproduces the value of his or her labor power. The measure of this value, which was calculated as a national average, was necessary for establishing the wage and a national system of wages. Thus, a relation between labor time, wage, and borders is essential to the construction of a national labor market. Just as the construct of a national market required the presence of a given stock of labor, which could be supplemented and appropriately sized by attempts to control migration, it also required elaborate calculations that would identify certain temporal values and parameters within a closed and bordered space. The border was an important mechanism of temporal management, which aimed through its spatial operations to synchronize multiple heterogeneous experiences of time into a regularly measurable and statistically manipulable time. Today, with the proliferation of borders we have traced, the role of bordering in regularizing time and the monetary value that is read off it has drastically changed. The expansion of informal, nonwage, and precarious labor, the global extension of production processes, and the role of migration in testing the borders between labor markets and establishing new borders within them have severed the linear relation between time and money. Even when averages and statistical regularities can be identified, the calculation of socially necessary labor time is no longer an accurate measure of value.

These changes in the relations between labor time, borders, and the production of value become particularly visible in the workings of transnational labor systems that establish new kinds of spatial connection and temporal control. In his book *Global "Body Shopping"* (2006), Xiang Biao provides an ethnographic account of the labor system known as body shopping for the transnational mobility of Indian IT workers. This is a complex system by which consultants and brokers around the world work to recruit IT workers from India, arrange their passage to different countries, and then farm them out to clients as project-based labor. By mediating between the needs of firms and the juridical arrangements regarding migration in host countries, this transnational labor system allows matching mobile labor to volatile capital, often by temporarily withdrawing workers from labor markets or preying on the underpaid labor or investments of family members in India. Recalling Manuel Castells's (2001) observation about how a digital divide separates labor and people around the world, Xiang contends that body shopping rather demonstrates "that how insiders and outsiders of high tech reach are *connected* is more significant than how they are divided" (Xiang 2006, 114). In particular, he stresses how it is "the invisible and undervalued work of . . . women, children and many other men that enables the Indian IT labor force to be produced at very low costs" (113). What Xiang means by this is that elaborate arrangements at "home" and thick social networks are at play in this process of production.

These are not the only arrangements Xiang highlights in his analysis. Processes of ethnicization, point-system migration schemes, questions of training, kinship relations, and the role of placement agencies all play a role in organizing and working the body shop system. What is of particular interest from the point of view of temporal borders is the part of Xiang's fieldwork conducted in Sydney. Focusing his analysis on the mechanisms and legislation loopholes used by body shop operators to facilitate the entry of their workers under the Australian 457 visa scheme, he is able to make a general point about the changing logic of labor supply and demand in the IT industry: "Whether or not there was a real gap between IT labor demand and supply, is less important; what matters more is employers' desire for an ever enlarging labor supply to maintain the momentum in their expansion. Unlike a real shortage, a *virtual* shortage like this can never be balanced out, as more supply is likely to create more shortage. Thus, the coexistence of a skilled shortage and a significant level of professional unemployment can be a long-term feature of the New Economy, a feature epitomized by the routine practice of benching workers in body shops even as more are being hunted" (17).

The practice of benching referred to here involves the holding in reserve of body shop workers, who are paid very small amounts while benched, for outsourcing to private and government enterprises. This system of benching and the creation of a virtual shortage implicit in it can be understood as a technology for the timing and pacing of IT labor supply with respect to demand. From the point of view of the benched workers, this is a time of forced suspension in which their expensively acquired cognitive skills are frittered away but also continuously updated as they perform supposedly unskilled tasks, such as taxi driving or shop assistance. In this case, we see the operation of temporal borders well beyond the geographical boundaries of the nation-state. These are internal borders that are not spatial in the classical sense and that function to subject migrant workers to programmed delays that raise the price of their labor while also creating demand that facilitates further transnational migration within the body shopping system. What is important is that supply and shortage do not correlate in a linear sense, which means that the value of the benched labor power cannot be calculated within a national system of averages. There are also other factors operating here, not least the temporary status of body shop workers in the Australian labor market. To understand these practices of benching, and the more general operation of temporal borders, it is necessary to interrogate the workings of contemporary migration systems and the changing role of skills in the global economy.

The Race for Talent

Studies of border politics have typically focused on the experiences and struggles of unskilled and often undocumented migrants and asylum seekers who encounter the full force of the border's filtering functions. By contrast, studies that deal with the question of skilled migration tend to evade the question of the border, emphasizing instead issues such as recruitment, remuneration, and even cultural integration. Often it seems as if skilled and unskilled migrants occupy different universes of migration, living in parallel worlds where the experiences and political stakes of their mobilities are radically incongruous. In many public discussions there is even a reflexive and fallacious tendency to correlate skilled migrants with documented mobility and assume that "illegal" migrants must be unskilled. If viewed from the perspective of temporal borders, this tendency to place a firm border between skilled and unskilled migration is increasingly problematic. Consider the benching of Indian IT workers. These are undoubtedly highly skilled individuals who have invested time and money—the latter often derived from family arrangements such as dowries—to acquire programming and other labor skills saleable through the body shopping system. But the practice of benching submits them to periods of delay in which they are compelled to perform tasks that are usually considered unskilled and are submitted to processes of bordering with implications for employment and exploitation within the juridical frame established by the Australian 457 visa for employer-sponsored skilled migrants. There is a controlled withdrawal of these workers from the skilled labor market, which as we argue later in the chapter exposes continuities between the temporal strategy of benching and the more violent practices of confinement and detention used to regulate the movement of migrants into national labor markets.

Body shop workers are particularly interesting figures of "cognitive labor" (Roggero 2011) because their patterns of work and mobility allow us to trace connections between current processes of economic transformation and capitalism's continued efforts to bind, restrict, or manage the movement of workers. A growing body of literature announces the arrival of "cognitive capitalism" as a critical alternative to overenthusiastic conceptions of information society, the new economy, or an economy based on knowledge and information. Carlo Vercellone (2006) identifies three aspects of the passage toward cognitive capitalism that are relevant for a consideration of temporal borders: the growing difficulty in giving a chronological measure to abstract labor, the fact that the labor time immediately dedicated to production is no longer necessarily the most important fraction within the overall social time of production, and the way the weakening of traditional boundaries between work and nonwork has broken the proportional relations between remuneration and individual labor (Vercellone 2006, 198). For Vercellone and other analysts of cognitive capitalism, the significance of these trends lies in their implications for monetary reform and new models of welfare at a time when the financialization of the economy creates growing insecurity for workers across the wage spectrum and in different kinds of employment arrangements. We want to emphasize something different: the role of temporal borders in the valorization and devalorization of labor power. This means analyzing how states have tried to adapt to the changing economic conditions described here, compensating for the fact that the "wealth of nations" tends increasingly to hinge on the activities of firms by differentially shifting the expenses of training and the risks associated with market fluctuations onto populations, especially migrant populations.

As the practice of benching shows, temporal borders do not necessarily coincide with territorial borders and their various extensions and externalizations. Nonetheless, the deployment of technologies of temporal delay and filtering has become central to the spatial functioning of many of the world's most contested borders. This is especially the case in instances where states pursue the dream of correlating migratory movements with perceived economic and social needs established by statistical analyses of labor market dynamics, demographic studies, and political priorities. Systems of detention and deportation are crucial devices in attempts to realize such dreams. Before offering a detailed analysis of these systems, it is necessary to account for the operations and diffusion of skilled migration policies that seek to attune flows of migrants to the real and imagined needs of countries of destination. As we will see, the control of international borders involved in such efforts also has marked effects on establishing internal administrative borders and categories that divide labor markets, separate migrant groups beyond and within the boundaries of ethnicity, and provide parameters within which individual migrants negotiate their biographies.

Across the world, there has been a turn away from traditional quota systems of migration regulation, which are increasingly recognized as inadequate to the new flexibility and interpenetration of labor markets and economic systems. The pursuit of a just-in-time and to-the-point migration now shapes migratory policies across diverse national and continental scenarios. One prevalent means of attempting to correlate migration flows with occupational gaps and "skills shortages" is point-system migration schemes. These have their origins in migration policies introduced by former settler colonies such as Australia and Canada in the 1970s as they moved from more racially based approaches to migration to ones that sought to match labor market needs to emergent social agendas of multiculturalism and integration (Hawkins 1991). The recent spread of such points systems to countries as diverse as the United Kingdom, Germany, Singapore, the Czech Republic, and the Netherlands attests to their currency within economic and political contexts in which a hunger for appropriately skilled labor is fueled by the onset of what Vercellone calls cognitive capitalism.

Point-system migration schemes give weight to the thesis that cognitive capitalism entails the expansion of productive labor time to include activities of social relation and reproduction. This is because although these schemes place emphasis on educational qualifications and labor skills for migration selection, they also control for many other qualities and attributes that promise to facilitate the migrant's productive integration into the social fabric: linguistic abilities, family connections, health, age, religion, monetary wealth, and even (by means of recently introduced citizenship tests in some countries) familiarity with national culture and values. Prospective migrants provide details of their statuses or accomplishments in each of these fields and are awarded points on a sliding scale that is subject to change with shifts in labor market needs, the number of applicants with similar attributes, and so on. Those who pass a certain threshold are accepted for immigration. For the most skilled and qualified applicants, there are additional incentives, including fast tracks to permanent residence and sometimes eventually citizenship. But many highly skilled migrants, such as the Indian IT workers studied by Xiang, are allowed only temporary access to national labor markets, being subject to visa conditions that, if violated, turn them into deportable subjects. Point systems thus not only manage the migration ambitions of countries that seek to adapt to conditions of cognitive capitalism. They also constantly redefine the borders between skilled and unskilled labor, establishing as we will see many gray areas, and expand and gradate the various subjective legal and political statuses that range from the citizen to the deportee. The fact that many individuals occupy a number of these statuses in their migration careers says much about the relation between point systems and temporal borders.

The operation of temporal borders is thus not restricted to territorial edges. Point systems identify migrants deemed worthy of international mobility and establish and police a series of administrative distinctions within national polities and labor markets. The passage of many migrants through different labor market and legal conditions is a built-in factor of these arrangements. For instance, a migrant may enter a country on a student visa, work informally while studying, apply for permanent residency on completion of his or her degree, and once this is achieved decide to move on to another country where this newfound status can facilitate entry and possible labor market opportunities. At any point in this trajectory, which we have simplified for purposes of exposition, there is a negotiation of temporal parameters, waiting, and the possibility of failure. In these processes of stretching and manipulating time, the tensions and contradictions that inhabit point systems become obvious. Take the student who works while studying toward a degree that promises to assist his or her migration ambitions. Such a subject often moves from the abject status of deportability, due to visa regulations that limit working hours, to becoming a valued permanent resident on the completion of studies and before the decision to leave for another destination (Baas 2010; Neilson 2009). The intervention of myriad brokers, middlemen, and recruitment agencies make this migratory landscape even more complicated. As governments adjust their point systems to maximize their ends, so migrants and the agents who assist and feed off them continually invent tactics to negotiate, exploit, and move through these hierarchized control devices. The blurring of the boundaries between legality and illegality is always at stake in these temporal contentions.

Point systems not only appeal to states that face the economic and social pressures associated with an increasingly cognitive capitalism and the related global race for talent, they also provide avenues for slipping through gaps and multiplying chances for mobility on the part of those who fall on the wrong side of what Ayelet Shachar calls the "birthright lottery" (Shachar 2009). This has important consequences in both so-called migration sending and receiving countries. One prominent feature of the international diffusion of point systems is the tendency for countries to borrow and imitate the taxonomies and calibrations established by their rivals in this scramble for young, educated, and talented workers (Duncan 2010). For instance, the official regulations that introduced the Canada Experience Class visa in 2008 state that it aims to attract "more temporary foreign workers and foreign students to Canada and retain them as permanent residents, thereby enhancing Canada's ability to compete against countries like Australia that have similar programs" (Government of Canada 2008). No longer is nation building the main driver of migration policy innovations. Imperatives of international competition and the influence of transitional communities of policy making and governance now rule the day. We return to a discussion of these governance trends and their complicated implications for the shifting maps of sovereignty and citizenship in later chapters. For now, we want to highlight how point systems introduce a two-way mobility between the categories of skilled and unskilled labor.

The question of what counts as skill is particularly pressed by actors who intervene in and work the ambiguities introduced by point systems. These actors tend to reverse engineer migration policies, often in ways that prompt developments and innovations within these schemes themselves. In so doing, they exploit the elusiveness of the concept of skill, which is increasingly difficult to define or quantify in economic contexts where generic human qualities such as sociability and adaptability are becoming crucial within productive processes. The growing slipperiness of the concept of skill is a problem that is now registered in official policy debates. As Bridget Anderson and Martin Ruhs (2008) note in a report prepared for the U.K. Migration Advisory Committee, "the term 'skills' is a very vague term both conceptually and empirically," because it can refer to "technical competencies" and also "to generic 'soft skills' (such as 'team-working skills') that are difficult to measure." "Demeanor, accent, style and even physical appearance" as well as "personal characteristics and attitudes" possessed by workers "who will be compliant and easy to discipline and control" become qualities that can be figured as "skills" (4). This clearly establishes a gray area in which the barrier between skilled and unskilled labor becomes porous and mobile, opening up new spaces of negotiation and paths for migrants and those who facilitate (and often contribute to exploiting) their movement.

The implications of this situation are double. Not only are those who are traditionally viewed as unskilled able to find gaps through which to negotiate skilled migration schemes, new techniques and forms of exploitation and labor market manipulation force those traditionally viewed as skilled workers into unskilled labor positions. For skilled and qualified workers, cross-border mobility often spells a radical devaluation of their competences. Even in cases where skilled workers move to access higher wages or citizenship entitlements, the boundary between skilled and unskilled labor is increasingly plastic. For this reason, the traditional division of migration studies into the parallel worlds of skilled and unskilled labor needs to be rethought. The ever more calibrated and technocratic rationality that spurs the introduction and fine-tuning of point systems tends to colonize the lifeworlds of migrants, whether they are categorized as skilled or unskilled. Though the skilled can accrue tremendous opportunities to reshape their biographies, the temporal borders that limit and pace their movements are part and parcel of more general border and migration regimes that deploy other forms of holding and delaying. Among these, detention is prominent.

Detention and Deportability

"No one is illegal." This slogan, which we mentioned at the beginning of chapter 3, was widely and successfully disseminated in the years following its original formulation in 1997. Only a year before, African migrants had occupied the Saint-Ambroise and Saint-Bernard churches in Paris, initiating the now-famous *sans-papiers* movement. Since the mid-1970s, when "boat people" from Vietnam first appeared on the global horizon, there emerged against the background of deep transformations to asylum and migration policies a new political figure—the "illegal" migrant. Our emphasis on processes of multiplication and fragmentation makes us highly suspicious of this label. Throughout this book we consistently use the term *migrant* to describe subjects who cross or negotiate the world's borderscapes, avoiding where possible the recourse to categories such as refugee, asylum seeker, or "illegal" migrant invented by state bureaucracies or their international counterparts. There is little hope of finding a single theoretical or administrative frame that can contain figures as diverse as Haitian and Cuban refugees, Chinese internal migrants, "clandestine" African workers in Italy, or the many people in transit across the world's migratory routes. Nonetheless, the slogan "No one is illegal" and the heated debates it occasioned managed to highlight a common thread that runs through the experiences and many struggles of migrants subjected to various degrees of illegalization. Aside from the many legal angles and frames in which such illegalization is established, the popular figure of the "illegal" migrant has grabbed the imagination (and fears) of governments, media, and publics throughout the world. While legal systems, in all their plurality, tend to label particular acts or conduct as illegal, this popular figure is distinguished by the fact that the label of illegality extends to its embodied subjectivity. To contest the attribution of this label is not just to strike against the myriad and sometimes microscopic prejudices that surround such naming but also to question the legal mechanisms responsible for the production of the figure of the "illegal" migrant. This is why such contestation has assumed a prominence and radicality across many different scenarios. In its simplicity, the slogan "No one is illegal" nicely captured this radicality. As this slogan circulated, theoretical debates about migratory movements placed questions and arguments about the "right to have rights" at center stage.

We return to these political and theoretical debates later. What we want to emphasize here is the way practices of detention and struggles against them have acquired a salience within the framework of illegalization processes. The temporality of migration is increasingly marked by the emergence of various zones and experiences of waiting, holding, and interruption that assume many institutional forms, among them camps and deportation facilities. As long as there have been passports, border control, and national labor markets, there have been subjects who flaunt these systems. The figure of the "illegal" migrant emerges on the world stage in the wake of tumultuous transformations of capitalism that began to unfold in the early 1970s (Anderson and Ruhs 2010; Bacon 2008; Dauvergne 2008; Squire 2011; Suárez-Navaz 2007, 23; Wihtol de Wenden 1988). Central to the emergence of this figure was a marked shift in public and policy discourses, a new international institutional environment for the generation of knowledge about and the forging of strategies to manage migration, a reorganization of labor markets to accommodate processes of informalization and flexibilization, and a disruption and multiplication of migratory routes and patterns across diverse geographical scales.

Part and parcel of these shifts were a series of challenges to the legal and political arrangements surrounding asylum seekers and refugees that had come into place after World War II. These arrangements had evolved against the background of humanitarian and political concerns and placed refugees and asylum seekers behind a secure boundary that separated them from so-called economic migrants. With the escalation of refugee movements, diversification and legal expansion of the category of the asylum seeker, and tightened migratory policies to account for these shifts, this boundary was increasingly tested. Growing attention to the concept of forced migration, which comprises the movements of trafficked and enslaved people as well as conflict- and development-induced displacement, was one symptom of the blurring of this boundary. The introduction of systems such as temporary protection visas, off-shore processing, and protection zones for "internally displaced persons" (IDPs) also deeply changed the humanitarian regime of refugee assistance and tutelage in ways that questioned its supposed foundations in apolitical ideals of universality and benevolence (Nyers 2006). These developments with regard to protection contributed to displace beyond the West the refugee crisis that had been increasingly discussed by scholars, governments, and public opinion makers from the late 1980s (Gibney 2010; Zolberg, Suhrke, and Aguayo 1989). As a result, holding camps for IDPs sprung up on the edges of countless crisis areas. According to the most cautious estimates the number of IDPs in 2008 was 26 million, approximately twice the number of refugees in the world. It is worth remembering that among the countries with the largest IDP populations are Somalia, Colombia, the Democratic Republic of Congo, and Sudan (Gibney 2010, 2–3). Human rights and asylum take on an uncanny shape in the mirror of this new geography of abjection and survival traced out by camps for IDPs.

Concerns of security, populist political rhetoric, and economic calculations concerning migration contributed to a situation in which the work of distinguishing the asylum seeker from the economic migrant was ever more surveyed while in some parts of the world legal developments presented new possibilities. In countries such as Germany, the United Kingdom, and Australia, the tightening of migration control was met from the end of the 1970s by attempts on the part of migrants and legal activists to widen the meshes of human rights regimes. These efforts almost always worked the boundary between economic migration and asylum, often in effective and inventive ways. As a reaction, conservative and populist provocateurs forged concepts such as the "bogus asylum seeker" or "queue jumper" (Hugo 2002; Neumayer 2005) in an attempt to reestablish this very boundary, which was increasingly being challenged by the scale and composition of refugee movements. In the gap between surveillance and the opening of new possibilities, the figure of the refugee was fragmented, leaving many asylum seekers stranded or detained in circumstances where their legal and political statuses verged on that of the "illegal" migrant. The restrictive constitutional reform of asylum in Germany in 1993, which removed the right to claim asylum for migrants entering from states signed up to the Geneva and European Human Rights Conventions (in effect, all of Germany's neighboring states) or from other third countries qualified as secure by an act of Parliament, can be considered a symbolic turning point in this regard (Bosswick 2000).

Many refugees and asylum seekers, indeed, are subject to processes of illegalization, often even before they enter countries that are considered privileged migration destinations. Looking at migration flows toward the European Union, one can observe a range of phenomena that make it very difficult to distinguish the asylum seeker from the labor migrant. On one hand, the experience of transit, along convoluted and often dangerous routes, is shared by migrants of many different stamps. Working in transit countries; facing police, armies, and detention; negotiating with smugglers and other facilitators; networking along the way; checking maps and changing directions—these are common experiences for many different types of migrants (Transit Migration Forschungsgruppe 2007). On the other hand, in the wake of the Dublin Convention of 1990 and its successive amendments a *cordonne sanitaire* of "safe third countries," in which asylum claims are supposedly technically possible, has been formed around the European Union. At the same time, camps and detention facilities have been established well beyond its official boundaries. This leads to a situation in which illegalization is a continuous threat, regardless of whether one seeks work or asylum. "Preemptive refoulement" is often the result of the combined action of these factors (Marchetti 2006).

The threat of illegalization, however, is not one that hangs only over the head of refugees and asylum seekers. Migratory systems and laws across diverse geographical scales have been increasingly shaped in the past decades by efforts to identify, expel, and even include the "illegal" migrant. If borders have moved to the center of our political lives, so the figure of the "illegal" migrant has become the driver of innovations in the sphere of border and migration control. As Nicholas De Genova remarks of undocumented Mexican migrants in the United States, there is "nothing matter-of-fact" about their "illegality." Indeed it is necessary to see illegality, in its contemporary configurations, as the product of "U.S. immigration law—not merely in the generic sense that immigration law constructs, differentiates, and ranks various categories of 'aliens,' but in the more profound sense that the history of deliberate interventions beginning in 1965 has entailed an active process of inclusion through illegalization" (De Genova 2005, 234). Such a vision presents a powerful contrast with familiar discussions of the U.S.–Mexico borderlands as a terrain in which "illegal" migrants are hunted down by border patrol agents, minutemen, or other armed vigilantes. It is important not to underestimate the scale and intensity of the deaths that occur in this space. But an analysis of the complex processes of illegalization and their intertwining with labor market dynamics, transnational community networks, and licit and illicit transborder flows cannot be delivered by mere attention to the violent spectacle of border reinforcement. Such a spectacle often functions as a kind of "ritualistic performance" that obscures the turbulent and seemingly ungovernable movements of migration beneath a screen of efficacy and exclusion (Andreas 2009, 143–44). By contrast, the notion of an active "inclusion through illegalization" draws attention to the temporal unevenness that characterizes the continuous inscription of differentiated subject positions within the U.S. juridical, political, and economic spaces.

The invocation of "an active process of inclusion through illegalization" is one that we see as applicable to other borderscapes throughout the world. Wherever the spectacle of border reinforcement is matched by filtering processes that capture migratory and laboring subjects in the net of illegality, it is possible to observe inclusive mechanisms of exploitation and subjugation that contrast but also complement the more familiar images of exclusion and expulsion. Such a legal production of illegality creates a range of subject positions, which correspond to the multiple ways migrants can be undocumented, including the fragile statuses they can acquire through certain employment arrangements or recognition on the part of public and private bureaucracies (for example, the possession of a driver's license or credit card). The "illegal" migrant also becomes a deportable subject, whose position in both the polity and the labor market is marked by and negotiated through the condition of deportability, even if actual removal is a distant possibility or a threat that has become the background to a whole series of lifetime activities.

Nicholas De Genova and Nathalie Peutz (2010) point out that the forced removal of "illegal" migrants, which has reached an unprecedented scale in the contemporary world, has a tangible impact upon countless others, who experience "illegality" not merely as "an anomalous juridical status but also a practical, materially consequential, and deeply interiorized mode of being" (De Genova and Peutz 2010, 14). Furthermore, the deportable migrant becomes entangled, even if only in a distant and implicit way, in a web of arrangements that involve actors and institutions, including police forces, nongovernmental organizations, airline companies, and other so-called carriers of migration. The geography of what De Genova and Peutz call the deportation regime involves a kind of reverse tracing of the actual routes forged by migrants who strike out for new destinations. Increasingly, the means and methods of deportation include even "voluntary repatriation" schemes that seek to entice return migration in periods of crisis with the offer of benefits and the implicit threat of forced removal (Andrijasevic and Walters 2010; Dünnwald 2010). But deportation does not necessarily involve repatriation. Creating "buffer zones" and spaces of "graduated securitization" facilitates the management of deportation across multiple borders, deeply connecting the deportation regime to processes of "externalization" and systems of detention in many different locations, particularly those that "border upon the borders" of regions of migration destination (De Geneva and Peutz 2010, 5). This has led to the design of different kinds of intergovernmental agreements and cooperation schemes that seek to coordinate processes of deportation with efforts of border control and interception targeted against migratory and other kinds of illicit flows. For instance, the governance of the U.S.–Mexico border is increasingly coordinated with the policing of the so-called *frontera olvidada* that joins Mexico to Guatemala and Belize. In the framework of intergovernmental agreements such as the Puebla Process (1996) and the Mérida Initiative (2007), this coordination forms part of a wider U.S.-led regional initiative that aims to control and make governable U.S.-bound migratory movements in Central American countries of origin and transit (Kron 2010).

Obviously deportation involves a set of physical and bureaucratic practices that are dependent on the wide global spread of spaces of holding and detention that are fundamental sites of investigation for any understanding of temporal borders. Since the early 1970s when the figure of the "illegal" migrant acquired a new global prominence, there has been proliferation and diversification of such spaces. From airport holding zones to vessels detained in harbors, from regular prisons to special-purpose facilities, these sites of detention have become objects of political anxiety and critical scrutiny, whether on the part of human rights groups, antiracist and migration activists, or concerned scholars. The figure of the camp, which famously has its origins in colonial practices of confinement and isolation, has almost monopolized the critical discussion of current practices of administrative detention. A growing archive of research, analysis, and political intervention has grown around this theme (Bernadot 2008; Dow 2004; Perera 2002; Pieper 2008; Rahola 2003). With heavy resonances with the Nazi *Lager* system of World War II, the analysis of contemporary detention sites from the theoretical and practical viewpoint offered by the camp has enabled a series of insights into the political workings of detention and its significance for wider questions of sovereignty, security, and biopolitics. This, in turn, has animated many different forms of political action and even artistic expression that have turned around the figure of the camp and its extraordinary emotive and historical implications.

The highly erudite and influential philosophical work of Giorgio Agamben has, since the publication of *Homo Sacer* (1998), elevated the camp to the status of the biopolitical paradigm of modernity. Building on the work of Hannah Arendt, Carl Schmitt, Walter Benjamin, and Michel Foucault, Agamben offers an extremely astute analysis of the camp and its juridical rooting in the state of exception and martial law. For him, the camp is a space opened up by a series of technologies and devices that strip away the rights of internees, robbing them of any political status and reducing them to a condition of "bare life" (Agamben 2000, 41). According to Agamben, this is a process at work across a wide variety of historical and contemporary sites, including the colonial camps in Cuba and South Africa, the Lager, refugee camps, *zones d'attente* in French international airports, detention centers for "illegal" migrants, temporary holding zones, certain outskirts of metropolitan areas, and special military prisons such as the one at Guantánamo Bay.

As far as camps for "illegal" migrants are concerned, the most fundamental and illuminating insight offered by Agamben concerns the way the camp catches its inhabitants in a legal order for the purposes of excluding them from this very same order. This process of exclusion through inclusion is an important instance of one of the main topics at stake in this book: the multifarious ways the border between inclusion and exclusion is stretched and reworked by the spatial and temporal dynamics of contemporary capitalism. Agamben's approach, however, centers on transhistorical and even ontological arguments that have little to do with such capitalist developments. By contrast, our focus on the relevance of global migration control and politics for current transformations of labor and capital raises questions about how practices of administrative detention link to the operation of temporal borders in the lives of deportable subjects who are not interned in camps. We believe that camps need to be analyzed not just from the transcendental perspective of sovereign power and its exceptions but also within the ever widening and complex networks of migration governance and management of which the "deportation regime" is an important element. The sometimes mechanical transposition of Agamben's arguments into critical discussions of refugees and migration politics has resulted in an almost unilateral focus on processes of exclusion, privation, and dehumanization that obscures what Foucault would call the more productive dimensions of the assemblages of power that target migratory movements (Rahola 2010). Let us not forget that even the "camp for foreigners" is a "social institution" that, as Marc Bernardot comments, is in a state of permanent recomposition before shifting circumstances and never fixes a definitive form (Bernardot 2008, 43). Struggles of migrants, both inside and outside detention facilities, figure prominently among these changing circumstances. Whether they involve dramatic actions, like sewing together the lips by nearly sixty detainees in Australia's notorious Woomera detention center in 2002, or deliberate acts of sabotage and escape, such as occurred when Tunisian migrants burned down a "reception center" and fled onto the streets of the Italian island of Lampedusa in 2011, these struggles force changes that show that the camp is by no means a fixed institution that deprives migrants of the capacity to rebel.

The sheer diversity and range of arrangements, institutions, and spaces that can attract the label of the *camp* is so vast that the term threatens to lose the analytical grip that stitches it into wider political and ontological schemes. There is a need to go beyond Agamben's emphasis on the sovereign exception and the stripping of rights by conducting more carefully focused investigations of different kinds of detention facilities and their roles in wider processes of migration governance, temporal bordering, and deportation. This means analyzing the apparatuses of power that bear on migratory movements, in particular the methods of selection and filtering that seek to match these movements to the real and phantom needs of cities, states, and regions. To highlight the temporal dimension of detention is to reconsider contemporary techniques of migration control in the light of asynchronous rhythms of transit, prolongation, and acceleration. These tempos and timings cross the subjective experiences of bodies and minds in motion and are also key to the inscription of this motion into labor market dynamics and the social and symbolic fabric of citizenship. As Efthimia Panagiotidis and Vassilis Tsianos write, "the governance of migratory movements aims to force their dynamic into temporal zones of hierarchized mobility in order to produce governable mobile subjects from ungovernable flows" (Panagiotidis and Tsianos 2007, 82). Rutvica Andrijasevic explains that this approach breaks "the progressive linearity by means of which migrants' journeys are commonly portrayed (i.e. a movement from A / origin to B / destination)" and draws attention to "interruptions and discontinuities such as waiting, hiding, unexpected diversions, settlements, stopovers, escapes and returns" (Andrijasevic 2010b, 158). Writing of the camps in the EU's southern neighboring countries, she corroborates our approach by contending that their purpose is not simply to prevent or block migratory movements in general but also to regulate the time and speed of migrations.

One way of conceptualizing the links between the system of administrative detention and the shaping of labor markets is to describe the detention center as a "decompression chamber" (Mezzadra and Neilson 2003) that equilibrates, in the most violent of ways, the constitutive tensions that underlie the very existence of labor markets. Returning to our earlier discussion of the practice of benching Indian IT workers by temporarily withdrawing them from the labor market, we can now draw a parallel between the temporal dimensions of this practice and the strategies of delay specific to administrative detention. The benching of body shop workers involves a form of bordering that separates them from regular IT workers in the national labor market, and it can also be considered a form of temporal holding that displays an uncanny contiguity with the temporal regulation practiced in detention camps. The condition of benched body shop workers parallels that of "illegal" migrants violently confined in such institutions insofar as both involve strategies of temporal delay that stratify movements into the national labor market and polity. Importantly, there are stark material and experiential differences between these instances of holding and detention, but the temporal borders they establish can be submitted to an analysis that also stresses their continuities. What this parallel suggests is that the zones of temporal holding created by benching mobilize similar processes of delay, deceleration, and pacing as the "temporal zones of hierarchized mobility" that detention systems create in league with other elements of migration policies such as point systems.

When the global dimension of the body shopping practice comes into view (the relation of these workers to relatives in India, to similar IT workers in Australia or the United States, to intermediaries in locations such as Singapore and Kuala Lumpur, etc.), it is possible to discern how these temporal processes are not necessarily coextensive with spatial borders but serve to reconfigure, strengthen, and attenuate them. Benching is only one of many devices that channel and filter the mobility of Indian IT workers in the body shopping system, restricting their access to freedom in specifically calculated and strategic ways that manipulate and twist the classical relation of supply and demand of labor. While the experience of detention centers allows us to understand something in the experience of benching, the opposite is also true. Seen through the reference to benching, detention centers seem to be much more related to the production and reproduction of labor power as a commodity than to the exercise of sovereign power on bare life. Here we find a dramatic instance of the difference that an analysis of temporal borders can make. Without losing sight of the violence enacted in the camp, the focus shifts to an examination of the roles played by the legal production of illegality and the condition of deportability in synchronizing the tumultuous movements of migration with the flexible and financialized logic of contemporary capitalism. This implies attention to international border crossings and also to how these movements resonate across the internal borders of nation-states and the urban territories of metropolitan space.

Internal Borders

Time runs at a different pace in the buildings of a global banking company and in a shantytown. While such different temporalities can intersect in daily life, the world is crossed by complex patterns of spatial segregation that work to manage and rule populations marked by poverty, destitution, and often racial discrimination. The spread of ghettos and favelas, "migrant villages," and slums cuts across geographical divides and provides an important instance of the proliferation of internal borders in the contemporary world. The apocalyptic picture provided by Mike Davis in his *Planet of Slums* (2006) can be contrasted here with more nuanced analyses of Indian shantytowns or *bustees* that emphasize the political negotiations pursued by inhabitants of these spaces. Partha Chatterjee (2004, 2011) develops the concept of "political society" to describe how the life of these marginalized populations is governed according to criteria that are fundamentally different from the rights and obligations that prevail in "civil society" and define the liberal subject. For the purposes of livelihood and struggle, Chatterjee argues, these subjects "make their claims on government, and in turn are governed, not within the framework of stable constitutionally defined rights and laws, but rather through temporary, contextual and unstable arrangements arrived at through direct political negotiations" (2004, 57). This approach may appear problematic from the point of view of the foreclosure of spaces of agency and autonomy on the part of the subaltern subjects it implies (Samaddar 2007a, 135–52). In the context of this chapter, however, it helps highlight the emergence of a fracture at the very heart of the concept of citizenship. The internal border between the bourgeois city and the slum appears to us as a border *within* citizenship and this sheds new light on the issues at stake in its policing. Mobility, its channeling, its management, and often its blocking figure prominently among these issues. One has only to recall Matthieu Kassovitz's film *La Haine* (1995) to get a sense of the temporal suspension and spatial holding, as well as the multifarious borders that shape life in such a place as a banlieue. When the three young protagonists of the film catch a train to Paris, they really seem to move across different worlds—and different *times*. "Le monde est à vous [the world belongs to you]," says a huge advertisement they see from the window of the train in an ironical reference to the classic gangster movie *Scarface* (both in the original version of 1932, directed by Howard Hawks, and in Brian de Palma's 1983 remake). It is telling that in an extreme gesture of hope and rebellion, before the tragic ending of the story, one of the three youngsters uses spray paint to change *vous* to *nous: the world belongs to us!*

The French *banlieues* present a particularly interesting case of spatial segregation that allows us to further investigate the working of temporal borders. Writing in the wake of the urban uprisings of 2005, Étienne Balibar emphasizes that *"the 'banlieue' as such is a frontier, a border-area and a frontline.* It forms a periphery at the very center of the great metropolitan areas" (Balibar 2007, 48). It is important to keep in mind the peculiarity of the banlieues, which reflects specific French patterns of urban and social development and is easily lost with English translations such as *suburbs* or *ghettos*. That Balibar goes on to associate them with South African townships indicates the possibility of locating the banlieues within a wider global framework of urban apartheid. "The proximity of the extremes" characteristic of the banlieues, the fact that the same word defines "rich, even very rich" and radically destitute neighborhoods, "often geographically very close to one another but separated by a social abyss and a permanent antagonism" (Balibar 2007, 48) allows parallels with other metropolitan landscapes. One thinks of the *conurbano* (the huge metropolitan periphery) of Buenos Aires, where gated communities for the rich (the so-called *countries*) and extremely poor neighborhoods (so-called *villas miseria*) shape and drive urban development (Vidal-Koppmann 2007).

The history of the modern banlieues runs parallel to the history of industrialization in France and the related history of migration, first from the countryside and other European countries, then from colonies and former colonies. From the time of the electoral victory of the Front Populaire in 1936, working-class banlieues became strongholds of the Left, with municipal governments led by the Socialist and particularly the Communist Party shaping the reality and the myth of the "red banlieues." Investments in social services and education were characteristic of these administrations, which attempted to create a "relatively homogeneous community, capable of elaborating a distinctive culture" (Dubet and Lapeyrronie 1992, 51). Migrants, especially those from Algeria, were always in a kind of subordinate position even in the red banlieues, often living in special buildings, the so-called *foyer* (Sayad 1980) that spatially marked their problematic belonging to the "community." Nevertheless, in the Fordist age there was a widespread recognition of the legitimacy of their presence as "immigrant workers," and their struggles in factories and society played a key role in further consolidating this recognition (Abdallah 2000, 14–31). In his book *Dis-Agreement*, originally published in 1995, Jacques Rancière effectively describes the dramatic transformation produced by the crisis of Fordism when he comments on new forms of xenophobia and racism emerging in France. "We had nearly the same number of immigrants twenty years ago," he writes. "But they had another name then: they were called migrant workers or just plain workers. Today's immigrant is first a worker who has lost his second name, who has lost the political form of his identity and of his otherness" (Rancière 1999, 118).

The rise of unemployment and dereliction of the urban fabric have characterized poorer banlieues around Paris and other major French cities since the end of the 1970s. The demographic composition of these areas has also changed, because those who had the opportunity to flee have moved to better-off neighborhoods. Ethnic minorities and poor whites are often the only inhabitants left, increasingly stigmatized in public discussions of criminality, exclusion, and more recently Islamism. Since the hot summer of 1981, riots have shaped daily life in the banlieues, providing a kind of counterpoint to these social processes and leading to stark intercommunal tensions. Active processes of what we could call bordering-from-below, often at work in such spaces, have been instrumental to an assertion of the right to self-defense, and they have also occasionally multiplied lines of division and partition within and between communities and territories. The stigma associated with living in banlieues makes mobility particularly difficult (Castel 2007), both in the literal sense of word (since the risk of being stopped by police officers and other surveillance agents is much higher and transport systems often make the travel to the city center uselessly long) and as far as social mobility is concerned (because the chances to get a good education or job are far less than for other French citizens). Above all this is true for youngsters with a family history of migration, although they are often formally fully fledged French citizens. François Dubet and Didier Lapeyronnie (1992, 7) noted at the beginning of the 1990s that "the problems of migration, juvenile criminality, and insecurity" had substituted for workers' strikes as the key topic in public debates on the "social question" of the banlieues. More recent discussions have been haunted by the specter of a racial inflection of this social question (Fassin and Fassin 2006), which is particularly disturbing for the hegemonic "republican" understanding of French citizenship.

The banlieues have come to be increasingly considered in French public discourse as a wasteland of exclusion. This image definitely grasps some of the developments that we have briefly sketched—from chronic unemployment to the limitation of spatial and social mobility. At the same time, there is a need to complicate the use of the concept of exclusion, because it risks obscuring other aspects of life in the banlieues. Independently of the fact that most of their inhabitants are French citizens, recent surveys show that these populations share cultural attitudes, preferences, and lifestyles with the wider French society (Castel 2007, 36–37). As far as youth culture, music (especially rap), films, and even literature (especially the new wave of crime novels known as *polar*) are concerned, the banlieues can be considered "the most important cultural laboratory of the country, a constant source of new talents and styles" (Caldiron 2005, 129). Thick networks of social cooperation and the experiences of social movements like the Mouvement de l'Immigration et des Banlieues and Ni Pute Ni Soumise (Neither Whores nor Submissives) lie behind this astonishing productivity, which allows the *banlieusards* to cope with conditions of economic precarity that are increasingly spreading to other sectors of the society (Revel 2008). We are confronted here with a paradoxical predicament in which the border area of the banlieues blurs the boundary between inside and outside or, rather, points to a field of subjective experience that continuously works that boundary. As the French sociologist Robert Castel writes, "the problem that young banlieusards face is not that they are *outside* the society. . . . But they are neither *inside* it, since they do not occupy any recognized place and many of them do not seem able anymore to manage one" (Castel 2007, 38).

Describing the combined action of class and race in defining this peculiar subject position, Balibar (2007, 57) contends that its effect is to constitute "those who occupy it as eternally *displaced* (*out of place*) persons, the *internally excluded*." Balibar's phrase nicely captures the intertwining of time ("eternally") and space ("out of place") in the peculiar production of subjectivity by the internal border of the banlieues, which not only circumscribes a space of segregation but also establishes zones of temporal suspension. This temporal dimension can be further qualified as far as the topic of race is concerned. It was notably Achille Mbembe (2009) who started a lively discussion on this issue with an article published in the days of the uprisings of November 2005, "The Republic and Its Beast." Mbembe pointed to the resurfacing of French colonial history in migration policies and in the management of populations with migratory background. It is not by accident that one of the most important movements that arose out of the 2005 riots adopted the designation Les Indigènes de la République (Natives of the Republic), referring to the Code de l'Indigénat (Natives Code), the French law regarding the subjection and government of colonial populations (Bouteldja and Khiari 2012; Le Cour Grandmaison 2010; Rigouste 2009). Considering the banlieues from this historical angle, French citizenship appears internally fractured by the reemergence of the colonial past (Blanchard et al. 2005) and the internal borders surrounding these blighted urban peripheries acquire a further temporal dimension. The figure of the colonial subject makes an untimely reappearance within the secularized space of French republicanism. Criminal law, police, and administrative measures shape the daily governance of populations living in these border zones.

Although the peculiarity of the French banlieues must always be kept in mind, a resurrection of the colonial distinction between citizen and subject under fully new postcolonial conditions can be traced in recent developments of citizenship and migratory regimes for the European Union as a whole (Mezzadra 2006). In this perspective, the problems of the banlieues are a specific inflection of more general questions regarding the position of second, third, and X generation migrants in the society where they live. Time is always at stake here: how long is a migrant a migrant, how long is he or she "different?" We cannot dwell on such questions here, as well as on the related formation of ethnic minorities or communities under different patterns of integration. Suffice it to say that from the point of view of the banlieusards the very concept of integration seems suspect. At least this is the position taken by Ahmed Djouder in *Désintegration*, a text published in 2006 and widely read as a kind of retrospective manifesto of the uprisings of the preceding year. Assuming an ironic tone that resonates with the everyday languages and street styles of the banlieues, Djouder declares that the French love the word *integration* because it makes them feel as if they are able to "domesticate" strangers who are treated as if they were "wild animals." "Asking us to integrate after we have been here for two or even four generations is a real kick in the ass," he writes. With this refusal of the ideology and practices of integration, Djouder grasps the disciplinary logic by which mainstream French society attempts to shape the subjectivity of unruly sections of the population. Interestingly, to make this point he mentions an institution with which readers of this chapter are familiar: "we won't integrate, because this word is repugnant. To be frank, it stinks of the prison camp" (Djouder 2007, 89–91).

The question of how long a migrant remains migrant—which is to say of how long the migrant remains an object of difference and hence a target of integration—is intimately related to the question of temporal borders. Such temporal borders stratify the space of citizenship. They are typically calibrated through the elusive concept of the generation, which, as Karl Mannheim famously wrote in an essay of 1928, describes a cohort that provides sources of opposition, challenges established norms and values, and is *"potentially* capable of being sucked into the vortex of social change" (Mannheim 1952, 303). Migration studies are replete with theories and empirical approaches to the question of how migrant experiences change across generations, with particular attention to the unstable and fragile condition of second generations, which emerged as a classical conundrum with the pioneering work of William I. Thomas and Florian Znaniecki (1918–20). More recently, concepts such as "segmented assimilation" (Portes and Rumbaut 2001; Portes and Zhou 1993) have been introduced to explore the variegated and fractured paths second-generation migrants tend to pursue even if they are members of the same ethnic community or group.

One important challenge for such studies, which is also crucial for the question of temporal borders, is to understand how the generational logic that scholarship attributes to migrant experience overlaps the tendency for migratory movements to correspond with wider historical and geographical patterns. From this perspective, generations and the social perspectives and experiences they bring are not just a matter of age. Encounters and often clashes between different temporalities of migration are often staged along the internal borders of cities, countries, and regions. Consider, for instance, the recent migration of young Indians to Australia, often on student visas after recruitment into that nation's "higher education export" industry (Baas 2010). Tempted by favored paths to permanent residency for students who qualify in nominated fields, these Indian migrants often take on family debt to facilitate their movement and are thus compelled to work while studying, making them deportable subjects if, as many do, they work more than the twenty hours a week allowed by their visas. Indeed, the overlaps between the Australian education and skilled migration systems has provided a window for a whole wave of migrants to enter the national labor market, many with motivations of work and permanent residency dominating over educational ambitions. These migrants tend to take on low-status and supposedly unskilled jobs such as taxi driver, security guard, shop assistant, kitchen hand, or babysitter. As it happens, their employers often turn out to be an older generation of Indian migrants who arrived in Australia in the 1960s and 1970s and have established themselves within business and community networks. Such patterns of intraethnic employment and exploitation are well documented in studies of migration chains and networks, where they are frequently connected with the formation of migrant enterprises, processes of ethnicization of labor markets, and the rise of ethnic enclaves in metropolitan areas (see, for instance, Light and Bonacich 1988; Model 1985; Portes and Jensen 1989; Werbner 1990).

What is interesting in this case is that this same older generation of Indian migrants has also brought up a second generation of younger Indian Australians who now have the same age and sometimes study in the same institutions as many of the newer arrivals. In 2008 and 2009, the more recently arrived Indian "students" began to stage spontaneous protests and sit-ins in reaction to violent attacks on them, exploitive work conditions, and the attempts of some of the higher education providers and colleges to extract extra fees by delaying their academic progress (Neilson 2009). These protests, which eventually spurred the Australian government to change its policy on student paths to permanent residency, gained wide media coverage in Australia and India, especially when the racial aspects of the violence were splashed all over the subcontinental media sphere. Although the second-generation Indian Australians were of the same age and ostensibly the same ethnicity of the protesting students and workers, the social and temporal barriers between them were manifest. At stake were a whole series of class and caste differences as well as worries about whether the hard-won standing of the Indian community within business circles and the national consensus of multicultural politics would be damaged by the angry and disruptive character of these protests by Australia's "new proletarians" (Thompson and Rosenzweig 2009). Temporal borders were clearly operating in the uneasy and mutually suspicious relations between these groups. Here we see how the working of time through different generations and successive migratory movements divides and stratifies migrants within wider vistas of citizenship and also divides them from each other, even when they occupy to all extents and purposes the same age group. Whether on the outskirts of Paris or the streets of Melbourne, internal borders take on a temporal form that contributes to the production of subjects and conflicts while also exposing the limits of theories and rhetorics of inclusion and integration.

Differential Inclusion

Whoever said the time of the nation-state is "homogeneous and empty"? The correlation of linear clock time with the history and destiny of modern states has become a commonplace of critical thought. Just as E. P. Thompson (1967) famously linked the imposition of straight temporal measure to industrial discipline, so the time of the nation-state has been associated with processes of imagination, seriality, and historical progress that sew diverse and unequal subjects into a single and compact community (Anderson 1991). In the previous chapter, our discussion unfolded within the space of tensions and incompatibility that separates abstract from living labor; the figures we follow in this chapter point to the inscription of these same tensions within the internally bordered spaces of contemporary cities, nations, and economic regions. These processes of internal and temporal bordering are the contemporary expression of the violence implicit in efforts to impose uniform patterns of time and temporality across vast stretches of the Earth's surface. We doubt that the "angel of history," celebrated in Walter Benjamin's (1969) famous invocation of a *Jetztzeit* (now time) capable of blasting through the "homogeneous and empty" time of historicism, can free us from this wreckage. Benjamin has inspired a number of important postcolonial interventions on questions of nationalism, migration, and difference (see, for instance, Bhabha 1994). But the moment of innovation implied in Jetztzeit, far from completely exploding the continuity of progressive time, can work as an internal supplement to this measure, covering it in a mystical and even charismatic mode.

Such messianic rhetoric is, for us, beside the point because the contemporary historical moment is crossed by temporal borders that make the nation-state no longer a consistent unit of time and space. The contribution of postcolonial critics such as Homi Bhabha or Partha Chatterjee (1986, 1993) to the understanding of this new constellation brought about by the proliferation of borders has been outstanding. This galaxy of critical thought asks whether the supposed linearity of national time can stand the spatial dimensions and heterogeneity of empire, pointing to the anomalous time lags and asynchronous historical rhythms of colonial modernity. Migration carries these uncanny and diverse temporal variations across and beyond the grid of latitude and longitude that establishes mean time from the former imperial center. Imagine asking the banlieusard, the detained migrant, the former peasant who runs a tea shop, or even the benched body shop worker about how their labors measure up against empty clock time. At every turn, they encounter temporal borders, whether imposed through coercion or more nuanced forms of suasion and baiting, which cross not only their biographies but also their daily lives. These encounters generate asynchronous, fragmented, and elongated experiences of time that unfold increasingly within the space of the nation. The benched worker who waits patiently to reenter the IT labor force is unlikely to share a sense of simultaneity-along-time with workers who are not subject to this same discipline of temporal withdrawal. Similarly, the tea shop proprietor whose opening hours are dictated by the rhythms of another time zone is likely to feel radically out of sync with the pace of life around him. The engagement of workers like this with the chronological time that allegedly sustains a national sense of community is always distributed across multiple frames of inclusion and exclusion that shade into and away from the master narratives and territorial coordinates of the state and its international order.

Surely the void time of the nation has always encountered such heterogeneous scatterings and temporal displacements. What is new about the perspective opened by border as method is that these anomalies are no longer merely disturbances. The homogeneous cross-time of national progress has been shattered by a series of internal borderings that force a rethinking of the capacity of collective historical narratives to fully subsume the less ordered and plural trajectories of singular historical experiences. This is not merely a matter of cultural and linguistic diversity. Nor is it an issue of the remainder that is always left over after policies of social inclusion have swept through metropolitan landscapes and mindscapes. The space and time of the nation are increasingly divided and tested. The boundaries between the dynamics of filtering, subordination, and labor market discrimination that once occurred at the international border and those that take place within the bounded spaces of national societies have been blurred. This means that the borders between inclusion and exclusion have also been pressed and become confused. There is thus an urgent need to question the widespread notion that inclusion is always an unambiguous good that facilitates a diminution of social and economic inequalities. As Djouder's comments on the French ideal of integration remind us, inclusion also serves as a means of discipline and control. While critical studies of borders and migration tend to emphasize the moment and technologies of *exclusion* as the decisive elements of differentiation and power relations, we take an alternative path. Our focus on what we call processes of *differential inclusion* entails a conviction that the figures who inhabit the world's borderscapes are not marginal subjects that subsist on the edges of society but central protagonists in the drama of composing the space, time, and materiality of the social itself.

The concept of differential inclusion has a complex and multiform genealogy that crosses the borders of migration studies and antiracist and feminist thought. Although it has assumed many names, this concept has long provided a means for describing and analyzing how inclusion in a sphere, society, or realm can be subject to varying degrees of subordination, rule, discrimination, and segmentation. In feminist thought and practice, it has been associated with pragmatic attempts to break the glass ceiling that limits women's ability to advance in the workforce and other social institutions as well as with the theoretical emphasis on difference that has informed critical approaches to issues of equality, rights, and power. The concept of differential inclusion is so widespread and intuitively understood in feminist circles that it is difficult to trace how it permeates the multiple branches of feminist thought and practice. We can, however, mention a few instances in which its surfacing is provocatively close to our own approach. In particular, we need to turn our attention to radical feminists, who criticize the liberal understanding of women's emancipation as a result of a linear integration into the public sphere. Particularly relevant here are U.S. feminists who "dared to be bad" (Echols 1989) and European feminist collectives suspicious of liberal political arrangements, such as those who declared "Do not believe you have rights" (Libreria delle donne di Milano 1987).

In her 1970 manifesto *Sputiamo su Hegel* (Let's Spit on Hegel), Carla Lonzi strongly challenges the holistic, organic, and absolutely inclusive tendency of masculine thought that she finds embodied in the philosophical work of Hegel. Her refusal to inscribe feminist thought within the dialectical framework, which integrates all differences into an overarching telos of totality, opens a space in which the liberal political anthropology of equality and rights appears to rest on a "legalized bullying" that seals women's inclusion in society (Lonzi 2010, 15). Lonzi's approach nurtured a series of attempts, especially by Italian feminists, to develop a political practice that strived not for women's integration in the male-dominated public sphere but to valorize women's difference as a positive and open movement that unhinges the divisions between nature and culture, psychic and social, and private and public that lie at the core of political modernity (Dominijanni 2005; Muraro 2004). Along a different line, inaugurated by the book of Mariarosa Dalla Costa and Selma James, *Power of Women and the Subversion of the Community* (1972), an emphasis on the "power-difference between women and men and the concealment of women's unpaid labor under the cover of natural inferiority" has shed light on "an accumulation of differences, inequalities, hierarchies, divisions, which have alienated workers from each other and even from themselves" (Federici 2004, 115). The unity of the working class thus appears fractured by what we can call a process of differential inclusion of female (unpaid) reproductive labor and by the use of (male) wage to command it within the family. In the important work of Carole Pateman, we find yet another critical analysis that brings the differentiating effects of "patriarchal subordination" to bear on the supposedly unifying capacity of modernity's social contract. Contesting the idea that patriarchy can be overcome by public laws and policies that treat women as if they are men, Pateman suggests that a view of the public and civil realm as "uncontaminated" by sexual difference can only reproduce the asymmetrical inclusion of women in this sphere (Pateman 1988, 17). The way these thinkers open the "hidden abode" of modern political anthropology and its attendant institutions finds a parallel in other excavations of

concepts such as civil society and citizenship, including those that emphasize racial differences.

The discovery of the multiplicity of subject positions lying behind the
signifier woman has opened a wide field of debates in the past few decades,
prompting an investigation of different degrees of subordination at the
intersection between gender, class, and race (Crenshaw 1991; McCall 2005).
This work shows how exclusion always operates in tandem with an inclusion that is never complete, fracturing and dividing identities in ways that
are not necessarily compatible and scattering differences across social and
political spaces. Stuart Hall's discussion of Antonio Gramsci's relevance for
critical studies of race and ethnicity provides a provocative means of linking
such processes of heterogenization to the operations of capital. Drawing on
examples from around the globe, he points to "differential modes of incor-
porating so-called 'backward' sectors within the social regime of capital"
(Hall 1986b, 24). This leads him to extend his analysis far beyond Gramsci's
invocation of the "southern question" in Italy by mentioning as instances of
such "differential incorporation" hinterland economies in Asia and Latin
America, enclaves within metropolitan capitalist regimes, and migrant labor forces within domestic labor markets. "Theoretically," he contends,
"what needs to be noticed is the persistent way in which these specific,
differentiated forms of *incorporation* have consistently been associated with
the appearance of racist, ethnically segmentary and other similar social
features" (25). This brilliant flash in Hall's essay verges toward a discussion
of what we call differential inclusion without ever fully developing an analysis of such incorporation with respect to borders, time, or subjectivity.
Subsequent attempts to extend and apply Hall's thought have made use of
the concept of differential incorporation to study emergent forms of transnationalism among migrant communities (Basch, Schiller, and Blanc 1994)
or have elaborated it to explore the body politics of capital (Cherniavsky
2006).

Within migration studies there has been a parallel and somewhat more
sociologized engagement with these questions. In this context, the question
of inclusive modes of incorporation has been subject to successive refinements and renamings, each with its own idiosyncrasies, strengths, and practical implications. Castles (1995) uses the term *differential exclusion* to describe the "policy model" of immigration applied across a range of nations.
These include former Western European guest-worker countries such as
Germany, Switzerland, Austria, and Belgium; Southern European countries
with a different history of migration; the Arab Gulf States; and Japan. Cas-

tles describes "a situation in which immigrants are incorporated into certain areas of society (above all the labour market) but denied access to others (such as welfare systems, citizenship and political participation)" (294). The key features of this particular version of the concept are an approach to migrant admission as a "temporary expedient" and the maintenance of a national policy frame as the most relevant context in which to consider disciplining migrants and their movement. Most important, Castles maintains a view of the labor market as an integral "area of society" to which migrants are admitted in opposition to other social institutions from which they are excluded. In other words, the differentiation in differential exclusion describes the uneven accessibility of various areas of society to migrants, but leaves these areas themselves intact and discrete, at least regarding issues of migrant access. The labor market, for instance, remains nationally bounded and migration answers its established modes of differentiation rather than unsettling them by introducing new temporal, internal, and transnational borders that cut between and across national limits.

We have already mentioned another important concept that emerges from migration studies and especially from scholarship on the "new second generation" in the United States—segmented assimilation. Unlike the differential exclusion model addressed to temporary migration arrangements and policies, studies that employ the concept of segmented assimilation strive to come to terms with the fate of "new immigrant children" amid the increasingly complex and differentiated terrain of race and ethnicity in U.S. society. As developed by Alejandro Portes and Min Zhou (1993), the concept points to the availability of different groups to which such immigrant children can assimilate and identifies divergent paths to this assimilation. This is really quite different from what we mean by differential inclusion. The concept of segmented assimilation can be understood as an elaboration of older theories of ethnic succession, which seek to seal the course of individual migrants with that of ethnic communities identified within a stable typology of migrant groups which are bound to be successively integrated into the wider national society. Alejandro Portes and Rubén G. Rumbaut (1996, 2001) identify different paths and patterns of assimilation: straight-line assimilation, downward assimilation, and selective acculturation. This effectively registers the deep transformation of the processes of inclusion and exclusion that regulate the reproduction of American society. Commenting on these same trends in a study of Cambodian refugees in the United States, Aihwa Ong goes a step further by showing how such changes radically challenge the images of citizenship and integration that animate theories of ethnic succession and segmented assimilation. "The different social and class positions of what are in fact a variety of immigrant populations explode any attempt to contain all of them within a single 'national community of fate' in the U.S." (Ong 2003, 259).

In offering the concept of differential inclusion, we go a step further again. It is not only that approaches assuming the inevitability of assimilation must be tested by pluralist and multiculturalist perspectives but also a matter of observing and accounting for the operations of borders across different geographical scales and continental vistas. Among these temporal borders are important because they stretch across and within the space of nation-states, elongating and fracturing the empty, homogeneous time assumed by theories of assimilation. The crisis and even failure of multiculturalism, which is currently discussed across many different spaces and scales, interests us as a symptom of these processes. We cannot dwell on the history of multiculturalism as a complex set of public policies ranging from more pluralist to more communitarian models of accommodating cultural diversity. Nor can we trace in detail the many theoretical debates that accompanied the rise and successive refinements of multiculturalism in several countries since the 1970s. It is important to note that already in the heyday of liberal multiculturalism, critical voices signaled the radical asymmetry between the ethnically neutral white citizen and those ethnic others who were to be recognized and tolerated within a multicultural frame (Žižek 1997). Writing of the Australian context, Ghassan Hage mobilized Lacanian concepts to define "white multiculturalism" as a "fantasy" that cannot incorporate the "multicultural Real" (Hage 1998, 133). The distinction proposed by Stuart Hall (2000) between *multiculturalism* and *multicultural* was another important critical contribution, which pointed to the tensions between governmental attempts to manage cultural diversity and the everyday reality of cultural difference. Paul Gilroy's (2004, 108–9) discussion of "ordinary, demotic multiculturalism" extended Hall's observations, arguing that "everyday exposure to difference" can give rise to heterogeneous and dispersed practices that are "not the outcome of governmental drift and institutional indifference but of concrete oppositional work: political, aesthetic, cultural, scholarly." This is an important point for us, especially considering the relevance of culture and creativity as fields of neoliberal governmentality in metropolitan areas across the globe (Rossi and Vanolo 2012). It is even more important, however, to understand the processes and stakes underlying current debates on the crisis of multiculturalism, which have been particularly bitter in the wake of the events of September 11, 2001.

It is perhaps too early to declare multiculturalism a movement of the past since the current impasses it has reached in the Anglosphere and Western European nations have not prevented a strong governmental interest in multicultural policy approaches in countries such as Malaysia and South Korea, where new migration pressures are changing the ethnic composition of populations. Nonetheless, the retreat from multiculturalism before agendas of integration, security, and immigration control in many powerful and wealthy nations cannot be ignored. As the discourses of European leaders such as Nicholas Sarkozy, Angela Merkel, and David Cameron show, the concept of integration in particular has emerged as a counterpoint to multiculturalism. At stake is an effort, which targets Muslim populations above all, to ensure the adherence of migrant and minority groups to supposedly shared national values and lifeways. As Alana Lentin and Gavan Titley (2011, 200) explain, integration "is profoundly a question of control and instrumental insertion, of managing flows of good and bad diversity, and of focusing on *compatibility* as the nexus of future social cohesion" (200). This is why matters of language, culture, and intercultural dialogue figure ever more prominently in migration and integration schemes along with professional skills, rendering the condition of a growing number of migrants precarious and their legitimacy suspect even independently of the passing of generations. Such a condition is quite different from the one of differential exclusion described by Castles with regard to the classical guest-worker systems of the Fordist age. On one hand, processes of fragmentation and precarization have seeped into the shape of citizenship under the pressure of the flexibilization of the labor market. This leads to an overlapping of multiple lines of inclusion and exclusion, blurring the boundary between them and destabilizing the existence of a unified and homogeneous point of reference against which the position of migrants can be ascertained. On the other hand, the stratification and multiplication of systems of entry, status, residence, and legitimacy, coupled in a seemingly contradictory ways with new kinds of demands for loyalty and homogeneity, foster processes of further diversification and bordering of migrants' subject positions.

Integration, Lentin and Titley write, has become "a border practice, beyond and inside the territorial border" (2011, 204). Our analysis of migration and border regimes in the next chapter investigates precisely such processes of bordering, which are constitutive of the concept of differential inclusion. In doing this, we take a rather different position from the wide-spread rhetoric that presents the border as a static wall. The notion of Fortress Europe, for instance, has played an important role in drawing attention to the warlike operations against migrants along the external borders of the European Union. But it is not adequate to describe the mobility of borders toward the inside of the European space and toward its multiple outsides that are crucial characteristics of contemporary regimes of migration and border management (Cuttitta 2007). Moreover, the metaphor of Fortress Europe drives the political imagination in a too unilateral way onto mechanisms of control and domination. There is a risk of obscuring how the external borders of the European Union are challenged by migrants along the multiple geographical scales of their stretching. As we show in the next chapter, filtering, selecting, and channeling migratory movements—rather than simply excluding migrants and asylum seekers—seems to be the aim of contemporary border and migration regimes. This involves deploying a huge amount of violence, the processes that we have called (with De Genova) inclusion through illegalization, the multiplication of detention camps, and thousands of deaths. The concept of differential inclusion attempts to grasp these processes from the point of view of the tensions, encounters, and clashes between the practices and movements of migrants and the workings of the various apparatuses of governance and governmentality that target them (Squire 2011).

These tensions, encounters, and clashes, which occur across mobile external borders, are key to the production of the internal and temporal borders that we analyze in this chapter. As we have seen through the discussion of figures such as benched body shop workers, "illegal" migrants, deportable subjects, banlieusards, and international students, such conflicts and encounters make the idea of a clear-cut distinction between inclusion and exclusion increasingly problematic. Furthermore, they force us to rethink the contemporary form of the nation-state, which has been reformatted but not eliminated by globalizing tendencies, beyond the monolithic shape of the holistic territorial unit that moves through chronological or calendrical time. The nation-state, in our estimation, is really much more adaptable, sly, and fragmented than the limited and sovereign community identified by theorists who imagine it in these terms. It is capable of harboring a multiplicity of times, temporal zones, and temporal borders. These facilitate its management of different temporal practices and rhythms, from those associated with the lightning speed and fiber optic–mediated transactions of cognitive capitalism to the slower and more biopolitical tempos arising from the demographic variations of populations. But the temporal multiplicity of the nation-state also explodes its spatial integrity, crossing it with internal borders that can no longer be conceived as mere social boundaries, cultural divisions, or sectoral limitations that structure the labor market and other economic institutions.

Our notion of internal borders has a very different inflection from that of the "internal frontier," which has been developed by Chantal Mouffe (2005) as the cornerstone of her political thought and by Ernesto Laclau (2005) as the basis around which "populist" movements revolve. "There is no consensus without exclusion," Mouffe writes, "there is no 'we' without a 'they,' and no politics is possible without the drawing of a frontier" (Mouffe 2005, 73). As we argue in chapter 9, these theoretical elaborations remain caught in the conceptual world and political trap of the modern state and are precisely predicated on the clear-cut distinction between inside and outside. Our analysis of internal borders and differential inclusion contributes to a broader attempt to map the emergence of a political world beyond the nation-state, which requires the elaboration of new concepts for rethinking questions of organization, political action, and contestation. Such an exercise, however, cannot be undertaken from the perspective of the state. Rather, it requires, to strategically alter the title of a famous book by James C. Scott (1998), seeing like a migrant. Only from the subjective viewpoint of border crossings and struggles can the temporal thickness and heterogeneity of the border be discerned. Writing from this angle is the gambit of border as method. Maintaining this perspective amid an analysis of the current mutations of sovereignty and governmentality is the task of the next chapter.

— *Chapter Six* —

THE SOVEREIGN MACHINE OF GOVERNMENTALITY

Tough but Humane

"Tough but humane"—this was the political sound bite offered in October 2009 by Australian Prime Minister Kevin Rudd to describe his government's approach to migrants attempting to reach Australia by boat. The pronouncement foreshadowed a series of events that reshaped the borderscape to Australia's north. The story involves two vessels: the *MV Oceanic Viking* and the *KM Jaya Lestari 5*. The first is an Australian customs vessel, which at Indonesia's request rescued seventy-eight Tamil migrants from a distressed craft in Indonesia's Search and Rescue Region. These migrants were transported to Bintan Island near Singapore, part of Indonesia's territory that hosts a detention center run by the International Organization for Migration (IOM) and partly funded by Australia. At that point, the passengers refused to disembark. A standoff of over two weeks was punctuated with hunger strikes, diplomatic tension, and threats to remove the migrants from the craft forcibly. Eventually it became clear that neither Australia nor Indonesia was prepared to deploy violent force. The incident was resolved when Australia offered to fast-track the asylum applications of the migrants on the boat.

The *KM Jaya Lestari 5* is a ten-meter boat that was carrying some 254 Tamil migrants when it was intercepted in Indonesian waters at Australia's request. The Indonesian Navy towed the vessel to the port of Merak, where again the Tamils refused to disembark. The standoff lasted for more than six months. During this time, the migrants were offered only limited food and medical care. About forty of them escaped, several fell ill, and one died before the impasse was resolved. Although Sri Lanka claimed to have identified former members of the Tamil Tigers aboard the boat and Indonesia threatened to remove the migrants, such violent intervention never occurred. Eventually the Tamils disembarked when UN officials agreed to begin the process of resettling them to a third country. They were transported to the same detention center on Bintan Island that the *Oceanic Viking* migrants had passed through. Just ten days before, the Australian government had suspended processing for all new asylum claims from Sri Lankan and Afghan arrivals. It was as if the plight of the *Jaya Lestari 5* migrants had been generalized. All undocumented arrivals from these countries would be forced to wait months before their claims could be processed.

Three months later, Australia removed the processing suspension for Sri Lankan migrants on advice from the United Nations that the country was safe to accept the return of those who had fled. By that stage, the Australian prime minister had changed, and one of the first announcements of the new prime minister, Julia Gillard, was the recommencement of offshore processing for migrants intercepted on their way to Australia. Her proposal to set up a "regional processing centre" in East Timor was rejected by that country's government. A subsequent plan to establish an asylum seeker swap with Malaysia was blocked by Australia's high court, which ruled in August 2011 that the immigration minister did not have the power to declare that Malaysia was a safe country for refugees. At that point, the decade-long episode of offshore asylum processing, which had been introduced by the Australian government in 2001 as part of its so-called Pacific Solution, was suspended until the reopening of detention centers on the Pacific island of Nauru and Papua New Guinea's Manus Island a year later. Over the course of that decade, the practice of external processing had become widespread across the world. It had emerged, for instance, as a mainstay of European migration management (Gammeltoft-Hansen 2007; Vaughn-Williams 2009) with the establishment of "transit camps" in northern Africa. Aside from the possibility of tracing connections between such instances of externalization, this chapter explores how changes to the policing and administration of borders register wider transformations to the workings of power across diverse geographical scales. Returning intermittently to the situation of the migrants on board the *Oceanic Viking* and *Jaya Lestari 5*, the chapter suggests that neither sovereign nor governmental conceptions of power are adequate to account for current border politics and struggles. This leads us to question the monolithic conception of sovereignty that tends to inform exceptionalist arguments and also to explore some of the limits of governmentality studies. Taking Karl Marx's concept of labor power as a strategic point of reference for the transformation of border and migration regimes, we argue that contemporary systems of migration control and detention blur the borders between norm and exception, governance and sovereignty.

The impasse surrounding the migrants on the *Oceanic Viking* and *Jaya Lestari 5* is only one instance in which migratory subjects experience indefinite periods of delay. In the previous chapter we developed a conceptual parallel between benched Indian information technology (IT) workers in Australia and migrants subjected to administrative detention. What distinguishes the *Oceanic Viking* and *Jaya Lestari 5* migrants from these groups is an act of refusal—their decision not to alight from the boats. The standoffs surrounding these vessels provide another example of temporal borders in action, but they trigger a series of actions and reactions that are difficult to account for within existing typologies of sovereign and governmental power. Far from prompting a sovereign decision, for instance in the form of a violent intervention, the vessels were held up by an abdication of sovereign power or an incapacity to decide. Neither Australia nor Indonesia was prepared to intervene, the former lest its toughness be perceived as inhumane and the latter presumably because it did not want to take administrative responsibility for the migrants. The vessels also fell into the gaps between normative governmental regimes, occupying an uncertain space where jurisdictional differences and the discrepancies between legal orders were contested. Nor did the efforts of private actors, nongovernmental groups, or international organizations prove more effective in ending the gridlock. As much as sovereign power, decentered governmental operations were unable to defuse the situation or avert its tragic consequences. How are we to account for the dual and seemingly complicit working of sovereignty and governance in these instances? Extending the discussion across a range of borderscapes and border struggles, our argument in this chapter is that sovereignty provides a necessary supplement for governance, particularly in cases where the latter fails to reproduce the framing of its operations, for instance, through appeals to humanitarianism.

In a 1981 address to the United Nations in Geneva, titled "Confronting Governments: Human Rights," Michel Foucault (2000) argued that the "suffering of men," which is all too often ignored by governments, legitimates a right to humanitarian intervention. Enthused by the activist humanitarianism of the 1970s and his work with Bernard Kouchner (then head of Médecins san Frontières/Médecins du Monde, and, until recently, France's foreign minister), Foucault envisioned the possibility of a new form of right liberated from sovereignty. The statement is interesting for two reasons. First, in registering an implicit link between humanitarian interventions and what Foucault calls the rights of "international citizenship," it contrasts the present day when humanitarian imperatives not only provide the frame for many governmental operations but also specify the border where sovereign interventions can be called on to supplement or supervene over governmental powers (Whyte 2012). This is not just the case in state military exercises that justify themselves as humanitarian interventions, such as those that occurred in Kosovo in the late 1990s or more recently in Libya. Sovereign intervention regularly crosses governmental rule in episodes of border policing and migration control, although in such instances humanitarian motives and justifications can pull in different and often discrepant ways. This brings us to our second point of interest in Foucault's text—the fact that he mentions, alongside Amnesty International and Terres des Hommes, the German nongovernmental organization (NGO) Cap Anamur, which was founded in 1979 when a group of concerned West German citizens, including writer Heinrich Böll, chartered the cargo ship *Cap Anamur* to rescue "boat people" fleeing from Vietnam. As it happens, twenty-three years after Foucault's address to the United Nations, a ship given the name *Cap Anamur* when purchased by the same German NGO, in memory of the original chartered vessel, sat at the center of a migration controversy. This incident proved crucial to the remaking of the southern borders of the EU and displays some uncanny parallels with the cases of the *Oceanic Viking* and *Jaya Lestari 5*.

On June 20, 2004, the second *Cap Anamur* interrupted its mission of transporting humanitarian supplies to Iraq to rescue thirty-seven Sub-Saharan migrants from a small boat that was sinking in international waters between Malta and the Italian island of Lampedusa. When the ship attempted to dock at Porto Empedocle, it was repulsed by the Italian navy and coast guard. An eleven-day standoff ensued. Migrants experienced nervous breakdowns and threatened to jump overboard as Germany (whose flag the *Cap Anamur* was flying), Italy, and Malta locked in diplomatic dispute. The German government argued that claims for asylum had to be lodged on their territory. Italy insisted that Malta accept the migrants because the *Cap Anamur* had crossed Maltese waters after the rescue. But Malta denied this claim and suggested that Italy should return the migrants directly to Libya. Eventually, when the captain of the *Cap Anamur* issued an emergency call, the vessel docked at Porto Empedocle. The main crew was immediately arrested and threatened with prosecution on the grounds that they were acting as illegal "people smugglers." The rescued migrants claimed asylum in Italy, but all their claims were rejected. After a short period of detention, they were removed to Ghana and Nigeria. In this episode, we see the humanitarian intervention of the *Cap Anamur* illegalized by Italy and Germany. There is a sovereign standoff while the ship is refused the right to land. After the vessel docks, Italy makes the sovereign gesture of arresting the crew and deporting the migrants. The upshot of these events was a reorganization of the EU border and migration management regime.

In July 2004, immediately following the *Cap Anamur* incident, German Interior Minister Otto Schily expressed support for a modified version of a U.K. proposal tabled at the European Council the previous year that advocated the establishment of "reception facilities" and "transit processing centers" in northern Africa. Widely recognized as inspired by Australia's Pacific Solution, this British plan and its subsequent elaborations by Germany were never explicitly endorsed at the EU level. However, at the European Council meeting held in Brussels on November 4–5, 2004, the heads of member states and governments officially declared their will to "continue the process of fully integrating migration into the EU's existing and future relations with third countries" (European Council 2004, 21). Importantly, Schily and his Italian counterpart, Giuseppe Pisanu, used the *Cap Anamur* case to call for steps to "humanitize" the management of the EU's external borders. This led the European Council to introduce so-called Regional Protection Programmes (RPPS) in cooperation with the UN High Commissioner of Refugees (UNHCR). Aimed at strengthening the "protection capacity" of the regions in question and instituting programs allowing refugees from selected target regions to settle in the EU, Schily and Pisanu saw RPPS as a "durable solution" to tackle the humanitarian problem of migrants drowning in the Mediterranean (Hess and Tsianos 2007, 34). The sovereign overriding of the *Cap Anamur*'s humanitarian mission was thus met by sovereign entities attempting to institute a regionally coordinated approach to migration management in a humanitarian frame. Unsurprisingly, this program of humanitarian and rational migration governance could only ever be a dream, leaving the violent face of sovereign power to intervene whenever this frame was broken or fractured in the gap that separates policy from practice.

Critical migration scholars refer to the displacement of border control and its technologies beyond the territorial edges of formally unified political spaces as externalization. Whether this involves the establishment of off-shore detention facilities, the interception and diversion of vessels, cooperation in deportation procedures, the surveillance of routes and so-called carriers of migration, or the use of digital databases in surveying migrant populations (Broeders 2007), the defining aspect of externalization is the involvement of third countries in the creation and management of the border regime. This is particularly apparent as far as the EU's southern borders are concerned. The period since 2004 has seen the establishment of a tight network of repatriation agreements, especially with countries of the Maghreb, the funding of extra-European detention facilities, and the export of police and border control techniques and knowledges branded as "best practices." "Conditional aid" is the key phrase of this process, which has facilitated the intertwining of migration and border control with "development cooperation." Under these conditions, Ali Bensaâd writes: "Europe wishes to 'deport' or 'delocalize' its contradictions. Seeking to make the Maghreb into a *limes* . . . it recruits the Maghreb countries for the role of 'advance guards,' calling on them to fill the function of dams holding back the flood of African migrations" (Bensaâd 2006, 16).

Although some of the EU member states, such as Italy through its "privileged" relationship with Libya until Gaddafi's last stand and violent fall in 2011, are particularly active in pushing this process forward, a project such as the CIGEM (Centre d'Information et de Gestion des Migrations), established in Bamako, Mali, in October 2008 and funded within the framework of the Ninth European Development Fund, is perhaps the best instance of the European philosophy shaping the process of externalization. The CIGEM is characterized by an attempt to involve the Malian government in the European border and migration regime under the aegis of the new connection between migration and development. The aim of this emerging regime is not to stop migration, but to filter and channel what the center's website calls the "human, financial and technical capital" of potential migrants (Janicki and Böwing 2010).

The CIGEM's use of such terminology registers the dream of remaking migration systems in the light of the economic and labor market needs of EU member states. While there have existed bureaucratic means of filtering migration flows and establishing degrees of informality in labor markets since the birth of the modern state, these mechanisms are becoming increasingly fine-tuned. The fantasy of a "just-in-time" and "to-the-point" migration nurtures the evolution of migration policies in many parts of the world. Xiang Biao (2008), for instance, describes how the "collective and camp-based" labor migration systems prevailing in East Asia from the 1960s to the 1980s have been displaced by the emergence of "sector-specific migration policies" that identify "without ambiguity" when and where migrants are going to work. Tracing the "transplanting" of Chinese migrant workers to Japan, South Korea, and Singapore, Xiang points to an "economicization of public policies," a blurring of internal and external economies, and to the role played in migration management by employers and intermediary agencies within the framework of a "governmentalization of society" (182–84). This kind of increasingly calibrated and directed regulation of migration is associated by William Walters, in an influential article on Europe's "Schengenland," with the emergence of a biopolitical function of the border. "The concept of biopolitical border," Walters writes, "tries to capture the relationship of borders, understood as regulatory instruments, to populations—their movement, security, wealth, and health" (Walters 2002, 562).

There is an important difference to be noted here between the concept of population and the concept of the people. This distinction, like the concept of biopolitics, comes from Foucault. We come back to it later in this chapter. Here we can note that while for Foucault the people corresponds to the "legal" logics of sovereignty and citizenship (and the language of rights), he posits population as the target of biopolitical government. To be governed, the population has to be known, and since it is an elusive, statistically unstable entity, it has to be continually traced in its movements and dissected into discrete groups. The more unstable and mobile the population to be governed becomes, the more finely tuned and sophisticated the knowledge devices deployed must become. In the case of migrants, a vast assortment of technologies have been assembled toward this end, including "passports, visas, health certificates, invitation papers, transit passes, identity cards, watchtowers, disembarkation areas, holding zones, laws, regulations, customs and excise officials, medical and immigration authorities" (Walters 2002, 572). New biometric and information technologies have been added to this panoply, inscribing the border onto migrants' bodies and prompting further the deterritorialization of borders (Amoore 2006; Feldman 2012, 117–49). It is important to remember that images of race and ethnicity are also continuously reshaped and reinscribed in the daily operation of border regimes across the world. As again Xiang writes: "the conflation of the 'primitive' obsession about skin and blood with the neo-liberal cosmopolitan interest in skill and brain presents a new technology of profiling in a selectively globalizing world" (2008, 182). The subjects produced at the border are thus constructed as highly differentiated, capable of providing "human capital" according to the changing and elusive needs of flexible economic systems and labor markets. As we shall see, the rhetoric of border and migration management presents the emerging regime of migration control as operating smoothly and facilitating the "freedom of movement" of its subjects. Although this rhetoric and this regime directly target labor migration, they increasingly shape the transformations of asylum and the mobility of refugees as well.

Our emphasis in this chapter is on the conflictual and coercive operations of the border that interrupt the dream of a smooth governance of migration. By drawing attention to these disruptive and often violent factors, we seek to contrast certain attempts to extend Foucauldian governmentality theory in ways that stress the emergence of paradigms of liberal governance in which values of self-responsibility and enterprise compel (or even force) subjects to conduct their lives as free agents. There is a wide debate in this area, but we can take as emblematic the work of Paul Rabinow and Nikolas Rose (2006), who use as their primary example the forms of governance that pertain to the extraction, circulation, and redistribution of genetic materials that are perceived to carry vital qualities. Informed consent, autonomy, voluntary action, choice, and nondirectiveness seem to describe the heart of the concept of governmentality that these scholars propose far beyond the field of biomedicine. It is important to point out that such a concept of governmentality not only "blurs the boundaries of coercion and consent," as Rose puts it in his book *The Politics of Life Itself* (2007, 74), but also blurs the boundary between ethics and power.

The difficulty with this approach is that it can only account for the infinite repetition of nuanced variations of the same version of subjectivity—that of the entrepreneurial liberal subject that dominates in advanced capitalist societies. What is absent from this picture is an account of how the production of such a subject is always accompanied by the production of other kinds of subjectivities for whom the moments of coercion and consent are far from indistinct. Those migrants who undergo the experience of interception and/or detention are one such group of subjects. What we can call with Achille Mbembe (2003) the "necropolitical" effects of governmental processes of border and migration management—that is, the thousands of often unreported deaths that occur every year across the world's borderscapes—are the shocking material reminder of the sovereign powers that interrupt this vision of liberal governmentality. While they dramatically show that the dream of a just-in-time and to-the-point migration is precisely a dream, they also point to the necessary supplement that is needed to keep the biopolitical border working. To grasp both the processes of governmentalization of borders and migration management and this necessary supplement, we introduce the concept of a *sovereign machine of governmentality*.

Governing the Border

Let us return to the credo with which we opened this chapter: "tough but humane." Although the fortunes of the politician who first uttered it have subsided, the formula is still effective when it comes to describing the changing means of policing the borderscape to Australia's north. Presumably toughness consists in the forceful patrolling of borders—that is, in intercepting boats and the system of detention. Humaneness, by contrast, would seem to suggest a lack of violent intervention—for instance, the reticence to use military force to remove migrants from boats. More important, humaneness implies a certain humanitarianism that might be claimed by policing borders according to UN protocols or observing principles of human rights. The formula "tough but humane" registers a process that seems to be happening to many borders across the world—they are both *hardening and softening at the same time* (Mostov 2008). Devices and practices of border reinforcing, to pick up the categories we took from Pablo Vila (2000), are increasingly shaping the conditions under which border crossing is possible and actually practiced and experienced.

Nevertheless, it would be a mistake to correlate toughness with border reinforcing and humaneness with border crossing. These attitudes or dispositions are operative in both episodes of border reinforcing and border crossing. Toughness is a quality associated not only with the violence of interceptions and border reinforcement but also with the forced border crossing implicit in practices of deportation and *refoulement* (De Genova and Peutz 2010). Humaneness, by contrast, is a quality associated with the international system of human rights, which plays an important role in migration management. Human rights provide the dominant frame for negotiating questions of borders and migration in the world today. This is particularly the case within certain activist circles, the NGO sector, and international and intergovernmental organizations such as the United Nations or the International Organization for Migration. To analyze the nexus of human rights and migration management means recognizing that human rights play just as much a role in establishing the conditions under which border crossing can be blocked or slowed as those under which it is facilitated. This is an important point: although human rights used to be considered *external* to the exercise of power, as a crucial element in the system of checks and balances that keep power at bay, we contend that they are increasingly becoming a key component in migration and border regimes worldwide. This means that they are increasingly becoming *internal* to the exercise of power insofar as processes of governmentalization of power are under way. This claim is crucial to our critical analysis of the modalities of the intertwining of the discourse of human rights and processes of governmentality, in particular at the border. It is important to note that an emphasis on such intertwining is central to the many critiques of humanitarianism that in recent years have targeted the principles of impartiality and neutrality of humanitarian interventions, especially in the case of the management of refugees (see, for instance, Nyers 2006).

A partial understanding of the role of humanitarianism in border control can be obtained by mobilizing the categories of governance and governmentality. If the moral practice of humanitarianism is viewed as one of the principal governmental regimes pertaining to migration management, it becomes possible to analyze its connection to other systems of governance operative at the border, whether they are transnational or national in scale, private or public in character. Borders are becoming increasingly governmentalized or entangled with governmental practices that are bound to the sovereign power of nation-states and also flexibly linked to market technologies and other systems of measurement and control. They are sites where multiple governmental actors come into play.

There can be little doubt that concepts such as governance, governmentality, and governmental regime, once they are critically understood, allow us to grasp some of the crucial political transformations that are connected to the global processes that crystallize on the borders. At the same time, taking the border as a site of investigation sheds light on what is often obscured in current debates on governmentality and governance. Foucault (2003) famously presents governmentality as emerging out of a crisis of sovereignty. In his lectures of 1977–78, he offers a threefold definition of the term. First, *governmentality* refers to the exercise of power that "has the population as its target, political economy as its major form of knowledge, and apparatuses of security as its essential technical instrument." Second, it designates the power of "government," which has become preeminent over all others and led to the formation of specific governmental apparatuses and bodies of knowledge. Third, it describes "the result of the process by which the state of justice of the Middle Ages became the administrative state in the fifteenth and sixteenth centuries" (Foucault 2007a, 108–9). Foucault's invention of the concept of governmentality was part of an attempt to criticize the "circular ontology of the state asserting itself and growing like a huge monster or automatic machine" (354), as he characterized the Hobbesian image of Leviathan as well as mainstream legal theories of sovereignty. It was also closely linked to his growing concern with neoliberalism, to which he dedicated his lectures of 1978–79 (Foucault 2008). From this point of view, it makes sense to draw a parallel between the Foucauldian concept of governmentality and the concept of governance that from the late 1960s increasingly becomes associated with neoliberal theories and policies.

Drawing above all from the field of corporate governance and the critical analysis of public administration in the United States, theorists of governance are careful to distinguish it from the concept of government. As Gerry Stoker writes, governance "recognizes the capacity to get things done which does not rest on the power of government to command or use its authority. It sees government as able to use new tools and techniques to steer and guide" (1998, 24). There is an analogy here with the Foucauldian insistence on the role of apparatuses, tactics, and power devices that operate at the microphysical level. For governance scholars, *government* means something very close to the ontology of the state criticized by Foucault.

There is another important feature of governance that needs to be highlighted. Following Stoker again in his attempt to provide a definition of the concept, we note that *governance* refers to "shifting patterns in styles of government," "in which boundaries between and within public and private sectors have become blurred" (Stoker 1998, 17). It seeks to grasp and map "a complex set of institutions and actors that are drawn from but also beyond government" (19). The widespread use in governance theory and policies of such words as *shareholders* and *stakeholders* corresponds precisely to this blurring of the boundary between public and private and to the mobility of the very definition of the subjects entitled to become actors in the processes of governance. The corporate language used to define these actors is far from neutral: it must be considered part and parcel of an attempt to spread the model, the language, and the rationality of the capitalist corporation throughout the whole fabric of global society and policies. Nevertheless, it describes fundamental transformations that we need to carefully follow and try to map in our investigation of emerging border and migration regimes.

There is a further feature of governance that deserves critical analysis here. Among interest groups and civil society networks that concur in processes of governance, both as consulting and as implementing bodies, "epistemic communities" play a key role (Shapiro 2001). Epistemic communities, John Gerard Ruggie writes, "may be said to consist of interrelated roles that grow up around an episteme: they delimit, for their members, the 'proper' construction of social reality" (Ruggie 1998, 55). Given the importance of risk definition, calculation, and management in patterns and processes of governance, bearers of "expert knowledge" capable of codifying risk (from natural to social science) are potentially entitled to become governmental actors (Joerges 2008, 7). Obviously, science has long played a constitutive and even constitutional role in the whole history of the modern state. One has only to think of the German experience, particularly at the turn of the nineteenth century, which has been considered paradigmatic in this respect (Schiera 1987). Nevertheless, it seems to us that the shift from government to governance signals a transformation in the general configuration of what can be defined in Foucauldian terms as the relationship between knowledge and power. The boundary between these two categories becomes increasingly blurred in processes of governance. To the framing of these processes through the language of expert knowledge there corresponds a kind of governmentalization of knowledge production. This can be observed, for instance, in the penetration of the rationality of risk management in the funding programs of the EU as well as in other national and transnational funding bodies in different parts of the world.

Turning now to the concept of the regime, we find it important to mention that its current use in social sciences has a genealogy that exhibits many points of overlap with the developments described so far with regard to governmentality and governance. Drawing from a recent essay by Serhat Karakayali and Vassilis Tsianos (2010), we can identify three sources for the current uses of the concept of the regime. In international relations it has been introduced to overcome the constraints of the neorealist school and to grasp the importance of informal bargaining in the analysis of global trade or currency management. In the French regulation school of economics, the concept of the accumulation regime was forged to come to terms with the problem of creating a consistency of relations between a set of heterogeneous and autonomous social processes converging toward the aims of capitalist accumulation. Perhaps more important for our purposes, the concept of migration regime was introduced in recent years as a kind of supplement for or substitute to the concept of migration systems (Papadopoulos, Stephenson, and Tsianos 2008, 164). According to Giuseppe Sciortino, the "notion of a migration regime allows rooms for gaps, ambiguities and outright strain: the life of a regime is the result of continuous repair work through practices. . . . The idea of a 'migration regime' helps to stress the interdependence of observation and action" (Sciortino 2004, 32).

It is easy to see how the concept of regime encapsulates the flexible, multiscalar nature of the processes of governmentality and governance already discussed, as well as the heterogeneity of their actors and the growing intertwining of knowledge and power that characterizes them. Moreover, as far as migration is concerned, it seems an effective analytic tool to describe the emergence of new patterns of migration management in different parts of the world. These new patterns are characterized by the growing awareness of the inability of traditional rigid governmental tools, such as quota systems, to come to terms on one hand with the "turbulence" of migration (Papastergiadis 2000) and, on the other hand, with the needs of an economic system reshaped under the pressure of processes of flexibilization of labor and production (Castles 2004). Since its formulation by Bimal Ghosh in 1993, following requests from the UN Commission on Global Governance and the government of Sweden, the concept of migration management has tried to cope with both of these challenges. "Migration management" has become a kind of synonym for "crisis management." In other words, it has codified migration in terms of crisis, and its aim is to flexibly manage this crisis in the attempt to produce "economically needed and beneficial flows" out of the "turbulence" of "unwanted migration" (Geiger and Pécoud 2010, 3).

It is thus tempting to apply the concept of regime to the management of borders themselves, as has notably been done by a group of German critical migration and border scholars (Hess and Kasparek 2010). Looking at the ways borders are controlled and managed from the angle of the regime means carefully investigating the set of heterogeneous social practices and structures, of discourses, actors, and rationalities that intervene in processes of governmentalization of the border. It also means that the unity of the border regime is not given a priori. Rather, such unity emerges through the ability to react effectively to questions and problems raised by dynamic processes, codified in terms of risk. Speaking the language of governance, one could say that states continue to be the main stakeholders in emerging border and migration regimes. Nevertheless they are increasingly (although differently in different parts of the world) confronted with an elusive environment of governance, within which a multiplicity of stakeholders play crucial and not always predictable roles. It is useful to remember here that migration and border regimes touch on key political questions, because they entail the distinction between citizens and aliens, as well as the crucial decision about whom to admit into the national territory. These features, as well as the control of borders itself, have been considered defining characteristics of sovereignty since the earliest formulations of this concept in the political theories of Jean Bodin and Thomas Hobbes. Even today, they belong to the prerogatives that are most jealously maintained by nation-states.

Therefore, we must be very careful in the analysis of what is often described as an emerging global migration and border regime (see, for instance, Düvell 2002). In our use of this formula, we do not refer to the emergence of an integrated political government of migration, nor do we try to imagine and normatively anticipate its features. Instead, we refer, in the frame of our analysis of governance, to the contradictory and fragmentary formation of a body of knowledge within disparate epistemic and political communities. We further refer to the circulation at the global level of administrative techniques of control, technical standards, and capacity-building programs forged within these communities, which deeply influence the formulation of migration policies and border control patterns. Governance presents itself within emerging border and migration regimes as a smooth process of persuasion without coercion according to neutral patterns of risk calculation and management, often emphasizing the "freedom of movement" of migrants (Bigo 2006; Rygiel 2010; Walters 2002). It is also important to keep in mind that "neoliberal political reason" is compelled to consider the subjects targeted by its governance strategies as autonomous actors, both at the national and at the international levels (Hindess 2004). The actors involved in these emerging regimes of border and migration control are themselves increasingly shifting and heterogeneous.

Looking at the European case, one can easily see how member states cooperate in the management of the external frontiers of the European Union. The aim, to put it in the words of a European Commission communication released in May 2011, is not "the establishment of a centralized European administration, but the creation of a common culture, of shared capacities and standards, supported by practical cooperation" (European Commission 2011, 7). One agency with which member states cooperate is the Warsaw-based Frontex, which is responsible for coordination of EU border protection efforts and describes itself on its website as "a *community body* having *legal personality* and *operational* and *budgetary autonomy*" (Frontex 2006; see Feldman 2012, 83–109, Kasparek 2010, and Neal 2009). As one of the keenest critical analysts of the politics of border control in Europe has stressed, the mere fact of increasing cross-border police actions "disturbs the categories of traditional understanding that depend on the radical separation between the inside and the outside" (Bigo 2006, 115). Both analyzing the so-called enlargement process of the European Union and critically investigating the variable and multiscalar scope of European border control policies, it is clear that the unity of what could be considered the European "territory" is increasingly destabilized by the structural mobility of borders (Beck and Grande 2007). In both cases, what tends to emerge are different degrees of internality and externality to the European space, which substitute and blur the clear-cut distinction between inside and outside that was produced by the traditional border of the nation-state. While distant and neighboring countries are increasingly involved in the management of the European migration regime, the legal and political systems of would-be member states are increasingly put under pressure by the EU. This implies a stretching of border devices, which is matched by their reinscription within the space of European citizenship through the differential inclusion of migrant labor (Cuttitta 2007; Rigo 2007). To put it in the words of Ilkka Laitinen, the executive director of Frontex: "activities before the border, at the border, across the border and behind the border are all crucial elements in effective border control" (Laitinen 2011).

At the same time, one has to note the increasing involvement in the governance of European borders of actors that are radically different from the ones traditionally involved in government: private transport companies known as migration carriers, which in many jurisdictions operate under threat of sanctions for the movement of unauthorized migrants, come first to mind (Feller 1989; Gilboy 1997; Scholten and Minderhoud 2008). Perhaps even more important is the role played in the emerging European migration and border regime by new global actors such as the IOM, by "epistemic communities" such as the International Centre for Migration Policy Development, and by "humanitarian" NGOs, which are crucial to the inscription and the governmentalization of the human rights discourse within the new border regime (Andrijasevic and Walters 2010; Georgi 2007; Transit Migration Forschungsgruppe 2007). Concerned with research and documentation, the provision of expertise and policy advice, and the execution of specific tasks and operations, these organizations tend to take a managerial and hence depoliticized approach to migration politics. Unlike states or UN agencies, they are not bound to treaties such as the Geneva Convention or the Universal Declaration of Human Rights. For this reason, they are "sometimes used by states that wish to avoid the obligations imposed by international law" (Geiger and Pécoud 2010, 13). One thinks of the role of the IOM in the execution of preventive refoulement or running externalized detention facilities. Despite this, these transnational agencies heavily mobilize human-itarian arguments to justify their initiatives. Martin Geiger and Antoine Pécoud observe an "almost systematic reference to international human rights law" in their discourses (12). Indeed, the prevalence of such language and the claim to neutrality on the part of these organizations is not lost on governments, who often cite their involvement—as well as the involvement of the UNHCR (Bigo 2002; Ratfisch and Scheel 2010)—in migration control initiatives to diffuse criticism or avoid political debate.

While many intergovernmental organizations, NGOs, and other agents of migration management work across a variety of fields, the majority acquire specialist orientations that lead them to confine their actions to distinct areas of intervention such as health, education, religion, labor, policy, crime, or media. In this respect they acquire a relative autonomy that facilitates the creation of social subsystems that tend to escape territorial confines and constitute themselves globally. Other actors active at the border include police, military, customs, and intelligence agencies. These usually fall under state control, but they can also acquire, as we began to show with the example of Frontex, a degree of autonomy through cooperation agreements or the assumption of responsibility for coordinating such agreements (Kas-parek 2010). In countering the movements of migrants and the operations of so-called carriers of migration, agencies such as this, or at least their operatives, tend to enter into systematic and symbiotic networks with clan-destine actors, leading them to further extend their powers beyond terri-torial borders and state control. There is also a tendency for the lines be-tween police, military, customs, and intelligence agencies to blur.

Added to this panoply of agencies are the many private organizations involved in securitizing the border. Apart from the transportation com-panies already mentioned (to which many informal and "illegal" carriers and networks should be added), these include private security firms that provide migration detention and escorting services for governments (Fernandes 2007; Huysmans 2006; Lahav 1998). They also include not-for-profit and charitable organizations that supply various social, legal, and psychological services (Flynn and Cannon 2009). Furthermore, an increasing number of private organizations, such as employer associations, play a role in the de-sign of migration policies (Menz 2009). The addition of such agencies to the other actors operative on the border means that private regimes of gover-nance also come to bear on migration politics. There is a multiplication of governmental agencies and regimes operating at the border. Discourses and practices of humanitarianism often provide the frame within which these agencies and regimes claim to operate. As we shall see, this frame rarely holds the conflicts and struggles that are constitutive of the border within the smooth and harmonious order of migration management. Sovereignty appears not merely as a supplemental power that intervenes when ungovernable migration flows cannot be tamed or negotiated but as a quality of governance itself—a governance that is prepared to live and let live only until it encounters a subject who will not freely abide its rule.

Regime Conflicts

How are we to understand the changing configurations of governance and sovereignty that take shape in borderscapes across the globe? How do these qualities of power interact, intersect, and work on each other to mediate the conflicts of labor and capital that unfold across the proliferating borders of the contemporary world? How do these operations of governance and sovereignty intersect the discourses and practices of law, rights, and humanitarianism that dominate the fields of migration and border politics? We suggest that these questions can be answered neither by an approach that assumes a world characterized by a full legal plenitude divided according to unambiguous jurisdictional boundaries nor by the assumption of a permanent state of exception in which sovereign powers indefinitely suspend normative arrangements. Adapting the work of German legal theorist Gunther Teubner, we argue that these developments should be understood in the context of a fragmentation of normativity, where a multiplicity of societal constitutions emerge outside of institutionalized politics and normative orders can no longer be firmly anchored to systems of law, either national or international (Fischer-Lescano and Teubner 2004, 2006; Teubner 2004, 2010). Such an approach supplements our efforts to make sense of border politics and struggles in terms of governance and governmentality without losing our central concern with the production of subjectivity. Exploring these developments implies two claims. First, borders are at once spaces of control and spaces of excess, at once sites for the restriction of mobility and sites of struggle. Second, borders are social institutions involved in producing the very conditions for governance and governmentality. Understanding the relation between these claims means analyzing how borders seek "to produce governable mobile subjects from ungovernable flows" (Panagiotidis and Tsianos 2007, 82).

To speak of a fragmentation of normativity is at once to recognize that normative arrangements do not necessarily derive from formal law and to account for the conflicts or collisions that can result between different normative regimes. Returning to our discussion of the diverse, increasingly globalized and privatized actors and regimes operative at the border, we can note how they increasingly generate their own normative structures and codes. Teubner observes the "rapid quantitative growth" of such private governmental regimes and their development of "a strong 'norm hunger,' an enormous demand for regulatory norms, which cannot be satisfied by national or international institutions" (Teubner 2010, 331–32). Take the case of an organization such as G4S, a private security firm involved in border control across jurisdictions such as Australia, Belgium, France, Israel, the Netherlands, the United Kingdom, and the United States. Along with its major competitor, SERCO, G4S has contracted with governments to administer migration detention and deportation services in many jurisdictions, operating in what it identifies as "asylum markets" (Grayson 2012). It has also been active in providing security at global mega-events such as the London 2012 Olympics, where among other things the employment of migrant workers played an important role. The company, however, tends not to publicly discuss the prevalence of migrants in its own workforce. Rather it represents migrants as victims that its control practices protect, using the language of humanitarianism and cultural sensitivity. In 2010, G4S became a signatory to the UN Global Compact, a strategic policy initiative that promotes "socially responsible business behaviour in the areas of human rights, labour, environment and anti-corruption" (G4S 2010, 4). It has actively developed corporate governance and corporate social responsibility protocols that cover areas such as human rights, the environment, local communities, business practices, accounting standards, labor relations, and diversity and inclusion (G4S 2010). In addition, G4S is a founding signatory of the International Code of Conduct for Private Security Providers, developed by the security industry, civil society representatives, and the Swiss, U.K., and U.S. governments (Leander 2012). This code has recently resulted in the drafting of a charter that specifies oversight mechanisms for the private security industry. Like intergovernmental organizations and NGOs, private governmental actors like G4S are not bound by international law or human rights declarations. Nonetheless, they actively fashion claims to humanitarianism, environmentalism, and labor justice through instruments such as charters, recommendations, best practices, and standards.

What needs to be noted is the way these diverse and increasingly globalized and privatized actors and regimes "make use of their own sources of law, which lie outside the spheres of national law-making and international treaties" (Teubner 2010, 332). Returning to the example of the Draft Charter of the Oversight Mechanism for the International Code of Conduct for Private Security Providers, we can note how the "Mechanism aims to support effective oversight of Private Security Services that are performed in areas where the rule of law has been substantially undermined, and in which the capacity of the state authority is diminished, limited or non-existent" (ICOC 2012, 2). While many thinkers make recourse to a distinction between hard and soft law (Shaffer and Pollack 2010), Andreas Fischer-Lescano and Gunther Teubner (2004) argue for abandoning "the assumption that global law exclusively derives its validity from processes of State law-making and from state sanctions, where these derive from State internal sources or from officially sanctioned international sources of law" (1010). This means extending the "concept of law to encompass norms lying beyond the legal sources of Nation-State and international law, and, at the same time, to reformulate our concept of the regime" (1010). What they have in mind are regimes that "result from the self-juridification of highly diverse societal fragments" (1012). These evolve in divergent social spheres, such as "the globalized economy, science, technology, the mass media, medicine, education and transport" (Teubner 2010, 331). As Fischer-Lescano and Teubner (2004) write:

> While courts occupy the centre of law, the periphery of the diverse autonomous legal regimes is populated by political, economic, religious etc. organizational or spontaneous, collective or individual subjects of law, which, at the very borders of law, establish themselves in close contact to autonomous social sectors. . . . In the zones of contact between the legal periphery and autonomous social sectors, an arena for a plurality of law-making mechanisms is established: standardized contracts, agreements of professional associations, routines of formal organizations, technical and scientific standardization, normalizations of behavior, and informal consensus between NGOs, the media and social public spheres. (1012–13)

We thus have a situation in which instruments such as professional agreements, standards, best practices, and routines acquire a quasi-legal status when rooted in autonomous social fragments that are delimited by sector and engaged in the production of norms. Encompassing not only private regimes but a whole host of civil society institutions, "epistemic communities," NGOs, and private-public actors, these "create a sphere for themselves in which they are free to intensify their own rationality without regard to other social systems or to their natural or human environment" (Teubner 2010, 330). The border is a site where these heterogeneous regimes tend to come into sharp conflict with each other as well as entering into various degrees of discord with state agencies, intergovernmental and international organizations, and the movements of migrants themselves.

Approaching the border in this way allows a greater understanding of the conflicts, struggles and stalemates that characterize contemporary border politics than a perspective grounded in either state legal rationalities or international law. In cases such as those we mentioned at the beginning of the chapter, the precedents of national and international law tell us little about the reasons for the impasses. As one legal expert explained during the *Oceanic Viking* standoff, "international law is silent on who has responsibility for disembarking the asylum seekers" from the vessel (Force Could Be Used on Oceanic 78: Academic 2010). Or, as another commentator put it, the episode exposed the "porous norms and mechanisms of international law" (Zagor 2009). To understand such cases, one has to follow a complex process of bargaining and crisis management, in which government agencies (including police, customs, intelligence, diplomatic corps, and military), NGOs, intergovernmental and international organizations, epistemic communities, activists, media, and the migrants aboard the vessels all have a say and a role to play.

The resolution to these situations tends to emerge not through a central power that issues a verdict or directive but by means of loose connections that are negotiated between the governmental actors involved. These often involve selective processes of networking that strengthen already existing factual networks between the various parties. Clearly there are situations in which these already existing linkages are strong, and in these cases borders tend to operate efficiently. But in those circumstances where conflicts ensue, the mediation between these relatively autonomous systems takes time to unfold. In the cases of the *Oceanic Viking* and *Jaya Lestari 5*, the decision of the migrants to stay on board the craft was the trigger that activated these regime conflicts. These were not passive reactions to changing circumstances but deliberate and strategic acts of refusal that confused and flustered both nation-states and international bodies. Despite the legal discrepancies introduced by the different jurisdictions in which the vessels were registered and the different locations at which the migrants were initially intercepted, the demands made by the people on board the two crafts were similar—both groups refused to disembark in Indonesia or return to Sri Lanka. The two groups of migrants also employed similar methods of protest and publicity, including hunger strikes, suicide threats, drawing attention to the plight of children, and speaking to the media when possible. These were properly political actions carried out in excess of the evolving system of migration control. They were also productive of a mobile and plural subjectivity that embodied the tensions, violence, and struggles that mark contemporary border regimes.

Perceiving the situation in this way delivers a very different picture of contemporary migration struggles than a rights-based approach that calls on the resources of international law. Teubner argues that the question of human rights needs to be recast as one about how the boundary conflicts between different societal regimes impinge on the rights of groups or individuals, rather than one about the violation of rights by specific legal personalities. As there is no paramount court for these conflicts, they "can only be solved from the viewpoint of one of the conflicting regimes," for example, when "the normative principles of one sector" is "brought into the other's own context as a limitation" (Teubner 2010, 340). This means that the attempt to confront the human rights problem using the resources of law is an impossible project. The "justice of human rights can . . . at best be formulated negatively. It is aimed at removing unjust situations, not creating just ones" (Teubner 2010, 340). Human rights do not provide "horizontal effects" that transfer guarantees of freedom between different sectors. Rather, the international system of human rights is only one governmental regime among others operative at the border. In some cases, it wins out, effectively providing a limiting context for other regimes and contributing to the system of border control. In other instances, it is disregarded or sidelined. As Didier Bigo comments, "discourses concerning the human rights of asylum seekers are de facto part of a securitization process if they play the game of differentiating between genuine asylum seekers and illegal migrants, helping the first by condemning the second and justifying border controls" (Bigo 2002, 79).

It would be a mistake to view the relation between the securitization of borders and humanitarian interventions as one of call and response where humanitarian actions are belated interventions that aim to address collateral damage. As William Walters notes, it is possible to observe not only conflict and the differentiation of aims and priorities among humanitarian agencies but also the materialization of security practices and effects within the institutions and practices of humanitarian governance. There is also a certain production of knowledge at stake in the humanitarian engagement with the border, one that is based on ad hoc missions, delegations, and gathering of data and testimony in the field. Humanitarianism has prompted innovation in governmental modes of administration, making border policing a more complex, polymorphous, and heterogeneous affair. It is thus necessary to ask how political struggles delineate the boundaries of humanitarianism, and to investigate how this involves a "tricky adjustment between different powers and subjectivities" as well as "transactions and imbrications between official governance and certain moves which contest it" (Walters 2009, 152, 154).

In this regard, it is important to ask how the governmentalization of power intersects the transformations of sovereignty. Far from being a site where sovereign logics fall away to make a way for a proliferation of biopolitical, disciplinary, and pastoral power, the border is a space where sovereign and governmental powers interact and are contested by the autonomous actions of migrants themselves. Just as it is necessary to account for the complexity of the conflicts between governmental regimes at the border, it is also important to recognize the presence of sovereign powers that can exercise coercive force over migrants without providing a comprehensive juridical frame that either legitimates such coercion or allows migration conflicts to be legally resolved. Indeed, it could be claimed that the collisions between different regime constitutions that unfold at the border, their organization and temporality, is precisely what is at stake in the operations of both sovereignty and autonomy within contemporary migration politics. An understanding of these dynamics must inform the critical debate about the role of borders and border struggles in the production of subjectivity.

At a very abstract level, we can say that the concept of sovereignty posits the existence of political unity as a condition of rule, whereas governmentality understands unity and coherence as results of its own action. The origins of sovereignty lie in that form of supreme power that has the capacity to decide over life and death within a social group. Although the political reality surrounding such power has been discussed, debated, and questioned from the time of Aristotle to the present day, it is really only at the dawn of the modern period that a proper theory of sovereignty begins to emerge. This theorization of sovereignty, which still supplies the inheritance for contemporary understandings of the concept, is closely linked to the emergence and development of the modern state. It is thus the case that although the material constitution of sovereignty has undergone various shifts and transformations over the ages, the dominant conceptual understanding of it has remained relatively stable since the eighteenth century. Sovereignty is usually understood as a final, absolute, and centralized form of political power vested in the territorial state. This view remains prevalent among many analysts of the concept, including those governmentality theorists who maintain that sovereignty is an outmoded but still operative form of power. Such an understanding also informs another prevalent view of sovereignty that in recent years has proved very influential in debates about the border and detention camps for migrants. The notions of bare life and *homo sacer* introduced by Giorgio Agamben (1998) have monopolized a certain way of approaching the politics of borders, migration, and camps, particularly in the worlds of academia, activism, and arts. These notions have played an important role in shedding light on the sovereign violence and the rule by force that permeate the policing of the border.

Agamben's understanding of sovereignty derives from his critical engagement with the exceptionalist approach established by Carl Schmitt in the 1920s. Adopting Schmitt's view of sovereign power as that which has the ability to suspend the law and affirming Walter Benjamin's claim that the exception has become the norm, Agamben aims to conceive a form of politics that reaches beyond the state. Notwithstanding this radical trajectory, his baseline argument remains heavily influenced by Schmitt's understanding of sovereignty as "the very condition of juridical rule and, along with it, the very meaning of State authority" (Agamben 1998, 18). In our assessment, this perspective risks wiping out the movements and struggles through which migrants challenge the border on an everyday basis, making the latter "the site of both the law . . . and its negative critique" (Lowe 1996, 35). Moreover, the exceptionalist approach is in many ways the flip side to the human rights perspective in migration politics, since Agamben's schema presupposes either a wholesale stripping of migrants and refugees (as exception) or the existence of a full legal plenitude (as norm). What is needed is therefore a concept of sovereignty that is less monolithic and apocalyptic in tone than the one Agamben proposes. We elaborate such a concept in the remainder of this chapter, first discussing in some detail the work of Foucault and then picking up again the writings of Teubner and other legal theorists.

Assemblages of Power

For both governmentality scholars and those who emphasize the sovereign exception, the maintenance of a state-centered concept of sovereignty suggests a reticence to examine how sovereignty has transformed itself under the current pressures of capitalism and globalization, not least at the border. A range of thinkers, among them Robert Latham (2000), Michael Hardt and Antonio Negri (2000), Saskia Sassen (2006), Dimitris Papadopoulos and Vassilis Tsianos (2007), and John Agnew (2009), have closely analyzed how sovereignty has changed with the evolution of transnational and denationalized formations of economy, politics, culture, and power. Examining these transformations means not only questioning the state-centered view of sovereignty that haunts exceptionalist arguments but also asking how theories of governance and governmentality have been unable to fully grasp sovereignty's mutations. We pursue this task by revisiting Foucault's writings on sovereignty and governmentality in the light of current capitalist transformations. Our analysis is informed by a reconsideration of Marx's conception of labor power. Furthermore, we introduce the concept of assemblages of power to critically analyze how borders bring together in unique and conflictual ways both governmental and sovereign forms of power.

That sovereignty is a form of power that has been subject to historical and political transformations is already evident in Foucault's discussions in the lectures published as *Society Must Be Defended*. In the lecture of January 14, 1976, Foucault argues forcefully for the study of power "outside the model of Leviathan, outside the field delineated by judicial sovereignty and the institution of the State" (2003, 34). He extends this argument by claiming that in historical terms, the theory of sovereignty has played four roles. First, it was "an actual power mechanism: that of the feudal monarchy" (34). Second, it "was used as an instrument to constitute and justify the great monarchical administrations" (34). Then, during the Wars of Religion, it "became a weapon that was in circulation on both sides . . . the great instrument of the political and theoretical struggles that took place around systems of power in the sixteenth and seventeenth centuries" (35). Finally, in the eighteenth century, with the work of Jean-Jacques Rousseau and his contemporaries, "its role was to construct an alternative model to authoritarian or absolute monarchical administration: that of the parliamentary democracies" (35).

What Foucault offers here is a schematic and highly truncated account of the transformations of sovereignty leading up to the time of the French Revolution. It would certainly be possible to flesh this history out in more detail, discussing events such as the signing of the Treaty of Westphalia in 1648 or adding names of protagonists such as Niccolò Machiavelli, Jean Bodin, Johannes Althusius, Thomas Hobbes, Baruch Spinoza, Samuel Pufendorf, John Locke, or Emer de Vattel. This would deliver a rich picture of the evolving theory of sovereignty as well as of the powerful alternatives to it that crisscrossed the early history of sovereignty (see, for instance, Bartelson 1995; Negri 1999). Our interest, however, is less in the early modern history of sovereignty than in its contemporary transformations. What is fascinating but also frustrating in Foucault's account is the way the history of sovereignty more or less stops with Rousseau and the French Revolution. With the emergence of the modern constitutional state, there appear new forms of power whose procedures and instruments are incompatible with the workings of sovereignty, namely, disciplinary power and biopower. But sovereignty itself remains essentially the same. Paradoxically, this unchanging quality is what gives sovereignty an ongoing role in the modern era. Speaking, for instance, of the "only existing and apparently solid recourse we have against the usurpations of disciplinary mechanics," Foucault identifies a misguided tendency to "return to a right that is organized around sovereignty, or that is articulated on that old principle" (2003, 39).

Sovereignty provides a threshold against which new forms of power emerge. Foucault advocates the search for "a new right that is both anti-disciplinary and emancipated from the principle of sovereignty" (2003, 40). What actually occurs in the eighteenth century, he contends, is that sovereignty becomes "a permanent critical instrument to be used against the monarchy and all the obstacles that stood in the way of disciplinary society" (37). Foucault's critique of sovereignty lies in his reversal of Carl von Clausewitz's claim that war is the continuation of politics. By rejecting this subordination of war to politics, which underlies sovereign power, he potentially undermines the whole modern edifice of statehood and its achievements: civil liberties, democracy, rule of law, republicanism, and so on. This is why he receives harsh criticism from thinkers like Jürgen Habermas (1989) and Beatrice Hanssen (2000), who worry that his view of politics as a war involving a multitude of force relations invokes the specter of Hobbes's war of all against all. In reality, the Foucauldian critique of sovereignty is more complex than this.

A good starting point to highlight the complexity of Foucault's approach to sovereignty is to pick up the vexed question of his relationship to Marx (Revel 2010, 246–57). "As far as I'm concerned," Foucault stated in a 1976 interview on geography with the editors of the French journal *Hérodote*, "Marx doesn't exist." He was quick to specify: "I mean, the sort of entity constructed around a proper name, signifying at once a certain individual, the totality of his writings, and an immense historical process deriving from him" (Foucault 1980, 76). This "entity constructed around a proper name" (and embodied in states and parties, in a political culture with its "organic intellectuals") was indeed one of Foucault's main polemical targets. At the same time, he was quite skeptical about attempts to "academicize" Marx, to make him "into an author": this would mean, Foucault said in the same interview, "misconceiving the kind of break he effected" (76). Marx was therefore a critical name to reckon with for Foucault. Nevertheless, we agree with Étienne Balibar that "in ways that were constantly changing, the whole of Foucault's work can be seen in terms of a genuine struggle with Marx, and that this can be viewed as one of the driving forces of his productiveness" (Balibar 1992b, 39).

Given the critical position of the name *Marx* in the French cultural and political landscape of the 1960s and 1970s, it is easy to understand why Foucault was quite sparing in his explicit references to Marx in his writings. It is therefore important that in one of the first texts where he employs the concept of biopolitics—"The Meshes of Power," a lecture he gave at the University of Bahia on November 1, 1976—Marx plays a major role in Foucault's attempt to develop a critical approach to merely "juristic" analyses of power. Foucault refers to "Volume II of *Capital*," where he finds a clear Marxian awareness that "there exists no *single* power, but several powers" (Foucault 2007b, 156): "Powers, which means to say forms of domination, forms of subjection, which function locally, for example in the workshop, in the army, in slave-ownership or in a property where there are servile relations. All these are local, regional forms of power, which have their own way of functioning, their own procedure and technique. All these forms of power are heterogeneous. We cannot therefore speak of power, if we want to do an analysis of power, but we must speak of powers and try to localize them in their historical and geographical specificity" (156).

Foucault's mention of the second volume of *Capital* here is quite puzzling, because he seems rather to be referring to the first volume (for instance, to sections on the working day, on cooperation, on machinery and industry, and on so-called primitive accumulation). Foucault was indeed referring to the second book of the French edition of the first volume of *Capital*, as suggested by Rudy Leonelli (2010, 126–27). Foucault states: "Marx continually insists, for example, on the simultaneously specific and relatively autonomous, in some way impermeable, character of the *de facto* power that the employer exerts in a workshop, in relation to the juridical type of power that exists in the rest of society. Thus the existence of regions of power. Society is an archipelago of different powers" (2007b, 156).

The point that Foucault makes here is interesting beyond the task of philological analysis, since the passage seems not only to point to the different topics dealt with by Marx in the first volume of *Capital* that we mentioned. It seems, above all, to refer to the seminal passage where Marx lays the foundations of his critique of exploitation. The text is well known. After describing the fabric of exchanges that take place in the sphere of circulation ("a very Eden of the innate rights of man," where "Freedom, Equality, Property and Bentham" rule), Marx invites his reader to "leave this noisy sphere, where everything takes place on the surface and in full view of everyone, and follow them into the hidden abode of production, on whose threshold there hangs the notice 'No admittance except on business.' Here we shall see, not only how capital produces, but how capital is itself produced. The secret of profit making must at last be laid bare" (Marx 1977, 279–80).

What is important to stress in the context of our analysis is the fact that this move from the noisy sphere of circulation into the "hidden abode of production" quite accurately corresponds to the shift from the analysis of what Foucault calls "the juridical type of power" to the analysis of the *"de facto* power that the employer exerts in a workshop" (Foucault 2007b, 156). To this move corresponds a fundamental shift in the field of what we call production of subjectivity: we can perceive here, Marx writes, a change "in the physiognomy of our *dramatis personae.* He who was previously the money-owner now strides out in front as capitalist; the possessor of labour-power follows as his worker. The one smirks self-importantly and is intent on business; the other is timid and holds back, like someone who has brought his own hide to market and now has nothing else to expect but—a tanning" (1977, 280).

As we will show in chapter 8, Marx's use of the words *dramatis personae* is strategic. Although the term refers to the theatrical stage where the individual is bearer of either money or labor power, it also implies the crucial role played by the *legal* concept of the person in shaping the exchange between money and labor power (through the *labor contract*) and in producing the *necessary* appearance of equality, of the "very Eden of the innate rights of man" (Marx 1977, 280). Foucault is right: "if we analyze power by privileging the State apparatus, if we analyze power by considering it as a mechanism of conservation, if we consider power as a juridical superstructure, we basically do no more than return to the classical theme of bourgeois thought, when it essentially envisaged power as a juridical fact. To privilege the State apparatus, the function of conservation, the juridical superstructure, is to 'Rousseau-ize' Marx" (Foucault 2007b, 158). State apparatuses and law continued to play an important role in Marx's critical thinking, but what counted more was their articulation with heterogeneous technologies of power such as the ones at work in the hidden abodes of production. Only by focusing on this articulation did it become possible for him to collocate and develop the analysis of power within the contested field of the production of subjectivity.

In his Bahia lecture, Foucault locates his own project of a "history of powers in the West" within this Marxian problematic, arguing that his aim is to develop Marx's approach by disentangling it from the "bourgeois and juridical theory of power" into which it has been reinscribed, particularly by European social democracy since the end of the nineteenth century. From this point of view, he sketches the rise of the technologies of discipline that filled the gaps of the global power of European monarchies and established "a continuous, atomistic and individualizing power: that each one, every individual himself, in his body, in his movements, could be controlled, in the place of global and mass controls" (Foucault 2007b, 158–59). This is the family of "anatomo-political" power technologies that Foucault had so effectively analyzed a year earlier in *Discipline and Punish*. But at Bahia, he further sketches the emergence since the eighteenth century of "another great technological core around which the political procedures of the West transformed themselves." Their mode of operation is not coercion, but regulation. Their target is not the individual, but the *population*. Foucault goes on to explain that the concept of population does not simply refer to "a numerous group of humans, but living beings, traversed, commanded, ruled by processes and biological laws. A population has a birth rate, a rate of mortality, a population has an age curve, a generation pyramid, a life-expectancy, a state of health, a population can perish or, on the contrary, grow" (161).

Sovereignty—discipline—biopolitics: do these concepts refer to a chronological development of modern technologies of power? Although there are surely passages in Foucault that seem to point in this direction, we do not think that this would be the most productive reading of the concepts Foucault proposed. In the text of the Bahia lecture, it is clear that the heterogeneous technologies of power that he labels "anatomo-politics" and "biopolitics" are articulated with each other while nonetheless retaining their specificity. Interrogating these two Foucauldian concepts with our rereading of the Marxian concept of labor power in mind, we can observe that their heterogeneous subjective targets (individuals and population) nicely correspond to the two sides of labor power: the "living body" produced as the "bearer" of labor power and the general human potency epitomized by the concept—or, from another point of view, the individualized experience of the laborer and his or her living in the reality of social cooperation. From this point of view, an emphasis on the heterogeneity of discipline and biopolitics as technologies of power cannot but go along with an attempt to grasp the unitary moment and rationality of their articulation.

In this regard, it is worth following the suggestion of Ann Laura Stoler, who has tested Foucault's "history of powers" beyond the Western context that remained the exclusive point of reference for the French philosopher (Mezzadra 2011e). According to Stoler, concepts such as sovereignty, discipline, and biopolitics maintain their value in an analysis of the colonial experience only if they are not understood as markers of different stages in the development of power, but if their intertwining and juxtaposition are emphasized. What is crucial is to critically investigate the "economy" of the shifting configurations of power and knowledge that arise from this intertwining and juxtaposition (Stoler 1995, 38, 61 and 64). Extending Stoler's argument, we can introduce the concept of assemblages of power to suggest how these different forms of power come to bear on border struggles and border politics. In this context, the term *assemblage* designates a contingent ensemble of powers that operate across different scales and political mappings. While the concept has a heritage in Gilles Deleuze and Félix Guattari (1987), our use is more directly influenced by the recent discussions of global assemblages offered by authors such as Aiwha Ong and Stephen Collier (2005) and Saskia Sassen (2006). What these authors point to is the way that new assemblages of power tend to reconfigure state territory and authority rather than completely displacing them. There is at once a disaggregation of powers that were once firmly lodged in the nation-state and a reconfiguration of them in specialized assemblages that mix technology, politics, and actors in diverse and sometimes unstable ways.

These processes of disaggregation and reconfiguration are particularly important for the dynamics of power at stake in the formation, patrolling, reinforcement, and crossing of borders. The assemblages of power that come together in these contexts are almost always highly differentiated— that is, they are hardly ever exclusive collections that consist merely of different varieties of sovereign power, different kinds of disciplinary power, or different biopolitical technologies. Rather, they bring together and even combine different forms of sovereign, disciplinary, and biopower in distinct and highly contextual formations. As Walters (2009) points out, it is also important to consider the recent elaborations of pastoral power within humanitarian border interventions. Although an assemblage that takes shape within a borderscape may involve the deployment of sovereign state powers, it may also involve the mechanics of discipline, say, in the formation of knowledge apparatuses, the deployment of pastoral power in the humanitarian efforts of NGOs or other migration management agencies, or the operation of biopower through practices of securitization or the application of technologies that shape populations through differential inclusion—for example, point-based migration systems. Equally such an assemblage may mobilize sovereign powers that have become detached from the state or are vested in intergovernmental, nongovernmental, or international organizations that work with states to effect the governmentalization of the border.

What is crucial from our perspective is how the governmentalization of the border links to different assemblages of power and the different forces of capital through which they are fragmented, recombined, and produced. This is why the border provides us with a conceptual and material field in which to stage an encounter between Marx and Foucault. Power devices and technologies that are central to the control of borders in the contemporary world also reshape the reality and the spatial reorganization of what Marx called the "hidden abode of production." Whereas the theoretical focus on labor power is clear in Marx's discussions of class struggle, Foucault tends to deploy and even displace this concept within a wider analytical field that encompasses the genealogical investigation of many different technologies of power. Nonetheless, the manifold processes of production of subjectivity that correspond to these technologies of power need to be analyzed and understood against the background of current transformations of global capitalism. Foucault (2008) himself works toward this realization in his lectures of 1978–79. Discussing the neoliberal concept of human capital, he describes the perspective of the concept's progenitor, Gary Becker, as follows: "the wage is nothing other than the remuneration, the income allocated to a certain capital, a capital that we will call human capital inasmuch as the ability-machine of which it is the income cannot be separated from the human individual who is its bearer" (2008, 226).

Although here Foucault addresses the concept of human capital rather than that of labor power, the indication of the impossibility of separating it from the embodied individual attests the proximity of his analysis to the conceptual field of labor power. This is especially apparent given his use of the word *bearer* (*Träger* in German, *porteur* in French), which is precisely that used by Marx (1977, 276) in designating the subject exploited in the hidden abode of production. Even more relevant for our purposes is Foucault's turn to include mobility, "an individual's ability to move around, and migration in particular," in the elements that make up human capital (2008, 230). Although Foucault develops this point in the context of an explication of neoliberal approaches to labor and innovation, this move to discuss migration and mobility is hardly accidental considering their importance in the shifting labor regimes of historical capitalism.

As Stuart Elden (2007) argues, the question of territory is consistently "marginalised, eclipsed and underplayed" in Foucault's late lectures (562). This means that Foucault pays little attention to the formation and politics of borders, both in historical terms and with regard to his own time. Walters speculates this is because borders in the 1970s "had yet to be constituted as a kind of meta-issue, capable of condensing a whole complex of political fears and concerns, including globalization, the loss of sovereignty, terrorism, trafficking and unchecked migration" (2009, 141). Historical developments in the control and management of migration since Foucault's time have shown that the formation and deployment of diverse assemblages of power is crucial to the emergence of contemporary borderscapes. Moving beyond Foucault, we want to suggest that a critical engagement with the concept of sovereignty as well as with its material and historical transformations over this same period is just as important for a critical understanding of the present as an analysis that deploys the concepts of discipline and biopolitics. On one hand, the technologies of power that have been forged under the name of sovereignty continue to play crucial and often necropolitical roles in the political landscape of the present. On the other hand, sovereignty can also be understood as the name of the articulation of the heterogeneous technologies of power that we have described under the names of governmentality and governance. Unsurprisingly, both this articulation and this sovereignty have become highly problematic in the present.

The Sovereign Machine of Governmentality

One thinker who has paid close attention to the multifarious tensions that are reshaping sovereignty within the processes of capitalist globalization is Saskia Sassen (1996). *Territory, Authority, Rights*, her book of 2006, produced a very important shift in the discussion of the political consequences of globalization. On one hand, Sassen made it clear that states are not bound to disappear in the near future, having been key players in the promotion of global processes and continuing to be important actors in the new assemblages of power into which they are increasingly incorporated. On the other hand, she effectively pointed out the great transformation of the functions and structures of states resulting from this incorporation. Above all, it is the claim of states to the exclusive monopoly of power within a specific bounded territory that is challenged by the processes of globalization. More and more the state is compelled to negotiate its power with local, transnational, international, and global agents of power as well as with sources of law (on the distinctions between these dimensions, see Ferrarese 2006). This leads to a situation in which, Sassen writes, "It is becoming evident that state sovereignty articulates both its own and external conditions and norms. Sovereignty remains a systemic property but its institutional insertion and its capacity to legitimate and absorb all legitimating power, to be the source of the law, have become unstable. The politics of contemporary sovereignties are far more complex than notions of mutually exclusive territorialities can capture" (Sassen 2006, 415).

It is particularly important for our present analysis that Sassen exemplifies this point by discussing a wide set of transformations in border regimes worldwide. She points to the "detachment" of bordering capabilities from geographic territory and to the existence of "multiple locations for the border, whether inside firms or in long transnational chains of locations that can move deep inside national territorial and institutional domains" (Sassen 2006, 416). These nongeographic bordering capabilities and multiple locations for the border represent crucial sites for the working of contemporary sovereignty. They also register the instability of its institutional locations, which "no longer assume a territorial correlate" (416).

One could note at this point that the transformations of state and sovereignty at stake in contemporary debates on globalization are not really new. A lively discussion on the crisis of sovereignty and the modern state developed in Europe at the end of the nineteenth century, precisely focusing on the limits increasingly produced for the sovereign state on one hand by the development of international law, and on the other hand by the increasing social and legal pluralism (Mezzadra 1999). The latter was linked to the rise of syndicalism and was analyzed by Harold Laski from the point of view of labor movements. In 1928, considering it alongside Italian fascist corporatism, William Yandell Elliott detected in such social and legal pluralism the sign of a "pragmatic revolt in politics." In 1909, the Italian jurist Santi Romano described the crisis of the state as emerging out of a situation in which "modern public law does not dominate, but is rather dominated by a social movement to which it is hardly able to adapt" (Romano 1969, 15). Such an important theoretical development in legal theory as the one represented by institutionalism—as well as the theories of law of Carl Schmitt and Hans Kelsen—must be understood against the background of these debates.

We are convinced that the contemporary situation is characterized by a qualitative shift (by the crossing of what we could call, in Sassen's terms, a "tipping point") with regard to the political landscape mapped by these earlier European debates. This is particularly apparent if we consider that legal and social pluralism today seems not to be a separate phenomenon but to intertwine with the very development of international law. Nonetheless, the alternatives outlined more than a century ago are still circulating in contemporary discussions, as demonstrated by the revival of interest in Schmitt's theory of sovereignty and Kelsen's theory of global law. Gunther Teubner, the German jurist that has provided many tools for the analysis we have offered of contemporary border regimes, feels the need to locate himself in the genealogical archive of the debates we have just mentioned. In an important essay published in 1997, Teubner criticized in a very sharp way Bill Clinton's project of a Pax Americana, which would globalize the rule of law on the basis of the worldwide hegemony of the United States. Teubner's criticism of Clinton, focusing on the structural inability of the United States to control the "multiple centrifugal tendencies" of globalization, seems even sharper today, when the awareness of a crisis of U.S. hegemony has become widespread after the bloody failure of the war on terrorism and the global economic crisis.

We are more interested here in the alternative model of legal globalization proposed by Teubner in 1997 under the label "global Bukowina." This is a reference to the province in the far east of the Austrian Empire that was the birthplace of Eugen Ehrlich, the jurist who published the first edition of his *Fundamental Principles of the Sociology of Law* in 1913. This work was in many ways related to the debates on social and legal pluralism as well as on institutionalism in fin-de-siècle Europe, and this link gave new meaning to insights that Ehrlich picked up from the German tradition of the historical school of law. Some of the most important points in Ehrlich's proposal for a sociological study of "living law" were indeed a radical criticism of what he considered to be the myth of the omnipotence of legislation. Importantly, he claimed that the "center of gravity of legal development" does not lie "in the activity of the state, but in the society itself" (Ehrlich 1936, 390). It is not surprising that Teubner finds the blueprint for his own theory of legal globalization in Ehrlich's idea of a multiplicity of legal orders arising from society itself. Though he is building on a different theory of the social, the one provided by Niklas Luhmann, he shares with Ehrlich, as we saw, the idea of a spontaneous growth of legal orders from the functional subsystems of society itself. Bukowina, the remote province of the Austrian Empire, becomes for him a metaphor of what he considers one of the most important features of these sector specific legal orders: the fact that they grow from the "margins" and "peripheries" of the system and remain dependent on them.

This is consistent with Ehrlich's criticism of the omnipotence of legislation, since Teubner's aim is precisely to marginalize the state, which continues to claim for itself the center of the legal stage: "A new living law growing out of fragmented social institutions which had followed their own paths to the global village seems to be the main source of global law. This is why, for an adequate theory of global law, neither a political theory of law nor an institutional theory of autonomous law will do; instead a theory of legal pluralism is required" (Teubner 1997, 7).

It is easy to see here the distance taken by Teubner both from Schmitt and Kelsen: neither a political decision nor an autonomous *Grundnorm* (basic norm) leads to the emergence of a global law, which rather appears *real* only insofar as it is structurally *contradictory* and *fragmented*. Legal fragmentation is the form taken by legal globalization. According to Teubner, this process can be neither curbed nor combated, and this is because legal fragmentation is itself "merely an ephemeral reflection of a more fundamental, multi-dimensional fragmentation of global society itself" (Fischer-Lescano and Teubner 2004, 1004). At best, a "weak normative compatibility of the fragments might be achieved. However, this is dependent upon the ability of conflicts law to establish a specific network logic, which can effect a loose coupling of colliding units" (1004).

We cannot really go into the technical details of what Teubner means by "conflicts law," a formula deriving from private international law, where it has been used since the nineteenth century to designate rules and procedures that aim to resolve the collisions between different national legal orders in such matters as marriage, inheritance, and economic transactions. In recent years, many jurists working from a perspective close to that of Teubner have used conflicts law as a method for understanding a whole set of crucial legal developments of the present time, most notably the problems implied by the emergence of European law and by European integration as such (see, for instance, Joerges 2011 and Nickel 2009). In the work of Fischer-Lescano and Teubner, conflicts law becomes the strategic key to the decoding of the "specific network logic" that can possibly account for the "weak normative compatibility of the fragments" of global law. The "selective process of networking" between the legal regimes is meant to increment and systematize "already existing factual networks" (Fischer-Lescano and Teubner 2004, 1017). Such networking is particularly fostered—it becomes a "symbiotic relationship"—when systems face an "increasing turbulence of their environments" (Fischer-Lescano and Teubner 2006, 60).

The systemic perspective of Teubner and Fischer-Lescano derives from Luhmann. Particularly important for our present discussion is their reference to an essay published by Luhmann in 1971, "Die Weltgesellschaft"

(The World Society), where they find a rare example of successful prediction of the future in social sciences. In that essay, they write, Luhmann "allowed himself the 'speculative hypothesis' that global law would experience a radical fragmentation, not along territorial but along social sectoral lines. The reason for this would be a transformation from normative (politics, morality, law) to cognitive expectations (economy, science, technology); a transformation that would be effected during the transition from nationally organized societies to a global society" (Fischer-Lescano and Teubner 2004, 1000).

The reference to cognitive expectations is important here because it is consistent with the developments we have described in this chapter (in general as well as with regard to emerging border and migration regimes) regarding governmentality and governance. If one looks at many of the empirical instances provided by Lescano-Fischer and Teubner (from the transnational copyright regime to the so-called *lex constructionis* and its standard contracts on transnational construction projects, from the *lex mercatoria* to human rights regimes), it is easy to see that they refer to fields that also play important roles in the literature on governmentality and governance. We are confronted with parallel although not entirely coincidental developments. Luhmann's shift from normative to cognitive expectations blurs the boundary between the legal, technical, and political dimensions of these legal and governmental processes. What matters is the systematic need to cope with and reduce the turbulence of the many different environments involved. Fischer-Lescano and Teubner acknowledge this and present the dynamic nature of the "relationship of the big functional system with the law" as the main source of the flexibility of global law and of its ability to adapt to shifting circumstances: "what is at stake is always an interplay between events external to law and normative chances internal to law" (2006, 38).

It should be clear that we find the approach Teubner developed, as well as the ones developed by scholars of governmentality and governance, particularly effective from a descriptive point of view. Our own analysis of the shifting regimes of border control shows how these approaches are able to grasp fundamental transformations of the ways that a constitutive prerogative of sovereignty is exercised nowadays. Nevertheless, the border is also the site where the internal limits of these theories emerge in a very clear way. The point is not that in many parts of the world the claim of sovereign nation-states to exclusively control their borders still shows a certain degree of effectiveness and is often the source of bloody wars and conflict: think of

Kashmir, just to make an example. Nor is it simply to contrast the rhetoric of border management and government with the reality of the multitude of women, men, and children who lose their lives every day in the attempt to cross borders worldwide. Clearly, this is an important point that needs to be remembered to shed light on the struggles for life and death that occur around the border. These struggles are structurally erased by the rhetoric of migration governance and management, which needs to be politically denounced for its complicity with some of the most violent forms of contemporary necropolitics. Nevertheless, there is a more general point to be made here: the very existence of processes of governance and governmentality, of an emerging fragmented global law, of the very articulation of the world society in functional systems and subsystems (to put it Luhmannian terms) relies on conditions, on a "framing" that transcends the modalities of their operation.

To name this framing, we think the concept of sovereignty, once the mystical mask that envelops it is removed, still retains its importance. Needless to say, as Sassen shows, we have not to look for sovereignty in the contemporary world only where it appears in its most traditional manifestations, which means where it is directly linked to the claims and actions of sovereign states. As Robert Latham (2000) argues, this means recognizing not only that sovereignty can exist without the state but also that states can "provide order without being sovereign in any robust sense of the term" (1). We must learn to map the scattered effects of sovereignty well beyond any methodical nationalism, and particularly where governance, governmentality, and global law fail to reproduce the framing of their operation. This is why we spoke of *internal* limits of the theories we have been discussing in this chapter. To make a very simple example: the fantasy of a just-in-time and to-the-point migration effectively produces a governmentalization of the border regime that can be analyzed following the multifarious ways a neoliberal economic rationality shapes its daily working. But this is just a fantasy, although it produces very real effects. To fill the gap between the fantasy and the reality, which means also to allow the fantasy to reproduce itself, a different form of power is required, often entering the stage in the form of a militarization of the border.

The reference to neoliberal economic rationality, to the market as transcendental scheme of operation of governmentality, governance, and global law, plays a crucial role here, because it points to the problem of the historically and theoretically complex relation between sovereignty and capital. In one of the most important critical investigations of sovereignty in the global age published in the last decade, Michael Hardt and Antonio Negri (2000) describe the rise of a new paradigm of power and of a new form of sovereignty. What they call "imperial" sovereignty is presented as coincidental with the sovereignty of global capital. We are convinced that Hardt and Negri's book grasps some fundamental characteristics of the political and legal problems arising from capitalist globalization (and this despite the many simplistic critiques by theorists of a new imperialism that emerged in the second Bush era). We have already stressed the importance of such concepts as the mixed and hybrid constitution of Empire, which nicely encapsulate many of the developments described in this chapter.

It is necessary to add that among the most important actors that now produce sovereign effects, we definitely find capitalist actors. The violence of financial capital itself, which has been evident in the global economic crisis, is able to act as a sovereign nowadays, dictating policies "from above" to nation-states (Fumagalli and Mezzadra 2010; Marazzi 2010). Just think of Greece or Italy in 2011! Nevertheless, this does not indicate that a full coincidence of sovereignty and capital has been achieved. To fully develop this point, it would be necessary to discuss in some detail the operation of sovereign funds as well as the current currency wars, which is beyond the scope of this book. More important for us is to insist on the fact that this coincidence would correspond once again to a fantasy, which means to the fantasy of a smooth space encircling the whole world. As we already argued earlier in this book, and as we further analyze in the next chapter, we are indeed confronted with radical transformations in the geography of the capitalist mode of production. Its spatial coordinates become more and more elusive, challenging established frames of center and periphery as well as the unity of bounded national territories. Nevertheless, these processes are accompanied by the multiplication of borders and the operation of zoning technologies that make the space of global capital all but smooth. Once again, the perspective of border as method opens up an angle from which such an important issue as the relationship between sovereignty and capital can be productively analyzed. One could say that the multiplication of borders in the space and time of capitalist globalization is an index of the existing and shifting tensions that continue to shape the relationship between sovereignty and capital.

It is important to stress that the sovereignty we are talking about is at the same time immanent to governmentality—because it tends to be subjected to its rationality—and transcendent to its devices—because it retains its autonomy, otherwise it would not possible for it to act as a supplement of governmentality. It is this paradoxical and "monstrous" apparatus that we call the *sovereign machine of governmentality*. Once again we need to emphasize that the Marxian concept of labor power provides a crucial angle from which this intertwining of the logics of sovereignty and governmentality can be critically analyzed—particularly at the border, which means at that strategic site where both of these logics intersect on bodies that are in the process of being produced as "bearers" of labor power. Marx interestingly defines labor power in terms of movement and unrest. He also posits labor power as the quintessence of the *potential* creative and productive attitudes that are contained in a living body. From the point of view of capital, this movement must at once be exulted and restrained to render it productive within the networks of capital accumulation.

This introduces an interesting problem because if we understand labor power with Marx in terms of movement and life, we must also posit the existence of a form of power that acts to restrain, detain, or, as Foucault writes, to concatenate, manage, or even arrest practices of mobility (1978, 93). The point is not to assert that power in the Foucauldian conception is simply a device of constraint or disciplining. The introduction of Marx's concept of labor power, however, can challenge much of the theoretical orthodoxy that has developed around Foucault's discussions of the inherent relation of power and resistance. This is because Marx's insistence on potentiality as a defining feature of labor power opens a scenario in which the field of exercise of power in the Foucauldian sense is always subjectively qualified and shaped by the existence of a prior power that cannot be encapsulated by the Deleuzean slogan "resistance comes first." Labor power, in this sense, is axiomatic for the analysis of the complex relation of sovereignty to governmentality precisely because it is axiological or, in other words, because it is the source of value that logically precedes all measure. Subjectivity, we might say, is the battlefield in which power comes head to head with power, creating a line of conflict drawn precisely by the alternative between the capture of life's potentiality and its appropriation as a common basis for a multiplicity of exit and escape strategies.

Chapter Seven

ZONES, CORRIDORS, AND POSTDEVELOPMENTAL GEOGRAPHIES

Corridors and Channels

The stowaway or clandestine migrant who hides on a sea vessel faces a different set of perils than does the terrestrial border crosser. So often our images of border struggles, deportation, and temporal bordering are shaped by an implicit land-hugging, even in cases where borders are forced by "boat people" and the various agents and carriers who bring them to the point where land meets sea. Take the question of repatriation for migrants who stow away on ships investigated by William Walters in his provocative essay "Bordering the Sea" (2008). Ships are mobile vessels that cross the many high seas, archipelagic waters, contiguous zones, and transit passages that are marked by the world's maritime boundaries and borders (Prescott and Schofield 2005). But as Walters shows, the processes and procedures for repatriating stowaways swing into action when maritime vessels reach port. This is because the opportunities for moving stowaways back to their point of origin, if such a location is identifiable, are vastly uneven in different ports of call. Assemblages of power and territory that connect port authorities, coast guards, political and legal orders, insurance firms, and shipping companies are at work in these situations. Walters tracks the operations of the "stowaway removal industry," pointing to the work of the Singapore-based shipping consultant called SEAsia, which has branded the notion of "repatriation corridors." Its publication *Stowaways: Repatriation Corridors from Asia and the Far East* (2005/6) provides a catalog that assesses the suitability of different coastal countries for the disembarkation and repatriation of stowaways. The manual contains "a map that geo-graphs Asian countries and their ports into regions of 'viable exit,' 'potential exit' and 'no exit'" (Walters 2008, 15).

What interests us about repatriation corridors is how they establish channels or pipelines of movement, which can be categorically identified, ranked, and sold by bodies such as SEAsia to shipping firms and other interested agents. The complicated role of maritime routes and routines in establishing new geographies of migration and regionalism becomes visible in this particular juncture between land and sea. Such a fractured and differentiated arrangement of time and space appears at many points of transit, departure, and arrival around the world, whether in airports, islands that sit along migration routes, train stations, or ferry terminals, to name a few. The variegated and diverse actors and processes that assemble themselves at these junctions increasingly work in ways that accord with what we have called the sovereign machine of governmentality. In the case of repatriation corridors for stowaways, the sovereign gesture of deportation is inscribed by multiple governmental processes, not least among them those involving insurance companies and their risk-management strategies. A prominent concern in identifying passages of repatriation is the logistical coordination of various factors to facilitate the successful and efficient removal of stowaways. This practice of logistical coordination is central to the instances of bordering, connecting, and stretching of heterogeneous spaces that we examine in this chapter. Logistics is about the management of the movement of people and things in the interests of communication, transport, and economic efficiencies. Its operations calibrate and coordinate movements across different populations and borders, taking into account the varying conditions that shape their formation. The aim is not to eliminate differences but to work across them, to build passages and connections in an ever more fragmented world. Gaps, discrepancies, conflicts, and encounters as well as borders are understood not as obstacles but as parameters from which efficiencies can be produced (Cowen 2010; Holmes 2011; Neilson 2012; Neilson and Rossiter 2011).

If the port is a privileged site of logistical operations, a space from which repatriation corridors can be established and maintained, it is also an important site in any genealogy of the free zones, enclaves, and "lateral" spaces that dot the contemporary world. The emergence of free ports in antiquity and the Middle Ages marks the beginning of a global geography that assumes a very different shape than that pertaining to territorial states but plays no less a role in the establishment of trade circuits and the ascendance of capital. Exemptions from taxes and tariffs were a key feature of these particular thresholds of land and sea, some of which organized themselves into sophisticated alliances of commerce and politics, such as the Hanseatic League, even before the rise of the modern state. The current proliferation of free trade and special economic zones, technology parks, and offshore enclaves (Easterling 2008) finds one of its most important precedents in such borderscapes. Ports have been historical holding zones where a multiplicity of techniques for filtering and surveying movements of people and things have been invented and refined, from the migration processing systems that evolved at sites like Ellis Island to methods of quarantine inspection and isolation.

As enclaves for the harboring of ships, ports were also peculiar legal spaces where different juridical orders came into interaction. In the fifteenth and sixteenth centuries, when the first modern empires were emerging, the ship was organized around the legal authority of the captain, who assumed an absolute power analogous to that of a monarch. As Lauren Benton explains, ships "played a dual role as sources of order in the oceans: they were islands of law with their own regulations and judicial personnel, and they were representatives of 'municipal' legal authorities—vectors of crown law thrusting into ocean space" (Benton 2005, 704). The discontinuous legal seascape resulting from the movements of these floating islands and from the projection of the territorial law of European monarchies across the oceans anticipated the peculiar relationship of modern empires with territory. These empires did not have a consistent or continuous means of establishing territorial limits or controls but unevenly covered a patchwork space that "was full of holes, stitched together out of pieces, a tangle of strings" (700). This gave rise to highly politically differentiated spaces in which the exercise of imperial power was not necessarily proportionate to the extension of territory or commensurate with the fixity of borders. "Though empires did lay claim to vast stretches of territory," Benton writes, often the control that reinforced these claims "was exercised mainly over narrow bands, or corridors, of territory and over enclaves of various sizes and situations" (700).

Such imperial assemblages of power, space, and law hinged on a relation with territorial logics and divides that, as we discussed in chapter 2, came to cover the world with the emergence of the Westphalian order and its gradual encroachment on all continents. The seam connecting land to sea remained a contested domain that crystallized tensions and conflicts that would lead to wider reorganizations of space and power. This is one reason the figure of empire has not disappeared from contemporary discussions of globalization, even if the question of the territorial workings or underpinnings of empire remains contested. The persisting relevance of discussions of empire for understanding and assessing the production of political space in today's world is strongly registered in Ann Laura Stoler's work on the degrees of imperial sovereignty, its historical gradations and unevenness. Stoler draws attention to the "legal and political fuzziness of dependencies, trusteeships, protectorates and unincorporated territories" that were "part of the deep grammar of partially restricted rights in the nineteenth- and twentieth-century imperial world." Those "who inhabited these indeterminate spaces and ambiguous places," she importantly notes, "were not out of imperial bounds" (Stoler 2006, 137). In Stoler's assessment, which we share, such political spaces reveal something paradigmatic about the political, legal, and even cultural workings of empire. Her emphasis on "imperial formations as supremely mobile polities of dislocation" provides a productive angle on the scattered forms of empire that crisscross the political spatiality of the present. Though Stoler's concern is to reinterpret the functioning of U.S. imperialism in this light, our focus in this chapter is on the role of such political spaces in the various practices of expansion, "primitive accumulation," and bordering that characterize the operations of capital in its current global moment.

A crucial question in this regard concerns the changing intersections between jurisdiction and territory and their relevance for understanding the political, economic, and legal constitution of such indeterminate and ambiguous spaces. All of the spaces that we have evoked here, from the free trade zone to offshore enclaves, appear as anomalous from the point of view of the modern state and its legal and political standards. Despite the fact that states still lay claim to the whole of the Earth's surface, including the submarine depths and ocean tops, there has been a proliferation of such spaces. The strange form of excision, by which states establish such zones and enclaves by removing them from ordinary normative arrangements, allows a plurality of legal orders, labor regimes, patterns of economic development, and even cultural styles to emerge. We argue that these zones, which have proliferated in number and type, invert the logic of exception that in recent times many thinkers have used to explain the new forms of securitization epitomized by the camp. Rather than being spaces of legal voidness, they are saturated by competing norms and calculations that overlap and sometimes conflict in unpredictable but also negotiable ways. The forms of accumulation they enable spur processes of spatial and social reorganization that extend well beyond their borders, making these sites paradigmatic for any serious political examination of the current global predicament.

The manifold borders that define and confine these zones have a radically different status than those that surround national territories. These are a special class of internal and temporal borders that create particular forms of life and economy within delimited spaces and have a particular relevance for the structuring and logistical organization of movements of people, labor power, information, and other commodities. Seen from this perspective, the current organization of global regions or, as we called them in chapter 2, continental blocs, and the changing balance of economic and political power between them appear in a different light. What is at stake is not a civilizational or regional logic of competing values or hegemonies. Nor is it merely a matter of strategic positioning in trade, industrial production, the exercise of soft power, or the building of economic spatial networks. Equally, the cultural and social politics of challenging Eurocentrism, for instance, through the positing of "alternative modernities" (Gaonkar 2001), confronts some of its internal limits in this context. While providing a necessary postcolonial foil to older and persistent theories of modernity and modernization, the critical task of displacing European modernity does not supply a theoretical and political apparatus adequate to the analysis of the regional formations that emerge from the intertwining, bordering, and multilevel articulation of such spaces. These formations are precisely postdevelopmental (Sidaway 2007) in the sense that they are entangled with heterogeneous postcolonial and capitalist conditions that cannot be framed within classical narratives of development or dependency. Looking at the workings of capital through this postdevelopmental optic involves a pointed and concrete analysis of the shifting relations between the frontiers of capital and multiple borders and boundaries. It also requires us to question the metaphor of flow that has almost monopolized critical discussions of globalization and global mobilities.

With its origins in Heraclitean notions of flux, the concept of flow has provided a powerful idiom for the analysis of forms and practices of mobility that exceed the borders of the modern state. We suggest that this conceptual image cannot adequately capture the variegated process of segmentation, hierarchization, and logistical coordination at stake in the production of the diverse spaces we examine in this chapter. Prominent ethnographic and anthropological works question the seeming ubiquity of the metaphor of flow by foregrounding cases and patterns of global connection and disconnection that seem better described with other conceptual tools and nomenclatures. Aihwa Ong's discussion of zoning technologies emphasizes the opening of spaces in which "market-driven calculations are being introduced in the management of populations" (Ong 2006, 3). Ong suggests that "the language of mobility—*flows, deterritorialization, networks*—has inadvertently distracted attention from how the fluidity of markets shapes flexibility in modes of control" (121). This resonates with the perspective of Anna Tsing, who argues that "world-making 'flows'" are "not just interconnections but also the recarving of channels and the remapping of the possibilities of geography" (Tsing 2000, 327). Tsing displaces the metaphor of flow, drawing attention to "the making of the objects and subjects who circulate, the channels of circulation, and the landscape elements that enclose and frame those channels" (337). The point is to emphasize that global connections are often created with great force, violence, and enterprise rather than simply following established tracks or chaotic patterns of swirl. In a later essay on what she calls "supply chain capitalism," Tsing abandons the language of flow altogether, concentrating on logistical processes and their interactions with patterns of spatial and social heterogeneity to "offer a model for thinking simultaneously about global integration, on the one hand, and the formation of diverse niches, on the other" (Tsing 2009, 150). Her attention to the generation of "new parameters for niche-making" and the way they link with "new figurations of labor power" parallels this chapter's investigations of zoning technologies, extraction enclaves, new towns, and other anomalous spaces that compose the global situation.

Mapping the multiplication of these spaces provides a new angle on the emerging spatiality of globalization, the logistical operations that make its production possible, and the multifarious bordering processes that channel practices of mobility and attempt to discipline working lives. We do not deny the importance of flows in shaping the reality of the contemporary world. What we question is the influential insight, presented for instance by Manuel Castells, that the dominant tendency nowadays is "toward a horizon of networked, ahistorical space of flows, aiming at imposing its logic over scattered, segmented places, increasingly unrelated to each other, less and less able to share cultural codes" (Castells 2010, 459). Such an image of global-space-in-the-making may have played a relevant role in prompting the awareness of the novelty of the challenges we are confronted with. But by positing a simple contradiction between the space of flows and segmented places, it suggests a disconnection between a homogeneous and smooth global space on one hand and politically, socially, and culturally fragmented local spaces on the other. This does not allow us to fully grasp the logics of contemporary global processes. What is missing in such a theoretical rendering of the global space of flows is precisely what Tsing (2005) calls "global connections," the continuous heterogenizing and fragmentation of space necessary for the articulation and grounding of global flows.

Explaining how his historical studies of colonial thinking and practice in Africa have induced skepticism toward the concept of globalization, Frederick Cooper writes that "to adopt a language that implies that there is no container at all, except the planetary one, risks defining problems in misleading ways" (Cooper 2001, 190). Our analysis in this chapter shows how global processes unfold through many containers, which are characterized by logics of spatial production profoundly different from those epitomized by the modern state. Opening up territories to global flows often implies, as Tsing shows in her research on the deforestation of vast tracks of the Indonesian island of Kalimantan, the establishment of new "frontier" spaces, which are characterized by "confusions between legal and illegal, public and private, disciplined and wild" (Tsing 2005, 41). Such a frontier condition exists with different degrees of violence and intensity across the huge array of special zones that articulate the connections as well as the disconnections between what Castells calls the space of flows and the space of places. It is important to note that connection and disconnection go hand in hand in articulating global processes in many parts of the world. Global links themselves, as James Ferguson writes in his work on resource extraction and "enclaves" in Sub-Saharan Africa, "connect in a selective, discontinuous, 'point-to-point' fashion" (Ferguson 2006, 14). Ferguson introduces the concept of global "hops" to describe how movements can efficiently connect "the enclaved points in the network while excluding (with equal efficiency) the spaces that lie between the points" (47). Here we find yet another conceptual image that questions the capacity of the metaphor of flow to meet analytical challenges thrown up by current global processes.

The global geography that emerges from the research of anthropologists like Ong, Tsing, and Ferguson is characterized both by the pressure of global forces and by multiple levels of spatial fragmentation. It implies the multiplication of connections as well as territorial, economic, social, and cultural disconnections. We are convinced that such spaces as special economic zones, corridors, and enclaves, far from being marginal and exceptional, provide a privileged perspective on globalization and its accompanying tensions, frictions, and conflicts. The bordering technologies that make these spaces possible intertwine with state borders and contribute to the formation of new territorial assemblages for the workings of governmentality and sovereignty. These emerging political spaces cannot be adequately grasped through such metaphors as verticality and encompassment, which are intimately associated with the history of the modern state (Ferguson and Gupta 2002). A process that simultaneously folds and unfolds spaces multiplies the statuses and units contained in formally unified territorial states, while new regional, continental, and transcontinental routes of connection further contribute to this uncanny stretching and overlapping of geographies. In what follows we focus on practices of labor control and mobility that traverse such spaces and routes, drawing particularly on Chinese and Indian case studies we had the opportunity to conduct in the frame of the research project Transit Labor (http://transitlabour.asia/).

Investigating changing patterns of labor and mobility in the whirlwind of Asian capitalist transformation, the Transit Labor project led us to establish and participate in "research platforms" in the cities of Shanghai and Kolkata. This involved organizing collaborative research activities between researchers, activists, and artists drawn from different parts of the world and local Chinese and Indian participants. By means of workshops, site visits, symposia, mailing lists, and online publishing, these collaborations focused on issues of zoning, migration, land acquisition, and logistics at the intersection of labor's transition and transitoriness. What we draw from these experiences is a sense of how multiple actors, norms, and labor regimes coexist within Chinese and Indian production zones as well as how various protocols, management styles, and governmental approaches pass between these sites. At stake is an analysis that moves beyond comparison, recognizing the discontinuous and relational movement of factors as diverse as architectural motifs, corporate codes, and methods of political organization. Our attention turns to questions of dispossession and resistance, loss and redeployment of livelihood, and the complicated issue of how to conceive exploitation in contexts where the subjectivity of labor no longer converges on a homogenized industrial worker. In this way, we track how multiple realms of influence interact within and between these spaces, giving them a strange form of proximity-in-distance and obfuscating the ruses of power that aim to keep labor in place.

In the Frame

It is hard to avoid the concept of neoliberalism in critical analyses of capitalist transitions and mutations over the past three or four decades. From the widespread use of this concept to explain various forms of plunder, dispossession, and scaling back of public resources (Harvey 2005; Klein 2008; Mattei and Nader 2009) to the more nuanced accounts of the later work of Michel Foucault (2008) and John and Jean Comaroff (Comaroff and Comaroff 2001), there has been a near monopolization of discussions of present forms of capitalism from this perspective. Perhaps the blanket laid by critical accounts of neoliberalism across many different geographical and historical instances of recent capitalist activity is what makes us wary of the concept. Doubtless there is something to be gained by examining the intellectual history of the thought collectives, think tanks, and foundations associated with the birth of this "doctrine" (Mirowski and Plehwe 2009). Likewise the line of criticism that emphasizes the break between neoliberal thought and classical liberalism provides a necessary counterbalance to the appropriation of the concepts of freedom and liberty by conservative political forces in many parts of the world. In the previous chapter, we drew on such elaborations of neoliberalism, specifically with regard to the intertwined formations of governmentality and sovereignty that they bring to the fore. Our present concern is to confront some of the ways the widespread infiltration of the concept of neoliberalism into the vernacular of critical thought has also blocked and obscured some important—indeed, vital—lines of analysis and intervention.

What we want to point out is not so much the confusion that inhabits discussions of neoliberalism that waver between and never quite decide if they are presenting an economic, ideological, or governmental analysis. Nor do we want to make the easy point that neoliberalism has many different contextual manifestations, both spatial and historical, that warrant close empirical analysis. Rather, our attention is drawn to arguments that present neoliberalism as an irregular or inconsistent development in the history of capitalism, contrasting it often with a Fordist or Keynesian norm that itself never had a universal scope or homogeneous existence. To our minds, such a rendering of neoliberal thought tends to gloss over the struggles and contradictions that always inhabited Fordist articulations of capital and labor and eventually led to its crisis. As a consequence, neoliberalism is reduced to a kind of ideology, and the multifarious attempts to organize new material constellations of production are obscured. Fortunately we now have analyses that stress how such patterns of production and exploitation have emerged across global and regional scales. The work of scholars such as Wang Hui and Aihwa Ong, who discuss the manifestations of neoliberalism in East Asian contexts and beyond, is notable in this regard. In the 1990s, discussions of the history and development of neoliberalism in Latin America, encompassing the work of the Chicago boys in Augusto Pinochet's Chile and the protracted moment of Menemismo in Argentina, set the tone for a wider global analysis. The legacies of Ronald Reagan and Margaret Thatcher, and their reverberations across many faces of institutionalized political power, including the regimes of Silvio Berlusconi, John Howard, and Vladimir Putin should also be mentioned. But it is the remarkable developments that followed Deng Xiaoping's pursuit of "perestroika without glasnost" in the Chinese context and their projections across the East Asian landscape that we focus on here. It seems to us that these permutations and shifts, which in our estimation cannot be approached in isolation from the parallel transmutations of the Indian economy, have a relevance that extends beyond the Asian region and the dramatic processes of rescaling that have crossed it in the past decades. The adventures of Chinese capital in Africa and Greece, the story of the Mittal steel family, the outsourcing of Indian call centers to Eastern European countries like Poland—all of these stories and many more like them are relevant in this regard. Our interest, rather, is in more paradigmatic lessons that can be learned from an analysis of the combination of different spaces, times, and calculations that have resulted from Asian experiments in being global. A multiplicity of borders, frontiers, and boundaries has been tested in these efforts of stretching and remixing different scales of accumulation, sovereignty, and governmentality.

We begin by focusing on the asymmetrical and asynchronous interaction of sovereignty and governmentality in the wide transcontinental spaces that Ong (2006) calls "latitudes." With this concept, Ong describes lateral spaces that stretch across continents and intersect processes of production and exploitation that involve processes of ethnicization, carceral modes of labor discipline, and the dominance of market over territorial rights. She has in mind, for instance, electronics manufacturing operated by Asian managers that is "dependent on both free-floating market networks and zones of incarcerated labor" (125). Such "high-tech production regimes are transpacific in scope, so that high-tech sweatshops in Silicon Valley are pitted against ever lower-cost manufacturing sites in China" (125). These transcontinental production regimes also involve the high-end mobility of managers and technocrats, including those who have made an enterprising return to China after working abroad to stay ahead of business and technology curves. What fascinates Ong about such lateral spaces is how they stretch the bounds of governmentality through the mobilization of market technologies that enable "a kind of transnational power rooted in mobile capital" (137). In her view, a central strategy of contemporary capital is the use of comparative market calculations to play off and exploit the differential opportunities for labor in various global locations, including those imposed by levels of pay, possibilities for unionization or other forms of organization, and gendered and ethnicized forms of discipline. Significantly, these market-driven calculations set up patterns of migration and mobility between distant sites, establishing privileged channels or corridors between them. For Ong, the spatial and temporal dimensions of these latitudes provide a powerful analytical angle on the evolution of neoliberalism in East Asia.

In the book we are discussing, *Neoliberalism as Exception* (2006), Ong's analysis of these calculations and dimensions occurs under the sign of exception. Differently from the well-known appropriation of this term from Carl Schmitt pursued by Giorgio Agamben (2005), Ong uses the concept of exception more broadly "as an extraordinary departure in policy that can be deployed to include as well as to exclude" (Ong 2006, 5). She investigates how this play between inclusion and exclusion, which importantly resonates with the analysis of differential inclusion we offered earlier in this book, disturbs existing patterns of sovereignty and citizenship. First and foremost in her analysis are the shifting processes of market governmentality that selectively target spaces and populations by working alongside but also sometimes at odds with strategies of demarcation pursued by sovereign powers. The split between what is accomplished by governmental powers, by which Ong usually means market powers, and the effects of sovereign manipulations is really quite crucial for understanding what she means by exception. Although she points to the role of nongovernmental organizations (NGOs) and corporations in the emerging assemblages of overlapping sovereignties that govern lateral spaces, the moment of bordering or demarcation seems to provide the primary instance of sovereign intervention. In the dual operations of such sovereign practices and market logics of governmentality (that is, in their powerful consonance or even in the gaps between them), exception appears not as a negative suspension of rights but as the positive creation of "opportunities, usually for a minority, who enjoy political accommodations and conditions not granted to the rest of the population" (101). Ong's examples range from the way "moderate Islam" allows a vigorous public presence for middle-class women in Malaysia to how NGOs safeguard the biological security of maids in Hong Kong and the role of Singaporean authoritarian rule in fostering experimentation and entrepreneurialism in biotechnology. By far her most relevant discussion for our purposes concerns strategies of so-called graduated sovereignty.

Explored not only in *Neoliberalism as Exception* but also in Ong's earlier work *Flexible Citizenship* (1999), "graduated sovereignty" refers to the practice, on the part of some East and Southeast Asian states, to set up special economic zones, in which labor market access, tax regimes, health and safety standards, industrial relations, environmental policies, and so on are regulated according to the market-driven logic of neoliberal governmentality. Such a logic, she explains, "induces the coordination of political policies with corporate interests, so that developmental decisions favor the fragmentation of the national space into various noncontiguous zones, and promote the differential regulation of populations who can be connected to or disconnected from global circuits of capital" (Ong 2006, 77). In such instances of zoning, it seems the sovereign moment is restricted to the actual establishment or demarcation of the space in which neoliberalism works. From the point of view of governmentality, however, this is just another kind of space within and across which market calculations can be effected and optimized. Such a view of how sovereignty and governmentality work off each other is not restricted to Ong's analysis of zoning technologies. It extends to her view of the various forms of migration and movement that establish the privileged corridors of lateral spaces. What are the implications of the exception that Ong believes to be generated by such combination for what we have called the sovereign machine of governmentality?

According to Ong, sovereign power "depends on a network of regulatory entities that channel, correct, and scale human activities in order to produce effects of social order." Rejecting the prevalent view of sovereignty as "a uniform effect of state rule," she associates it with "the contingent outcomes of various strategies" (2006, 100). From this perspective, which encompasses the emergence of what she calls "postdevelopmentalism," graduated sovereignty is not merely a refinement or qualification of modern nation-state sovereignty but takes on some of the decentralized features of governmentality. It is "a more dispersed strategy that does not treat the national territory as a uniform political space" (77). By the same token, the very concept of graduated *sovereignty* suggests that the deployment and operation of zoning technologies cannot be wholly reduced to the logic of governmentality. Here we see something more than the parallel functioning of sovereign and governmental powers. Rather, these powers begin to blur. Ong describes the opening of an exception that gives "corporations an indirect power over the political conditions of citizens in zones that are differently articulated to global production and financial circuits" (78). By pointing to a heterogeneous constitution of sovereignty that mixes state, corporate, and nongovernmental actors as well as international organizations such as the World Trade

Organization, she moves the concept of sovereignty closer to those of govern-mentality. Indeed, she often begins a sentence using one term only to shift to the other toward the end. "Grasping how sovereignty functions in practice," she writes, "requires an understanding of the different mechanisms of gover-nance beyond the military and the legal powers" (76). In such moments, Ong comes quite close to the concept of the sovereign machine of governmen-tality we elaborated in the previous chapter. But there are also important differences at work here, which we now wish to explore precisely through an analysis of the juridical arrangements that pertain in Chinese production zones and the uneven and irregular overlapping of economic and legal spaces that occurs in these contexts.

One of the puzzles of investigating the foreign corporate involvement in Chinese special economic zones is the fact that these capitalist actors do not always choose to use the bottom lines of labor, health, and environmental standards that zoning technologies afford them. In a world where con-sumers as well as producers are highly aware of the complicated trade-offs between such standards and the value of commodities and brands, there are distinct economic benefits for firms that adopt ethical stances as strategies for fashioning their identities in the context of global humanitarian and environmental rhetorics. These ethical stances and the "values" they refer to become part and parcel of the process of generating economic value. In an interesting essay on corporate codes and their relevance for labor condi-tions and standards among multinationals operating in China, Pun Ngai (2008) registers the growing importance of private governance regimes un-der globalization. For Pun, these codes present "a form of reorganized mor-alism in an increasingly globalized Chinese context." She explains: "the principle of reorganized moralism involves reworking neoliberal principles operating at the micro-workplace level not only to rearticulate labor rights practices from the corporate point of view but also to move into the sphere of labor rights and labor protection, a domain supposedly belonging to the role of the state and civil society" (Pun 2008, 88). Pun sees such governmen-tal strategies as a "moral façade" that "creates the impression that transna-tional capital is protecting the rights of Chinese labor from a despotic re-gime" (88–89). Although this certainly catches an important aspect of the situation, our discussion of Gunther Teubner's theory of legal pluralism in the previous chapter also suggests the need to highlight the maze of com-peting norms that cross the spirit and material operations of contemporary capitalism.

In an essay specifically devoted to corporate codes, Teubner observes a deep transformation of these charters from performative "public relations strategies" to what he calls "genuine civil constitutions" (Teubner 2009, 263). Existing alongside other partial global regimes in which "private actors make rules," including *lex mercatoria*, Internet law, and construction law, corporate codes have a "binding nature" that "is not guaranteed by state power," yet they also "display a high normative efficacy" (263). Transferring Teubner's observations into the context of Chinese production zones, we can note a fragmentation as well as potential contradictions between the multiple normative regimes operative in these spaces. Often this gives rise to complex and uncanny blame games by which different actors displace and attempt to transfer onto each other moral responsibilities for labor conditions or environmental transgressions. For instance, in rhetorical exchanges that followed the widely publicized suicides at Foxconn and massive strikes at the Foshan Honda factory in 2010, it was the Chinese party-state that stood up to present itself as "protecting the rights of Chinese labor" from transnational capital. Aside from such moral and political positioning, the fragmentation implied by the legal pluralism into which corporate codes insert themselves shows the trace of sovereign power within the very constitution of the special economic zone.

We are confronted again with an important problem we mentioned in the previous chapter. Although a sovereign gesture is definitely implied in the bordering that makes the existence of special economic zones possible, the framing of the operations of the multiplicity of actors and normative orders involved in the governance of these spaces also bears the traces of sovereignty. Such framing is not necessarily or not only a spatial maneuver. It clearly exists in a spatial sense at the borders of the zone but is also intensively manifest within them. A corporate code, for instance, pretends to apply across all the locations and activities of a multinational firm, but in its local translations it necessarily enters into tight tussles with adjacent and competing orders, material circumstances, and regimes. The frame of this translation is what requires further analysis. The limits of a multiscalar approach become apparent here. The geographical switch between the global and the local is not sufficient to account for the workings of such translation and the ways they cross arrangements of power that are materially and often violently implicated in the tension between unifying and dispersing tendencies. Asian experiments in being global do not escape this tension. In agreement with but also with dissonance from Ong, we believe it is important to focus on the frames that organize (or at least attempt to organize) this tension, making it productive for capital. In these frames the vexed question of the relationship between state and capital takes on its contemporary shape and idiosyncrasies. Here the question of sovereignty rests neither on the mystical veil of exception nor on the monopoly powers of law and violence. Rather, it superimposes itself on normative regimes and governmental networks in ways that attempt to orchestrate and work the boundaries between them.

It is no accident that talk of *orchestrating networks* has assumed prominence in both management discourses and international relations. In a widely read essay by Anne-Marie Slaughter, the capacity to make and maintain connections "above the state, below the state, and through the state" is seen as the prerogative of the "central player, able to set the global agenda and unlock innovation and sustainable growth" (Slaughter 2009, 95). Slaughter does not write directly of sovereignty, but the fact that her essay addresses the prospects for the United States to remain a dominant global power in the face of claims for a coming Asian century shows how close her concerns are to those that are traditionally analyzed in the frame of this concept. Importantly, she notes how contemporary arrangements of power are caught in the crossfire between centralizing and dispersing forces. The United States, she argues, has an edge because "it faces no threats to its essential unity," and its immigrant history, culture of openness, and capacity to connect to other regions position it strategically in "a world that favors decentralization and positive conflict" (102, 109). In this view, the ability to orchestrate rather than dictate or directly control is the key to the maintenance of global power and purpose. Slaughter's vision remains rooted in the language of international relations, but it effectively registers the kind of framing or orchestrating devices that we see as essential to the workings of the sovereign machine of governmentality. From our perspective, the tensions between unifying and decentralizing power tendencies are even more evident in the case of anomalous spaces such as zones. These spaces crystallize the problems and dynamics of contemporary global regionalism. This is not only because they are magnets for migration that almost always exist with shantytowns on their peripheries. It is also because they are sites of unusually intense connections where competing norms and networks overlap and exist in excess of spatializing strategies that attempt to contain them. Analyzing the bordering processes that constitute and cross these spaces draws attention to the ways they enable and empower processes of accumulation, dispossession, and exploitation. With this in mind, we turn our investigations to China and India.

Last Train Home?

Anyone who has seen the film by Lixin Fan, *Last Train Home* (2009), knows something about the pains and dreams, struggles, hopes, and deceptions that make up the fractured lives of the more than 150 million migrant workers that spur China's ascendance as a global economic power. Moving from factory to factory, "roaming around the world" as one character says in the film, these internal migrants have been key actors of development since the beginning of China's economic reforms in the late 1970s. Channeled and controlled through the household registration system established in 1958 (the so-called *hukou*), migration has also been used by the Chinese government to manage and exploit the historical divide between the city and the country. By the rules of the hukou system, the difference between a rural and urban household is particularly important in establishing the entitlement to social services provided by local authorities (Chan 2010; Fan 2008, 40–53). Registered as "temporary residents" in industrial cities, most migrants retain an ambiguous status while the system "ensures the labor supply even as it limits the pressure of population migration on the urban social structure" (Wang 2003, 70). Starting the journey from their new home in the booming coastal cities to the rural villages they left several years ago, the protagonists of Lixin Fan's film share the destiny of millions of migrant workers at Chinese New Year. The country they traverse seems to contain different worlds. There are multiple geographical and temporal borders crossed, and clashes between modernity and tradition must be constantly negotiated.

Last Train Home invites us to approach from the migrants' point of view some of the most important topics at stake in the intellectual debates that have surrounded China's dramatic growth in the past decades. Migrant workers embody some of the most striking characteristics of the Chinese "transition." As we will see, they are constructed by state policies as members of a transitory working class, circulating from the factory to the countryside. Often they inhabit temporary and exceptional spaces such as segmented "migrant villages" (Xiang 2005) or labor dormitories that facilitate "the temporary attachment or capture of labour by the companies, but also the massive circulation of labour" (Pun 2009). The concept of "unfinished proletarianization" has been proposed to come to grips with these processes, which produce a continuous proliferation of "ambiguous identities" characterized by an extreme fragility of residence status and hence of access to welfare services (Pun, Chi Chan, and Chan 2010). Although it is important to note that "partial proletarianization" has a long history under capitalism outside of the West (Amin and Van der Linden 1997), here we are confronted with a peculiarity of Chinese development in recent years that cannot easily be accommodated within a generic concept such as neoliberalism. Emphasizing the need to dispose "of the myth that the Chinese ascent can be attributed to an alleged adherence to the neo-liberal creed," Giovanni Arrighi (2007, 353) has made an important contribution to our understanding of contemporary China. In so doing, he has also problematized the concept of neoliberalism as such, which has served as a kind of catch-all notion in political and economic debates of the past decades. Though we do not always agree with the tone of Arrighi's analysis, which is often close to the mainstream Chinese discourse, we recognize the importance of many of the elements he stresses in his attempt to understand the economic and social model underlying China's ascent—from the role of diasporic Chinese capital to the contribution of "Township and Villages Enterprises," from the historical rooting of China's economic resurgence in the East Asian "Industrious Revolution" to the combination of "knowledge-intensive" and "labor-intensive industries" in Export Processing Zones.

Having said this, the concept of neoliberalism retains an analytic validity if we recognize, as Wang Hui writes, that "there is no way to adduce convincing conclusions by merely summing up [its] character at an abstract level" (Wang 2003, 44). Wang has provided one of the most striking and passionate analysis of the ways in which, after the crackdown on the Tiananmen movement in 1989, the market gradually became "the basic motive power behind promotion of the transformation of the mechanisms of the state and the reform of the legal system" (119). The role played by the violence of 1989 in prompting market and monetary reforms shaped a relationship of exchange between political power and the market, which made up what Wang (2009, 32) calls "the secret history of the mutual entanglement of neo-liberalism and neo-authoritarianism in China." Though a deep depoliticization of society was the main condition of this entanglement, an "intertwining of the processes of state factionalization and the formation of social factions and special interests" (31) became a crucial characteristic of Chinese development, risking the involvement of the Communist Party itself. New assemblages of governmentality and sovereignty also emerged under conditions shaped by complicated relationships between central and local authorities, the state and NGOs, as well as by the proliferation of special zones of economic activity and development.

It is interesting to note that since the 1990s, critiques of neoliberalism and marketization have been closely associated in China with a reassessment of modernity. The work of Wang Hui is dominated by an attempt to disclose the rich archives of "modern Chinese thought," investigating the encounter with Western imperialism and capitalism in the nineteenth century and analyzing the history of more ancient Chinese traditions. A prominent feature of this work is its attempt to displace the alternative between a narrative of Chinese history centered on empire and a narrative centered on the nation-state. Wang explains the difference between these two models of political organization in terms of the explicit borders characteristic of nation-states, observing that empires by contrast "understand both sides of borders or the various shared frontiers as their own." From the point of view of this clear-cut distinction, Wang finds it striking that already in 1689, with the Treaty of Nerchinsk, two empires such as China and Russia "clearly deployed methods of drawing boundaries." The mention of a fugitive slave law in the treaty signifies that "people from each side of the border are prohibited from fleeing to the other, and that the governments on each side are prohibited from granting asylum to fugitive slaves" according to a distinct "administrative jurisdiction in frontier territories." Speaking more generally of China under the Qing Dynasty, Wang adds that many regions "had frontiers; yet many regions also had explicit boundaries, precisely because they had to resolve ownership and trade questions within the minority populations in their border regions. This was a very complex system and set of practices" (Wang 2009, 131–32).

This system and set of practices regarding borders and frontiers sets an important historical precedent for an organization of contemporary Chinese space, which is very different from the standard relationship between the nation-state and its territory in the Western political experience. Invoking such notions as "trans-systemic society" and "trans-societal system," Wang (2011a) frames the question "what is China?" in a regional perspective. Working through the differences between different renderings of the multiple territorial divides that have shaped Chinese history within a wider regional framework, such as the "Great Wall–centric" and the "Yellow River–centric" theories, Wang stresses what he calls the "perspective of fluidity" (180) and the structural instability of center–periphery relations. What we find particularly useful in his essay is its emphasis on the necessity to dispose of the homogeneous and void time of the nation-state to make sense of Chinese history and the present within a regional perspective. "Epistemologically," Wang writes, "only when time is liberated from the vertical relationship and situated in a multilevel horizontal movement can we find a temporal dimension for the spatial concept of region. The aim of this is to place the ambiguity, fluidity, hybridity, and overlap of region at the center of our reflection on history" (193). This image of a deep heterogeneity of space and time, to which multiple temporal and territorial borders correspond, provides a key to a new understanding not only of Chinese history but also of the present. It allows an analytic grasp on the peculiarities of Chinese development that is far more productive than the one provided by familiar narratives of modernization or by mainstream concepts such as totalitarianism or even the metonymy of "the world's factory."

While the image of China as the world's factory captures the booming of export-oriented industrial production after the economic reforms, its implications are far too simplistic because it isolates industrial production and labor from the deep heterogeneity of space and time within which it is embedded. In his important research on the "Chinese condition," French scholar Jean-Louis Rocca has emphasized this heterogeneity from the point of view of the multiple labor regimes and subject positions that coexist in contemporary China—ranging from "formal" to despotic domination of labor, from relatively protected forms of labor in public enterprises to the spread on a massive scale of processes of precarization and flexibilization that have been described elsewhere as characteristic of "post-Fordism" (Rocca 2006, 56–67, 97–104). The articulation of (or attempt to articulate) these profoundly heterogeneous forms of labor control and regulation comprises the peculiarity of Chinese development. Moreover, far from being free, the labor market is "bonded" by geographic and gender determinations, with family and community networks playing a major role in channeling social and territorial mobility (Rocca 2006, 100). Powerful processes of multiplication of labor are the result of these complex assemblages. Huge concentrations of cognitive labor arise in metropolitan areas around "creative industries," often characterized by processes of stratification and segmentation that correspond to a multiplicity of contractual arrangements with high degrees of mobility of laboring subjects and precarity for university graduates (Ross 2009, 53–76).

One has only to take a look at Zhongguancun, the "Chinese Silicon Valley" in the northwest of Beijing, to get a sense of the limits of the image of the world's factory. In *The Inside Story of China's High-Tech Industry* (2008), Yu Zhou demonstrates the pitfalls of any interpretation of China's ascent as predicated exclusively on participation in the "international division of labor" through cheap labor and export-oriented production (15–18). The making of Zhongguancun, which in 2005 was home to over seventeen thousand new technology enterprises (60 percent of them in information and communication technology or related sectors), cannot be explained in this way. Its development has been dominated by domestic technological firms and driven by the domestic market, according to a model that is best described in terms of a synergy between "import substitution and export upgrades" (21). In Yu's description, the development of Zhongguancun has not followed "a state-issued blueprint of transformation" but has been "cyclical, evolutionary, and often chaotic and haphazard." This reflects a framework of "institutional uncertainty" that recalls the theories of governance and governmentality we discussed in the previous chapter: "The actors including state, MNCs [multinational corporations], local firms and local research institutions are locked in a quadrangular innovation system in which each sees its influence wax and wane, and each is challenged by others and by the changing political and institutional environment. New institutions have emerged, only to become inadequate a few years later. In short, like a reptile shedding its own skin, Zhongguancun grows by generating and testing new identities, organizations, and strategies and by accumulating knowledge on technological management and innovation" (25).

Confrontations and complex processes of bargaining and conciliation are at stake in the rise and development of this particular economic and technological enclave, which attracts and mobilizes a workforce seemingly at the pinnacle of the developments described by contemporary theories of cognitive capitalism and labor. It would be misleading, however, to position Zhongguancun as an absolute exception with regard to other enclaves, such as the special economic zones (SEZs) that have driven the economic development in China since the early 1980s. It is important to recall that Chinese SEZs are different from export processing zones in Asia and other parts of the world, being "more functionally diverse and covering much larger land areas" and having been designed since the beginning as "a complex of related economic activities and services rather than uni-functional entities" (Yue-man, Lee, and Kee 2009, 223). While export-oriented manufacture was definitely prominent since the establishment of the first SEZs in 1980, processes of multiplication of labor and intertwining of regimes of production that seem to pertain to different epochs in the history of capitalism are dramatically apparent here. This is the reality that emerges from Leslie Chang's book *Factory Girls* (2008), once it is read against the apologetic intentions of its author. Through her research among young female migrants in the city of Dongguan, located in central Guangdong Province, Chang documents how the lives of these workers are shaped not only by practices of territorial mobility but also by a continuous crossing of the boundaries between heterogeneous labor regimes (from sweatshop to factory, from formally independent labor in the consulting or financial sectors to the circuits of *shanzhai*, the imitation of brands and goods, particularly electronic). The deep heterogeneity of space and time characterizing contemporary China acquires new dimensions in the light of these phenomena.

The establishment of multiple internal boundaries has been a key element in the articulation of heterogeneous labor regimes in China. Since the establishment of the first SEZs in the Dengist period, there has been a multiplication of zones with special status, ranging from "free trade" to "development zones." A multilevel system of filters, connections, and disconnections is the result of this zoning activity. At stake has been an attempt to combine different paces of economic development, articulate heterogeneous regimes of governmentality, and manage the practices of mobility that traverse these overlapping and hierarchized spaces. These zones and the multiple border technologies associated with their establishment and management have also been reproduced in the course of China's projection of economic power outward, in Africa and elsewhere (Bräutigam and Tang 2011). In Pun's study of women factory workers in Shenzhen, we find a striking analysis of the ways the proliferation of internal borders operates to create the workforce on Shenzhen's production lines. Pun emphasizes the way in which the hukou system, with its differentiation between permanent, temporary, and "illegal" residents (subject to deportation until 2003), renders the condition of migrant workers structurally fragile. Combined with the requirement for factories to register and pay the Shenzhen Labor Bureau for the labor certification of their workers, this system "provides population and labor control that favors global and private capital" (2005, 5). Workers become dependent on the company for their legal presence in the SEZ and this, in turn, institutes further bordering practices at the moment of selection and hiring, such as controls for language ability, marital status, nimble fingers, as well as general attitudinal qualities (established through probing interview techniques) such as "politeness, honesty, and obedience" (53).

Pun shows how these factors produce the Shenzhen female working subject as a transient presence, usually laboring in this context for no more than four or five years. The fact that this window of time often coincides with "women's transitional life period between puberty and marriage" shows how the "individual life cycle" meshes "with social time, the transitional period of the socialist economy fusing with global capitalism" (Pun 2005, 32). In other words, the time of the state and the time of capital are coordinated with the time of patriarchal control of women's lives in rural China to produce the tight coordination and regulation of labor time in the factory. Indeed, these temporalizing dynamics are strikingly similar to what we discussed in chapter 5 as temporal borders, since they establish within both working and biological lives a time of suspension that is, in this case, also a time of hard labor. But, as Pun argues, the experience of working in these factories is for many women not just one of near incarceration but also one of escape. Her ethnographic interviews reveal that many women workers experience their passage to the Shenzhen zone as a means of fleeing domestic circumstances in which their opportunities were limited and lives subject to traditional forms of gendered oppression. From the point of view of many of these women migrant workers, the current transition in China is a deeply conflictual process. Pun goes as far as to speak of a "silent 'social revolution' in Chinese society that is challenging the existing rural-urban divide, reconfiguring the state-society relationships, restructuring the patriarchal family, and remaking class and gender relations in particular" (Pun 2005, 55). The processes of subjectivation at stake in these migratory and laboring experiences cannot fully be accounted for in terms of processes of proletariatization and alienation, or even of the "unfinished proletarianization" mentioned by Pun. Though they certainly involve a class dynamic, they also embody gendered, ethnicized, and spatialized relations that contribute to the making of class and likewise shape the conflictual practices that drive the current transition in China.

Since Pun undertook her research in Shenzhen, there have been many attempts to reform and to make the hukou system more flexible under pressure from migrant workers. Nevertheless, it "remains integral to China's socioeconomic and development strategy" (Chan 2010, 362). At the same time, the formation of a second generation of migrant workers—more educated, experienced, and ready to participate in various forms of collective action and struggle—has been a crucial element in the dynamics and composition of recent labor struggles in China (Pun and Lu 2010). As has often been noted, since the beginning of the 1990s migrant workers have been responsible for "marked increases in protests and strikes, or what the Chinese authorities vaguely refer to as 'spontaneous incidents'" (Lee 2007, 6). Nevertheless, the movement of strikes that started in May 2010 at the Honda plant in the southern Guangdong city of Foshan signaled a new quality of struggle or what the researchers of the *China Labor Bulletin* describe as "the galvanizing impact of the new generation of migrant workers" (*China Labor Bulletin* 2011, 5). It is too soon to assess the consequences of the workers' struggles in 2010, which took place against the background of the suicides of more than a dozen young workers at Foxconn factories in China. However, huge increases in wages and attempts to reform the labor contract and industrial relations system show that a shift in social and economic power to the advantage of workers has taken place. As has often been the case in history, this dramatic wave of strikes and labor struggles, which has been one of the most important on the world scale in the twenty-first century, was in many respects a wave of migrant struggles. At stake in these strikes were border struggles across and against the multiple boundaries that cut and crossed the composition of living labor in China and elsewhere.

Interestingly enough, the time of the 2010 labor unrest in China coincided with a visit we made as participants in the Transit Labor project to a Hong Kong–owned factory that manufactures printed circuit boards in the Songjiang Industrial Zone on Shanghai's southwest fringes. Located in an Export Processing Zone established in 1992 and subsequently rezoned several times, this is a production site for rigid flex, HDI-1 and HDI-2 printed circuit boards required by high-end communications equipment and consumer electronics. The factory is part of an assembly and production chain that extends across mainland China, Hong Kong, and Japan, and supplies OEMs (original equipment manufacturers) such as Pioneer, Ericsson, NEC, Fujitsu, Apple, Alcatel, Sanjo, Canon, Foxconn, and others for the production of mobile phones, personal digital assistants, notebook computers, and digital cameras. The workers we met on this occasion were bound by strict confidentiality agreements, but they were able to tell us that they were aware of the suicides at Foxconn and that they were a topic of conversation in their dormitories. Of interest to us was also the presentation offered by management before we entered the factory, which detailed adherence to industry and client-determined protocols for environmental practice, quality management, and labor standards. This is relevant to our earlier discussion of corporate codes, reorganized moralism, legal pluralism, and the mutations of sovereignty and governance that become visible in Asia's production zones. The certificates we were shown demonstrated adherence to a number of standards such as ISO 14001 for the promotion of "effective and efficient environmental management," ROHS (Restriction of Hazardous Substances Directive), and WEEE (Waste Electrical and Electronic Equipment Directive). Some of these were issued by organizations such as the Hong Kong Quality Assurance Agency or the Business Standards Institute. Others were awarded by the OEMs to which the factory supplies circuit boards. Among these, for instance, was the Sony Green Partner Certificate demonstrating compliance to ss-00259, a Sony Corporation Technical Standard pertaining to environment-related controlled substances.

Here we find a situated instance of the way corporate codes and standards, once introduced into the logistical operation of supply chains, become instrumental in the production of value. The moral and environmental vigilance attested by such certificates as well as the logos and other green branding devices that mark consumer products containing circuit boards manufactured in this factory mean that OEMs can demand a higher price for these commodities. What is interesting is how this creation of value occurs through a multiplicity of industry and individual regulation mechanisms, increasingly monitored by private agencies as well as sovereign entities more directly subject to political control. Standards such as ISO 14001, RoHS, and WEEE, whatever their rigor, are not enough. There must also be ss-00259, directly mandated and controlled by Sony, because this is a much more efficient mechanism for corporate branding and even for potential "green washing." In the factory space of the Songjiang Industrial Zone, there is a saturation of conflicting and overlapping norms. What interests us are the framing of these multiple regimes and the way their orchestration makes possible the productivity of capital. This has implications for labor conditions in the factory space. As Tsing astutely observes, "the diversity of supply chains cannot be fully disciplined from inside the chain" and "this makes supply chains unpredictable—and intriguing as frames for understanding capitalism." Under these circumstances, "the exclusions and hierarchies that discipline the workforce emerge as much from *outside* the chain as from internal governance standards" (Tsing 2009, 151). Thus, the presence of certificates tells us little about labor conditions in the factory. We cannot say for sure what the labor conditions are like in this site, although from what the management was keen to communicate to us, they certainly seemed more amenable than those documented by Pun and other witnesses to the dormitory labor system. We could only discern through observation and the subtle economy of gesture and eye contact the experiences of workers who were contractually gagged from telling us about their lives and pay packets. Precisely in such moments, we sense the traces of sovereign power among the multiple governance regimes of the SEZ.

Between Cognizant and Infinity

Standing between the Cognizant and Infinity buildings in Kolkata's Sector V information technology (IT) hub, one could be forgiven for imagining one was in Beijing's Zhongguancun or some other Chinese technology zone. The architectural styles of linear metal and glass with imposing angles, land-scaped gardens, and widened streets seem almost as if they were designed by the same Hong Kong–based firms. Only the street vendors splitting open coconuts and selling other Bengali staples betray the location of this technology park established on Kolkata's northeast fringe in the 1990s. Indeed, resistance to a "Chinese model" of development including land grabs and accelerated urban expansion has been a hallmark of recent peasant struggles in West Bengal (Roy 2011). One thinks particularly of the conflicts that unfolded at Singur and Nandigram in 2006–7 when peasant movements successfully blocked the West Bengal government's acquisition of village and agricultural lands for the "public purpose" of establishing an automobile factory in the first instance and an SEZ in the second. These struggles resounded loudly in Indian and West Bengali public life, igniting debates about primitive accumulation among Kolkata's intellectual class (Chatterjee 2008; Samaddar 2009; Sanyal 2007) and eventually contributing to the fall of the state's long-standing Left Front government in May 2011. Elsewhere on Kolkata's fringes, resistance to land acquisition and the Chinese model of development has not been so successful. The huge area of land known as Rajarhat or New Town, which sits to the city's northeast and borders on Sector V, is a barren monument to failed peasant movements. Dotted by empty housing estates, shopping malls, special IT zones, "service villages" inhabited by populations left without livelihoods, and vast stretches of arid land, Rajarhat has much to teach us about mobile styles of governing, trans-mutations of capital and labor, and the violent production of space that accompanies informational strategies of accumulation.

The proposition that the development of SEZs, new towns, and other urban experiments in India follows a Chinese model is largely a matter of impression and criticism. Despite the popular construct of "Chindia" that is used to indiscriminately lump these two countries together, there is little evidence of a direct or technocratic process of knowledge or policy transfer. Both nations have precedents for zoning exercises in their colonial histories, including the concessions and treaty ports that emerged in China following the Opium Wars of the nineteenth century and the presidency towns established on the subcontinent by the British East India Company. Though the Kandla Export Processing Zone established in Gujarat in 1965 is frequently mentioned as one of the world's first, the Chinese SEZs did not emerge until the late 1970s and early 1980s under the impulse of Deng's open door policy (Chen 1995). Nevertheless, the visit of Indian Commerce Minister Murasoli Maran to China in 2000 is a landmark event in the history of Indian SEZs.

Impressed by what he saw in China and by his discussions with officials there, Maran introduced a new export-import policy in April 2000. This provided the precedent for the controversial 2005 SEZ Act by converting India's existing Export Processing Zones into SEZs replete with social facilities such as schools, housing, hospitals, and retail developments. In reality, the zoning experiments pursued in India over the past decade differ from the Chinese model in a number of important respects, including the preponderance of private investment and public-private partnership initiatives as opposed to publicly driven development, the location of most SEZs close to existing industrialized and urban areas, and the relatively small size of Indian SEZs in comparison to their Chinese counterparts (Jenkins 2007). Nonetheless, the materialization of planners' impressions, circuits of architectural design, and the cultural and management styles carried by the presence of many of the same employers and corporations lend the development zones in India and China an uncanny resemblance. As Keller Easterling observes, rather than circulating in the "proper and forthright realm of political negotiations," these reverberations tend to result from "unofficial currents of market and cultural persuasion" (Easterling 2008, 297).

The SEZs that have multiplied their presence across the Indian subcontinent since the middle of the last decade join an array of other spaces that are fundamental to the reorganization of labor forces, labor processes, and the social relation of capital well beyond the national scale. These spaces include Export Processing Zones, Free Trade Zones, new towns, IT hubs, freight highways, and industrial corridors. Understanding how these spaces connect to and disconnect from each other is crucial for assessing the saturated normative arrangements that pertain in them, their significance for sovereign and governmental powers, the logistical operations that link them to each other as well as into wider global circuits, and the various forms of labor, exploitation, and dispossession they facilitate. Important factors in this regard are the competition between Indian states to attract direct foreign investments (Sharma 2009; Tripathy 2008), the role of development commissioners and other administrative bodies in the governance of these spaces, the use of the Land Acquisition Act of 1894 to acquire the land for such developments as a "public purpose" (Bhaduri 2007), the displacement of peasant and sharecropper communities (Chakrabarti and Dhar 2010), intergovernmental agreements that facilitate vast infrastructure implementations (for instance, between India and Japan in building the Delhi–Mumbai Industrial Corridor), the assignation of differential citizenship rights and their role in the precarization of the workforce (Dey 2010), and the significance of knowledge work and virtual migration in building up these spaces (Greenspan 2004; Remesh 2004). This is not the occasion to undertake a comprehensive survey of the postdevelopmental rescaling and respatialization of labor and production that has crossed the Indian subcontinent since the economic reforms of 1991 (Sen and Dasgupta 2009). Suffice it to say that there has been a persistence of unorganized and informal work (involving in many instances the incorporation of informal arrangements into the formal sector through casual contracts, etc.), a reinforcement of the sexual division of labor, and a swelling in the ranks of internal migrant workers, particularly those who subsist at the point where the frontiers of capital impinge on urban heartlands and fringes (Samaddar 2009). In spaces such as Rajarhat, where the development of the urban fringe has abandoned all industrial pretensions, these tendencies come together. We thus focus our attention on the experiences and knowledge we garnered in this site as part of the Transit Labour project.

As a new town established on Kolkata's fringes, Rajarhat is not technically an SEZ. Although it contains a number of SEZs established for the IT and IT-enabled services (ITES) sectors, it is rightly classified with the other new towns that have grown up along the edges of Indian metropolises: Navi Mumbai for Mumbai, Gurgaon for Delhi, and so on (Bhattacharya and Sanyal 2011). Initially conceived by the West Bengal government to relieve the city's housing problems, its development was charged to a new administrative body, the West Bengal Housing and Infrastructure Development Corporation, which was set up in the late 1990s and granted broad powers to acquire and sell land, install infrastructure, construct housing, supervise the building of commercial premises, and maintain the future city. Moving through Rajarhat today, one has the impression of Chinese development in slow motion. Stalled by the economic crisis of 2007/8, a distinguishing feature of the area is unfinished or uninhabited apartment blocks. These lack basic infrastructural supply such as electricity but nonetheless have become the object of real estate speculation, mostly on the part of nonresident Indians hoping to cash in on the area's future growth. One also encounters shopping malls, private schools and hospitals, bus terminals, and office buildings slated for occupation by IT and related service firms, such as Accenture, Wipro, Infosys, and Tata Consultancy Services.

Perhaps the most striking features of Rajarhat are the desolation of this once lush and biodiverse farming and fishing area, the destruction of water sources, and the barrenness of the land. Former peasants and sharecroppers have been forced to sell their land at supposed market prices, which were quickly exceeded by five- or sixfold in subsequent sales. Those who resisted usually met the force of riot squads or local goons. Now many of them have been gathered into so-called service villages, where their current state of dispossession is preemptively figured as cheap labor for the middle-class communities who are yet to inhabit the new town's residential towers. As we noted at the beginning of chapter 5, some of these former peasants have redeployed themselves by setting up tea shops and other makeshift stores to cater to the new workforces employed in the area. Others offer themselves for sundry labor tasks along the road every day or have turned to sex work or the various forms of thuggery that facilitate and accompany such urban development. Lacking the skills and know-how to participate in the construction of Rajarhat's buildings and infrastructure, a task largely performed by mobile workforces coming from elsewhere in West Bengal, these are populations for whom transition is an empty proposition. The roads back to peasant cultivation and forward to industrial work are blocked. Their biographies do not follow the classical script of primitive accumulation.

To traverse the heterogeneous spaces of Rajarhat, from the IT SEZ to the tea shop, the shopping mall to the service village, or the drenched rice paddy to the empty apartment block, is not only to cross the borders separating labor regimes but also to negotiate the contours of "postcolonial capitalism" (Samaddar 2012; Sanyal 2007). The fragmentation and splintering of this space, as well as the multiple and indefinite borders that separate it from Kolkata proper and join it on one side to the Sector V IT hub and on the other to the unkempt bazaar, eating place, and banking center called Baguihati, far exceeds what Ernst Bloch in a famous text of 1932 called the "synchronicity of the non-synchronous" (Bloch 1977). Caught in the vortex of globalized time, Rajarhat is a densely bordered space where the very narrative that separates past from present modes of production is shattered. Devoid of peasant cultivation and never imagined as a site of industrial manufacture, this is a space where times, temporalities, and temporal borders can neither be arranged along a progressive timeline nor flattened on to the dead time of co-presence. Who is to say that the service village and the empty high rise are nonsynchronous but made to exist side by side? How can we say that the ITES firm in the SEZ and the tea shop across the road from it exist in different stages of social and economic development when the workers in both are obliged to labor according to the rhythms of other time zones and thus inhabit lateral spaces that stretch way beyond Rajarhat and the subcontinent itself?

One way of tracking these patterns of stretching and global connection is to consult the literature produced by firms that set up in this environment. A pamphlet titled "Global Delivery: A Course to High-Performance in a Multi-Polar World," published by the technology, consulting, and outsourcing firm Accenture, describes the need "to access new engines of talent, and manage an around-the-world and interconnected workforce to achieve global delivery and ultimately reach high performance" (Haviland 2008, 2). This pamphlet's slick language of teamwork, interconnection, and multidirectionality is the smiling face of the corporate capital that touches ground in Rajarhat. In February 2011, Accenture opened a Delivery Centre in the Infospace development, an unfinished IT park with SEZ status in Rajarhat's Action Area III. Frequenting the tea shops that cling to the borders of this space and visiting nearby Baligari service village, one sees the materialization of the ideology embodied in this document. It is certainly necessary to analyze the kinds of work that occur in IT/ITES companies such as Infosys under the sign of cognitive capitalism. This means noting the positive spin that presents the "workplace as yet another campus" (Remesh 2004, 492), the attempts of trade unions and other labor groups to organize in these sectors (Stevens and Mosco 2010), the "liquification of labor" implied by "virtual migration" (Aneesh 2006, 9), as well as the precarious work conditions, sociocultural adjustment, and exploitation of the reserve of English-speaking graduates easily absorbed into this sector (Upadhyay and Vasavi 2008). Such an analysis, however, cannot ignore the devastation of surrounding communities and ecosystems affected by the very developments that enable such work processes. Consequently the economic and political category of cognitive capitalism, at least as elaborated in the global context of subcontinental labor struggles and transitions, makes no sense if it is not simultaneously articulated to an analysis of postcolonial capitalism, of its fragmented and overlapping spaces, heterogeneous labor regimes and laboring subjects, as well as of the political and cultural constitution of its precarious legitimation.

Without doubt, the prevalent means of analyzing the displacement of peasant and sharecropper communities affected by the new forms of informational and logistically driven capitalist developments in India makes recourse to the concept of "accumulation by dispossession" introduced by David Harvey (2005). Swapna Banerjee-Guha, for instance, approaches the establishment of SEZs in India as a "classic unfolding" of this process, involving "a mode of production based on the relation between labor and capital expressing a time-space compression" (Banerjee-Guha 2008, 52). Though Harvey uses the phrase "accumulation by dispossession" to indicate the continuation and proliferation of accumulation practices described as primitive or original by Marx, the debate on primitive accumulation has taken on particular twists and turns in the Indian context, where the developments in Rajarhat and similar economic spaces have taken center stage. Writing of primitive accumulation as what he calls the "immanent history of capital," Kalyan Sanyal conceptualizes "capitalist development as a process that in its own course produces pre-capital." At stake is a process of primitive accumulation that goes beyond the "narrative of transition" (Sanyal 2007, 39). Seeking to "inscribe the wasteland of the excluded into the narrative of capital's coming into being," Sanyal points to a scenario "in which direct producers are estranged from their means of production . . . but not all those who are dispossessed find a place in the system of capitalist production" (47, 52). Primitive accumulation does not necessarily oblige the peasant to become a wage laborer. Rather, what allows such accumulation to continue is what Sanyal terms its governmental reversal. Under the sign of development and the dominant discourse about the necessity of growth, there is a global consensus that basic conditions of life should be provided to people everywhere and that those dispossessed of their means of labor should not be left without subsistence. Thus, when national or local governments do not intervene, there are other states, international agencies, or NGOs that step in with governmental programs and measures that seek to meet the livelihood needs of the dispossessed, and, in so doing, enable the very continuation of primitive accumulation. As Sanyal puts it, "development can now claim the legitimacy of capital's existence only by addressing poverty and deprivation in terms of governmental technologies with the aim of ensuring subsistence to the dispossessed, to the inhabitants of the wasteland that surrounds the world of capital" (174).

In *Lineages of Political Society* (2011), Partha Chatterjee extends this argument by relating it to the transformed structures of political power in India, including changes in the framework of class dominance, the state's susceptibility to the political-moral sway of the middle classes, and the penetration of state and other governmental technologies into peasant communities. For Chatterjee, this enablement of primitive accumulation by its governmental reversal is a process played out in what he calls "political society," where peasants play an active role in agitating for their livelihood needs. In these negotiations, which often involve a "calculative, almost utilitarian use of violence," what peasants frequently invite "is for the state to declare their case an exception to the universally applicable rule." This makes "the governmental response to demands in political society . . . irreducibly political rather than merely administrative" (Chatterjee 2011, 229–

31). In a provocative way, Chatterjee's argument reverses the claims for neoliberalism as exception. While he associates the classical "imperial prerogative" of the Raj with "the power to declare the colonial exception" (250), referring to the techniques of "enlightened despotism" that characterized British rule, he understands the governmental maintenance of processes of primitive accumulation precisely as the negotiation of exceptions to normal administrative processes crisscrossed by both the politics of dispossession and the politics of "the governed" (Chatterjee 2004).

Chatterjee's argument gives rise to a vision that is close to ours insofar as it gives us an analytical approach to the normative arrangements that penetrate into economic zones. What remains underemphasized in this approach are the very spatial strategies employed in the ongoing processes of primitive accumulation and the conflictual and overlapping relations between normative regimes that not only crystallize in such zones but also *exceed them*. This means that the dispossession effected by these developments must always be analyzed in relation to the forms of exploitation they allow both within and beyond their borders, whether or not governmental initiatives that seek to assuage the effects of dispossession are effective. To put it in terms relevant to Rajarhat, peasant politics and the precarious state of IT/ITES workers must be understood with reference to each other. As Jamie Cross recognizes, the "most significant achievement of India's new economic zones . . . is to render visible and legitimize the conditions under which most economic activity in India already takes place" (2010, 370). By this he means that the absence of regulation and protection for workers in the wider informal economy is laid bare in the zone where it is rendered as deregulation and flexibility. Seen from this perspective, the continuing processes of accumulation by dispossession must be analyzed in relation to ongoing processes of accumulation by exploitation as well as the normative governmental arrangements that articulate these accumulation strategies and the processes of the production of subjectivity they entail. This is an analysis we undertake in the next section, where an emphasis on the bordering processes that connect zones and other anomalous economic spaces to wider national, regional, and global economies crosses the question of political subjectivity.

Borderzones

The spaces we have investigated in this chapter can be aptly defined as borderzones. Multiple and heterogeneous bordering technologies are at play in their establishment and existence. Geopolitical borders are a crucial lever for state powers that decide to excise portions of their sovereign territories to open them up to regional and global circuits of capital accumulation. Through this decision, sovereign power enters shifting assemblages of governmentality and becomes enmeshed in a plurality of normative orders whose boundaries have to be continuously policed. The coexistence of several labor regimes often shapes the productive landscape of contemporary special economic zones. There is an increasing diversification of these spaces, even though certain precedents and models continue to spread. For instance, the model of the *maquila*, the industrial export-oriented production zones that have dotted the U.S.–Mexico border since the negotiation of a bilateral agreement in 1965 (Peña 1980, 1997; Sklair 1994), continues to spread in Central American and Caribbean countries as well as to sites in Africa and Asia. While it is important to keep in mind that the spaces we have analyzed or mentioned are profoundly heterogeneous, they share a certain kind of normative saturation that makes them laboratories for the production and articulation of new norms. These spaces cannot be considered spaces of exception if we equate exception with a normative void. Nevertheless, they retain something exceptional if we consider them as sites where norms can be analyzed in the making and in their constant adjustment to changing circumstances, including their relations and conflicts with other norms. To recall Tsing's (2005) analysis of Kalimantan, a certain frontier spirit shapes life and labor in these sites, where the boundaries between legal and illegal, licit and illicit, are often blurred and the nested scales of local, national, regional, and global no longer hold tight.

The intersection of multiple spatial scales, the very geographical disruption that lies at the core of current global processes and transitions of capital, can be observed with a particular relief in these borderzones. This is especially the case as far as the emergence of new regions and regionalisms is concerned. Take the Great Mekong Subregion (GMS), recently investigated by geographers Dennis Arnold and John Pickles (2010). Since the Asian Development Bank launched the GMS Economic Cooperation Program in 1992, free trade and investment in the region along the Mekong River have been promoted to facilitate the area's economic growth. According to Arnold and Pickles, these patterns of trade and investment provide "a particularly clear illustration of the complex intertwining of supply chain dynamics and state practices." Though policies associated with the GMS program of the Asian Development Bank are established by international organizations and national authorities, they "are implemented by the local, national and trans-national regional organizations that manage the flow of labor and investment" (Arnold and Pickles 2010, 1604–5). New institutions of cross-border governance and development infrastructure emerge across the region, combining neoliberal rationality with authoritarian political styles. Importantly, borders are tested and reworked in this process of regional integration, which attempts to transform them from sites of potential conflict and war into strategic junctures for the convergence between regionalization and globalization. In the GMS, Arnold and Pickles write, such convergence "is articulated in localized spaces conducive to mobile capital and investment that, on the one hand, straddle and blur national boundaries, and on the other, redefine and reify borders, particularly in terms of flows of migrant labor" (1599).

What Arnold and Pickles observe here is a softening of the border as far as its geopolitical function and its role in the control of the flows of capital and commodities are concerned. To this there corresponds a new rigor in the control of labor mobility. The establishment of new SEZs near Thailand's borders provides an empirical setting from which an analysis of these transformations can be carried out. Focusing on the Mae Sot–Myawaddy zone near the Thai border with Burma (Myanmar), which has been an important textile and garment production center since the early 1990s, Arnold and Pickles show how a combination of practices of border reinforcement (due to geopolitical tensions between Thailand and Burma) and border crossing (due to well-established routes of illicit trade in gems, timber, and other natural resources) create the conditions for the exploitation of huge reserves of migrant workers on which the whole economy of Mae Sot relies. A multiplicity of boundaries surrounds the life and labor of these migrant workers from Burma, ranging from widespread racism to differentiated legal statuses, from prohibitions on the use of cell phones or motorbikes to restrictions on holding cultural events. A "partial border citizenship" emerges, which displaces the costs of reproducing the labor power of these migrant workers away from the state and employers. Along with this come low wages that make their conditions particularly fragile and precarious (Arnold and Pickles 2011, 1615). At stake in the highly monitored movement of these workers is a production of flexible subjectivity that is enmeshed in complex legal, cultural, and economic arrangements. Though Arnold and Pickles are keen to analyze the strong role of state policies in Mae Sot, as well as across all forms of regional integration in the GMS, they also provide an excellent case study of the multifarious ways an SEZ inserts itself into classical political maps and at the same time blurs and complicates them. The multiple boundaries at play in Mae Sot rework the meaning of the geopolitical border between

Thailand and Burma, stretching the territorial edge of the nation-state and opening it up to regional and global circuits of capital accumulation. At the same time, they trace new demarcations within the national territory. Different patterns of global connection can be observed in the coastal regions on the Thai-Malaysian border where the shrimp farming and sea food processing industries lead to the dispossession of villagers and environmental degradation (Horstmann 2007, 150–51) or in the metropolitan area of Bangkok, where finance, real estate, and other high-value sectors are concentrated. Multiple bordering technologies are at work in the articulation and policing of relationships between these heterogeneous patterns of global connection and related economic and labor regimes.

"For much of the twentieth century," writes James D. Sidaway, "development was conceptualized as a national project of becoming," which "rested on a broad homology of territory and economy." The spaces we analyze in this chapter are part and parcel of the emergence of new postdevelopmental geographies, within which "this coupling of nation and development has become less stable" (Sidaway 2007, 350). This process is visible in many parts of the world and takes a particularly grim shape in some African countries, where "the links between resource-extraction enclaves, chronic warfare, and predatory states" results in the "destruction of national economic spaces" and the "construction of 'global' ones" (Ferguson 2006, 13; see also Reno 1999). The multiplication of such bounded and enclaved spaces seems to be a more general characteristic of the emerging spatiality of globalization. As we have shown, this is also the case in countries such as India and China, where the nation undoubtedly remains an important symbolical and political reference. Sidaway observes how "sub- and transnational spaces, nodes and networks, marked by a variety of fractures and boundary practices" superimpose themselves on and rework the roles of "national narratives and schemes" (Sidaway 2007, 355). What is described by many scholars, most notably Ong, as a process of gradating sovereignty corresponds to the opening of states to processes of governance that transcend any national denomination—a trend we have tried to grasp in the previous chapter through the concept of the sovereign machine of governmentality. The multiplication, selective reworking, reinforcement, opening, and heterogenization of borders and boundaries are crucial features of these postdevelopmental geographies.

We agree with Sidaway that "graduated sovereignty is not therefore only about new boundaries *per se*, but is a complex and uneven experience of selective boundary crossings, subjectivities and exclusions" (Sidaway 2007, 352). What interests us is precisely the role played by borders in producing and shaping subjects as well as the ways practices of mobility crisscross the multiple border struggles that challenge the sovereign machine of governmentality and its entanglement with shifting regimes of exploitation. In the next chapter we focus on the implications of new assemblages of sovereignty and governmentality and of the multiplication and heterogenization of borders for the important political concept of citizenship. Migration and mobilities are crucial forces operating in these processes as well as in the emerging postdevelopmental geographies we have been analyzing here. Latin America offers some interesting illustrations of how such postdevelopmental geographies insert themselves into urban, national, and regional environments. This is true even though the term postdevelopment has taken on a different significance in the Latin American context, designating the search for a kind of normative alternative to the perceived failings of mainstream development discourses and practices. Arturo Escobar explains his use of the term as follows, "by postdevelopment, I mean the opening of a social space where these premises [the premises of mainstream development discourses and practices] can be challenged, as some social movements are doing" (Escobar 2010b, 20).

An interesting instance of a postdevelopmental geography in Latin America is La Salada, an informal market established in the early 1990s in Loma de Zamora, at the administrative border between Buenos Aires and its huge metropolitan *conurbano*. Considered the hugest informal market in Latin America (in 2009 its earnings were more than double the earnings of all the shopping centers of Buenos Aires), La Salada is a site in which heterogeneous spaces, corridors, networks, and flows meet. The Buenos Aires–based collectives RallyConurbano and Tu Parte Salada, mainly featuring architects and urban scholars, have proposed the concept of "logistical urbanism" to define the peculiar space of La Salada (D'Angiolillo et al. 2010). Operating at night, the market offers mainly textile products that are produced on a daily basis (but over the years the commodities for sale have greatly diversified, including household appliances and cell phones) for buyers coming not only from Buenos Aires and other Argentine cities but also from Peru, Chile, Uruguay, and Bolivia. The importance of this informal market in the establishment of transnational and regional routes for the circulation of commodities cannot be overestimated. It has been possible to trace connections not only with the informal markets of Los Altos in La Paz, Bolivia, but even with Nigeria and China (D'Angiolillo et al. 2010).

As Verónica Gago (2011) shows, the establishment and booming of La Salada have been possible due to the encounter between different forms of popular and subaltern resistance to the varieties of neoliberal capitalism that have arisen in Argentina through interaction with regional and global processes. The dramatic spread of informal exchange, trade, and barter in the wake of the crisis and uprisings of December 2001 created the conditions for the scale upgrading that allowed La Salada to become what it is today. A wide fabric of what Gago calls "proletarian micro-economies" supports the logistical operations of the market, which are particularly evident once one considers the role of Bolivian migrants in the establishment and maintenance of La Salada. The transnational spaces opened up since the mid-1980s by the migration of dispossessed peasants and mine workers from Bolivia have been spaces of resistance, social, and even economic self-organization in the face of the violent transformation and destruction of the material conditions for the reproduction of whole subaltern and proletarian communities. At the same time there is a need to note that processes of neoliberal restructuring in Bolivia led to a crisis of discourses and policies of modernization and developmentalism and to an attempt to combine in a new hybrid capitalist framework heterogeneous regimes of labor and accumulation. The social scientist and current vice president of Bolivia Álvaro García Linera speaks in this regard of a "baroque modernity," which "unifies in an echelon-like and hierarchized form productive structures of the 15th-, 18th-, and 20th-centuries" through the exploitation of domestic and communitarian forces (Linera 2008, 270). The emergence of a wide informal economy, often promoted through the spread of micro-credit, has been a key component of this emerging baroque modernity in Bolivia, crisscrossed by multiple encounters, clashes, and hybridizations between "proletarian micro-economies" and capital's accumulation.

It is important to keep these developments in mind when looking at La Salada. As Gago writes, in the case of Bolivian migration "there is also a 'communitarian capital' that migrates and reformulates itself. This 'communitarian capital' is characterized by a deep ambivalence: it can work as a resource for self-management, mobilization, and insubordination and *at the same time* as a resource for servitude, submission, and exploitation" (Gago 2011, 282). Exploring this ambivalence, Gago shows the connections between the "logistical urbanism" of La Salada and a series of bounded spaces that surround it and make the very existence of the regional networks and flows it articulates possible—from the slums in which many Bolivian migrants live to the clandestine sweatshops where the textiles and garments for sale there are produced. A peculiar form of indentured labor is prevalent in these productive sites, which are very often owned and run by Bolivians. The workers are directly recruited in Bolivia through radio announcements and "employment agencies" but above all through community and family networks. Contractors organize the travel, provide low-grade accommodation and food, and hold the passports of the workers, who are compelled to work for a certain period without wages (251–53). But the slums and the sweatshops are not only sites of confinement and exploitation; they are also sites of struggle. While the mainstream press often associates the use of "enslaved labor" with the falsification of brands at La Salada and with an ethnic and marginal economy, a radically different picture emerges in the words and actions of Bolivian migrants and workers' associations that challenge the passivity and unilateral subordination implied by this label. The textile industry in Argentina, which was dismantled during the Menem era through the import facilitated by the parity between the peso and the U.S. dollar, reorganized itself around outsourcing to clandestine sweatshops that often produced commodities with both "false" and "authentic" labels. Far from being marginal and ethnically specific, the economy of La Salada has become a mirror of the transformations and multiplication of labor in Argentina beyond the predominance of wage labor. The enmeshment of capital in dense, complex, and ambivalent proletarian microeconomies, which originated in the neoliberal age in Bolivia, has loomed in the mirror of the "post-neoliberal" Argentina of recent years.

The borderzones we explore in this chapter are all specific sites in which multiple boundaries and scales intersect to foster a new expansion of what we call the frontiers of capital. This expansion is structurally linked with the resurfacing of many processes and forms of so-called primitive accumulation. Capital continues to open new spaces and circuits of accumulation disrupting social and natural "environments," to recall a term used by Rosa Luxemburg (2003, 348), which have often already been shaped by capital in preceding moments of its history. What distinguishes these current processes from the classical primitive accumulation analyzed by Marx is precisely the fact that what is at stake today is not so much a transition from a noncapitalist to a capitalist mode of production but, as we saw in the baroque modernity of the Bolivian case, a reworking of different epochs of capital on the variegated scales of its contemporary operations. Land and the extraction of natural resources are still very much at stake in current manifestations of primitive accumulation. But today's "enclosures" also crisscross knowledge and life, operate in dismantling welfare systems, and take abstract shape in the working of financial devices such as subprime mortgages (Sassen 2010). The multiple boundaries that circumscribe and cross the zones and other anomalous spaces analyzed in this chapter are profoundly enmeshed in these processes. From the point of view of border as method, we have approached them as crystallizations of the tensions, conflicts, and struggles that invest the emerging articulations of the frontiers of capital and territorial borders. In this way, we have attempted to provide material illustrations of the workings of what we call the sovereign machine of governmentality. Although there is a widespread tendency in the literature concerning the contemporary forms of primitive accumulation to treat dispossession and exploitation as counterposed practices (Harvey 2003), the boundaries we investigate tend to work as devices to articulate these two terms or moments of capital's operations. In the experiences, practices, and struggles of mobile subjects living and working in and across zones, corridors, and other postdevelopmental geographies, such articulation becomes visible.

—— Chapter Eight ——

PRODUCING SUBJECTS

Stakhanov and Us

Whatever happened to the concept of exploitation? There was a time in the not too distant past when labor politics drew its strength and energy from the reality of exploitation in the workplace. It was the age of the industrial worker in which the search for the "hidden abode of production" veiled by markets and contracts promised to unleash a revolutionary class struggle. Maybe it was the collapse of actually existing socialism in 1989, or perhaps it was the continuation of so-called primitive accumulation into the present, but this politics and this search seem to have experienced steady diminishing over the past decades. Unless immunized with the prefix *self-* and embedded in an analysis that emphasizes the worker's complicity in the production of surplus value, the word *exploitation* appears naive or at least to hark back to an earlier period of capitalist development. This is not simply the result of neoliberal orthodoxy. The drift away from a political analysis of capitalism grounded in relations of exploitation is a tendency that marks even some of the most radical analyses of the global present. As long ago as the early 1990s, Stuart Hall (1992) noted the propensity of cultural studies to focus more on power than on exploitation. Without a doubt, Michel Foucault's emphasis on the positive and productive nature of power was an important influence here. But a shift away from an analytics of exploitation is also a feature of many Marxian approaches to contemporary globalization. We have mentioned more than once David Harvey's conviction that "accumulation by dispossession" has "moved to the fore as the primary contradiction within the imperialist organization of capitalist accumulation" (Harvey 2003, 172). It cannot be denied that "primitive accumulation" is a key element of current capitalist expansion, whether it pertains to the dispossession of peasants, the enclosure of genetic materials, the expropriation of natural resources, the monetization of exchange or taxation, or the use of the credit system to discipline entire populations. Though Harvey points to a qualitative shift spurred by capital's inability to reproduce the conditions that fueled the postwar boom, he is careful to indicate that the accumulation of capital continues to accompany accumulation by dispossession. Nonetheless the question remains: what has become of exploitation?

It is our conviction that an important analytical and political key for understanding the present operations of capital lies in critically examining the articulation between practices of dispossession and practices of exploitation. Tracking how these different processes of accumulation join, disconnect, work together, and work off each other is a vital part of border as method. This is a task that cannot be fully accomplished in the frame of an analysis that limits itself to national or regional economies. The crucial role played by the globalization of financial markets, which command contemporary accumulation strategies, is not the only reason for this. Equally important is the part of migration and various forms of internal and temporal bordering in shattering the assumption that, while financial markets are global, labor markets are inherently national in their workings and extent. The continual interplay of space and scale in cutting, dividing, and multiplying labor markets within and beyond putatively national bounds is a critical factor to observe in tracking how capital works the edges between different accumulation strategies. In the previous chapter, we examined how the existence of different kinds of pockets, enclaves, and corridors above and below the national scale brings these relations to the fore. The techniques of sovereignty and governance applied in establishing and administrating special economic zones, for instance, enables not only dispossession but also the control of surplus labor. In this chapter, we emphasize the implications of these developments for the subjects of labor, asking how they position workers as political and legal subjects, citizens, and persons. This prompts a consideration of different kinds of border struggles and the relevance of the politics of translation within them. To begin, however, it is necessary to show how capital's pursuit of accumulation across the borders of dispossession and exploitation has disarticulated the position and status of the citizen from that of the worker.

Karl Marx provocatively describes primitive accumulation as a "secret" (Marx 1977, 873). But he makes no secret of the fact that capital deploys dual methods of squeezing absolute and relative surplus value from labor. Classically the former has been associated with extensive methods of accumulation, which is to say with the expansion of the spatial and temporal dimensions of production. The latter has been associated with the intensification of production methods, for instance, through techniques of scientific management that seek to increase productivity and efficiency. A thinker like Harvey recognizes that "it is the particular manner in which absolute and relative strategies combine and feed off each other that counts" (Harvey 1989, 186–87). There is also a need to understand the particular ways the accumulation of capital joins and works off the processes of primitive accumulation. We tend to agree with Anibal Quijano when he writes that "any relation of production (as any other entity or unity) is in itself a heterogeneous structure, especially capital, since all the stages and historic forms of the production of value and the appropriation of surplus value are simultaneously active and work together in a complex network for transferring value and surplus value" (Quijano 2008, 201–2). Once this is recognized the question of the historical predominance of one form of accumulation over the others becomes less relevant than detailed examination of their heterogeneous combination in different temporal and spatial contexts.

Returning to the question of exploitation, we need to pay attention to the production of both absolute and relative surplus value as well as their articulation to primitive accumulation. This means recognizing that some of the elements identified by Harvey as accumulation by dispossession, including financialization and privatization, extend beyond the processes Marx described as primitive accumulation and can potentially be considered as part of accumulation by exploitation. Again, the mix is important because it establishes the complex and always contextual joining of different strategies of accumulation in "the production of value and appropriation of surplus value." It is limiting to constrict an analysis of primitive accumulation to the processes described by Marx in the last section of *Capital*, volume 1, for the case of the Industrial Revolution in England. Indeed, Marx states that the "history of expropriation, in different countries, assumes different aspects, and runs through its various phases in different orders of succession, and at different periods" (1977, 876). Similarly, as we have emphasized in our engagements with global labor history, the workings of exploitation cannot be assumed to converge on a homogeneous industrial worker. This makes it difficult to draw a firm conceptual border between dispossession and exploitation or even assume that primitive accumulation results in the emergence of an urbanized workforce bound to the wage relation. Harvey rightly questions "the idea that the politics of primitive accumulation and by extension accumulation by dispossession belong to the prehistory of capitalism." Giving the example of the tested relations between the Landless Workers' Movement and urban-based Workers' Party in Brazil, he sees the barriers to an alliance between "struggles against accumulation by dispossession" and "more traditional proletarian movements" arising mostly from the rigid organizational structures of the latter (Harvey 2010, 313). Once we recognize the extension of exploitation beyond the wage relation, the possibilities for political alliances that join struggles against dispossession with struggles against labor exploitation become greater, even as they face the more complex task of negotiating multiple and shifting lines of connection and association.

One of the most entrenched barriers to the formation of such political alliances is the embeddedness of labor relations, wage systems, and the institutions that govern them in the national frame. We have already questioned the adequacy of such institutions to address the turbulent, hierarchized, and differentially bordered operations of contemporary labor markets. We have also critically interrogated the concept of the international division of labor that implies the worldwide extension and interrelation of such nationalized systems for labor organization, arbitration, and regulation. Now we need to add that the very form of these institutions, whether nationally based like industrial arbitration commissions and most trade unions or international in scope like the International Labor Organization, tends to prevent meaningful cooperation with movements struggling against the growing stakes of dispossession in the contemporary world. Movements that address issues of accumulation by dispossession tend to either be extremely locally oriented in their battles or acquire a decentralized, transnational, and networked form. The most successful are able to work across these scales. Though nothing inherently prevents them from operating at the state level or even through state institutions, they frequently face the reality that states are key players in facilitating the practices of dispossession they struggle against.

Consider the role of governments in India, which have been involved in a kind of race to the bottom in acquiring agricultural lands from peasants and making them available to industry and commerce (Sharma 2009). Or think about the difficulties of movements that address issues of labor, migration, and borders finding voice in state institutions or ones that operate in the shadow of the state and tend to assume the equivalence of the citizen and the worker. The traditional indifference of trade unions to the struggles of migrant, noncitizen, or irregular workers is only one instance of this. As Janice Fine (2007) shows, such ingrained attitudes are shifting. This is the result of innovative organizing strategies on the part of labor movements that manage to address issues of dispossession and exploitation faced by migrants and mobilize workers in ways unachievable by traditional trade unions (Alzaga 2011). It is also the effect of a more general disarticulation of the figure of the citizen-worker. Indeed, this very figure tends to stitch the subject into the national frame. This is the case even though the figures of the citizen and the worker can have separate elaborations that cross many scales. Across the twentieth century, however, the figure of the citizen-worker, alongside the related figure of the citizen-soldier (Cowen 2008), is what threatened to monopolize the field of subjectivity in all three of the state forms that assumed historical prominence after the defeat of fascism in World War II: the democratic welfare state, the socialist state, and the developmental state. To tell the story of the disarticulation of the citizen-worker is to explore from the point of view of subjectivity the transitions and transformations of these three different versions of the state. First it is necessary to identify the contradictions, conflicts, and borders that always crossed this figure. We do this through a brief consideration of the Soviet Stakhanovite worker of the 1930s and the twentieth-century U.S. industrial worker.

The emergence of the citizen-worker was a long and variegated process with its roots in nineteenth-century nationalism, industrialization, and workers' struggles. One thinks of the Stakhanov moment in the Soviet Union; the heyday of U.S. industrial towns such as Flint, Michigan; the disciplined working subject of India's Nehru plans; or the *operário padrão* celebrated by the Getúlio Vargas government in 1950s Brazil. This is not the occasion to investigate the historical complexities surrounding these specific intersections of labor and citizenship. But a short investigation of the Soviet and U.S. instances throws light on the paradoxes and tensions that invest the figure of the citizen-worker and eventually led to its undoing.

Susan Buck-Morss observes of the Stakhanovite worker of the 1930s Soviet Union that the "physical suffering that hollows out the individual for the sake of the collective is the ecstasy of the Soviet sublime" (Buck-Morss 2000, 182). Alexey Stakhanov was a miner who in 1935 performed the record-breaking feat of hewing 102 tons of coal in less than six hours and was promoted by Joseph Stalin as a model worker whose efforts should be replicated across other branches of the economy. Eventually half the Soviet workforce, women as well as men, became Stakhanovites, with individuals such as tractor driver Pascha Angelina or champion beet grower Maria Demchenko emerging as "ordinary celebrities" who entered a "magical Potemkin realm" (Fitzpatrick 1994, 274). But this was clearly a highly constructed sphere of national heroism. In his book *Magnetic Mountain*, Stephen Kotkin observes that workers "could scarcely fail to see that Stakhanovism resembled a sweating campaign, placing inordinate strain on managers and creating much friction between managers and workers, as well as between foremen and workers —with often questionable results in production" (Kotkin 1995, 213). It didn't take long before Stakhanovites were denouncing managers. They also had their machines sabotaged in factories by other workers and became the butt of jokes. In offering the fetish of individual performance as a sign of political solidarity and citizenly duty, Stakhanovism undermined patterns of industrial cooperation in a situation of growing interdependence between producers and production processes. As Lewis H. Siegelbaum shows, this particular intersection of labor and citizenship was unsustainable, and "police terror largely replaced Stakhanovism as a device for bringing pressure on industrial cadres" (Siegelbaum 1990, 247).

In *Citizen Worker* (1993), the U.S. historian David Montgomery traces the rise in the nineteenth century of a society based on wage labor and the ways it was enabled and constrained by the voting rights and freedom of association enjoyed by working men as well as the dismantling of the personal bonds of subordination associated with slavery and retracing the "color line" in new forms after Emancipation. He concludes that the citizenly struggles of workers challenged but never defeated a new form of class rule disguised by freely contracted market and familial relationships that were sanctioned by courts, military and police forces, and the criminalization of unemployment. Evelyn Nakano Glenn also shows how in the United States "the concepts of liberal citizenship and free labor developed and evolved in tandem." She emphasizes how labor and citizenship emerged as "intertwined institutional areas in which race and gender relations, meanings, and identities" were "constituted and contested" (Glenn 2004, 1). Following Glenn's lead, we can identify how the figure of the U.S. citizen-worker was crossed by race and gender divides in ways that eventually placed stress on the political and legal categories that held it together. In a context like Flint, Michigan, the General Motors company town, the intense class conflict that culminated in the Depression-era strike of 1936–37 became muted by post–World War II consumer culture (Fine 1969). The unevenness that continued to invest the articulation of labor to citizenship in the United States became evident in other sites of the company's operations.

The *De Graffenreid v. General Motors* case of 1977, in which the court rejected the claim of five black women that the company's seniority system discriminated against them, is a famous instance here. As Kimberlé Crenshaw explains, the court's refusal to acknowledge "combined race and sex discrimination" rested on the assumption "that the boundaries of sex and race discrimination doctrine are defined respectively by white women's and black men's experiences" (Crenshaw 2011, 28). This internal differentiation of workers' statuses within the sphere of citizenship needs to be read against the strategies employed by General Motors during the period of deindustrialization of Flint and other towns that became part of the so-called Rust Belt in the 1980s, when many manufacturing jobs were shifted to the *maquilas* of Mexico (Dandaneau 1996). Here the field of labor crosses multiple citizenships as well as spaces and scales. The differential inclusion that gradates the space of national citizenship is stretched to a kind of breaking point, and the disarticulation of citizens from workers is begun.

What Frances Fox Piven and Richard A. Cloward call *The Breaking of the American Social Compact* (1997) replicates itself in many national contexts around the world. In this case, as in many others like it, we can recognize the partial undoing of the dyadic schema of the citizen-worker, which received its most formal conceptualization in the work of the British sociologist T. H. Marshall soon after World War II. Marshall (1950) conceived the social rights of citizenship to be intimately connected to the national labor market. "Today all workers are citizens," he wrote in 1945, "and we have come to expect that all citizens should be workers" (Marshall 1964, 233). Marshall saw social rights, distinct from civil and political rights, as a material qualification of what he called the "universal status of citizenship." In the postwar Britain of which he primarily wrote, he saw such a status as offering a bundle of obligations and entitlements that protected individuals from the vagaries of the capitalist marketplace, specifically through the mechanisms of the welfare state. Marshall is often criticized for viewing citizenship as a means of mitigating rather than overcoming the social inequalities of class and for underestimating the role of racial and sexual divisions within national societies (Barbalet 1988; Crowley 1998). He is also held to task for fashioning a sacrificial approach to work as a social duty and obligation of citizenship, a perspective that underwent deep questioning and, indeed, attracted the refusal of an entire generation in 1968 (Mezzadra 2002). What concerns us more is the problem of Marshall bypassing the question of noncitizens as well as his inattention to the borders of citizenship and the multifarious processes of differential inclusion that regulate them. To be sure, these are issues that have come to the fore with what Bryan Turner (2001) calls the "erosion" of Marshallian citizenship, which has accompanied the globalization of capital and deeply influenced patterns of work, war, and familial relation. What we want to emphasize is the disarticulation of the figure of the citizen-worker that provides the very unit on which Marshall builds his influential theory.

It is not that this connection between the citizen and the worker has been fully ruptured now. There is still undeniably a nexus of citizenship and labor, whether manifest in paths to citizenship that pass coercively through the labor contract, regular forms of collective bargaining practiced through nationally organized trade union systems, or the newer forms of Anglo-Saxon "mutual obligation" that mandate third-way schemes, such as "work for the dole." What has changed is that this citizenship-labor nexus can no longer be fully captured by the dyadic subject citizen-worker and the sexual division of labor that sustained its reproduction. Both citizen and worker have been invested by diffuse processes of division and multiplication. This is evident in the presence across many political spaces of migrant workers who are not citizens (and may not desire to be citizens). It is also manifest in the augmented possibilities through points schemes and the race for talent for many subjects to become citizens of certain countries through capital investment as well as fulfilling other requisite controls (e.g., health, education, labor skills, absence of criminal record). More generally, the relation between labor and citizenship in advanced capitalist societies has ceased to produce the materiality of what Marshall called the "status of citizenship," which was meant to balance the principle of contract in shaping social relationships. In the context of the postdevelopmental spaces and states we discussed in the previous chapter, (wage) labor has ceased to provide the key that allows the access to full citizenship. Consequently, the subjective positions of both citizens and workers must be rethought outside the dyadic structure of citizen-worker, which can no longer be taken for granted and underlies the construct of the national labor market. Though we have previously analyzed these processes from the perspective of the production of space and the multiplication of labor, it is also important to consider their relevance for *the production of subjectivity*. As we will see in the remainder of this chapter, this is a task that takes us well beyond the debates concerning citizen and stranger, into a realm where we have to consider some of the most radical contemporary approaches to the subjective dimensions of politics, law, and labor. It is a journey in which we encounter different, quite fragmented, and even irreconcilable figures of the political subject, the legal persona, and the worker. The question is whether it makes any sense to try to put these figures together again.

The Subject of Politics

The dyadic figure of the citizen-worker has long monopolized the political imagination, especially within the Left. The analysis we have pursued in this book can be read as a contribution to the description of the explosion of the relation between labor and citizenship epitomized by this dyadic figure. A triple crisis—of the democratic welfare state, the socialist state, and the developmental state—opens the political history of globalization. At stake in each moment of this crisis is precisely the disruption of the citizen-worker as the bearer of political development and constitutional arrangements. This does not mean that labor has ceased to colonize human action and experience. Rather, social life and cooperation are subdued to the imperative and rationality of labor as never before. The concept of multiplication of labor that we elaborated in chapter 3 attempts to grasp this process, which has made labor "*the* common substance" of society (Hardt and Negri 1994, 10). At the same time, this concept provides a critical angle on the steady marginalization of labor from the center of political and constitutional processes. Multiplication also means heterogenization. It entails the production of diverse subject positions and boundaries that crisscross the composition of living labor and insert themselves within shifting assemblages of knowledge and power.

Precisely at the point when labor threatens to colonize the whole of life and become the common substance of human activity, its representation has become a riddle for social scientists as well as for trade unions and political parties. As neoliberalism has reworked the social nexus between individuals in ways that are often described using concepts such as human capital, debt, and risk, citizenship itself has undergone profound transformations. Migration is a crucial site of investigation from this point of view. The concept of differential inclusion attempts to come to grips with the undoing of the unitary figure of the citizen and the corresponding production of multiple conditions of "partial citizenship" or denizenship (Hammar 1990; Standing 2011, 93–102). The blurring of the boundary between inclusion and exclusion that we register in our discussion of this concept points to a displacement of the code of social integration. Concurrently, the post-developmental geographies we explored in the previous chapter provide an effective angle for analyzing the emerging articulations of the frontiers of capital and territorial borders as well as a means of assessing the repositioning of the nation, the historical terrain, and the political form long inhabited by the citizen-worker.

The search for new figures of political subjectivity has been a fundamental topic in critical debates of the past two decades. For us, writing of subjectivity means writing in the spirit of Marx, who always attempted to combine an analysis of the "specific process of the constitution of the subjectivity in the age of capital, and therefore the specific technologies or practices shaping this process of constitution" with an exploration of "the theme of the liberation of subjectivity, in other words the theme of revolutionary subjectivity" (Samaddar 2010, xxviii). This implies, as we can say adapting and elaborating on Foucauldian terms, that for us subjectivity is a battleground, where multiple devices of subjection are confronted with practices of subjectivation. Constituted by power relations such as those that operate in processes of dispossession and exploitation, the subject is always constitutive or characterized by a moment of excess that can never be fully expropriated. To locate our investigation within this battleground means to take into account the material determinations of the emergence of political subjectivity. It also means to take seriously the two senses of the genitive in the phrase "production of subjectivity." Once it is located at the foundations of the capitalist mode of production, Jason Read writes, the production of subjectivity describes "the constitution of subjectivity, of a particular subjective comportment and in turn the productive power of subjectivity, its capacity to produce wealth" (Read 2003, 102).

In our eyes, the concept of the multitude (Hardt and Negri 2000, 2004; Virno 2003) nicely captures these two sides of the production of subjectivity under capitalism. Thinkers who use this concept have tried to develop an analysis of the changing composition of the working class, drawing on the *operaista* tradition. An important aspect of its elaboration concerns the way it has been excavated from the philosophical and political controversies surrounding the rise of the modern state in the seventeenth century, involving such authors as Thomas Hobbes and Baruch Spinoza (see Negri 1991). Posited against the concept of the people, which prevailed in those controversies and later became a key word for the definition of the political subjectivity of individuals in the ages of revolution and constitutionalism, the multitude pointed to a radically different articulation between singularities and the common. The transition from the industrial working class to the multitude therefore opens a scene within which what Paolo Virno (2003, 22) calls the "mode of being of the many" becomes the eminent ground on which power and exploitation redefine themselves. At the same time, it challenges us to invent new forms of struggle and political organization, beyond the influence exerted by the form of the state (and its shadow, the people) over the experience of labor movements. We keep these important points in mind. At the same time, several years after its original formulation, there is a need to test the concept of the multitude in the context of the wide critical discussion it has initiated. In many ways this debate has run parallel to the one on "immaterial labor," which we mentioned in chapter 4. Our own concepts of the multiplication of labor and the proliferation of borders contribute to further interrogate the idea of the unity of the multitude, pointing to the multifarious lines of division and potential conflict that crisscross the composition of contemporary living labor.

What we find important about the concept of the multitude is the way it materially roots politics in the field of forces constituted by the double meaning of the genitive in the phrase "production of subjectivity" that we mentioned. This contrasts the tendency in discussions of neoliberalism to posit "politics" as simply the positive other of neoliberalism, often ending up with an identification of politics and an idealized image of the welfare state. One of the reasons for this widespread inflection of critical thought, as Wendy Brown notes in an influential essay, is the fact that neoliberalism tends to be considered as "little more than a revival of classical liberal political economy" and is reduced to "a bundle of economic policies with inadvertent political and social consequences" (Brown 2005, 38). Following Foucault, Brown rightly emphasizes that the *neo-* in *neoliberalism* points to a "constructivist project" (40), which attempts to reorganize the social around the paradigm of *homo economicus*. This means that neoliberal policies blur the boundary between the economic, private, and political spheres that classical liberalism considered insurmountable. The autonomy of the political and its identification with the state appear radically challenged under these conditions. What we are confronted with is a displacement of politics, which needs to be reflected in critical theory. On one hand, neoliberal rationality and governmentality permeate bodies and souls of subjects in an absolutely material, physical way, to which multiple practices of subjectivation correspond. On the other hand, the financialization of capitalism has crystallized moments of political command outside of the structures of the state and its constitutional arrangements. These two dimensions, the materiality of politics and financialization, must figure prominently in any discussion of political subjectivity. This does not mean that the state is not an important element in contemporary political assemblages. It clearly plays multiple roles in the articulation of such assemblages, but it has been displaced from the center of politics. With this, the autonomy of politics (or of "the political") has been radically destabilized.

From this point of view, some of the most astute positions in debates on political subjectivity appear problematic, including the ones Slavoj Žižek has critically branded with the label "pure politics" (Žižek 2006, 55–56; see also Žižek 1999, 171–244). We do not think that Žižek's trenchant criticism of an important book like Jacques Rancière's *Dis-Agreement* (1998), which has been among other things a source of inspiration for scholars and activists engaged with migration, provides grounds for a total dismissal of this work. As is well known, *Dis-Agreement* provides a fascinating reading of Western political philosophy as a succession of attempts to neutralize the destabilizing and subversive discovery of the "ultimate equality on which any social order rests" (Rancière 1998, 16). Oversimplifying Rancière's elaborate and sophisticated argument, we can say that this neutralization gives rise to heterogeneous regimes of "police," which are all predicated on a specific distributive architecture—on an administrative "ac/count of the parts." Politics, as opposed to police and the consensus surrounding it, is for the author of *Dis-Agreement* the result of the subjectivation of the part with "no part" in a specific regime of "police," which reactivates "the contingency of equality, neither arithmetical nor geometric, of any speaking beings whatsoever" (28). Keeping in mind Rancière's striking analysis of the transformations produced in the position of migrants by the crisis of Fordism, a topic we also discussed in chapter 5, it is easy to see that "illegal" migrants are among the most obvious candidates to play the role of the part with no part. Indeed, it is difficult to resist the temptation to read *Dis-Agreement* through the lens of the *sans papiers* movement of 1996, which occurred one year after the original publication of the book in French.

Along with Étienne Balibar's notion of *égaliberté* (Balibar 2010), Rancière's reading of politics at the point of intersection between equality and the insurgence of a partial subject (the part of those who have no part) has been very influential, nurturing interesting attempts to rethink the concept of the universal (Butler, Laclau, and Žižek 2000). What we find problematic in Rancière's work is, on one hand, that the partial subject of politics seems to be deduced in a negative way from the concept of police, and on the other hand that politics only exists in the temporality of the "event," of the "singularity of a political moment" that "interrupts the temporality of consensus" (Rancière 2009, 7–9). Although this emphasis on rupture is definitely important and fascinating, there is a need to further investigate the materiality of the practices and struggles that produce the conditions for the emergence of the political subject and for its constituent action. This is a problem we find even more pronounced in the recent attempt by Alain Badiou to rethink the "communist idea" as the "potential force of the becoming-Subject of individuals" at the intersection between his theories of the event and truth (Badiou 2010, 242).

If we turn our attention instead to Ernesto Laclau (2005), who has built his political theory and attempts to grasp the "heterogeneity of the social" on such notions as the "empty" and "floating signifier," we are confronted with an inverse problem. Consistently with the theory he elaborated with Chantal Mouffe in *Hegemony and Socialist Strategy*, the moment of "artic-ulation" is what gives "character" to social struggles that, "whether those of workers or other political subjects, left to themselves, have a partial charac-ter" (Laclau and Mouffe 2001, 169). Laclau and Mouffe's critique of tradi-tional Marxism refuses the idea of the existence of a unique privileged position for thinking and practicing the transformation of society (meaning the position of the working class and the contradiction between capital and labor). This risks leading to a kind of transmutation by which the privileged position that has been traditionally occupied by the state (and the party) becomes a theory of the primacy and autonomy of the moment of articula-tion. Implicit in this position are a defense of the "old rights of sovereignty" and a commitment to "democratic rights of self-government" that can only be imagined within the institutional framework of the modern state (Mouffe 2005, 101). The emphasis on what Laclau calls "constitutive antagonism," or the "radical frontier" fracturing social space (Laclau 2005, 85), inscribes politics within a horizon dominated by the production of unity (of the people)—"the political act par excellence" (154). The ghost of the state looms behind Laclau's people.

Considering Rancière and Laclau together, one has the impression that both the insurgence of the part of those who have no part and the performa-tive production of a "chain of equivalence" between heterogeneous social demands inscribe themselves within an institutional framework that is never really questioned. One of the problems with Rancière's understanding of the relation between politics and police is, indeed, that it is difficult to imagine the result of the rupture "through which egalitarian logic comes and divides the police community from itself" (Rancière 1998, 137) as some-thing different from yet another regime of police. The point is even clearer when it comes to Laclau, who equates politics with a moment of articulation of or equivalence between heterogeneous social struggles and demands. As we show in the next chapter, this argument relies on a transcendental perspective that is at once posited and withdrawn, replicating the position of the state in the mainstream of modern political philosophy from Hobbes to Hegel. The problem we have with such important theoretical contributions is that they seem to disavow the deep transformations that the institutional framework of the state is undergoing in the present. These involve the insertion of the state in global assemblages that tend to exceed it as well as more micropolitical contestations that have led to what Foucault calls the governmentalization of the state. Our analysis sheds light on some of these transformations, following the thread of a multiplicity of subjective figures whose movements, struggles, and conditions are symptomatic of the vacillation of boundaries of the institutional form we have inherited from the modern state. One of the ways political philosophy has registered such transformations is through an intensified concern with the exclusionary function of the border and with the legitimacy of the division between members of a polity and foreigners (Cole 2000; Hashmi and Miller 2001; Mezzadra and Neilson 2012).

Citizenship studies, in particular, have contributed in a crucial way to challenging the clear-cut distinction between citizens and noncitizens and have highlighted the agency of strangers, outsiders, and aliens as a crucial force driving the development of citizenship (Isin 2002). From a historical and a theoretical point of view, the attempt has been made to work through the ambiguity of the concept of citizenship, which increasingly appears not as a "unitary or monolithic whole" but as a "divided concept" (Bosniak 2006, 3). The tension between citizenship as legal status and a multiplicity of practices of citizenship has been increasingly recognized as constitutive of the concept (see, for instance, Honig 2001, 104). Parallel to the process of violent disarticulation of the figure of the citizen-worker, which means first of all the diminution of social rights, citizenship has been reshaped and flexibilized (to recall Aihwa Ong's analysis). A multiplicity of statuses tends to explode its unitary profile, making the citizen an elusive character. "Who is the citizen?" becomes an increasingly problematic question for contemporary theories of citizenship (Isin and Turner 2008, 8). Under these conditions, Saskia Sassen argues, a full understanding of the tensions and conflicts that mark contemporary citizenship can emerge only from an analysis that works from the edges of the space of citizenship, not from one that operates from the legal plenitude of its center. That political subject who is "unauthorized yet recognized" (Sassen 2006, 294) or, in other words, the "illegal" migrant, is not only subject to exclusion but also becomes a key actor in reshaping, contesting, and redefining the borders of citizenship. An emphasis on the fact that such a subject *acts* as a citizen independently of his or her legal status has characterized theoretical elaborations of "acts of citizenship," as well as of the activist dimension of citizenship expressed in "insurgent citizenship" (Balibar 2010) or the "right to *claim* rights" (Isin 2008, 2009).

An important aspect of the contribution made by citizenship studies to the debate on political subjectivity is that they allow us to move beyond a binary understanding of politics in terms of a simple opposition between inclusion and exclusion. Defined as a field of tension and conflict, the concept of citizenship provides an angle both on the proliferation of hierarchies and internal boundaries within the space of a polity and on the political struggles of subjects along and across those hierarchies and boundaries. This is why the concept of citizenship must always be broached in relation to the question of borders. What remains problematic in many contemporary approaches to citizenship is the assumption of a dialectical relation between practices and statuses, which throughout the span of citizenship studies have been understood to provide the two sides of the political figure of the citizen. It seems paradoxical that while citizenship studies tend to trace disconnections and drifts between practices and statuses of citizenship, for instance, in the claims of noncitizens (Isin 2009; McNevin 2006, 2011), it is precisely this moment of disconnection that seems to provide the impetus to reinstate the citizen as the political subject par excellence. Moreover, what needs to be remarked is the inability of many practices identified as *practices of citizenship* to secure or hold in place any kind of *citizenship status*. It is useful in this perspective to take as a point of reference the interpretive framework of modern politics proposed in a memorable essay by Balibar, which in many ways has influenced discussions of citizenship. In that essay, "'Rights of Man' and 'Rights of the Citizen,'" Balibar contends that modern politics appears structurally divided by a permanent oscillation between an "insurrectional politics" and a "constitutional politics" (Balibar 1994, 51). The problem of the mediation between these two constitutive sides of modern politics was historically solved in many ways, among them constitutional arrangements that aimed at making class struggle productive within the "contentious democracy" epitomized by the welfare state, or what Balibar (2003b, 125–34) calls the "national (and) social state." The very possibility of such a mediation seems to be vanishing nowadays.

Labor/Power

Many times in this book we have evoked the name Balibar with regard to borders, "racism without race," the ideological tensions marking universalism, the "internally excluded" inhabitants of the French *banlieues*, and Foucault's struggle with Marx. But Balibar's works are also a key reference in the debates on citizenship and subjectivity. In a series of essays written across the past two decades, he shows how the shadow of subjection, the original meaning of the Latin word *subjectus* as a synonym of *subditus*, has never faded in the adventures of the modern "sovereign subject." Even citizenship, historically and conceptually constructed in opposition to the vertical relation of domination that produces the subject as subditus, is constantly and structurally troubled by the "return" of subjection (Balibar 2011, 5–7). This is not just because sovereignty retains the characteristic of an autonomous and transcendent power in the face of the individual members of the community of the citizens who have theoretically instituted it. The very shape of the citizen, Balibar shows, is the result of multifarious processes of bordering that are played out on an "anthropological" terrain. These processes produce the figure of the "normal" citizen, excavating it from a human that is constantly divided and selectively interpreted according to criteria such as class, gender, race, security, or foreignness (465–515). In this perspective, citizenship appears as a "difference machine" (Isin 2002). To track how it produces new stratifications and hierarchies, there is a need to analyze how this machine intertwines anthropological with territorial boundaries. For instance, complex assemblages of gender and race are at work to produce the subject position of the migrant care workers we discussed in chapter 4, whose foreignness is often translated into a precarious or irregular legal status. Concerns of security mingle with racial fantasies in public debates on "illegal" migration, while certain groups of migrants are more accepted than others (and therefore in a position to better negotiate their partial citizenship) due to considerations of language, nationality, or religion. Not only the status of subjects but also the spaces of action available to them as activist citizens are deeply influenced by these factors.

To deepen our critical analysis of citizenship as a difference machine and its related production of subjectivity, it is necessary to articulate it with a reinterpretation of Marx's critique of political economy. As Balibar suggests, the "correlation between *sovereignty* and *subjection* lying at the heart of the modern social relation that seemingly marks the triumph of free individuality" indicates the need for a radical theoretical displacement (Balibar 2011, 315). Marx deploys a whole set of political concepts elaborated by modern theorists of the social contract in his analysis of market exchange relations. If one reads the section on "The fetishism of the commodity" in *Capital*, volume 1, from the point of view of the production of subjectivity, the problem at stake appears to be the formation of a power capable of representing the social nexus between individuals and the social characteristics of their labor. The double character of the commodity as both a natural thing and a social object replicates the split between heaven and earth analyzed by the young Marx in *The Jewish Question* as constitutive of modern politics and the modern citizen. It also insinuates this split into the daily exchanges that make up the fabric of capitalist society. Not by accident are theological references so important in both texts. To find an analogy for "the fantastic form of a relation between things" assumed by "the definite social relation between men" through the dominance of the commodity form, Marx writes in *Capital*, "we must take flight into the misty realm of religion" (Marx 1977, 165). A double process of representation is at work in the commodity form and in the exchange relations underlying the specific form of sociability corresponding to it. On one hand, each commodity represents, in its "phantom-like objectivity," a "congealed quantity of homogeneous human labor" abstracted from any concrete determination. On the other hand, "as crystals of this social substance, which is common to them all" (128), commodities need their value to be represented to make the exchange relation among them possible. Working on a striking phrase Marx employed in his analysis of the origin of money as the "universal equivalent," "the social action of all other commodities" (180), Balibar shows that we are confronted with a reworking of the script of the social contract elaborated by modern political philosophy. Money emerges as a universal and representative power from a process of mutual recognition between individual commodities. It becomes the sovereign of a commercial society whose unity is made possible by its very existence (Balibar 2011, 330–31).

Speaking of the social action of commodities is less extravagant than it may appear from the point of view of the Marxian theory of subjectivity. Rather, it is perfectly consistent with his analysis of the commodity form and its phantom-like objectivity. The problem arising from this analysis is precisely the need to investigate the subjective figures that inhabit this objectivity. "Commodities," writes Marx at the beginning of the second chapter of *Capital*, volume 1, "cannot themselves go to the market and perform exchanges in their own right. We must, therefore, have recourse to their guardians, who are the possessors of commodities." To describe these guardians and inaugurate the analysis of their relationships, Marx introduces the term *persons*. This word is not employed here in a generic sense. Rather, it refers to a "juridical relation, whose form is the contract," through which the "guardians" of commodities "recognize each other as owners of private property." The phantomlike objectivity of the commodity form penetrates the legal form, shaping the subjective figures produced by law. Here, Marx writes, "the persons exist for one another merely as representatives and hence owners, of commodities." It is worth quoting at length the conclusion of this dense paragraph: "as we proceed to develop our investigation, we shall find, in general, that the characters who appear on the economic stage are merely personifications of economic relations [*daß die ökonomischen Charaktermasken der Personen nur die Personifikationen der ökonomischen Verhältnisse sind*]; it is as bearers [*Träger*] of these economic relations that they come into contact with each other" (Marx 1977, 178–79).

The word *Charaktermaske* employed by Marx is particularly telling here (see Haug 1995). The reference to the "mask," which is lost in the English translation, strengthens the theatrical reference and allows us to better understand Marx's use of the phrase *dramatis personae* with regard to the owner of money and the possessor of labor power. Hobbes also stressed the relation between the mask and the concept of person in chapter 16 of *Leviathan* ("Of Persons, Authors, and Things Personated"; 1981) and transformed this relation into the cornerstone of his theory of representation. Later, Marcel Mauss investigated it from an anthropological point of view (Mauss 1985). The use of the word *Charactermaske* in the passage just quoted must be understood within this context. The concept of person is here used in its technical meaning as a legal construction that at the same time makes possible and circumscribes the liberty of subjects. Concurrently, behind this legal construction looms the powerful determination of the "economic relations" that shape the commodity form of the objects whose guardians these same subjects pretend to be. The autonomy of these relations from the will of individuals allows Marx to speak of *Charaktermasken* and at the same time of a social action of commodities. As Evgeny Pashukanis showed in the 1920s in his remarkable work on law and Marxism, "if objects dominate man economically because, as commodities, they embody a social relation which is not subordinate to man, then man rules over things legally, because, in his capacity as possessor and proprietor, he is simply the personification of the abstract, impersonal, legal subject, the product of social relations" (Pashukanis 2002, 113). This double bind, which stitches the commodity form and law, finds its subjective expression in the abstract figure of the person, which importantly applies both to individuals and to corporations. It further evolves in the production of a double sovereign representative, the state and money, whose relations are both constitutive and problematic, as we have demonstrated earlier in the book with the discussion of territorial borders and frontiers of capital.

Considering the concept of the person as the epitome of this double bind provides a way of critically assessing contemporary discussions of citizenship and human rights. We do not mean to abandon and dismiss these concepts. What interests us is the production of the frame and discourse of citizenship and human rights. This allows an investigation of the differential positioning of subjects within that frame, which is often missed by analyses that work from the concept of personality without critically analyzing its implications. The multiplication of borders in the contemporary world, fracturing both the unitary figure of the citizen and the human in human rights, is a crucial factor in this regard. It is worth recalling the perspective of Roberto Esposito, who has undertaken a biopolitical critique of the discourse of human rights through an investigation of the theological and juridical genealogy of the concept of person that figures prominently in it. Esposito analyzes the multifarious ways in which "the dispositif of the person appears to be an artificial screen that separates human beings from their rights," demonstrating the problematic nature (Esposito claims the impossibility) of "something like 'human rights'" (Esposito 2012, 83). Taking the approach suggested by Marx's analysis of the commodity form allows us to materially ground the investigation of the production of subjectivity that plays itself out behind the mask of the person and at the same time sustains that mask.

In the world of commodities, there are for Marx two hyperbolic manifestations of the commodity form. One is money, the universal equivalent that as a sovereign regulates exchanges, representing and measuring the exchange value of each individual commodity. The other one is labor power, the commodity "whose use-value possesses the peculiar property of being a source of value" (Marx 1977, 270). Money and labor power can be defined as hyperbolic commodities because they partake in the world of the commodities only insofar as they occupy an excessive position within it, making its very existence possible. It is not by accident that they are at the same time, as we discussed in chapter 1, the two poles of the divided production of subjectivity that takes place behind the mask of legal personality and the related exchange relations that shape the world of commodities. Another important meaning of the concept of the person comes to the fore here—

the one implied by John Locke's theory of the "property in his own person" as the distinguishing feature of "every man" (Locke 1988, 287). We have already argued that Marx at once accepts this theory and displaces it, showing that owning one's own person has a radically different meaning for subjects who relate to themselves and the world through the mediation of social power crystallized in money and for subjects who are instead compelled to rely on their potentiality, that is, on labor power. To this we have added in chapter 4 that there is a need to question the Marxian image of the "bearer" of labor power as constructed on the concept of the legal person, as the free owner of his or her labor power enabled to sell it through a free contract.

As Stephen Best shows in his remarkable *The Fugitive's Properties* (2004), it is not easy to trace a firm boundary between the free wage laborer and the slave by claiming that the former owns his or her person and the second does not. Working on legal controversies and political debates surrounding fugitive slave laws in the United States in the mid-nineteenth century, he demonstrates that a distinction between the person of the slave, which was not to be considered property, and his or her labor, which was, gradually emerged. It is precisely such heterogeneous domains as slave law and intellectual property, "as two spheres eccentric to the law of real property and emphatic about property's extension into the fleeting and evanescent," that according to Best helped "redefine the very essence of property in nineteenth-century America" (2004, 16). This legal work on the body of the slave and its duplication through the use of a concept of the person that is both "fleeting and evanescent" can be considered one of the primary precedents for the more flexible forms of personality that are emerging with current capitalist developments. Lisa Adkins argues that "the relations between property and people are being restructured" and, more particularly, "qualities previously associated with people are being disentangled, are the object of processes of qualification and re-qualification" (Adkins 2005, 112). Such a reorganization of property and personhood involves not only a retreat of the significance of the labor contract but also a "reworking of the relations between persons and the ownership of labour" (119). This occurs through forms of authorship and performance that are increasingly measured through "socio-technical devices such as the customer audit, customer benchmarking, customer surveys, customer focus groups and job descriptions and job training schemes" (122). If, as Adkins suggests, this spells "the end of property in the person," it is important to reaffirm that the production of labor power as a commodity continues to exercise a social action that sustains the processes of subjection and subjectivation that drive capitalist production.

It should not be forgotten in the foregoing discussion of the relation between the commodity form and the legal concept of the person that labor power itself is a commodity. To realize this is to open a field of investigation and analysis that provides a window on the production of subjectivity that is significantly different from, if also related to, the one provided by the framework of citizenship and state. Behind the mask of the legal person, there is a mix of variegated and historically differentiated circumstances that compel embodied subjects to commodify their labor power. This differentiation, however, occurs across a common material background. As we discussed in chapter 1, the specificity of labor power as a commodity is inseparable from the living body of its bearer. This remains true across a wide range of situations in which labor power is put to work under capital's command—from the classical contractual arrangements Marx described to the coercion of slavery, from the manifold intermediate forms between free and forced labor to the hired and casual labor that occupies many contemporary workplaces. Dispossession and exploitation are always at play in such situations, although in different combinations. Importantly, the former always haunts the latter as a trace of the specific production of subjectivity that is needed to control the supply of labor power as a commodity. This is why the figure of the worker, understood in this expanded sense, can never be equated with that of the citizen. At the same time, this figure cannot be reduced to the legal person, both because juridical modes of regulating labor are coexistent with other forms of labor control (one recalls the "tanning" mentioned by Marx in *Capital*, volume 1, at the end of the chapter "The Sale and Purchase of Labor Power") and because many labor relations escape standard regulation through the contract. The borders between the juridical and the nonjuridical here are as important as the borders between jurisdictions. Equally they are as important as the territorial borders that are related to but increasingly disjointed from such jurisdictional demarcations.

The irreducibility of the subject that bears labor power to the legal person on one hand and to the citizen on the other is due not just to the powers that swirl around the labor relation. It is also an effect of the excess that characterizes this specific production of subjectivity and which means that the bearer of labor power can never be fully identified with the commodified form of that same labor power. As we already argued, there is a need to approach labor power as precisely a form of power that exceeds, and in a certain sense precedes, processes of discipline and control, dispossession and exploitation. Many names have been given to this excessive moment, which as we mentioned earlier in our discussion of class cannot be mapped as an effect of mere social stratification. What we can add now is that this excess always exists in relation to and in tension with the figures of subjectivity that are its correlates in the legal and political realms. From here derives the difficulty of translating the bodily woes and joys of the worker into the abstract languages of law and political theory. Perhaps because of this difficulty, we have seen many different attempts to invent the new legal or political subject: from the resuscitation of the citizen to the resignification of the people, from the "part that has no part" to the new cosmopolitan subject. What matters is not so much whether any one of these concepts is more enabling or more empirically grounded than the others. Rather, we need to understand the historical circumstances that give rise precisely to such a proliferation of different approaches to the subject. Approaching this as a problem of translation gives us an entry point for interrogating the thorny problem of the unity of such a subject at the same time as it raises another important issue that so far we have not sufficiently discussed: the problem of political organization.

Border Struggles

"You just fucked with the wrong Mexican," declares Machete, the ex-narc *cum* vengeful border hero played by Danny Trejo in the eponymous film directed by Robert Rodriguez (2010). Machete strips bare the hard-line Texas senator who sets him up and runs an antimigration campaign. He also runs amok among this senator's minutemen allies, utterly eliminating them in an old-style shootout featuring a motorcycle mounted with a bazooka. The exaggerated comic book style of this movie stretches masculine antics to the point of irony and registers in an inverse way the excess that characterizes the migration control regime in the southern borderlands of the United States. Walls, vigilantes, satellite surveillance, and border police are all part of this assemblage, while state migration laws have subjected migrant workers to ever harder forms of exploitation from Arizona to Alabama. Significantly, it is a female voice that rallies the troops prior to Machete's decimation of his foes. "We didn't cross the border, the border crossed us," shouts Sartana, the ex–border cop who sides with Machete, in a clear reference to one of the slogans that was prominent in the Latino struggles that swept the United States in 2006. We return to this slogan later; for now we want to note that border struggles and the production of subjectivity they entail exist in excess of the law and the many forms of regulation and legitimacy that crystallize at the border. If in *Machete* this excess takes the form of a pronounced irony, in many actual border struggles it assumes consequential, even tragic forms that work the line between life and death that is always at stake in such conflicts.

Previously we argued that relations of subjection and subjectivation compose the subject as a battlefield. In the case of border struggles, the conflicts and tensions that cross this battlefield have effects that go well beyond the specific conditions that apply at the location of the border. Indeed, border struggles are not simply, or not only, fought at the border. They have consequences and resonances that extend into and even manifest themselves at the very center of formally unified political spaces. The proliferation and heterogenization of borders we have discussed in this book are met by a multiplication of border struggles. Whether we are dealing with urban divides, internal borders, or even cognitive borders, there is a conflictive moment to the social relations that span the two sides of every border. Take the movements and struggles in Paris's *banlieues*, the Chinese labor strikes of 2010, or the ongoing actions since 2006 by the Association Malienne des Expulsés in Bamako against the deportation of migrants from northern African countries to Mali on the basis of EU readmission treaties. In all of these cases, the role of borders and boundaries in the production of subjectivity is highlighted and contested. National borders and the border struggles that surround them are undoubtedly important, but the struggles that unfold around these other demarcations are no less intense. Whether they center on border crossing, border reinforcement, or the intersection between the two, such struggles intervene in the field of tension that comprises the border, often highlighting its permeability but also displaying its tendency to congeal and solidify in ways that attempt to close off possibilities and paths of negotiation. Struggle, in this sense, refers not only to organized movements and political actions but also to social practices and behaviors that can be fundamental preconditions for such movements and actions but are often assigned to the realm of the prepolitical. As Nestor Rodríguez passionately argues in an article titled "The Battle for the Border" (1996), the mundane "self-activity" of migrants often assumes the characteristics of a struggle that allows them to resist and negotiate the ways in which borders mark and constrain their lives.

Migrants and refugees are often the protagonists of border struggles that tend to be interpreted in the frame of human rights, citizenship, or racism. But something more is always at stake in these conflicts. As we showed earlier in the book, migration and border control play constitutive roles in the formation and regulation of labor markets. We agree with Angela Mitropoulos (2006) when she writes that "jurisdictions, currencies and the hierarchical links between them are manifest in *every* pay packet." Every struggle played out along a border intervenes in the complex assemblages that sustain labor markets and the related production of subjectivity. The commodity of labor power circulates in a space that is neither a global domain without borders nor a purely national demesne. In this increasingly heterogeneous space, which is crossed by the frontiers of capital in ways that articulate with a multiplicity of boundaries, border struggles must be analytically located and politically interrogated. If we look at the relation between capital and labor from the perspective provided by the production of subjectivity, it should be clear that such an investigation cannot be limited to the point of production. It must rather follow the very processes that bring labor and labor forces into being—processes that often involve and have implications for people who do not work. As we have emphasized many times before, these processes work the boundaries established by gender and race in absolutely nonsecondary ways. The intertwining of such boundaries with the borders under consideration here is a crucial factor in producing hierarchies and fragmentation within the composition of living labor. Any attempt to rethink and translate the multiplicity constitutive of living labor into terms that can yield a unified political subject must therefore pay due attention to border struggles.

Obviously, border struggles assume many different shapes and forms. We have already mentioned urban conflicts, labor strikes involving internal migrants, and contestations surrounding processes of deportation. To be certain, not all border struggles involve issues of migration, and not all question the right of states to control their borders and territories or to exclude and deport migrants. Nonetheless, questions of migration tend to come to the fore in these struggles. A great many actors involved in border struggles, including academics, the media, nongovernmental organizations, trade unions, and lay individuals (both citizens and noncitizens), maintain a state-centered view of migration, often uncritically adopting policy-related labels such as "guest worker," "illegal migrant," or "refugee" as if they were analytical categories (Scheel 2011). There is, however, a variety of border struggles, prominent among activist networks and their allies, that call for the abolition of borders, pointing precisely to their role in sustaining nation-states and the globalization of capital. Under the loose label of No Border, which served for many years as the name of a diffuse network of European border activists, these struggles have provided some of the most radical and inspiring instances of political action around and on borders with implications extending far beyond migrant issues. From the organization of border camps at strategic sites of migration control to campaigns against agencies involved in migration management, from direct actions aimed at detention centers to attempts to build "underground railroads" for the safe passage of subjects in transit, these initiatives have crossed our political experiences and in many ways informed our approach to borders. In an article that attempts to take stock of No Border politics, Bridget Anderson, Nandita Sharma, and Cynthia Wright (2009) develop a number of analytical propositions that are close to our own. These authors approach borders as molds that attempt "to create certain types of subjects and subjectivities." Recognizing the temporal operations of borders and their extension across and beyond as well as around national domains, they show how border controls can force people "to live in an eternal present" in ways that intensify "their working time and effort." They thus view borders as "productive and generative" in ways that push border activism beyond humanitarian stances or perspectives based on citizenship rights. Moreover, they see such border politics "as part of a broader, reinvigorated struggle for the commons" (6–12).

These theoretical propositions presented by Anderson, Sharma, and Wright are ones that we share. However, when it comes to the practical elaboration of No Border politics, there often emerge other factors that can draw attention away from these carefully developed points. No Border struggles sometimes approach the border as an object to be eliminated rather than as a bundle of social relations that involve the active subjectivity of border crossers as much as the interdictory efforts of border police and other control agencies. This can give rise to a certain fixation on power and domination that paradoxically risks reinforcing the spectacle of the border. At the same time, the genuine commitment of many No Border activists to a radical understanding of human rights and the normative illegitimacy of the border is also an element that distances their approach from the one we elaborate in this book (Hayter 2004). There is the danger that No Border emerges as a kind of political logo that threatens to detach border activism from a wider political program by promoting primarily symbolic actions. Without doubt, there is a need to produce such actions in a social context that tends ever more toward symbolization and spectacularization. But in our opinion, the construction of the common must involve something more than the desire to eliminate borders. Though we take up the complex issue of the relations between the common and borders in the next chapter, we note for now that we do not share the usual criticisms of No Border politics: that it is utopian or threatens to erode democratic privileges that have been hard won in many states around the world. Nonetheless, we take sympathetic distance from the argument of Anderson, Sharma, and Wright that No Border is a practical political project in its own right, since we see a strong need for its articulation to other political struggles —those surrounding intellectual property, for instance, or the extraction of rent through the labors of cognitive capitalism. Insofar as we see a proliferation of borders in the contemporary world, we judge their political elimination as unlikely. But we are not realists in the usual sense of the word. Our focus is on the intensity of struggles surrounding the proliferation of borders, within which the refusal to abide the dictates of the border is an everyday occurrence. We valorize No Border for the political spaces it has opened while we note that the radical activity surrounding its networks has now mutated into projects that tend to attract different labels. It is precisely what many critics of No Border regard as utopian or romantic that we understand to be its most valuable aspect, since the elimination of borders realistically corresponds to the desires and practices underlying a multitude of border struggles. The problem is how to stitch such refusals and practices of desire into a wider program for the construction of the common.

Although we have expressed reservations about some of the more normatively inflected versions of No Border politics, we do not propose that normative arrangements have no relevance for the approach of border as method. As we mentioned, political philosophy itself has been increasingly compelled to come to terms with the politicization of the issues surrounding borders and the fluctuation of their legitimacy. In his book *Philosophies of Exclusion*, Philip Cole has proposed a detailed criticism of the series of "asymmetrical arguments" (that is, arguments based on a radical asymmetry between the position of members and foreigners, of insiders and outsiders) developed by the liberal theory of justice to overcome its unease before the exclusionary function of the border (Cole 2000, 53–55). One way to explain this embarrassment of liberal theory is to recall the intertwining of territorial borders and anthropological boundaries that, following Balibar, we earlier identified as constitutive for the figures of the citizen and legal person as well as for their articulation with money and labor power. Only by understanding how the border is productive of subjectivity, rather than acting as a mere limit on already-formed subjects, can we critically understand its capacity to act as a brake on justice as well as a conduit of injustice. This means we can begin to analyze how the border materially shapes the actual and always far from ideal passage of justice precisely because of its exclusionary function, rather than despite it. To the extent that the machinery of the border imposes limits on justice at the same time it enables the administration of justice, it operates as much as a means of inclusion, which always involves the production of multiple subject positions, as a device of exclusion.

One way to map out different varieties of border struggles is to situate them not only with respect to the heterogeneity and vacillating nature of borders but also in relation to the threshold that separates procedural justice from claims and desires that are often expressed in the language of justice (Mezzadra and Neilson 2012). The identification of such a threshold to justice has been a feature of many vibrant discussions of this important philosophical, political, and legal concept. One has only to think of the influential essay by Jacques Derrida, "Force of the Law" (1989–90), which stresses the structural excess that invests the concept of justice with respect to every historically given regime of justice or law enforcement. Clearly the relation between borders and this threshold of justice can take different forms. For instance, many kinds of migration politics and border activism assume both the border and the limits of procedural justice as stable, if not entirely coincident, lines. This is particularly the case in campaigns that appeal to an authentic and just idea of national community as the sole or primary basis for contesting decisions about exclusion and other forms of border control. In instances where one of these limits is conceived as mobile and the other as stable, there is a great variability of political horizons. These cases include campaigns that operate primarily around the discourses and legal instances of human rights to denounce the effects of new kinds of mobile border regimes. They also encompass political stances that understand current migratory movements as the reciprocal effects of the colonial adventure, denouncing the implication of actually existing justice-giving systems but reproducing the stable divide between metropolis and colonies (for instance, under the sign of the slogan "We are here because you were there").

Far more interesting and challenging are those border struggles that view both borders and the threshold immanent to justice as mobile, permeable, and discontinuous. Although it is difficult to identify such struggles in a pure form, we see in the interplay of these complex mobilities and arrangements the most hopeful possibility for forging a border politics that is adequate to contemporary processes of differential inclusion and the multiplication of labor. If we think of the slogan we already mentioned in our discussion of the film *Machete*—"We did not cross the border, the border crossed us"—there is an implicit connection between the claim for the mobility of the border and the question of which jurisdiction or legal process might be adequate to any claim for justice. That this slogan has a possible nationalist reading (referring to the U.S.–Mexican War and the Treaty of Guadalupe Hidalgo of 1848) does not detract from the more radical force of this interpretation. We see similar dynamics in migrant struggles that have unfolded in many different borderscapes: from the *sans papiers* movements in France and several other European countries (Suárez-Navaz 2007) to the Justice for Janitors and Justice for Cleaners movements that sprung up in southern California and reached different locations in the United States and Western Europe (Alzaga 2011) to the struggles of Indian "student-migrant-workers" in Australia (Neilson 2009) and the involvement of "illegal" migrants in labor strikes in France and Italy (Barron et al. 2011; Mometti and Ricciardi 2011). In all of these struggles and many more like them, the capacities and attitudes embodied in labor power are complexly crossed with the production of subjectivity at work in the bordering of the figures of the citizen and the legal personality. It is not a matter of the intensities involved in these struggles attempting to fuse these figures into a single body, whether individual or collective. Rather, the very force that at once separates and holds together these diversely bordered figures brings them into a relation that cannot be grasped from the theoretical perspective of articulation. To understand these relations as well as the political potentialities inherent in them, it is necessary to turn to the question of translation, a concept we elaborate on in the next section, stressing its material dimensions beyond any linguistic or even cultural reductionism.

The Labor of Translation

"In 1921 Ilich, in dealing with organizational questions, wrote and said (more or less) thus: we have not known how to 'translate' our language into the European languages" (Gramsci 1995, 306). Referring to Vladimir Ilich Lenin as Ilich, a practice adopted by Antonio Gramsci in his *Prison Notebooks* to evade fascist surveillance, this passage marks the importance of translation for issues of political organization. Apart from being a communist leader and intellectual, Gramsci was a trained linguist, and many of his most important political concepts, such as hegemony, bear the traces of this training (Ives 2004; Lo Piparo 1979). Issues of translation and "translatability," between "natural," national, and "scientific and philosophical" languages, figure prominently in the *Prison Notebooks* (Boothman 2004). The reference to Lenin opens a section titled "Translation of Scientific and Philosophical Languages" in Gramsci's most philosophical notebook (Notebook Eleven), written in late 1932. The political concept of translation evoked by his memory of Lenin's speech becomes the key to a sophisticated engagement with the constitution of theoretical concepts and their pretense to have universal validity. Gramsci writes: "Every truth, even if it is universal, and even if it can be expressed by a mathematical formula of an abstract kind (for the tribe of the theoreticians), owes its effectiveness to its being expressed in the language appropriate to specific concrete situations. If it cannot be expressed in such specific terms, it is a Byzantine and scholastic abstraction, good only for phrase-mongers to toy with" (Gramsci 1971, 201).

This moment of clash between concepts and the materiality of specific concrete situations requires translation and a theory of translatability that goes way beyond a merely linguistic approach to this problem. For Gramsci, translation is above all a social praxis, involving a kind of labor that works through linguistic borders but is never exhausted by this task. It demands an awareness of the interplay between economic, cultural, and political forces underlying the production of meaning in any given society and not just in the moment of contact between two languages. Translation, in its political transposition, is not an organizational technique dictated by leaders but a material practice forged from below within struggles. Particularly in border struggles, as we shall see, it provides an organizational lattice through which all other political practices tend to pass. Far from restricting itself to the linguistic-cultural domain, it is a grounding principle that links struggles to concrete situations even as they work or draw inspiration from past or distant political experiences.

To speak of the labor of translation is not merely to evoke a capacity for intercultural dialogue but to draw attention to material, political, and legal conditions that bring us back to a series of problems that we have already mentioned. "All Contract is mutuall translation, or change of Right," writes Hobbes in *Leviathan* (1981, 194). This recalls the sense of the Latin term *translatio*, which refers not only to a "transfer of meaning" but also a "transfer of property" (Best 2004, 124). While Hobbes reminds us of the legal and political implications of translation, it is also necessary to stress the more economic connotations of the concept. In a striking passage of the *Grundrisse*, Marx draws an implicit parallel between translation and the role performed by money in making possible the circulation and universal exchange of commodities. He refers to "ideas which have first to be translated out of their mother tongue into a foreign language in order to circulate, in order to become exchangeable." The "foreignness of language" furnishes, for Marx, an analogy with prices, which enable the buying and selling of commodities by separating out their "social character" from their materiality (Marx 1973, 163). The web of translations that surrounds the commodity form (turning concrete into abstract labor, abstract labor into exchange value, and exchange value into price) presents a series of transformations for Marx. These successive translations are also at stake in the production of subjectivity that relates to the commodity form and the sovereignty of money. Keeping the materially dense implications of translation in mind allows us to observe and analyze its operations as a social practice in ways that extend beyond the primarily linguistic concerns of translation studies (Snell-Hornby 1988). The explorations of thinkers like Emily Apter (2005), who points to a "translation zone" of cultural conflict and negotiation, are relevant to our approach insofar as they question the usually harmonious resonances of the term *cultural translation*. By highlighting the internality of translation to the operations of law, state, and capital, we also aim to interrogate its role in the production of borders, drawing on the work of Naoki Sakai (1997), who locates translation in the very center of the semantic field of the border, arguing that it serves as both a bridging and a separating device between languages, cultures, and indeed subjectivities.

Returning to Gramsci's comment about Lenin, we can note that "organizational questions" prompt his meditations on translation and translatability. Lenin himself, in the speech from which Gramsci paraphrases ("Five Years of the Russian Revolution and the Prospects of the World Revolution," actually delivered in November 1922), remarks that a resolution on "organizational structures" adopted by the Communist International in 1921 is illegible for foreigners not because of the quality of linguistic translations but due to the fact that "everything in it is based on Russian conditions." "We have not learnt," he claims, "to present our Russian experience to foreigners." This admission about the translatability of experiences, not languages, needs to be read in the light of Lenin's deep understanding and engagement with the political, economic, and social situation pertaining in Russia. Contrary to stereotypical images of party rigidity and postrevolutionary stringency, the statement displays a capacity and a will to flexibly adapt to changing conditions. Lenin declares: "I think that after five years of the Russian revolution the most important thing for all of us, Russian and foreign comrades alike, is to sit down and study" (1965, 430–31). His commitment to grounding organization in the shifting dynamics of class relations and political power, however, runs up against the problem of translation. At stake are the questions of internationalism and the modes of organization that might be appropriate and applicable in an international context that extends beyond the already heterogeneous Soviet assemblage of peoples, nations, and territories. Lenin is well aware that the methods that have served the Russian revolution and its aftermath cannot simply be transplanted into other specific concrete situations. He thus posits the political labor of translation as an ineludable aspect of revolutionary organization. Lenin's point is even more valid today. In a world of proliferating borders, the task of the translator and the task of the political organizer often tend to converge. Imagine organizing a labor struggle among the contemporary proletariat of Moscow—a city where more than one and a half million migrants are registered as residents, deportation of "illegal" migrants is a daily practice, and the composition of the workforce is crossed by linguistic, ethnic, and national boundaries. The problems of translation and organization Lenin identified with regard to the international situation in 1922 today manifest themselves even at the scale of a single city.

Wherever labor forces congregate and especially where migration shapes their composition, the question of translation is constitutive for political organization. The "fare rise" taxi strike of 2004 in New York City, which we discussed at the very beginning of this book, is just one of many labor actions and social struggles that confront translation in everyday practices of organization and in the workings of capital. Anyone who has been involved in such actions and struggles will be aware of the continuous need for translation, of the laborious effort, the negotiations, and even misunderstandings that characterize these situations. In a world obsessed with linking and networking, in practices of work and political organization, it is important to remember the relations established in moments of disconnection, discontinuity, and confrontation with the untranslatable. While capital labors under the illusion of translating everything into its language of value, living labor is continually crossed by discontinuities and differences. "It is within our differences that we are both most powerful and most vulnerable," writes Audre Lorde, "and some of the most difficult tasks of our lives are the claiming of differences and learning to use those differences as bridges rather than as barriers between us" (Lorde 2009, 201). Such a process of claiming and learning produces a subjectivity that is very different from the figures of the political subject developed by Rancière, Laclau, and others that we discussed above. This is not only because difference crosses and splits the subject internally but also because the social practice of translation, which always risks turning bridges into barriers, creates a collective subject that must continually keep open, open in translation, and reopen the processes of its own constitution. In these practices of opening and translation, there emerges a figure of power that does not search for legitimacy in the languages of inclusion and exclusion, the jargon of part and whole, or the horizon of a "pure politics" that plays itself out in the *demos* or the state. It is, rather, the power of a common that is not given by nature, history, or culture but must be politically invented and reinvented.

The radical strike for political possibility that translation creates as "a relation at the site of incommensurability" (Sakai 1997, 13) is a strike against capital, which is precisely the social relation that attempts to turn both bridges and barriers into conduits for exploitation and dispossession. This is an old ruse that appears in contemporary guise. Take Pun Ngai's discussion of the linguistic boundaries that cross the Chinese dormitory labor regime. Noting how regional, kin/ethnic, and linguistic networks are "often manipulated by the production machine to create a division of labor and job hierarchies" in the factories of southern China, she stresses that this involves competition among groups of workers interested to preserve and promote their regional identities. Such "self-disciplining" is often combined with other strategies for managing ethnic and linguistic boundaries to promote the "submissiveness" of female workers and to use "them against each other to prevent labor resistance" (Pun 2005, 121–23). In the very different borderscape created by the labor migration of men from India to Gulf state countries such as Bahrain, a similar dynamic can be observed. In his account of the *kafala* system of migration, which binds migrant workers to a particular job and legal sponsor, Andrew M. Gardner explores how linguistic and cultural barriers impose "limits to the agency of guest workers" and thus engulf them in inequitable relations. Companies are careful "to draw labor from a variety of regions, for the linguistic, national, cultural, and ethnic differences help build a more docile workforce—a workforce with less of an ability to organize and strike" (Gardner 2010, 216). Again, it needs to be stressed that this is an old strategy. As Marcus Rediker reminds us in his striking "human history" of the slave ship, American and European slave traders deployed similar methods. Rediker quotes Richard Simson, a late-seventeenth-century ship's surgeon who kept a log book: "The means used by those who trade to Guinea, to keep the Negros quiet, is to choose them from severall parts of ye Country, of different Languages; so that they find they cannot act jointly . . . in soe farr as they understand not one another" (quoted in Rediker 2007, 276). Many slavers were disappointed by these tactics, because the subjects who were their chattels became masters at the arts of improvisation and adaptation, even aboard the slave ship, fashioning a common language, a language of translation, that sustained and nurtured their resistance and played a role in the organization of their rebellions.

Pidgin English, Lascar *zubben*, and a multitude of other improvised patois were the underlings' inventive response to the divide and rule tactics imposed not only on slaves, convicts, and coolies in the "many middle passages" that made the modern world (Christopher, Pybus, and Rediker 2007) but also on sailors and the "motley crew" of maritime workers. The very notion of the crew describes a labor force collected on a vessel and despotically commanded by a quasi-military rule and also a collective subject in the making. As Bruno Traven writes in his classic novel, *The Death Ship* (1934), "living together and working together each sailor picks up the words of his companions, until, after two months or so, all men on board have acquired a working knowledge of about three hundred words common to all the crew and understood by all" (quoted in Linebaugh and Rediker 2000, 153–54). In such labor practices and experiences, we find a precedent for the capacity of translation to create the common. What needs to be emphasized here is once again the embodiment of translation in a whole series of social and material practices. What matters more is not so much the three hundred words that linguistically facilitate the communication of the sailors but the working knowledge that arises through living together and working together. Such knowledge corresponds to what we call the labor of translation. Forging a new idiom through a mutual process of picking up the words of companions involves a very peculiar kind of translation, which even when considered in linguistic terms is different from the traditional model of a transfer between source and target languages. Far from representing a movement between national languages or normative grammars, this is the discourse of foreigner to foreigner, which creates a language that is common precisely because it is forever in translation and rooted in material practices of cooperation, organization, and struggle.

Postcolonial writers and critics are well aware of the implications of such processes of continuous translation for the material constitution of languages and subjects. Édouard Glissant (1997), who emphasizes the importance of slavery and the plantation as a founding moment of modernity, analyzes the processes by which multiplicity infiltrates the principle of the unity and uniqueness of the language. He attributes this to the manifold practices of "relation" constitutive of subaltern struggles and cultural practices in the Caribbean. For Glissant, a moment of detour and translation is constitutive of language itself, giving way to processes of "creolization" that resist the politics of identity and provide the potential basis for an open understanding of subjectivation. Our own use of the concept of translation registers and attempts to multiply such an anti-identitarian inflection of creolization, which clearly distinguishes Glissant from other contemporary theorists of *creolité* or hybridity. At the same time, our emphasis on the role of translation in the operations of capital provides another framework for analyzing the conditions under which translation can become a tool for the invention of a common language for contesting capital. We should add to this, going back to Traven's *Death Ship*, that the production of such a common language is only one aspect of the wider production of subjectivity that constitutes the crew as an autonomous and multiple gang of workers. Bodily gestures, affective exchanges, rhythmic expressions, and the sharing of pain, sufferance, and joy are also at work in this labor of translation, which is again always enmeshed with capital, state, and law. Here we see the chance to generate a political subject adequate to meet the challenges of the bordering processes that cut and cross not only the high seas of past centuries but also the migratory and financial turbulences that disturb the capitalist waters of present times. In the next and final chapter, we confront the theoretical and practical task of fabricating this common.

─── *Chapter Nine* ───

TRANSLATING THE COMMON

Whose Method?

What is the relation between the common and borders? In this book we have tackled the question of borders from many angles, an approach necessitated by what we have called the heterogenization of global space, the multiplication of labor, and the proliferation of borders. The concept of the common has often been evoked as a key counterpoint to these processes and to the effects they have on the contemporary world. For instance, our discussion of the continuing reality of so-called primitive accumulation has pointed to multifarious means of appropriating the "commons." This is a topic that was at the center of Karl Marx's analysis of enclosures and the role of the state in the origins of modern capitalism. Today it has acquired a new salience in theoretical debates and social struggles. One thinks of peasants' resistance against land acquisitions and land grabbing in West Bengal, Africa, or Russia; struggles against the privatization of water and gas in Bolivia; Indigenous struggles against biopiracy in the Amazon; metropolitan struggles to establish and maintain sites of social, cultural, and political organization against the encroachment of rent; or digital struggles against the proprietization of information and knowledge in networks. The various efforts to resist the dismantling of state welfare systems both in postsocialist transitions and those of advanced capitalism are also important examples of struggles to defend the commons or, to be more accurate, to protect common goods, which are established within the frame of public law. All of these struggles, whether successful or otherwise, have their theoretical moments, which can by no means be collapsed into a "mathematical formula of an abstract kind," to recall again the words of Antonio Gramsci (1971, 201). To trace the relations between these struggles, we need a conceptual nomenclature adequate to the task of translating the common. This means not just tracking how or whether such struggles are linked, say, at the level of resources, communication, ideologies, or the involvement of people. It also means understanding how they require a production of subjectivity that is at once potentializing and destabilizing, which brings them into relations of translation that can never be fully mastered or organized by a single subject or institution. Already we have mentioned terms such as the *common*, the *commons*, *common goods*, the *public*, and the *private*. To these we add further concepts that help us specify the political stakes of translating the common; for now we want to work through this proliferation of terms surrounding the common to understand its relation to borders.

The concept of the common is not an umbrella that covers the other terms but a fundamental notion that enables the development of a radical perspective on social, juridical, and political matters pertaining to the commons, common goods, the public, and the private. The turn between the singular and the plural that marks the conceptual difference between the common and the commons is important here. The former signals a process of production, entirely immanent and material, by which instances of the latter acquire extension in time and space. At the same time, it gives to these plural instances an intensive quality that brings them into relation in contingent and also constitutive ways. Different commons can have radically different kinds of legal and political constitution. The evolution of different historical traditions of juridical regulation, such as common law and civil law systems, is only one mark of this. In many parts of the world the uneasy superimposition of colonial law on Indigenous ways of sharing and establishing normative modes of organizing social arrangements further complicates struggles and controversies surrounding the commons. The unstable divide between natural and artificial commons is also often at stake in these struggles, which in their negotiation of different forms of organization, distribution, and management necessarily move beyond the preservation or conservation of pregiven "goods." It would be of little use if a necessary resource like water were recognized as a common good but there were no means for its equitable distribution. Here we confront technical issues of infrastructure, logistics, and even measurement that, although usually confined to the realm of artificial goods, are susceptible to enclosure and thus become an integral consideration in any struggle against the privatization of water. This is true also for the political and social relations within which such technical assemblages are enmeshed. State-centered solutions to these questions, built around the logic of public law and public goods, can also be considered from this point of view as forms of enclosure. When it comes to supposedly artificial commons such as the welfare systems associated with the social state, this problem is particularly pronounced. Struggles for the preservation of such public systems are not necessarily or not yet struggles for the common. For them to become so, there must be a fundamental questioning of the processes of differential inclusion and exclusion that are constitutive of the public and its subjective figurations epitomized by citizenship. This is why the question of the common must always involve an interrogation of the question of borders.

We have said many times that borders connect and divide. Our discussions have shown that, in so doing, they also establish relations, which is to say that they create politically charged and highly contingent forms of sociality and vulnerability. To recognize that borders perform this work and that processes of sharing always involve moments of division is not to claim that borders enable or create the common. We do not adhere to a notion of a global or universal common, as sometimes imagined by the happier theorists of cosmopolitanism or global democracy. Nor do we subscribe to a version of the common that is strictly contained and subjected to the logics of border policing, as in the twentieth-century doctrine of socialism in one country or the multifarious attempts to protect the state and national communities from finance capital. However, we do not think that the fabrication of the common always and in all circumstances requires or can effect the elimination of borders. Borders will continue to cross the common. And the common will continue to contest borders. What is at stake is not a zero-sum game or a Manichean struggle. The problem for us is not to propose a "softening" or even a "democraticization" of borders, because empirically we know that borders are often hardening and softening at the same time. Rather, it is the quality of the social relations that are constituted and reproduced by and through borders that matters. We do not believe that the ethics of hospitality and welcoming can shift the social relation of capital that is invested in every border in the contemporary world. This is why we posed the question of the border as one of method. One of the best questions we were ever asked about this postulation was: whose method, capital's or yours? Such a provocation must attract a double answer.

Clearly capital pursues relations of bordering as a means of organizing and reinforcing its operations. This is by no means a simple matter of division, whether of labor or space, because as we have argued many times, borders are crucial devices of articulation that enable capital's circulation and support the expansion of its frontiers. The stretching of productive chains, the establishment of economic zones and corridors, and the encroachment of capital on ever smaller scales of bodily matter all turn on the proliferation of borders. We can thus say definitively that the border is a method for capital. But to posit border as method as a concept for radical political thought and action is not merely to make subversive use of the master's tools. It is, rather, to point to the necessity of taking capital's use of the border as a serious and inescapable point of contention. To suggest that borders are essential to capital's operations is to identify a strategic line of struggle, which reaches far beyond the territorial and jurisdictional edges of nation-states or regions. At stake is not just a struggle against the repressive violence that permeates borderscapes and border control regimes across the world, although this is undeniably a crucial aspect in any border struggle. Once the productive dimension of the border is emphasized, a whole series of further fields of contention emerge. In the *fabrica mundi* of the contemporary world, borders are instrumental in producing space, labor power, markets, jurisdictions, and a variety of other objects in ways that converge on the production of subjectivity. Border as method for us means focusing on the contentious aspects of these productive processes. It means showing how border struggles serve to crystallize the most intense tensions surrounding the social relation of capital and how they are played out in many contexts, often far away from geographical borderlands.

If capital holds a necessary relation to the border, it does not mean that borders can necessarily contain capital. As Marx famously writes when discussing the creation of the world market, capital approaches every limit "as a barrier to be overcome" (Marx 1973, 408). Borders are certainly some of the most important among these limits. Continuously overcoming them, capital is nevertheless caught in complex dynamics that make every moment of overcoming also a moment in which borders proliferate. The limiting function of the border, its capacity to mark out or define a territory, whether conceptual or material, is not given in a straightforward manner. If we recall Étienne Balibar's observation that defining a border risks "going round in circles," because the production of concepts is itself an act of bordering (Balibar 2002, 76), this complexity acquires a new significance. The task of making this kind of circular motion into a resource rather than an obstacle for radical struggles against capital is one that border struggles confront on a daily basis. An examination of how these struggles work and how they negotiate the equal and opposite capacity of capital to use borders to its advantage thus provides insights that can assist in the invention of a new politics of the common. Such a politics must extend beyond any rhetorical invocation of a world without borders. It must also renounce any attempt to turn the border into a justice-giving institution.

As we showed in the previous chapter, the question of translation is paramount in the organization of border struggles. In our discussion of the motley crew, pidgin English, and the working knowledge of life at sea, we referred to a politics of translation that sought to create a common language of subjects joined in labor and struggle. It is important, however, to remember that capital also affects a kind of translation, coding human activity according to the measure of abstract labor and its insertion within the nexus of exchange value and price. At this point, it is useful to introduce some more conceptual terminology to distinguish between these types of translation and the forms of address they imply. In his seminal work *Translation and Subjectivity*, Naoki Sakai (1997) identifies two different modes of address pertaining to translation, which means two different ways audiences or listeners are implied in acts of translation: homolingual and heterolingual address. Though these modes of address have cultural ramifications, they also have material effects on the social and political planes. At stake in the question of address is "the basic terms in which we represent to ourselves how our translational enunciation is a practice of erecting or modifying social relations" (Sakai 1997, 3).

Let us begin with homolingual address, which is "a regime of someone relating herself or himself to others in enunciation whereby the addresser adopts the position of representative of a putatively homogeneous language society and relates to the general addressees who are also representative of an equally homogeneous language community" (Sakai 1997, 4). In situations of translation, such a mode of address actively forges a border between different language communities and in so doing constitutes them as separate and homogeneous. For Sakai, translation conducted in this way constructs a "co-figurative schema" that interpellates subjects into civilizational partitions, between the West and the rest, for instance, or between Europe and Asia—divisions that are fully implied in the "violent transformative dynamic" of modernity "that arises from social encounters among heterogeneous people" (Sakai 2000, 799). It is also possible to observe that the translation accomplished by capital functions in a similar way, because it produces subjects and social relations by reducing the qualities of diverse activities, forms of life, and languages to the homogeneous measure of value. Thus, while commodities have a social life and cultural peculiarities, they are constituted by a particular form—the commodity form—that ensures a particular kind of translatability and stitches them into the circuits of general equivalence established by money. Between practices of translation that insert subjects into civilizations and those accomplished by capital there exists a material parallel. At stake is the way translation establishes and transforms social relations. In this regard, it is important to remember that capital itself is a social relation. The terms by which it is established and the ways it might be displaced or altered are deeply implicated in the politics of translation.

Not all translation functions in this homogenizing fashion. We already discussed how translation can be productive of a heterogeneity that troubles and flusters the workings of capital and its homolingual address. Sakai gives us a more precise language with which to analyze such translation and its implications for the production of subjectivity and the common. He contrasts homolingual address with what he calls heterolingual address. This refers to a situation of address in which an implied audience is not a homogeneous language community but is composed of foreigners from many different backgrounds, who do not necessarily share the means to communicate among themselves. Importantly, the addresser becomes just one more foreigner in this circumstance, which requires continuous translation and countertranslation. As a result, there is no generation of a definitive border between languages or across the line of address. Heterolingual address "does not abide by the normalcy of reciprocal and transparent communication, but instead assumes that every utterance can fail to communicate because heterogeneity is inherent in any medium, linguistic or otherwise" (Sakai 1997, 8). This gives rise to what Sakai calls a "nonaggregate community of foreigners" (9) or what, writing with Jon Solomon, he names "the multitude of foreigners" (2006, 19). These novel and unstable subjective formations involve a radically different use of the plural first-person pronoun than that implied in homolingual address. "In a nonaggregate community," Sakai explains, "we are together and can address ourselves as 'we' because we are distant from one another and because our togetherness is not grounded on any common homogeneity" (1997, 7). Although this is a loose use of the word *common*, Sakai later gives the term a more precise conceptual formulation. Recognizing that cultural differences have no primordial status, he points to the manner in which they can connect and disconnect "in new and accidental ways," mobilizing "various fragments" that are "heterogeneous to one another." Even if these kinds of arrangements are "represented in the name of an acknowledgment of difference and separation," he contends, there is "necessarily an inauguration of the being-in-common, of a *communism*" (122).

"Communism," mentioned by Sakai with a reference to the work of Jean-Luc Nancy (1991), has been in recent years at the center of an intense philosophical debate, most notably linked (as we recalled in the previous chapter) with the name of Alain Badiou. This debate has been characterized by a gap between communism as a philosophical idea and communism as a political name. While for some of the participants in the debate (and definitely for Badiou himself) this gap has to be maintained as a condition of political renewal, our work on translation and the common aims at reconstructing the material basis of a new communist politics. This is consistent with Sakai who moves from a discussion of Nancy to briefly mention the notion of articulation elaborated by Ernesto Laclau and Chantal Mouffe in their work *Hegemony and Socialist Strategy* (2001). What interests us more than the theoretical references mobilized by Sakai is how this inauguration of being-in-common opens a new continent of theoretical and political investigation. This includes but extends well beyond the question of cultural difference to ask how social relations established by heterolingual address and translation impact on issues of borders, capital, and the common. Such a political engagement with the question of translation implies a development of the concept that is always aware of the material and social density of this practice. Far from being the task of an interpreter or a mediator—a third person that necessarily intervenes in the translational exchange—it involves an immediate and often painful galvanization arising from a continuous negotiation of differences and smashing of constituted identities. This removal of a neutral arbiter also has implications on the political plane, radically questioning the transcendentalizing movement that collapses material and social differences into a *volonté générale*. Translation, in this sense, cannot be contained by any formal or representative scheme, be it epistemic, cultural, or political.

In the next section we contrast the implications of this political, material, and social conception of translation with theories built up around the notion of articulation. This generates a new way of approaching spaces of the common, which emphasizes the role of border struggles and the subjective dimensions always at stake in the fabrication of the common. Far from grounding the common in the linguistic-cognitive faculties of the human species, this approach implies a confrontation with processes of bordering that continually differentiate the human, both internally and in its unstable separation from the nonhuman. Differences appear as the ground on which the common can be built. To use again the terminology of Sakai (2011), this means moving beyond the distinction between *humanitas*, which seeks to know humanity in general and discern the contours of the universal, and *anthropos*, which entails the production of specific knowledge about particular communities. Only by short-circuiting the complicity of such universalizing and particularizing tendencies does the common come into view.

Articulation, Translation, Universality

How far can the theory and practice of articulation assist us in the fabrication of the common? The concept of articulation, whose invention is often retroactively attributed to Gramsci, was strongly elaborated in the 1970s and 1980s by thinkers such as Louis Althusser, Étienne Balibar, Gilles Deleuze and Félix Guattari, Ernesto Laclau, and Stuart Hall. We have employed this concept many times in our discussions of the border and its capacities to connect and disconnect. Indeed, precisely such a process of connecting and disconnecting, of constructing provisional and contingent unities that are always in negotiation and context-specific, is what the concept of articulation attempts to describe. For Althusser and Balibar, writing in *Reading "Capital"* (1970), the concept of articulation was employed to discuss the internal organization of the capitalist mode of production and the issues it raised regarding structure, superstructure, and the relation between different levels and temporalities of society. In the work of Laclau, however, the concept begins to take a shape that influenced many subsequent debates, for instance, in cultural studies and political debates about populism, social movements, and (radical) democracy.

An early elaboration of Laclau's approach is found in *Politics and Ideology in Marxist Theory* (1977). In this book, Laclau confronts the reductionist logic of some aspects of the classical Marxian theory of ideology, which even in its Althusserian elaboration posited a determination of social relations in the last instance by economic forces. The concept of articulation serves to place relations of class in a wider social context, where contingent connections between different practices, ideological elements, social forces, and social groups are seen to be in a constant process of aggregation, assemblage, and change. Laclau was beginning to elaborate a theory of the relations between class struggle and popular democratic movements, and the concept of articulation provides a means of trying to explain not only how the latter were "overdetermined" by the former but also why class struggles had to compose themselves as popular-democratic movements to have any chance of political success. An important aspect of Laclau's theory emerges at this point and remains present throughout his work, often in a muted sense. In seeking to relate class contradictions to popular contradictions, he tends to place the latter in a national frame. Thus, in describing the production of subjectivity that results from the articulation of class interests and popular objectives, he explains that the "'German working class,' or 'Italian,' 'English' etc., has then, an irreducible specificity because it is the condensation of a multiplicity of condensations which cannot be reduced abstractly to Marxism-Leninism" (Laclau 1977, 109). In these moments, where the concept of articulation opens a discursive field in which to think the heterogeneity of the social but simultaneously casts the shadow of nationally bounded peoples over this field, we begin to discern its limits for a new approach to the common. There is no attempt here to come to terms with the operations of bordering or their relation to the frontiers of capital—issues that are fundamental for us and which, as we have shown, have a strong presence in the works of both Marx and Lenin. Doubtless Laclau's approach strongly reflects his experience of Peronism, which, as he notes, "was undeniably successful in constituting a unified popular-democratic language at the national level." Although he questionably remarks that "this was due to the social homogeneity of Argentina, exceptional in the Latin American context" (190), he shifts his theoretical apparatus across a wide range of contexts precisely to explain how populism manages the differences that cross the social field.

These tendencies are even more pronounced in *Hegemony and Socialist Strategy* (2001), the influential work penned by Laclau and Mouffe. In the previous chapter we discussed how Laclau and Mouffe's reengineering of the concept of hegemony is haunted by the state and the party. Their development of the concept of articulation is an attempt to formulate a discursive approach to the "openness of the social." Renouncing the view that a "discursive structure" is merely a cognitive entity, Laclau and Mouffe understand discourse as "an *articulatory practice* which constitutes and organizes social relations." In "advanced industrial societies," they locate a "fundamental asymmetry" between "a growing proliferation of differences—a surplus of meaning of 'the social'—and the difficulties encountered by any discourse attempting to fix those differences as moments of a stable articulatory structure" (Laclau and Mouffe 2001, 96). They thus face the problem of where this proliferation of differences stops or at least rests. Their solution to this problem is to disavow the very notion of *society* as a "self-defined totality" in which the social fixes itself. They point to the ways articulatory practices construct privileged discursive points of "partial fixation," what they call "*nodal points*," which "*partially fix meaning*" and allow specific formations of the social to take shape (111–13).

At stake in this conception of the social is an effort to deploy the notion of articulation in a way that goes beyond and avoids some of the dialectical problems posed by concepts such as mediation and determination. We do not discuss in detail the Lacanian acrobatics performed by Laclau and Mouffe to confront the problem of how fixities, however partial, can emerge from a situation that turns on a process of continuous opening and unfixing. Suffice it to say that just as the master signifier lurks behind Lacan's insistence on flux along a signifying chain, so the "impossible object" of society as a fully sutured totality is always at stake in the constitution of the social, which can only exist "as an effort to construct that impossible object" (Laclau and Mouffe 2001, 112). For Laclau and Mouffe, articulation is a strategic border concept that is generated at this threshold between the possible and the impossible. Here "the problem of the political" appears as "the problem of the institution of the social," which is to say that the "reproduction and transformation of social relations cannot be located at the determinate level of the social" (153). But how, in this perspective, is the social instituted? If the social is a system of proliferating differences, where is the point that it meets a difference that it cannot merely absorb? How is it bordered? For Laclau and Mouffe, this involves a contradictory process of exclusion—one that at once establishes a border that marks a difference that is something more than difference and at the same time reduces differences to equivalences in which identities can emerge. The problem of the political emerges here as the problem of the transcendental conditions of the play between articulation and equivalence that constitutes the social. This transcendental moment is replicated in the workings of political articulation in hegemonic projects of coalition and alliance that take place within increasingly unstable political spaces, "in which the very identity of the forces in struggle is submitted to constant shifts, and calls for an incessant process of redefinition" (151).

In an interview with Lawrence Grossberg, Stuart Hall raises reservations about Laclau and Mouffe's approach that resonate with our own. Recognizing that there is much to gain by "rethinking practices as functioning discursively," he worries about the emergence of a perspective in which "there is no reason why anything is or isn't potentially articulatable with anything" (1986a, 56). According to Hall, Laclau and Mouffe introduce a discursive reductionism that overcompensates for the economic reductionism that characterizes some versions of Marxism. Laclau and Mouffe's "discursive position," he suggests, "is often in danger of losing its reference to material practice and historical conditions" (57). Thus, although Hall deploys the concept of articulation in his own work, he is always careful to remain attentive to questions of historical embeddedness. For instance, in the analysis of the Rastafarian movement he offers in this same interview, he emphasizes how it arises as the result of an articulation between various elements (musical, racial, religious, etc.) without losing focus on "the experiences, the position, the determinations of economic life in Jamaican society" (55). One could say that his reservations about Laclau and Mouffe's tendency to approach "society as a totally open discursive field" (56) lead him to raise concerns about bordering. Hall's discussions of the popular and popularism do not assume a national frame but take on issues such as "intercultural understanding" (1985) and diaspora (1990, 2006). When he does discuss how populism operates in national contexts in his critical political engagement with Thatcherism, he notes that he is dealing with the "national-popular" (Hall 1988, 55)—a term he adopts from Gramsci that implies analytical attention to how populism articulates with nationalism, which is to say to how and why popular movements can become nationally bordered rather than being born as such.

Laclau's interests by contrast drift toward the question of the universal. This is a concern that emerges in *Emancipation(s)* (Laclau 1996) and comes to the fore in *Contingency, Hegemony, Universality* (Butler, Laclau, and Žižek 2000). Focusing on what he calls the "proliferation of particularisms" in social and political struggles, Laclau argues that "the assertion of a pure particularism, independently of any content and of the appeal to a universality transcending it, is a self-defeating enterprise" (1996, 26). Particularistic struggles require an appeal to the universal that implies a moment of transcendence, but at the same time universality cannot exist apart from the particular. Here the striving for an impossible transcendence seals the political institution of society. This means that an ambiguity invests all forms of radical political struggle: "the opposition, in order to be radical, has to put in a common ground both what it asserts and what it excludes, so that the exclusion becomes a particular form of assertion" (29–30). But what kind of a common ground is this? It is one that rests on an exclusion that marks a difference that cannot be included and thus turns all those differences that are included into equivalents. It is a common forged within the terms of a hegemonic formation in which something visible makes present the invisible and something particular is made to signify the universal. Tendentially this common ground shares the transcendentalizing structure of the Hobbesian commonwealth, as Laclau makes clear: "I am thinking essentially of the work of Hobbes. Hobbes, as we have seen, presented the state of nature as the radical opposite of an ordered society . . . as a result of that description, the order of the ruler has to be accepted not because of any intrinsic value it can have, but just because it is *an* order, and the only alternative is radical disorder" (45).

Importantly, Laclau also distances himself from Hobbes. Pointing to "the unevenness of power in social relations," he maintains that "civil society" is "partially structured and partially unstructured and, as a result, the total concentration of power in the hands of the ruler ceases to be a logical requirement" (Laclau 1996, 45–46). But he continues to argue that "the only possible universality is the one constructed through an equivalential chain" (Butler, Laclau, and Žižek 2000, 304). Moreover, the impossible transcendence that this implies, which seals the very possibility of the political, presupposes an ontology that starts from the concept of demand. This becomes clear in *On Populist Reason*: "The smallest unit from which we will start corresponds to the category of 'social demand'" (Laclau 2005, 73). As José Luis Villacañas Berlanga remarks, the "liberal basis of his approach is clear" (Villacañas Berlanga 2010, 166). Laclau tends to assume that globalized capitalism "leads to a deepening of the logics of identity formation" as well as the political logic of antagonism around which they purportedly turn (Laclau 2005, 231). His aim, which resonates highly with that of Mouffe in *On the Political* (2005), is "to transform competition, the antagonism dislocated and in continual proliferation, into a visible and dualistic antagonism" (Villacañas Berlanga 2010, 161). Villacañas Berlanga doubts that such antagonism is likely to eventuate under the neoliberal governance of "a market based on the entrepreneurial production of equivalences that necessarily integrate demands—because they are anticipated" (165). We agree with this diagnosis. But it is necessary to add that the way Laclau and Mouffe frame the relation of social struggles to political articulation replicates a model in which the former are merely *particular* and therefore incapable of producing new political forms. As we saw in the previous chapter, it is indeed only through articulation that struggles lose their "partial character" (Laclau and Mouffe 2001, 169). Articulation functions as the moment of capture of this particularity and partiality in a pattern of equivalence, which is not questioned and can only be forestalled by its contamination of the universal. What Laclau and Mouffe call the "chain of equivalences" gives this proliferation a conceptual name and provides a simplified model of the social in which political actions are diminished by their multiplication. As Laclau explains, the "specificity of equivalence is the destruction of meaning through its very proliferation" (Laclau 1997, 305). The concept of articulation thus at once monopolizes the field of meaning and names the only possible way of conceiving and/or practicing a hegemonic or counterhegemonic politics.

To this model of articulation we oppose a concept of translation that does not abide the logic of equivalence. Because there are different forms of translation and translation can function as a form of articulation, there is a need for conceptual focus here. We have insisted that articulation disconnects as well as connects different social elements, demands, and situations. But unlike translation, it cannot do both at the same time. Indeed, the bordering function of translation, which connects and divides in one moment, makes it give rise to such contingent and elusive social relations. As Sakai puts it, "translation gives birth to the untranslatable." Its "essential sociality" (Sakai 1997, 14) is highly unstable and cannot be brought under the control of a supposed sovereignty, or, as Laclau would have it, a master signifier, however precarious the hegemony it establishes. We understand translation as a form of political labor that produces a *"subject in transit."* To quote Sakai again: the translator can be a subject in transit first because "she cannot be an 'individual' in the sense of *individuum* in order to perform translation, and second because she is a *singular* that marks an elusive point of discontinuity in the social, whereas translation is the practice of creating continuity at that singular point of discontinuity" (13).

Such a subject in transit is very different from the "subject before subjectivation" described by Laclau and Mouffe (2001, xi), which is always in danger of being swallowed by a "discursive identity" on the one hand and by the "subjectivity of the agent" on the other (121). Equally the singularity marked by this "subject in transit" cannot be specified within the articulation of universalism and particularism that, for Laclau, is "ineradicable" in the "making of political identities" (1996, viii). As Sakai explains: "Precisely because both are closed off to the singular, who can never be transformed into the subject of what infinitely transcends the universal, neither universalism nor particularism is able to come across the other; otherness is always reduced to the Other, and thus, repressed, excluded, and eliminated in them both" (1997, 157). It is by such a closure to the other that we detect in Laclau's assertion that the limits of the social are established by exclusion. By announcing a relative universalism that forces "a partial surrender of particularity, stressing what all particularities have, equivalentially, in common" (Laclau 2005, 78), Laclau comes close to conflating the universal with the common. It is not just that this perspective fails to account for what we have called differential inclusion and the role of borders in articulating as well as breaking flows and other kinds of global mobilities. It is also that it remains closed to a politics of translation that functions differently to that of articulation. By suggesting that the play of articulation and equivalence supplies the common ground on which political contestation takes place, Laclau is constrained to think the conflictual dimension of politics within the limits established by existing institutional arrangements.

In this regard, it is important to distinguish the universal from the common, as does Paolo Virno "both from a logical and an ontological point of view" (Virno 2010, 204). While the universal comes into being through an act of the intellect and exists as a predicate attributed to already formed individuals, Virno explains, the common "is a reality independent of the intellect. It exists also when it is not represented" (205). This is to say that a theory of the common is rooted in a materialist ontology, which considers the emergence of a multitude of singularities as a process that at the same time enriches and never exhausts the common being that they share as the condition of their existence and further development. The mutual constitution of the common and the singular, foregrounded in Sakai's conception of translation, is operative here. If we think of the movement between the common and the commons, for instance, there is at stake a process of what Michael Hardt and Antonio Negri call "generation" (2000, 386–89) or what we have described as opening and reopening in translation. The common is only richer and stronger for its production of plural commons with different spatiotemporal extensions and different legal and political constitutions. Indeed, the intensive implication of these different singularities, their "non-dialectical synthesis" (Casarino and Negri 2008, 70), provides the ground on which the common is produced and indeed alters the constitution of the common itself. By contrast, if one thinks about pluralizing the universal to create universals, there is no such feedback or strengthening of the abstract principle of universality. The universal is strengthened only by the proliferation of particularities (say, for instance, of culturally differentiated and alternative interpretations of such universal concepts as freedom and equality) that merely replicate its abstract claims to unity in concrete situations.

In effect, this is what Laclau and Mouffe suggest when they state that the function of universality "is not acquired for good but is, on the contrary, always reversible" (Laclau and Mouffe 2001, xiii). If, as this statement suggests, universals are more than one, that they come and go, there is a questioning of the "everywhere and forever" claim that invests the singular of the universal. Here we see the effects of what Balibar calls the "insurmountable *equivocity*" of the concept of the universal (Balibar 2002, 146). Recognizing that the "*ideal universal* is *multiple* by nature" (173), he seeks to discern an "intelligible order" that articulates the difference between universals and the "scattered meaning" implied by the universal (146–47). For Balibar, this is a problem that "philosophy cannot solve" (174), which means not that the universal is "relative" but that it can have no "'absolute' unity" and is thus "a permanent source of conflict" (173). A similar point can be made about Aiwha Ong's insistence on the existence of "multiple universalisms" (Ong 2009, 39), which parallels arguments about multiple modernities inflected by different cultural and spatial arrangements. In this case, the universal is refracted through particularisms that tend to think of themselves as universals. What we see in all of these different ways of posing the question of the universal is a movement between the abstract and the concrete in which the meaning of the universal is scattered while its essential claim to unity remains unaltered by its fall into the material world. By contrast, the relation of translation that we find crucial to the composition of the common involves a constant feedback of the energies and struggles involved in the building of commons. The material constitution of the common cannot be assimilated to the logic of the universal and particular. This is why we can speak of translating the common, which is not only to point to how it produces commons but also to mark how it simultaneously connects and divides the singularities that constitute it.

Bordering the Common

We repeat the question we asked at the beginning of this chapter: what is the relation between the common and borders? To answer this question, we find it first necessary to take stock of the constitutive role played by the tracing of multiple lines of demarcation and bordering in the destruction of the commons and the formation of the public and private spheres, which continue to shape the political imagination and legal developments in the present. It is not necessary to go into the controversies surrounding Marx and Friedrich Engels's notion of a primitive communism to understand how the common has become both a marker of the original condition of humankind and a radical challenge for legal and political theory. The idea that "All Things . . . were at first common" is formulated with a reference to the authority of Justin at the beginning of the section of Grotius's *De Jure Belli ac Pacis* (first published in 1625) devoted to the illustration of his theory of property (Grotius 2005, 420). Positing "occupancy" (*occupatio*) as a source for the establishment of property, Grotius provided an argument that proved influential for the legitimation of colonial conquest and violent appropriation of land. Interestingly, in his *Perpetual Peace* (1795), Immanuel Kant speaks of a "common right of possession of the surface of the earth," arguing that because "it is a globe, we cannot be infinitely scattered and must in the end reconcile ourselves to existence side by side" (Kant 2010, 18). Whereas Grotius refers primarily to the origin of private property, taking land as a paradigmatic example, Kant's argument allows us to reflect on the role of political borders in the partitioning of the surface of the Earth, which underlies the formation of political and legal territories, states, and "peoples." Kant's elaboration of a "cosmopolitan" theory of "universal hospitality" (the third "definitive article of perpetual peace") is predicated on the establishment of such borders. Indeed, hospitality, for Kant, means "the claim of a stranger entering foreign territory to be treated by its owner without hostility" (17–18; see, for instance, Benhabib 2004, 25–48, and Rigo 2007, 162).

A cut across the common is the constitutive gesture of both private property and public law. If one recalls the classical definition of the right of property provided by William Blackstone in *Commentaries on the Law of England* (1765)—"the sole and despotic dominion which one man claims and exercises over the external things of the world in total exclusion of the right of any other individual in the universe" (Blackstone 1825, 1)—the structural parallel with the relation of state to territory becomes clear. A process of bordering the common is the condition for the establishment of both forms of property. Long before the formulation of Grotius's theory of occupancy, the age of modern enclosures, and colonial conquest, the role of complex practices of bordering and tracing lines of demarcation was widely recognized in Roman law. A multitude of land surveyors, a "technical" figure that emerged at the boundary between the sacred and the profane (Schiavone 2005, 53), were at work in ancient Rome to make the establishment of private property possible through a *limitatio* (lit., the tracing of a *limes*, of a border) of common land (Bonfante 1958, 193). Once established, the preservation of this property as well as the adjudication of disputes between proprietors continued to require the work of land surveyors in the framework of what Roman jurists called *actio finium regundorum* (action to regulate boundaries), which much later entered the modern civil law of many continental European countries.

Under the totally different conditions produced by modern capitalism, the model of private property constructed by Roman jurists was enormously influential in the development of bourgeois civil law from the sixteenth century on, as is already clear in the theories of Grotius and Blackstone. The bordering and appropriation of the common on which that model was predicated found its violent modern equivalent in the enclosures discussed by

Marx in the section of *Capital* dedicated to so-called primitive accumulation as well as in the colonial occupancy of Indigenous land. The borders of private property were not only established and generalized with the direct of involvement of the state. There is, rather, a historical and a logical parallel between the concept of private property and the tracing of territorial borders constitutive of sovereignty. Giambattista Vico, in his *Scienza nuova* (1744), perhaps most strikingly mobilized the concept of the border to trace the continuity between the establishment of private property and the formation of the state. In the section of his work titled "The Guarding of the Confines," he writes that "it was necessary to set up boundaries to the fields in order to put a stop to the infamous promiscuity of things in the bestial state. On these boundaries were to be fixed the confines first of families, then of gentes or houses, later of peoples, and finally of nations" (Vico 1984, 363).

"State sovereignty and private property," writes the Italian jurist Ugo Mattei, "share an identical structure, one of exclusion and sovereign discretion" (Mattei 2011, 45). Far from being the other of, or more simply the limit to, state power, private property constitutes and develops itself within the same framework, whose establishment is made possible by multifarious processes of bordering the common. To recall what we wrote following Evgen Pashukanis in the previous chapter, a kind of double bind characterizes the historical and conceptual evolution of civil and public law in modern times. It is certainly true, as we saw in Marx's analysis of enclosures, that the establishment of private property and civil law is made possible by the direct and violent intervention of the state. Moreover, as we can say playing with the terminology of Roman law, the role of the state is not only crucial in the moment of *limitation* but also extends across each *actio finium regundorum*, each act of regulating the relations between proprietors, because the sovereignty of the state on its territory is the condition for the existence of civil law itself. At the same time, when we look at the structure of civil law from the angle provided by Pashukanis's analysis of the relation between law and the commodity form, it appears that "the hardest core of legal haziness (if one may be permitted to use such an expression) is to be found precisely in the sphere of civil law. It is here above all that the legal subject, the 'persona' finds entirely adequate embodiment in the real person of the subject operating egoistically, the owner, the bearer of private interests" (Pashukanis 2002, 80). To accept Pashukanis's analysis does not mean to dismiss the importance of public and constitutional law as terrains on which the arbitrary character of both sovereignty and private property has been historically subjected to limits, obligations, and regulations. But it does mean to recognize, as Hardt and Negri write in *Commonwealth*, that "the concept of property and the defense of property remain the foundation of every modern political constitution," even if with the advent of the welfare state "public property" acquires a crucial role in the regulation of Fordism (Hardt and Negri 2009, 15).

The concept of the legal personality of the state was pivotal to the construction of public property in a way that replicated the structure of private property and mirrored its exclusive character. This means that the borders of the state were inscribed onto the very concept of public property, distinguishing it in a radical way from the semantics of the common. Moreover, as momentous and ubiquitous processes of the privatization of public goods have demonstrated in the past few decades, a structural unbalance characterizes the legal construction and protection of private and public property. While the former is surrounded by a series of protections, qualifications, and guarantees, the alienation of the second is usually an ordinary business for governments and does not require particularly complex procedures (Mattei 2011). This moment of unbalance has become even more pronounced with the growing accumulation of property and rights owned by the legal personality of the corporation, which has given rise to the emergence of new actors, whose power and wealth exceed the borders, jurisdiction, and power of states (Soederberg 2009). Apart from leading to a weakening of public law and powers, these processes have fostered a blurring of the boundaries between private and public, as well as the emergence of new hybrid legal regimes and new assemblages of territory, authority, and rights within which states find themselves increasingly enmeshed. Theories of governance and legal pluralism we discussed earlier in this book attempt to grasp these new constellations of power and heterogeneous normative orders. If the boundary between private and public blurs due to these developments, it is hard to deny that property continues to rule the contemporary world.

The ascendance of the corporate personality as the owner of property rights is not a new phenomenon, but it has reached unprecedented levels. The intertwining of this process with the financialization of capital has fostered a dematerialization of property, which runs parallel to its delinking from the reference to an individual, embodied subject. This is not to say that property is no longer a fundamental criterion of division between individuals. The opposite is true, since we are well aware of the skyrocketing polarization in the distribution of wealth and property in most of the world. But because property and property rights have become more and more anonymous and immaterial and float elusively according to the dynamics of global financial markets, a major transformation has occurred in their social, political, and even anthropological functions and status. What seems to be undergoing transformation is the legitimating role that property has performed in bourgeois thought since the formulation in the seventeenth century of what Crawford B. Macpherson calls "possessive individualism"—the theory that imagined society as a web of commercial exchange relations between "a lot of free equal individuals related to each other as proprietors of their own capacities and of what they have acquired by their exercise" (Macpherson 1962, 3).

Against this background we must locate the so-called new enclosures. This term was proposed by the Midnight Notes Collective in 1990, amid the idyllic rhetoric of a "new world order" and a "borderless world" that surrounded the end of the Cold War, to grasp "the large-scale reorganization of the accumulation process which has been underway since the mid-1970s" (Midnight Notes Collective 1990, 3). Defined by Peter Linebaugh (2008, 306) as "the action of surrounding land with a fence or hedge, the means of conversion from common land to private property," the term *enclosure* implies a reference to land that is still crucial in many contemporary developments and conflicts surrounding the "new enclosures." At the same time, it is important to focus on what Linebaugh calls the moment of "conversion from common land to private property" to understand the possibility of a less literal use of the word *enclosure* that refers to any process in which private property is created through a violent gesture of appropriation. This use of the word becomes clear if one thinks of capital's new frontiers, such as the knowledge economy and biocapital. In these cases, there is an enclosure of common (or "tacit") knowledge produced in networks (Benkler 2006) and of "life-as-information" (Rajan 2006, 16). Interestingly, the analysis of new enclosures proposed by the Midnight Notes Collective took the debt crisis and structural adjustment programs in Africa as its point of departure. "Seizing land for debt" was an old strategy that in the 1980s took new forms in many African countries as part of a more general attempt to foster a "wide-ranging reorganization of class relations, aimed at cheapening the cost of labor, raising social productivity, reversing 'social expectations' and opening the continent to a fuller penetration of capitalist relations" (Midnight Notes Collective 1990, 4, 12). Two decades later, although under different conditions, the debt crisis reached the United States and Western Europe with subprime mortgages and the sovereign debt crisis. This resulted in millions of home foreclosures and cuts to social services that had come to be widely regarded as social commons, created "as a result of past social movements and later formalized by institutional practices" (De Angelis 2007, 148). The widely visible operations of new enclosures in these instances need to be analyzed as signals of deeper processes and attempts at social and political restructuring.

The bordering of the common is always at stake in new as well as in old enclosures. This process can create material and immaterial lines of demarcation that did not exist before. It can also rework existing boundaries, such as those circumscribing public spaces in cities, transforming them into new borders of private property. It is often the case that these processes of urban bordering are aimed at keeping undesirable subjects out of specific areas, constructed as valuable through the combined investments and efforts of financial capital and real estate. Among these subjects, migrants figure prominently. In their experiences, the action of these processes of bordering replicates and articulates itself with the action of other borders. The proliferation and spread of enclosures in the contemporary world produces a huge amount of violence, sufferance, and pain, intensifying both dispossession and exploitation. At the same time, at least conceptually, these enclosures provide an important perspective on the fragile legitimacy of private property as societal rule. In any act of enclosure, literal or otherwise, this legitimacy is affirmed. Struggles against enclosures and for the commons across the globe show the reverse side of this conceptual moment in an absolutely concrete and antagonistic way.

A powerful array of theoretical tools has been forged in the past decades to justify the destruction of the commons and their subordination to the logics of private property. These range from the "neo-Malthusian" argument of the "tragedy of the commons" summarized in an influential essay of Garrett Hardin in 1968 to the so-called law and economics approach, which originated in the United States and played a crucial role in the global transplanting of a rule of law that was reduced to the "rule of property" (Mattei and Nader 2008, 88–99). We do not underestimate the continuing influence and power of these theoretical constructions. Nevertheless, the fact that Elinor Ostrom was awarded the Nobel Prize in Economics in 2009, in the midst of the global economic crisis, signals that a certain confusion has become manifest even in mainstream economic theory. Ostrom is credited for having scientifically demonstrated the fallacy of what has long been considered a kind of received wisdom—the idea that the commons are structurally doomed to environmental and economic self-destruction and must therefore be either regulated by the state or privatized.

Governing the Commons, the book Ostrom published in 1990, has drawn attention to the existence and possible development of multiple forms of co-operative, community-based, collective forms of management of the commons, which are neither public nor private. The intellectual movement surrounding the establishment of "creative commons," and above all the work of Lawrence Lessig (2004), is another important source of the new interest attracted by the notion of commons in academic and public debates. Attempts to build a juridical typology of common goods, often connected with the actual development of struggles against enclosures and privatization, should be also mentioned here (Marella 2012; Mattei 2011). All these intellectual efforts oscillate between a search for an intermediate domain between the public and private spheres, which replicates the construction of a "social law" by European jurists in the early twentieth century (see, for instance, Gurvitch 1932) and more radical approaches. They have resulted in the creation of conceptual taxonomies of commons and common goods, which usually partition the common into the natural and the social, or the material and immaterial. In a more sophisticated way, Nick Dyer-Witheford (2006) traces what he calls the "circuit of the common," analyzing "how shared resources generate forms of social cooperation—associations—that coordinate the conversion of further resources into expanded commons." These include for Dyer-Witheford "*terrestrial commons* (the customary sharing of natural resources in traditional societies); *planner commons* (for example, command socialism and the liberal democratic welfare state); and *networked commons* (the free associations of open source software, peer-to-peer networks, grid computing and the numerous other socializations of techno-science)."

We have nothing in principle against this intellectual labor around the common. What needs to be pointed out, as Mattei (2011, 54) advises, is that any classification and legal construction of common goods should be handled with care, given the conceptual proximity of goods and commodities in a capitalist world. Dyer-Witheford's emphasis on the forms of social cooperation connected to what he calls the "circulation of the common" is important here. Far from being reducible to the status of "objects," which inheres in the legal concept of goods, the commons—even the most natural, as we saw with the example of water—cannot exist independently of a complex web of human activity devoted to their production and reproduction. This means focusing on the moment of excess that characterizes the common with regard to the commons. Such a moment is without doubt constitutive of rights and institutions, but it can never be exhausted by this juridical dimension. "Revolutionary becoming," Cesare Casarino writes in his conversation with Antonio Negri (2008, 22), "is living the common as surplus." Rooted in the antagonistic reality of labor, dispossession, and exploitation, the generation of this surplus can only take the shape of a political subjectivity capable of giving a new, common meaning to the memorable definition of labor provided by the young Marx (1988, 76): "life-engendering life."

Cooperatives, Community Economies, and Spaces of the Common

What we call the translation of the common allows a further specification of what Dyer-Witheford calls the circulation of the common. In a later article about labor cooperatives written with Greig De Peuter, Dyer-Witheford describes the circulation of the common as a process by which forms of association "organize shared resources into productive ensembles that create more commons, which in turn provide the basis for new associations" (De Peuter and Dyer-Witheford 2010, 45). This process mirrors and reverses the circulation of capital, substituting the common ("a good produced to be shared") for the commodity ("a good produced to be exchanged"). The common is thus understood as the "cellular form of society beyond capital" (44). It is clear, however, that the circulation of the common must also involve a moment of translation, which is what De Peuter and Dyer-Witheford specify as a transformation of this cellular form not into money but into association. How does this translation operate? We have contrasted the heterolingual translation that composes the common with the homolingual translation underlying capital's operations. Heterolingual translation is a process that not only inverts capital's reproductive circuits but functions according to a very different logic, one that implies the impossibility of a full and transparent translation of "a" common into "an" association. It points to a production of the common that involves the negotiation of multiple borders and the recognition that associations must always confront questions of political constitution and power. Neither the imagination of a social plenitude beyond capital nor the radical democratic vision of an articulation predicated on a lack provide the theoretical and practical resources to confront the reality of borders and bordering implied in the daily functioning of capital.

De Peuter and Dyer-Witheford are careful to consider how the circulation of the common must take into account questions of critical mass, and they note that even the state can play a role in the expansion of commons. Nevertheless, they maintain that "growth and interconnection of the commons have to precede such state interventions, to prefiguratively establish the necessary preconditions." At the same time, they emphasize that the commons must "grow beyond the moment of such direct interventions, in a proliferation of self-starting components that exceeds centralized control" (De Peuter and Dyer-Witheford 2010, 47). Their discussion of worker cooperatives is a welcome contribution to the debate about the commons because it directly confronts questions of labor politics and injects a good dose of realism into a discussion that is often dominated by theoretical abstractions. What needs to be considered to take this pragmatic approach further is the dimension of autonomous political organization that must invest experiments and initiatives in building commons. Such organization needs always to position itself not only with regard to the state but also in relation to a variety of other political forms and actors that can involve themselves in the management of commons: trade unions, nongovernmental organizations, community bodies, local governments, and so on. The reason such positioning is important, and must often take the form of a radical opposition, is that commons are by no means in themselves immune to the allures of capital and political corruption. Precisely this vulnerability makes the commons an important battleground on which struggles for the common are played out. And it is important to note that the corruption that can invest commons is a key matter to account for in the conceptualization of the common. The latter is not a figure of the morally good or a utopian horizon against which social struggles unfold. As we have affirmed before, the reproduction of borders within the commons—whether they take the form of lines of political division or ones of gender domination, racial difference, or indeed social class—can never be excluded. They must always be fought against. This is why the production of the common is always a political and not merely an ethical proposition.

"[A] friend of mine stole my idea for a book on Creative Commons" (Pasquinelli 2008, 122). With this joke, Matteo Pasquinelli points to the conflicts that invest the creation of commons. He focuses on the difficulties of organizing cooperation among creative workers and the limits of the Creative Commons intellectual property license in providing "the regulatory conditions for a real common to emerge" (78). But his quip sheds light on the way the common "falls into a field of forces surrounded and defined by the laws of value and production" (13). We see this same dynamic at play in many other spaces of the common where commons are built up or experimented with: workers' cooperatives, community economies, participatory economies (parecon), local exchange trading systems (LETS), or the barter schemes that proliferated in Argentina following the country's debt crisis of

2001. Writing of Kôjin Karatani's (2005) advocacy of LETS (a system for local exchange of nonmonetary credits and labor), Slavoj Žižek worries that it is difficult to see how it would avoid "the trap of money which would no longer be a fetish, but would serve just as 'labor money,' a transparent instrument of exchange designating each individual's contribution to the social product" (Žižek 2006, 57). There are multiple dimensions in which such spaces of the common can accommodate capital. Workers' cooperatives, for instance, are constrained to compete in market economies and can indulge in practices such as the employment of hired workers, among them lowly paid migrants. It would appear that the line between money and association is hard to draw. Furthermore, as David Ruccio argues, starting from contemporary experiences of occupation and recovery of workplaces in Argentina, the "emergence of communal forms of production constitutes a fundamental change in one social relationship, in that the workers who create the surplus now appropriate the surplus, but it doesn't speak to the distribution of the surplus and therefore the wider society within which communal enterprises exist" (Ruccio 2011, 338). This is why, in our opinion, it is important not to dismiss the valuable contribution of workers' cooperatives to building up commons, but it is unrealistic to view them as key organizations for overcoming capitalism.

Nonetheless, the building of commons provides the only grounds on which the common can be generated. Recognizing the limits of these enterprises and experiments does not mean dismissing their contribution to the political struggle of producing the common. The question of how different instances of commons coordinate, connect and disconnect, or translate into this wider political project remains. The work of Julie Graham and Katherine Gibson (writing as J. K. Gibson-Graham) is important in this regard because it emphasizes not only the need to "start where we are" in politicizing economic relations but also the challenge of working across "multiple heterogeneous sites of struggle" to "resignify *all* economic transactions and relations, capitalist and noncapitalist, in terms of their sociality and interdependence" (Gibson-Graham 2006, 97–98). Gibson-Graham's argument concerning the role of what they call "community economies" in "the task of thought of signifying communism" needs to be understood in relation to their wider vision of capitalism as an uncentered aggregate of practices (98). Joining figures such as John Chalcraft (2005) who think about capital in a plural way, they pull away from a globally coordinated politics of resistance, opposition, and transformation to embrace an alternative politics based on recognition of economic diversity. Their writing thus presents numerous and valuable instances of everyday people rethinking and reenacting economies. At the same time, it offers an attempt to grapple with the role of communities in translating between commons and the common.

Inevitably, in confronting issues of community, Gibson-Graham run up against the question of borders. Any attempt to "fix the fantasy of common being," they write, "to define the community economy, to specify what it contains (and thus what it does not) closes off the opportunity to cultivate ethical praxis" (Gibson-Graham 2006, 98). Furthermore, they recognize that "a politics aimed at building and extending community economic practices" confronts "the dangers of posing a positivity, a normative representation of the community economy, in which certain practices are valued to the exclusion of others" (98). Borders, in this vision, although they are mentioned very little by Gibson-Graham, are clearly devices of exclusion. But the question of how such a positivity or normative representation of community might be avoided, if indeed it can be avoided, is left open. Gibson-Graham describe the commons as "a community stock that needs to be maintained and replenished." They signal how the "ethical practice of commons management" creates and reproduces "the 'common substance' of the community while at the same time making a space for raising and answering the perennial question of who belongs and is therefore entitled to rights of decision" (97). But without an account of the political and legal constitution of the commons created by community economies, such an ethical vision is unable to fully come to terms with how such rights and entitlements are assigned. Nor is it able to adequately confront the question of how the borders of community are established, maintained, crossed, or challenged. The question of the relation of the common to borders is left aside.

To be sure, Gibson-Graham do not support an immunological or identitarian vision of community. They make reference to Giorgio Agamben's notion of a "coming community" as an "inessential commonality, a solidarity that in no way concerns an essence" (Agamben 1993, 19). Like Sakai, they approvingly draw on Nancy's idea of communism, of being-in-common. But the means they propose to achieve this are unclear. They propose a political project of "resubjectivation," which means "the mobilization and transformation of desires, the cultivation of capacities, and the making of new identifications" (Gibson-Graham 2006, xxxvi). This means organizing and meeting people in community settings to "make a new kind of universal that might guide the process of building different economies" (166). The practice is built on the conviction that many forms of noncapitalist economy already exist and are submerged under a metaphorical iceberg that the mainstream economy and even radical anticapitalist politics maintain. Yet the question of how such actually existing noncapitalist practices are articulated to capitalist economic activity remains muted.

Gibson-Graham's vision is hopeful and enabling insofar as it advocates and provides intellectual resources for living partly, if not fully, beyond the social relation of capital. But the dimension of autonomous political organization is less obvious. They pay scant attention to the common's susceptibility to economic and political corruption. Nor does their vision of economic diversity account for what in chapter 3 we follow Deleuze and Guattari in calling the "axiomatic of capital." As previously discussed, this axiomatic introduces isomorphy across increasingly heterogeneous situations. The existence of alternative economies does not mean that capital is no longer capable of working through an abstract matrix that continually reshuffles relations between economy and culture, politics, and law. In our view, it is precisely the operations of the axiomatic of capital that need to be taken into account if community economies are to become grounds on which struggles for the common can be successfully conducted. On one hand, it is important to remember, as Deleuze and Guattari write, that "capital as a general relation of production can very easily integrate concrete sectors or modes of production that are noncapitalistic" (Deleuze and Guattari 1987, 455). The financialization of capitalism has further increased capital's ability to capture forms of life and economic activity that were originally not subdued to the imperatives of valorization and accumulation. On the other hand, although Deleuze and Guattari's analysis refers primarily to the relation between capital's axiomatic and states as "models of realization" of that axiomatic (454), today there is a need to recognize that the alchemy of deterritorialization and reterritorialization constitutive of capitalism has moved beyond an international system centered on states as homogeneous cells. This does not mean that capital's axiomatic has created a smooth global capitalism. Rather, it continues to work through and produce radically heterogeneous conditions, which arise from capital's encounter with peculiar political, social, and cultural settings. It is important to pluralize the analysis of capitalism, both historically and in the present (Chalcraft 2005). But this should not lead us to underestimate the moment of unity that pertains to the very concept and logic of capital—to its "axiomatic."

The proliferation and heterogenization of borders we map in this book correspond to a geographical disruption at the core of contemporary global processes. New experiences of space, often mediated by new information and communication technologies; new practices of mobility; new assemblages of authority, territory, rights (Sassen 2006); new articulations be-

tween the frontiers of capital and territorial boundaries—all concur to produce a geography of power, accumulation, and struggle that challenges analytical frameworks centered on notions such as the international division of
labor, center and periphery, or the space of flows and the space of places.
This geographical disruption has political consequences that become clear
once we recognize that a specific production and bordering of political
space was one of the crucial features of the modern state in the West. The
basic concepts that still shape our political languages, from citizenship to
sovereignty, from constitution to representation, are all predicated on "implicit spatial representations" deeply embedded in the history and theories
of the modern state, which means in its *borders* (Galli 2010, 4). This is also
true for the concept of democracy, especially as far as the concepts and
institutions of political representation, sovereignty of the people, and the
nation are concerned. Once we look at existing national spaces from the
point of view of border as method, it becomes clear that they are traversed
by multiple flows and channels that escape the regulation of the state. They
are also crossed by a plurality of legal and normative orders with heterogeneous sources and by processes of increasing spatial heterogenization.
Moreover, they are all subject in different ways and with different intensities
to the action of powers that exceed national denominations. This means
they can no longer be fully governed by the logics of political representation
or be contained by a web of constitutional checks and balances operating at
the national level.

While the exclusionary dimension of the nation-state, symbolized and
implemented by the border, is still very much present in the contemporary
world, there still are "defensive" struggles, for instance, for social commons,
that are fought at the level of the state. This is probably rightly so. But
independently of what we have written about the structural antinomy between the public and the common, the political production of space historically associated with the state no longer offers an effective shield against
capital. This means it is a matter of realism for the political project of the
common to refuse the idea of positioning itself within existing bounded
institutional spaces and to look for the necessary production of new political
spaces. This is an awareness that has widely circulated in debates on democracy and the global order or disorder. Writing in 1995, for instance, David
Held maintained that "the meaning and place of democratic politics, and of
the contending models of democracy, have to be rethought in relation to
overlapping local, national, regional, and global structures and processes"
(Held 1995, 21). The attempt to globalize democracy and rethink cosmopol-

itanism undertaken by Held and other scholars in the following years has led to many proposals, widely discussed within the social movements that flooded the World Social Forum, to "democratize" the United Nations as well as agencies of global governance such as the World Bank, the International Monetary Fund, and the World Trade Organization. This is not the place to discuss the details of these proposals, which often imply the involvement of nongovernmental organizations and unions in attempts to introduce criteria of transparency and accountability into the structures of global governance. We do not want to dismiss these efforts, although we do want to register the difficulty of translating the principle of political representation, constitutive of the modern experience of democracy, onto the global level. Unless one thinks of cosmopolitanism in terms of a global state and a global people, which is unrealistic and in our eyes also undesirable, the mediation of the state seems indispensable to theories of global democracy, as proposals to reform the United Nations make clear. The globalization of democracy is often presented as the construction of overlapping levels of institutional organization moving from an imagined figure of the state that does not exist anymore. One of the problems we have with such theories regards the fact that the spatial scales distinguished by Held ("local, national, regional, and global") are taken as already given and fixed, without investigating the continuous and tumultuous processes of their constitution.

From the point of view of border as method, a politics of the common can only be imagined and constructed as one that works through all these scales and invests processes of bordering across and among them. In recent years, the new salience of regional and continental or subcontinental spaces in the framework of globalization has led to many attempts to rethink cosmopolitan and radical democratic projects on this scale and to assume the region as a space for "counter-hegemonic globalization" (Balibar 2003b; Beck and Grande 2007; Chen 2010; De Sousa Santos 2009; Escobar 2008). We find these attempts particularly interesting insofar as they emphasize the role of movements and struggles in processes of regional constitution and focus on what Wang Hui, speaking of Asia, calls "the ambiguities and contradictions" of the idea of the region itself (Wang 2011b, 59). In this sense, the discussion of European integration has perhaps been too much shaped by the specific spatial and institutional configuration taken by Europe in the framework of the European Union. Reading Ulrich Beck and Edgar Grande's *Cosmopolitan Europe*, originally published in 2004, one finds an interesting discussion of the "variability" and "shifting" of borders as a distinctive feature of what they call the European "cosmopolitan Empire" as opposed to the modern state (Beck and Grande 2007, 64). Unfortunately, this discussion is entirely constructed on the blueprint of the institutional processes of the so-called European enlargement and neighborhood policy, without any consideration of the new border regime accompanying them.

It would be too easy, but no less true, to maintain that the current crisis of European integration makes the huge intellectual investments since the early 1990s in the postnational citizenship emerging in its frame at least overproportioned. This is not to say that we do not see a chance for the political project of the common in the gaps of official institutional structures, which are themselves in-the-making, multilevel, and crisscrossed by multiple crises in Europe and elsewhere in the world. We are convinced that social struggles can nurture a new political imagination capable of working through current processes of regional integration and of opening them toward a reinvention of internationalism and a new global dimension (Chen 2010, 15). The role of border struggles in this opening is crucial, because they often insist on the boundaries that cross any region and at the same time question the bounded nature of the region itself. In a thought-provoking essay, titled "Europe as Borderland" (2009), Balibar proposes a crossover pattern for the interpretation of contemporary political spaces. He speaks of three "open overlapping spaces," which may be called "Euro-Atlantic," "Euro-Mediterranean," and "Euro-Asiatic" without forgetting that "these are symbolic rather than realistic nominations," to show how they "intersect over the projected territory of Europe" (Balibar 2009, 200). He is careful to add that this analytical framework is a projection of ideas forged within contemporary critiques of a pure cultural identity as well as in the work of geographers, writers, and political and social theorists who "examine the prospects of 'border zones' of the new Europe" (200). We find in this elaboration of a crossover pattern a suggestion that is valid not just for Europe. We know that border zones are at the same time "contact" and "translation zones" (Apter 2006; Pratt 2008). We also know that they are no longer found only at territorial edges of states and regions. Struggles developing in and around these zones therefore become even more crucial for an investigation of the possible spaces of the common.

In Struggle for the Common

In this chapter we have examined the complex feedback between the common and the commons from a variety of angles. This has meant positioning ourselves with respect to previous arguments about the common, commons, common goods, and the public and the private offered by thinkers such as Hardt and Negri (2009), Dyer-Witheford (2006), and Mattei (2011). It has also involved a critical engagement with works by Laclau and Mouffe and Gibson-Graham. To tell the truth, these critiques are not hard to write. The greater achievement is to find common ground with these intellectual and political projects. This is why we have tried to show what we share with these thinkers while we demonstrate what divides us from them. It is probably a good thing that struggles against the privatization of water in Bolivia and Italy or fights against the appropriation of land in India do not turn around esoteric questions such as whether the ontology of the common is constituted by an excess or a lack. Nonetheless, the question of how we translate between multifarious and heterogeneous struggles and attempts to build the commons is at the heart of the approaches to the common we have considered. Border struggles are prominent among struggles to establish and maintain commons, because the latter necessarily face questions of limitation, space, scale, and capital. Especially in cases where border struggles press the question of what constitutes territory or jurisdiction, they pose a strong challenge to understandings and practices of the common predicated on the appeal to an already existing and forever bound community. Independently of the sophisticated theoretical debates surrounding the notion of community, it is important to note that the invocation of community can be incredibly enabling for social and political struggles. But it can also be a trap. The relation of community to capital is often obscured in contemporary attempts to build alternative forms of social and economic association. The tendency of communities to close themselves is evident in xenophobic nationalisms and localisms and can also surface in radical political experiments (Joseph 2002). This is why border struggles provide a kind of political fulcrum in struggles for the common, exhibiting in particular how they turn around questions of subjectivity.

There is also the question of the borders between the multifarious struggles and movements that compose the contemporary politics of the common. What do struggles to protect alternative political spaces in European cities from rent have to do with peasant land struggles or labor struggles in Chinese factories? What does the attempt to build digital commons through free and open-source software share with Indigenous struggles against biopiracy or efforts to forge a genetic commons? It may be possible to identify analogies or homologies between these struggles at an abstract level. But what about the question of whether they offer each other intellectual, politi-

cal, or physical resources? Does it make sense to try to connect these struggles in a kind of network of networks, to recall a concept that circulated
in debates about transnational political organization in the "global movements" that swelled up after the iconic protests in Seattle and Genoa more
than ten years ago? Is connection alone enough to galvanize political collaboration and alliance if it does not lead participants to establish relations
across struggles, which is to say to become involved in the mutual constitution of a larger political subjectivity? Or do local struggles to build commons
immediately confront the global dimension of capital and contribute to the
construction of the common even if they are not linked up or related to
concurrent struggles?

These are questions that hark back to our discussion of international
solidarity and unity in chapter 5. But to ask them from the perspective of the
common is to add a new dimension. More than ten years ago, Hardt and
Negri provocatively characterized "the most radical and powerful struggles
of the final years of the twentieth century" as "incommunicable." By this
they meant that these struggles could not "be linked together as a globally
expanding chain of revolts" because "the desires and needs they expressed
could not be translated into different contexts" (Hardt and Negri 2000, 54).
Although many attempts were made to address this problem of translation
—for instance, in the context of the World Social Forums that started in
Porto Alegre in 2001—the encounter with the untranslatable that invested
these efforts was never avoided or overcome. At stake, to recall the invocation of Lenin by Gramsci that we mentioned in the previous chapter, was
not the translatability of languages but the deep rooting of struggles in
heterogeneous material networks and settings. Here we should be clear that
heterogeneity does not simply mean fragmentation. Rather, it points to a
proliferation of struggles that can potentially be a source of strength. This is
not to deny that the risk of a debilitating dispersion exists. Capital, insofar as
it works as a device of articulation and homolingual translation, exploits and
constantly reproduces this risk. This is why even struggles that are not
immediately conceived and fought as struggles against capital are always
haunted by its operations. Only by confronting the workings of capital can
such struggles enter potentializing relations with others, starting a process
in which the production of the common becomes a political possibility. The
best resources for translating between struggles often arise from within
struggles themselves, percolating up from below rather than being imposed
by leadership or a vanguard. Border struggles are perhaps the best example

of this. It is precisely because they are almost always confronted with the material need to translate that they have become crucial for the political project of the common.

Over the past ten years we have witnessed a rich sedimentation of experiences, networking tools, and exchanges between struggles and movements across many different scales and spaces. These efforts have made a material difference to the way that many movements organize and conceive of themselves. There is now less of a tendency for political movements to see themselves as operating through a set of nested scales moving from the local to the global. There is also more opportunity for movements to forge transversal relations across a multiplicity of borders. This has made the question of translation and its limits even more pressing for political organization. It is not that these experiences have increased confidence in the possibility of transparent translations between different struggles. To the contrary, the difficulties and paradoxes of translation are ever more present. This is true even within highly localized struggles, for instance, those involving migrant workers in metropolitan contexts where a dense multiplicity of experiences, languages, and organizing methods intersect. Indeed, it has become difficult to disentangle such struggles from their transnational dimensions, and the borders between struggles have become ever less clear and defined. The encounter with the untranslatable is a daily occurrence in these contexts. But, as Sakai allows us to see, the untranslatable "cannot exist prior to the enunciation of translation" (Sakai 1997, 14). It is not simply an obstacle but also a knot of intense social relations where processes of collective subjectivation are necessarily confronted with material differences that continue to proliferate and emerge anew despite the communicational possibilities enabled by translation. It is not a paradox that it is precisely in this encounter with the untranslatable that processes of networking and establishing links between struggles are confronted with their highest potentialities and their most forbidding limits.

"In a way that goes beyond metaphor," writes the Observatorio Metropolitano of Madrid, "the European revolution, if it happens, will have begun in North Africa" (2011, 110). This observation on the part of a "hybrid collective" of activists and researchers involved in the uprisings and occupations that swept Spain in spring 2011, registers the importance for these movements of the revolutions that occurred in Tunisia and Egypt earlier in the same year. At stake in this declaration is not just the inspiration arising from the Arab movements, whose effects resonated on the global scale, extending as far as Greece, the United States, London, and even metropolitan China. There was also an intense process of exchange between movements on the two shores of the Mediterranean, working across one of the most heavily patrolled and deadly borders in the contemporary world. This involved the organization of political meetings in cities such as Paris and Tunis, struggles around trans-Mediterranean migration (which markedly increased following the revolutions in north Africa), intellectual and political transfers passing through universities and social centers, the wide dissemination of materials and slogans on the Internet, and the translation of pamphlets, blogs, revolutionary handbooks, and other tools of rebellion. In all of these contexts and processes, there was a tense confrontation with the question of political translation.

While the revolutions in north Africa were highly mediatized, the lines of communication involved in the global dissemination of images and information about these events (even if carried out on Facebook and Twitter as well as CNN and Al Jazeera) left the border between Africa and Europe untouched, and arguably led to its reinforcement. The translation carried out between movements had a radically different aim, and, even if a series of issues regarding regime change, labor, education, debt, and gender dominated, the question of the border and the struggles surrounding it was a constant point of reference as well as contention. In this continued invocation of the border as a field of struggle, the element of untranslatability as a limit to communication compelled and fired political fervor on both sides of the Mediterranean. Doubtless this confrontation with the untranslatable was a social experience, fraught with affective joys and difficulties. But it also inspired and even required reopening translation in the face of material circumstances that exposed the limits of linguistic communication, tearing and renting established political subjectivities away from themselves (and from comfortable positions and contexts) and producing new vistas of struggle and organization. Despite the frictions and difficulties that haunted this process, it is in such moments that the possibility of translating the common emerges. The multiplication of struggles that followed these encounters did not forge a universalistic cause. Occupations and protests in different parts of the world engaged with different issues and employed different methods to struggle against dictatorships and financial capital. This multiscalar expansion of struggles (including the Occupy movement, the Indignados, and the continuations of the Arab revolutions) involved translation as a necessary moment. A continued encounter with the untranslatable supplied resources for the strengthening of revolts and a fabrication of the common that came into being precisely through the confrontation with borders. This remains true despite the changes experienced by these movements as they mutated, faced postrevolutionary regime changes, began new social initiatives beyond the staging of occupations, and temporarily disappeared from the screens of the mainstream media. In the contemporary globalized and networked world, the problem of continuity and discipline in the organization of collective opposition to capitalism cannot be addressed without confronting the discontinuity and rupture implicit in practices of translation and bordering. Indeed, it is only from the constant and critical work of organization, or what we have called the labor of translation, that a new sequence of struggles is likely to emerge.

Precisely in this grappling with borders, translation, in the political understanding of its heterolingual modality that we are proposing, always implies a transformation of subjectivity. Far from appealing to a sovereign machine of mediation or to a transcendental scheme, the workings of this kind of translation remain immanent to the constitution and proliferation of struggles. In this book, we have taken multiplicity as the material reality that structures the field on which the social relation of capital and struggles against capital are played out. The heterogeneity of global space, the multiplication of labor, differential inclusion, and border struggles are some of the concepts that have allowed us to grasp the political stakes and potentials of this multiplicity, which we have analyzed by following the thread provided by the tension between abstract and living labor. Focusing on the production of labor power as a commodity across a variety of borders, borderscapes, and border zones, we have pointed to the ways this tension is ever more pronounced for contemporary working subjects. It is no secret that this scenario introduces challenges, vulnerabilities, and even resistance to efforts of political organization and the creation of new institutional forms adequate to the networked conditions of current capitalism and struggles for the production of the common. These points of fragility are a small price to pay for the vast material potency that can be generated from this irreducibly heterogeneous array of spaces, times, subjectivities, and scales.

At stake is a making of the world, fabrica mundi, which works against the transcendentalizing impulse of both state and capital and the various configurations of their borders and frontiers. We are aware of the pitfalls and regressions that confront philosophical attempts to deal with the question of the many and the one. At the same time, we are convinced that the construction of a transcendental escape route, whether by means of a social contract or dialectical devices, leads to the imposition of unities from above —unities that can only hold by fiat of the violence and power that have been invested in their production and reproduction across the modern era. Constituted powers and the official philosophies that sustain them have always been scared by attempts to confront the problem of multiplicity and unity that do not make recourse to such transcendentalizing mastery and which threaten to produce a political subject that is at once multiple and potent. The image of the sixteenth-century philosopher Giordano Bruno burning on the stake in Rome's Campo de' Fiori is just one reminder of this fear. Bruno attempted indeed to show "how there is unity in the multiplicity [*moltitudine*], and multiplicity in the unity, how being is multimodal and multi-unitary, and how it is, finally, one in substance and truth" (Bruno 1998, 10). He added that "the one, the infinite—that being, that which is in all—is everywhere, or better still, is itself the *ubique* [everywhere], and that, therefore, the infinite dimension, since it is not magnitude, coincides with the undivided individual, as the infinite multitude, since it is not number, coincides with unity" (11). If this heretical whisper from a distant past continues to inspire materialist philosophies of immanence, the flames that licked at Bruno's feet are no less hot.

Moving between the poles of multiplicity and unity, struggles for the common today continue to draw on such subterranean and repressed strains of thought, whether they derive from traditions of anticolonial resistance, Indigenous narratives, strategies of *marronage*, or past experiences of subaltern and working-class movements. From the perspective of border as method, the crucial element in all of these struggles is the production of subjectivity that at once sustains and drives them. Approaching struggles in this way is important at a time when the borders between political experiences and social worlds are at once more evident and more porous. Border struggles in very real ways have expanded and sit no longer at the margins but at the center of our political lives. While they challenge any closed notion of political subjectivity in the struggle for the common, they also confront us with the continued production of other limits that run across societies, labor markets, and jurisdictions. Class division, for instance, continues to traverse these fields, even as the multiplicity that invests class struggle plays an essential role in struggles for the common. This is because such struggles are necessarily against capital and thus require a radical reformatting of social relations, liberating them from exploitation and dispossession and from the sexed and raced logics of domination that are deeply embedded in these modes of capitalist extraction and displacement. The fact that border struggles have come to the political fore does not mean they are about to end. To the contrary, they are mounting and escalating. The deaths that daily occur along the world's borders are testimony to this. We should not forget them even as we realize that border struggles are not played out only at the border and in many ways the battle has just begun.

REFERENCES

16Beaver. 2005. *Continental Drift Seminar Part I—Brian Holmes.* Accessed May 19, 2011. http://www.16beavergroup.org/events/archives/001590print.html.

Abdallah, Mogniss. 2000. *J'y suis, J'y reste!: Les luttes de l'immigration en France depuis les Années Soixante.* Paris: Reflex.

Adkins, Lisa. 2005. "The New Economy, Property and Personhood." *Theory, Culture & Society* 22 (1): 111–30.

Agamben, Giorgio. 1993. *The Coming Community*, trans. Michael Hardt. Minneapolis: University of Minnesota Press.

———. 1998. *Homo Sacer: Sovereign Power and Bare Life*, trans. Daniel Heller-Roazen. Stanford, CA: Stanford University Press.

———. 2000. *Means without End: Notes on Politics*, trans. Vincenzo Binetti and Cesare Casarino. Minneapolis: University of Minnesota Press.

———. 2005. *State of Exception*, trans. Kevin Attell. Chicago: University of Chicago Press.

Aglietta, Michel. 1979. *A Theory of Capitalist Regulation: The US Experience*, trans. David Fernbach. London: New Left Books.

Agnew, John. 2008. "Borders on the Mind: Reframing Border Thinking." *Ethics and Global Politics* 1 (4): 175–91.

———. 2009. *Globalization and Sovereignty.* Lanham, MD: Rowman and Little-field.

Akalin, Ayşe. 2007. "Hired as a Caregiver, Demanded as a Housewife: Becoming a Migrant Domestic Worker in Turkey." *European Journal of Women's Studies* 14 (3): 209–25.

Allen, Theodore W. 1994–97. *The Invention of the White Race.* London: Verso.

Althauser, Robert P., and Arne L. Kalleberg. 1981. "Firms, Occupations, and the Structure of Labor Markets: A Conceptual Analysis." In *Sociological Perspectives on Labor Markets*, ed. Ivar Berg, 119–49. New York: Academic Press.

Althusser, Louis, and Étienne Balibar. 1970. *Reading "Capital,"* trans. B. Brewster. London: New Left Books.

Alzaga, Valery. 2011. "Justice for Janitors Campaign: Open-Sourcing Labor Conflicts

Against Global Neo-Liberalism." *Open Democracy.* Accessed January 4, 2012. http://www.opendemocracy.net.

Amin, Shahid, and Marcel van der Linden, eds. 1997. *"Peripheral" Labour?: Studies in the History of Partial Proletarianization.* Cambridge: Cambridge University Press.

Amoore, Louise. 2006. "Biometric Borders: Governing Mobilities in the War on Terror." *Political Geography* 25: 336–51.

Anderson, Benedict. 1991. *Imagined Communities. Reflections on the Origin and Spread of Nationalism.* London: Verso.

——. 2005. *Under Three Flags. Anarchism and the Anti-Colonial Imagination.* London: Verso.

Anderson, Bridget. 2000. *Doing the Dirty Work?: The Global Politics of Domestic Labour.* New York: Zed Books.

——. 2003. "Just Another Job? The Commodification of Domestic Labour." In *Global Woman: Nannies, Maids, and Sex Workers in the New Economy*, ed. Barbara Ehrenreich and Arlie Hochschild, 104–15. London: Granta Books.

Anderson, Bridget, and Martin Ruhs. 2008. *A Need for Immigrant Labour? The Micro-Level Determinants of Staff Shortages and Implications for a Skills Based Immigration Policy*, Migration Advisory Committee. Accessed November 3, 2008. http://www.ukba.homeoffice.gov.uk/mac.

——. 2010. "Researching Illegality and Labour Migration [editorial]." *Population, Space, and Place* 16: 175–79.

Anderson, Bridget, Nandita Sharma, and Cynthia Wright. 2009. "Editorial: Why No Borders?" *Refuge* 26 (2): 5–18.

Andreas, Peter. 2009. *Border Games: Policing the U.S.-Mexico Divide*, 2nd ed. Ithaca, NY: Cornell University Press.

Andrijasevic, Rutvica. 2010a. *Migration, Agency and Citizenship in Sex Trafficking.* London: Palgrave.

——. 2010b. "From Exception to Excess: Detention and Deportations across the Mediterranean Space." In *The Deportation Regime: Sovereignty, Space, and the Freedom of Movement*, ed. Nicholas De Genova and Nathalie Peutz, 147–65. Durham, NC: Duke University Press.

Andrijasevic, Rutvica, and William Walters. 2010. "The International Organization for Migration and the International Government of Borders." *Environment and Planning D: Society and Space* 28: 977–99.

Aneesh, Aneesh. 2006. *Virtual Migration: The Programming of Globalization.* Durham, NC: Duke University Press.

Anggraeni, Dewi. 2006. *Dreamseekers: Indonesian Women as Domestic Workers in Asia.* Jakarta: Equinox Publishing Indonesia.

Anzaldúa, Gloria. 1987. *Borderlands/La frontera.* San Francisco: Aunt Lute Books.

Appadurai, Arjun. 1996. *Modernity at Large: Cultural Dimensions of Globalization.* Minneapolis: University of Minnesota Press.

Apter, Emily. 2006. *The Translation Zone: A New Comparative Literature.* Princeton, NJ: Princeton University Press.

Arendt, Hannah. 1951. *The Origins of Totalitarianism.* New York: Harcourt, Brace.

Arnold, Dennis, and John Pickles. 2010. "Global Work, Surplus Labor, and the Precarious Economies of the Border." *Antipode* 43 (5): 1598–624.

Aronowitz, Stanley. 2003. *How Class Works: Power and Social Movement*. New Haven, CT: Yale University Press.

Arrighi, Giovanni. 1994. *The Long Twentieth Century: Money, Power, and the Origins of Our Times*. London: Verso.

———. 2007. *Adam Smith in Beijing: Lineages of the Twenty-First Century*. London: Verso.

Artaker, Anna. 2010. "WORLD MAP." In *Das Potosí-Prinzip. Wie können wir das Lied des Herrn im fremden Land singen?*, ed. Alice Creischer, Max Jorge Hinders and Andreas Siekmann, 231–233. Cologne: Verlag der Buchhandlung Walter König.

Baas, Michiel. 2010. *Imagined Mobility: Migration and Transnationalism among Indian Students in Australia*. London: Anthem Press.

Bacon, David. 2008. *Illegal People: How Globalization Creates Migration and Criminalizes Immigrants*. Boston: Beacon Press.

Badiou, Alain. 2010. *The Communist Hypothesis*, trans. David Macey and Steve Corcoran. London: Verso.

Bair, Jennifer, ed. 2009. *Frontiers of Commodity Chain Research*. Stanford, CA: Stanford University Press.

Bakewell, Peter. 1984. *Miners of the Red Mountain*. Albuquerque: University of New Mexico Press.

Balibar, Étienne. 1991. "Is There a 'Neo-Racism.'" In Étienne Balibar and Immanuel Wallerstein. *Race, Nation, Class: Ambiguous Identities*. 17–28. London: Verso.

———. 1992a. *Les Frontières de la Démocratie*. Paris: La Découverte.

———. 1992b. "Foucault and Marx: The Question of Nominalism." In *Michel Foucault Philosopher*, ed. T. J. Armstrong, 38–56. New York: Routledge.

———. 1994. *Masses, Classes and Ideas. Studies on Politics and Philosophy Before and After Marx*, trans. J. Swenson. London: Routledge.

———. 2002. *Politics and the Other Scene*. London: Verso.

———. 2003a. *We the People of Europe. Reflections on Transnational Citizenship*. Princeton, NJ: Princeton University Press.

———. 2003b. *L'Europe, l'Amérique, la guerre. Réflexions sur la médiation européenne*. Paris: La Découverte.

———. 2007. "Uprisings in the Banlieues." *Constellations* 14 (1): 47–71.

———. 2009. "Europe as borderland." *Environment and Planning D: Society and Space* 27 (2): 190–215.

———. 2010. *La proposition de l'égaliberté*. Paris: PUF.

———. 2011. *Citoyen sujet et autres essais de anthropologie philosophique*. Paris: PUF.

Banerjee, Paula. 2010. *Borders, Histories, Existences: Gender and Beyond*. New Delhi: Sage.

Banerjee-Guha, Swapna. 2008. "Space Relations of Capital and Significance of New Economic Enclaves: SEZs in India." *Economic and Political Weekly* 43 (47): 51–59.

Barbalet, Jack M. 1988. *Citizenship: Rights, Struggle and Class Inequality*. Milton Keynes, UK: Open University Press.

Barber, Brad M., and Terrance Odean. 2001. "Boys Will Be Boys: Gender, Overconfidence, and Common Stock Investment." *Quarterly Journal of Economics* 116 (1): 261–92.

Bartelson, Jens. 1995. *A Genealogy of Sovereignty*. Cambridge: Cambridge University Press.

Barth, Fredrik. 1979. *Ethnic Groups and Boundaries: The Social Organization of Cultural Difference*. Oslo: Universitetsvorlaget.

Barr, Michael D. 2002. *Cultural Politics and Asian Values: The Tepid War*. London: Routledge.

Barron, Pierre, Anne Bory, Sébastien Chauvin, Nicolas Jounin, and Lucie Tourette. 2011. *On bosse ici, on reste ici. La grève des sans papiers, une adventure inédite*. Paris: La Découverte.

Basch, Linda, Nina Glick Schiller, and Cristina Szanton Blanc. 1994. *Nations Unbound: Transnational Projects, Postcolonial Predicaments, and Deterritorialized Nation-States*. Langhorne, PA: Gordon and Breach.

Bauder, Harald. 2006. *Labor Movement: How Migration Regulates Labor Markets*. New York: Oxford University Press.

Beck, Ulrich. 2000. *What Is Globalization?*, trans. Patrick Camiller. Cambridge: Polity Press.

Beck, Ulrich, and Edgar Grande. 2007. *Cosmopolitan Europe*, trans. Ciaran Cronin. Cambridge: Polity Press.

Becker, Gary S. 1962. "Investment in Human Capital: A Theoretical Analysis." *Journal of Political Economy* 70 (5): 9–49.

Belnap, Jeffrey, and Raul Fernández, eds. 1998. *José Marti's "Our America."* Durham, NC: Duke University Press.

Benhabib, Seyla. 2004. *The Rights of Others: Aliens, Residents, and Citizens*. Cambridge: Cambridge University Press.

Benjamin, Walter. 1969. *Illuminations*, ed. Hannah Arendt, trans. Harry Zohn. New York: Schocken Books.

Benkler, Yochai. 2006. *The Wealth of Networks. How Social Production Transforms Markets and Freedom*. New Haven, CT: Yale University Press.

Bensaâd, Ali. 2006. "The Militarization of Migration Frontiers in the Mediterranean." In *The Maghreb Connection. Movements of Life across North Africa*, ed. Ursula Biemann and Brian Holmes, 12–20. Barcelona: Actar.

Benton, Lauren. 2005. "Legal Spaces of Empire: Piracy and the Origins of Ocean Regionalism." *Comparative Studies in Society and History* 47 (4): 700–724.

Berg, Ulla. 2008. "Practical Challenges of Multi-sited Ethnography. *Anthropology News*, May. Accessed October 25, 2010. http://www.aaanet.org/pdf/upload/49-5-Ulla-Berg-In-Focus.pdf.

Berger, John, and Jean Mohr. 1975. *A Seventh Man: A Book of Images and Words about the Experience of Migrant Workers in Europe*. Harmondsworth, UK: Penguin.

Berman, Edward H. 1983. *The Idea of Philanthropy: The Influence of the Carnegie, Ford, and Rockerfeller Foundations on American Foreign Policy*. Albany: State University Press of New York.

Bernardot, Marc. 2008. *Camps d'étrangers*. Bellecombe-en-Bauges, France: Éditions du Croquant.

Best, Stephen. 2004. *The Fugitive's Properties: Law and the Poetics of Possession*. Chicago: University of Chicago Press.

Bhaduri, Amit. 2007. "Development or Developmental Terrorism?" *Economic and Political Weekly* 42 (7): 552–53.

Bhabha, Homi K. 1994. *The Location of Culture*. London: Routledge.

Bharucha, Rustom. 2009. *Another Asia: Rabindranath Tagore and Okakura Tenshin.* New Delhi: Oxford University Press.

Bhattacharya, Rajesh, and Kalyan Sanyal. 2011. "Bypassing the Squalor: New Towns, Immaterial Labour and Exclusion in Post-colonial Urbanization." *Economic and Political Weekly* 46 (31): 41–48.

Bigo, Didier. 2002. "Security and Immigration: Toward a Critique of the Governmentality of Unease." *Alternatives* 27: 63–92.

———. 2006. "Globalized-in-Security: The Field and the Ban-opticon." In *Translation, Biopolitics, Colonial Difference*, ed. Jon Solomon and Naoki Sakai, 109–55. Hong Kong: Hong Kong University Press.

Blackstone, William. 1825 [1765]. *Commentaries on the Laws of England*, Book the Second, 16th ed. London: printed by A. Strahn for T. Cadell and J. Butterworth and Son.

Blair-Loy, Mary, and Jerry A. Jacobs. 2003. "Globalization, Work Hours, and the Care Deficit among Stockbrokers." *Gender and Society* 17 (2): 230–49.

Blanchard, Pascal, Nicolas Bancel, Olivier Barlet, and Sandrine Lemaire, eds. 2005. *La fracture coloniale. La société française au prisme de l'héritage colonial.* Paris: La Découverte.

Bloch, Ernst. 1977 [1932]. "Nonsynchronism and Its Obligation to Its Dialectics." *New German Critique* 11: 22–38.

Bloch, Marc. 1953. *The Historian's Craft*, trans. Peter Putnam. New York: Knopf.

Bojadzijev, Manuela. 2008. *Die windige Internationale. Rassismus und Kämpfe der Migration.* Münster: Westfälisches Dampfboot.

Boltanski, Luc, and Eve Chiapello. 2005. *The New Spirit of Capitalism.* New York: Verso.

Bonfante, Pietro. 1958. *Storia del diritto romano*, 2 vols. Milan: Giuffrè.

Boothman, Derek. 2004. *Traducibilità e processi traduttivi. Un caso: A. Gramsci linguista.* Perugia: Guerra.

Bosniak, Linda. 2006. *The Citizen and the Alien: Dilemmas of Contemporary Membership.* Princeton, NJ: Princeton University Press.

Bosswick, Wolfgang. 2000. "The Development of Asylum Policy in Germany." *Journal of Refugee Studies* 13 (1): 43–60.

Bouteldja, Houria, and Sadri Khiari, eds. 2012. *Nous sommes les indigènes de la République.* Paris: Éditions Amsterdam.

Bowman, Isaiah. 1942. "Geography vs. Geopolitics." *Geographical Review* 32 (4): 646–58.

Brandt Commission. 1980. *North-South: A Program for Survival, a Report of the Independent Commission on International Development Issues.* Cambridge, MA: MIT Press.

Braudel, Fernand. 1979. *The Perspective of the World.* New York: Harper and Row.

Bräutigam, Deborah, and Tang Xiaoyang. 2011. "African Shenzhen: China's Special Economic Zones in Africa." *Journal of Modern African Studies* 49 (1): 27–54.

Braverman, Harry. 1974. *Labor and Monopoly Capital: The Degradation of Work in the Twentieth Century.* London: Monthly Review Press.

Broeders, Dennis. 2007. "The New Digital Borders of Europe: EU Databases and the Surveillance of Irregular Migrants." *International Sociology* 22 (1): 71–92.

Brotton, Jerry. 1998. *Trading Territories: Mapping the Early Modern World.* Ithaca, NY: Cornell University Press.

Brown, Wendy. 2005. *Edgework: Critical Essays on Knowledge and Politics*. Princeton, NJ: Princeton University Press.

———. 2008. "Porous Sovereignty, Walled Democracy." Paper presented at University Roma Tre, March 27.

———. 2010. *Walled States, Waning Democracy*. New York: Zone Books.

Bruno, Giordano. 1998 [1584–91]. *Cause, Principle and Unity. And Essays on Magic*, ed. R. J. Blackwell and R. de Lucca. Cambridge: Cambridge University Press.

Bryan, Dick, and Michael Rafferty. 2006. *Capitalism with Derivatives: A Political Economy of Financial Derivatives, Capital and Class*. London: Palgrave Macmillan.

Bryan, Dick, Randy Martin, and Mike Rafferty. 2009. "Financialization and Marx: Giving Labor and Capital a Financial Makeover." *Review of Radical Political Economics* 41 (4): 458–72.

Buck-Morss, Susan. 2000. *Dreamworld and Catastrophe: The Passing of Mass Utopia in East and West*. Cambridge, MA: MIT Press.

Butler, Judith, Ernesto Laclau, and Slavoj Žižek. 2000. *Contingency, Hegemony, Universality: Contemporary Dialogues on the Left*. London: Verso.

Caffentzis, George. 2005. "Immeasureable Value? An Essay on Marx's Legacy." *The Commoner* 10: 87–114. Accessed January 17, 2012. http://www.commoner.org.uk/10caffentzis.pdf.

Caldiron, Guido. 2005. *Banlieue: Vita e rivolta nelle periferie della metropoli*. Rome: Manifestolibri.

Calichman, Richard F., and John Namjun Kim. 2010. "Interview with Naoki Sakai." In *The Politics of Culture: Around the Work of Naoki Sakai*, ed. Richard F. Calichman and John Namjun Kim, 225–50. New York: Routledge.

Carens, Joseph. 2010. *Immigrants and the Right to Stay*. Cambridge, MA: MIT Press.

Casarino, Cesare, and Antonio Negri. 2008. *In Praise of the Common: A Conversation on Philosophy and Politics*. Minneapolis: University of Minnesota Press.

Castel, Robert. 2007. *La discrimination negative: Citoyens ou indigènes?* Paris: Seuil.

Castells, Manuel. 1996. *The Rise of the Network Society*. Cambridge: Blackwell.

———. 2001. *The Internet Galaxy: Reflections on the Internet, Business, and Society*. New York: Oxford University Press.

———. 2010. *End of Millennium: The Information Age: Economy, Society and Culture*, vol. 3, 2nd ed. Oxford: Wiley-Blackwell.

Castles, Stephen. 1995. "How Nation-states Respond to Immigration and Ethnic Diversity." *New Community* 21 (3): 293–308.

———. 2004. "Why Migration Policies Fail." *Ethnic and Racial Studies* 27 (2): 205–27.

Castles, Stephen, and Mark J. Miller. 2003. *The Age of Migration*, 3rd ed. Basingstoke, UK: Palgrave Macmillan.

Cella, Gian Primo. 2006. *Tracciare confini: Realtà e metafore della distinzione*. Bologna: Il Mulino.

Cetina, Karin Knorr. 1997. "Sociality with Objects: Social Relations in Postsocial Knowledge Societies." *Theory, Culture and Society* 14 (4): 1–30.

Chakrabarti, Anjan, and Arup Kumar Dhar. 2010. *Dislocation and Resettlement in Development: From Third World to World of the Third*. London: Routledge.

Chakrabarty, Dipesh. 1989. *Rethinking Working-Class History: Bengal, 1890–1940*. Princeton, NJ: Princeton University Press.

———. 2000. *Provincializing Europe: Postcolonial Thought and Historical Difference.* Princeton, NJ: Princeton University Press

Chalcraft, John T. 2005. "Pluralizing Capital, Challenging Eurocentrism: Toward Post-Marxist Historiography." *Radical History Review* 91: 13–39.

Chan, Kam Wing. 2010. "The Household Registration System and Migrant Labor in China: Notes on a Debate." *Population and Development Review* 36 (2): 357–64.

Chang, Leslie. 2008. *Factory Girls: Voices from the Heart of Modern China.* London: Picador.

Chase-Dunn, Christopher. 1989. *Global Formation: Structures of the World-Economy.* New York: Basil Blackwell.

Chatterjee, Partha. 1986. *Nationalist Thought and the Colonial World: A Derivative Discourse.* Minneapolis: University of Minnesota Press.

———. 1993. *The Nation and Its Fragments. Colonial and Postcolonial Histories.* Princeton, NJ: Princeton University Press.

———. 2004. *The Politics of the Governed: Reflections on Popular Politics in Most of the World.* New York: Columbia University Press.

———. 2008. "Democracy and Economic Transformation in India." *Economic and Political Weekly* 43 (16): 53–62.

———. 2011. *Lineages of Political Society.* New Delhi: Permanent Black.

Chen, Kuan-Hsing. 2010. *Asia as Method: Toward Deimperialization.* Durham, NC: Duke University Press.

Chen, Xiangming. 1995. "The Evolution of Free Economic Zones and the Recent Development of Cross-national Growth Zones." *International Journal of Urban and Regional Research* 19 (4): 593–621.

Cherniavsky, Eva. 2006. *Incorporations: Race, Nation, and the Body Politics of Capital.* Minneapolis: University of Minnesota Press.

Chiaruzzi, Michele. 2011. "'Fas est et ab hoste doceri.' Motivi e momenti della prima geopolitica anglosassone." *Filosofia politica* 25 (1): 45–56.

China Labor Bulletin. 2011. *Unity Is Strength: The Workers' Movement in China, 2009–2011.* Hong Kong: China Labor Bulletin.

Chow, Rey. 2006. *The Age of the World Target: Self-Referentiality in War, Theory, and Comparative Work.* Durham, NC: Duke University Press.

Christopher, Emma, Cassandra Pybus, and Marcus Rediker, eds. 2007. *Many Middle Passages: Forced Migration and the Making of the Modern World.* Berkeley: University of California Press.

Clarke, Simon. 1990. "What in the F—'s name Is Fordism?" British Sociological Association Conference, University of Surrey. Accessed January 17, 2012. http://www.warwick.ac.uk/~syrbe/pubs/Fordism.pdf.

Coates, John M., and Joe Herbert. 2008. "Endogenous Steroids and Financial Risk Taking on a London Trading Floor." *Proceedings of the National Academy of Science USA* 105 (16): 6167–72.

Cochrane, James L. 1979. *Industrialism and Industrial Man in Retrospect.* New York and Ann Arbor, MI: Ford Foundation.

Cohen, Robin. 1987. *The New Helots: Migrants in the International Division of Labour.* Aldershot, UK: Avebury.

Cole, Philip. 2000. *Philosophies of Exclusion: Liberal Political Theory and Immigration.* Edinburgh: Edinburgh University Press.

Collier, Stephen J., and Aiwha Ong, eds. 2005. *Global Assemblages: Technology, Politics and Ethics as Anthropological Problems*. Oxford: Blackwell.

Comaroff, Jean, and John L. Comaroff. 2001. *Millennial Capitalism and the Culture of Neoliberalism*. Durham, NC: Duke University Press.

Connery, Christopher Leigh. 2007. "The World Sixties." In *The Worlding Project: Doing Cultural Studies in the Era of Globalization*, ed. Chistopher Leigh Connery and Rob Wilson, 77–107. Santa Cruz, CA: North Atlantic Books.

Constable, Nicole. 2007. *Maid to Order in Hong Kong: Stories of Migrant Workers*. Ithaca, NY: Cornell University Press.

Cooper, Frederick. 2001. "What Is the Concept of Globalization Good For? An African Historian's Perspective." *African Affairs* 100 (399): 189–213.

Cowen, Deborah. 2008. *Military Workfare: The Soldier and Social Citizenship in Canada*. Toronto: University of Toronto Press.

———. 2010. "A Geography of Logistics: Market Authority and the Security of Supply Chains." *Annals of the Association of American Geographers* 100 (3): 600–620.

Crenshaw, Kimberlé W. 1991. "Mapping the Margins: Intersectionality, Identity Politics, and Violence against Women of Color." *Stanford Law Review* 43 (6): 1241–99.

———. 2011. "Demarginalising the Intersection of Race and Sex. A Black Feminist Critique of Anti-discrimination Doctrine, Feminist Theory, and Anti-racist Politics." In *Framing Intersectionality: Debates on a Multi-Faceted Concept in Gender Studies*, ed. Helma Lutz, Maria Teresa Herrera Vivar, and Linda Supik, 25–42. Farnham, UK: Ashgate.

Cross, Jamie. 2010. "Neoliberalism as Unexceptional: Economic Zones and the Everyday Precariousness of Working Life in South India." *Critique of Anthropology* 30 (4): 355–73.

Crotty, James. 2011. "The Bonus-Driven 'Rainmaker' Financial Firm: How These Firms Enrich Top Employees, Destroy Shareholder Value and Create Systemic Financial Instability." Working paper, Political Economy Research Institute, University of Massachusetts Amherst. Accessed January 2, 2013. http://www.peri.umass.edu.

Crowley, John. 1998. "The National Dimension of Citizenship in T. H. Marshall." *Citizenship Studies* 2 (2): 165–78.

Curzon, 1st Marquess Curzon of Kedleston. 1908. *Frontiers [The Romanes Lecture 1907]*. Oxford: Clarendon Press.

Cuttitta, Paolo. 2006. "Points and Lines. A Topography of Borders in the Global Space." *Ephemera* 6 (1): 27–39.

———. 2007. *Segnali di confine: Il controllo dell'immigrazione nel mondo-frontiera*. Milan: Mimesis.

Dalla Costa, Mariarosa, and Selma James. 1972. *The Power of Women and the Subversion of the Community: A Woman's Place*. Bristol, UK: Falling Wall Press.

Damrosch, David. 2003. *What Is World Literature?* Princeton, NJ: Princeton University Press.

D'Anania, Giovanni L. 1582. *L'Universal Fabrica del Mondo Overo Cosmografia*. Naples: San Vito.

Dandaneau, Steven P. 1996. *A Town Abandoned: Flint, Michigan, Confronts Deindustrialization*. Albany: State University of New York Press.

D'Angiolillo, Julián, Marcelo Dimentstein, Martín Di Peco, Ana Guerin, Adriana Massidda, Constanza Molíns, Natalia Muñoa, Juan Pablo Scarfi, and Pío Torroja. 2010.

"Feria La Salada: Una centralidad periférica intermitente en el Gran Buenos Aires." In *Argentina: Persistencia y diversificación, contrastes e imaginarios en las centralidades urbanas*, ed. Margarita Gutman, 169–208. Quito: OLACCHI.

Dauvergne, Catherine. 2008. *Making People Illegal: What Globalization Means for Migration and Law*. New York: Cambridge University Press.

Davis, Mike. 2006. *Planet of Slums*. London: Verso.

De Angelis, Massimo. 2007. *The Beginning of History: Value Struggles and Global Capital*. London: Pluto Press.

de Certeau, Michel. 1984. *The Practice of Everyday Life*, trans. Steven Rendall. Berkeley: University of California Press.

De Genova, Nicholas. 2005. *Working the Boundaries: Race, Space, and "Illegality" in Mexican Chicago*. Durham, NC: Duke University Press.

———. 2010. "The Deportation Regime. Sovereignty, Space, and the Freedom of Movement." In *The Deportation Regime: Sovereignty, Space, and the Freedom of Movement*, ed. Nicholas De Genova and Nathalie Peutz, 33–65. Durham, NC: Duke University Press.

De Genova, Nicholas, and Nathalie Peutz. 2010. "Introduction." In *The Deportation Regime: Sovereignty, Space and the Freedom of Movement*, ed. Nicholas De Genova and Nathalie Peutz, 1–29. Durham, NC: Duke University Press.

DeLanda, Manuel. 2006. *A New Philosophy of Society: Assemblage Theory and Social Complexity*. London: Continuum.

Deleuze, Gilles, and Félix Guattari. 1983. *Anti-Oedipus: Capitalism and Schizophrenia*, trans. Robert Hurley, Mark Seem, and Helen R. Lane. Minneapolis: University of Minnesota Press.

———. 1987. *A Thousand Plateaus: Capitalism and Schizophrenia*, trans. Brian Massumi. London: Athlone Press.

Denning, Michael. 2004. *Culture in the Age of Three Worlds*. London: Verso.

———. 2007. "Representing Global Labor." *Social Text* 25 (3): 125–45.

De Peuter, Greig, and Nick Dyer-Witheford. 2010. "Commons and Cooperatives." *Affinities: A Journal of Radical Theory, Culture, and Action* 4 (1): 30–56.

Derrida, Jacques. 1978. *Writing and Difference*, trans. Alan Bass. Chicago: University of Chicago Press.

———. 1989–90. "Force of the Law." *Cardozo Law Review* 11: 920–1045.

De Sousa Santos, Boaventura. 2009. *Una epistemología del Sur*. Buenos Aires: Editorial Siglo XXI.

Dey, Ishita. 2010. "Negotiating Rights within Falta Special Economic Zone." In *Globalisation and Labouring Lives*, Policies and Practices 34. Kolkata: Calcutta Research Group.

Dicken, Peter, Philip F. Kelly, Kris Olds, and Henry Wai-Chung Yeung. 2001. "Chains and Networks, Territories and Scales: Towards a Relational Framework for Analysing the Global Economy." *Global Networks* 1 (2): 89–112.

Djouder, Ahmed. 2007. *Disintegration*, trans. Ximena Rodriguez. Milan: Il Saggiatore.

Dominijanni, Ida. 2005. "Rethinking Change: Italian Feminism between Crisis and Critique of Politics." *Cultural Studies Review* 11 (2): 25–35.

Dow, Mark. 2004. *American Gulag: Inside U.S. Immigration Prisons*. Berkeley: University of California Press.

Dreiser, Theodore. 1912. *The Financier*. New York: Harper and Brothers.

Drucker, Peter F. 1969. *The Age of Discontinuity: Guidelines to Our Changing Society*. London: Heinemann.

Dubet, François, and Didier Lapeyronnie. 1992. *Les quartiers d'exil*. Paris: Seuil.

Du Bois, W. E. B. 1920. *Darkwater: Voices from within the Veil*. New York: Harcourt, Brace and Howe.

———. 1992. [1946]. *The World and Africa: An Enlarged Edition, with New Writings on Africa by W. E. B. Du Bois, 1955–1961*. New York: International Publishers.

———. 1995. [1928]. *Dark Princess: A Romance*. Jackson, MS: Banner Books.

———. 2002 [1940]. *Dusk of Dawn: An Essay Toward an Autobiography of a Race Concept*. New Brunswick, N.J.: Transaction Publishers.

———. 2005. *Du Bois on Asia. Crossing the World Color Line*, ed. Bill V. Mullen and Cathryn Watson. Jackson: University Press of Mississippi.

Ducey, Ariel, Heather Gautney, and Dominic Wetzel. 2003. "Regulating Affective Labor: Communications Skills Training in the Health Care Industry. *Research in the Sociology of Work* 12: 49–72.

Duncan, Natasha T. 2010. "Give Me Your Young, Your Educated, and Your Talented: Explaining the International Diffusion of the Points Immigration System." Ph.D. diss., Purdue University.

Dünnwald, Stephan. 2010. "Politiken der 'freiwilligen' Rückführung." In *Grenzregime. Diskurse, Praktiken, Institutionen in Europa*, ed. Sabine Hess and Bernd Kasparek, 179–99. Berlin: Assoziation A.

Düvell, Franck. 2002. *Die Globalisierung des Migrationsregimes*. Berlin: Assoziation A.

Dyer-Witheford, Nick. 2006. "The Circulation of the Common." Paper presented at the Conference on Immaterial Labour, Multitudes, and New Social Subjects, King's College, Cambridge, April 29–30. Accessed January 3, 2012. http://www.thefreeuniversity.net/ImmaterialLabour/withefordpaper2006.html.

Easterling, Keller. 2008. "Zone." In *Writing Urbanism: A Design Reader*, ed. Douglas Kelbaugh and Kit Krankel McCullough, 297–302. New York: Routledge.

Echols, Alice. 1989. *Daring to Be Bad: Radical Feminism in America, 1967–1975*. Minneapolis: University of Minnesota Press.

Edney, Matthew. 1999. "Reconsidering Enlightenment Geography and Map-making: Reconnaissance, Mapping, Archive." In *Geography and Enlightenment*, ed. David N. Livingstone and Charles W. J. Withers, 165–98. Chicago: University of Chicago Press.

Ehrenreich, Barbara, and Arlie Hochschild, eds. 2003. *Global Woman: Nannies, Maids, and Sex Workers in the New Economy*. London: Granta Books.

Ehrlich, Eugen. 1936 [1913]. *Fundamental Principles of the Sociology of Law*. Cambridge, MA: Harvard University Press.

Elazar, Daniel J. 1998. *Constitutionalizing Globalization. The Postmodern Revival of Confederal Arrangements*. Lanham, MD: Rowman and Littlefield.

Elden, Stuart. 2007. "Government, Calculation, Territory." *Environment and Planning D: Society and Space* 25: 562–80.

Elliott, William Yandell. 1968. *The Pragmatic Revolt in Politics: Syndicalism, Fascism, and the Constitutional State*. New York: Howard Fertig.

Ellis, Brett Easton. 1991. *American Psycho*. New York: Vintage.

Escobar, Arturo. 2008. *Territories of Difference: Place, Movements, Life, Redes*. Durham, NC: Duke University Press.

———. 2010a. "Planning." In *The Development Dictionary: A Guide to Knowledge as Power*, ed. Wolfgang Sachs, 145–60. London: Zed Books.

———. 2010b. "Latin America at a Crossroads: Alternative Modernizations, Post-Liberalism or Post-Development?" *Cultural Studies* 24 (1): 1–65.

Esposito, Roberto. 2012. *Third Person: Politics of Life and Philosophy of the Impersonal*, trans. Zakiya Hanafi. Cambridge: Polity Press.

Esteva, Gustavo. 2010. "Development." In *The Development Dictionary: A Guide to Knowledge as Power*, ed. Wolfgang Sachs, 1–23. London: Zed Books.

European Commission. 2011. "Communication on Migration," COM (2011) 248 final (May 4). Accessed March 20, 2012. http://ec.europa.eu/home-affairs/news/intro/docs/1_EN_ACT_part1_v11.pdf.

European Council. 2004. "Presidency Conclusions of the Brussels European Council" (November 4/5, 2004), 14292/1/04 Rev 1 (December 8). Accessed March 20, 2012. http://www.consilium.europa.eu/uedocs/NewsWord/en/ec/82534.doc.

Faist, Thomas. 2000. *The Volume and Dynamics of International Migration and Transnational Social Spaces*. Oxford: Oxford University Press.

Fan, Cindy. 2008. *China on the Move: Migration, the State, and the Household*. London: Routledge.

Farinelli, Franco. 2003. *Geografia: Un'introduzione ai modelli del mondo*. Turin: Einaudi.

———. 2009. *La crisi della ragione cartografica*. Turin: Einaudi.

Fassin, Didier, and Eric Fassin. 2006. *De la question sociale à la question raciale?* Paris: La Découverte.

Febvre, Lucien. 1962 [1927]. "Frontière, le mot et la notion." 1927. In *Pour un'histoire à part entière* 11–24. Paris: Sevpen.

Federici, Silvia. 2004. *Caliban and the Witch*. New York: Autonomedia.

Feldman, Gregory. 2011. "If Ethnography Is More Than Participant-Observation, Then Relations Are More Than Connections: The Case for Nonlocal Ethnography in a World of Apparatuses." *Anthropological Theory* 11 (4): 375–95.

———. 2012. *The Migration Apparatus: Security, Labor, and Policymaking in the European Union*. Stanford, CA: Stanford University Press.

Feller, Erika. 1989. "Carrier Sanctions and International Law." *International Journal of Refugee Law* 1 (1): 48–66.

Ferguson, James. 2006. *Global Shadows: Africa in the Neoliberal World Order*. Durham, NC: Duke University Press.

Ferguson, James, and Akhil Gupta. 2002. "Spatializing States: Toward an Ethnography of Neoliberal Governmentality." *American Ethnologist* 29 (4): 981–1002.

Fernandes, Deepa. 2007. *Targeted: Homeland Security and the Business of Immigration*. New York: Seven Stories Press.

Ferrarese, Maria Rosaria. 2006. *Diritto sconfinato: Inventiva giuridica e spazi nel mondo globale*. Rome: Laterza.

Ferraresi, Furio. 2003. *Il fantasma della comunità: Concetti politici e scienza sociale in Max Weber*. Milan: Franco Angeli.

Ferraresi, Furio, and Sandro Mezzadra. 2005. "Introduzione." In Max Weber, *Dalla terra alla fabbrica: Scritti sui lavoratori agricoli e lo Stato nazionale*, vii–lii. Rome: Laterza.

Ferrari Bravo, Luciano. 1975. "Vecchie e nuove questioni nella teoria dell'imperialismo." In *Imperialismo e classe operaia multinazionale*, ed. Luciano Ferrari Bravo, 7–67. Milan: Feltrinelli.

Fine, Janice. 2007. "A Marriage Made in Heaven? Mismatches and Misunderstandings between Worker Centers and Unions." *British Journal of Industrial Relations* 45 (2): 335–60.

Fine, Sidney. 1969. *Sit-Down: The General Motors Strike of 1936–1937*. Ann Arbor: University of Michigan Press.

Fischer-Lescano, Andreas, and Gunther Teubner. 2004. "Regime-Collisions: The Vain Search for Legal Unity in the Fragmentation of Global Law." *Michigan Journal of International Law* 25 (4): 999–1046.

———. 2006. *Regime-Kollisionen: Zur Fragmentierung des globalen Rechts*. Frankfurt: Suhrkamp.

Fitzpatrick, Sheila. 1994. *Stalin's Peasants: Resistance and Survival in the Russian Village after Collectivization*. Oxford: Oxford University Press.

Flynn, Michael, and Cecilia Cannon. 2006. "The Privatization of Immigration Detention: Towards a Global View." A Global Detention Project Working Paper. Accessed October 25, 2010. http://www.globaldetentionproject.org/fileadmin/ docs/GDP _PrivatizationPaper_Fina15.pdf.

"Force Could Be Used on Oceanic 78: Academic." 2009. *Australian National University News*, October 29. Accessed September 4, 2010. http://news.anu.edu.au/?p=1751.

Forcellini, Egidio. 1771. *Totius Latinitatis lexicon*, consilio et cura Jacobi Facciolati, opera et studio Aegidii Forcellini, 4 vols. Padua: Typis Seminarii, apud Joannem Manfrè.

Ford Foundation. 1999. *Crossing Borders: Revitalizing Area Studies*. Washington, DC: Ford Foundation.

Foucault, Michel. 1978. *The History of Sexuality. Volume 1: An Introduction*, trans. Robert Hurley. New York: Vintage Books/Random House.

———. 1980. "Questions on Geography." In *Power/Knowledge: Selected Interviews and Other Writings, 1972–1977*, ed. Colin Gordon, 63–77. New York: Pantheon Books.

———. 1989. *The Order of Things: An Archaeology of the Human Sciences*, trans. Alan Sheridan. London: Routledge.

———. 2000. "Confronting Governments: Human Rights." In *Power, Essential Works of Foucault*, vol. 3, ed. James Faubion, 474–75. New York: New Press.

———. 2003. *Society Must Be Defended: Lectures at the Collège de France, 1975–76*, trans. David Macey. New York: Picador.

———. 2007a. *Security, Territory, Population: Lectures at the Collège de France, 1977–1978*, trans. Graham Burchell. Houndmills, UK: Palgrave Macmillan.

———. 2007b. "The Meshes of Power." In *Space, Knowledge and Power: Foucault and Geography*, ed. Jeremy W. Crampton and Stuart Elden, 153–62. Aldershot, UK: Ashgate.

———. 2008. *The Birth of Biopolitics. Lectures at the Collège de France, 1977–1978*, trans. Graham Burchell. Houndmills, UK: Palgrave Macmillan.

Fröbel, Folker, Jürgen Heinrichs, and Otto Kreye.1980. *The New International Division of Labor*. Cambridge: Cambridge University Press.

Frontex. 2006. Background information. Accessed August 8, 2010. http://www.frontex .europa.eu/more_about_frontex/.

Fumagalli, Andrea. 2007. *Bioeconomia e capitalismo cognitivo: Verso un nuovo paradigma di accumulazione*. Rome: Carocci.

Fumagalli, Andrea, and Sandro Mezzadra, eds. 2010. *Crisis in the Global Economy: Financial Markets, Social Struggles, and New Political Scenarios*, trans. Jason McGimsey. Cambridge: Semiotext(e).

G4S. 2010. "Securing Your World: Corporate Social Responsibility Report 2010." Accessed March 19, 2012. http://www.g4s.com.

Gago, Verónica. 2011. *Mutaciones en el trabajo en la Argentina post 2001: Entre la feminización y el trabajo esclavo*. Tesis para optar al título de Doctor en Ciencias Sociales, Facultad de Ciencias Sociales Universidad de Buenos Aires, 2011.

Galli, Carlo. 2010. *Political Spaces and Global War*, trans. Elisabeth Fay. Minneapolis: University of Minnesota Press.

Gallicchio, Marc. 2000. *The African American Encounter with Japan and China: Black Internationalism in Asia, 1895–1945*. Chapel Hill: University of North Carolina Press.

Gammeltoft-Hansen, Thomas. 2007. "The Extraterritorialisation of Asylum and the Advent of 'Protection Lite.'" Working Paper 2007/2. Danish Institute for International Studies. Accessed September 3, 2010. http://www.diis.dk.

Gaonkar, Dilip Parameshwar. 2001. *Alternative Modernities*. Durham, NC: Duke University Press.

García Canclini, Néstor. 1999. *La globalización imaginada*. Mexico City: Paidos.

Gardner, Andrew M. 2010. "Engulfed: Indian Guest Workers, Bahraini Citizens, and the Structural Violence of the *Kafala* System." In *The Deportation Regime: Sovereignty, Space and the Freedom of Movement*, ed. Nicholas De Genova and Nathalie Peutz, 196–223. Durham, NC: Duke University Press.

Geiger, Martin, and Antoine Pécoud. 2010. "The Politics of International Migration Management." In *The Politics of International Migration Management: Migration, Minorities and Citizenship*, ed. Martin Geiger and Antoine Pécoud, 1–20. Houndmills, UK: Palgrave Macmillan.

Georgi, Fabian. 2007. *Migrationsmanagement in Europa*. Saarbrücken, Germany: VDM.

Gereffi, Gary, and Miguel Korzeniewicz. 1994. *Commodity Chains and Global Capitalism*. Westport, CT: Greenwood Press.

Ghosh, Amitav. 1998. *The Shadow Lines*. London: Bloomsbury.

Gibney, Mark. 2010. *Global Refugee Crisis: A Reference Handbook*, 2nd ed., Contemporary World Issues. Santa Barbara, CA: ABC-CLIO.

Gibson-Graham, J. K. 2006. *A Postcapitalist Politics*. Minneapolis: University of Minnesota Press.

Gilboy, Janet. 1997. "Implications of 'Third-party' Involvement in Enforcement: The INS, Illegal Travelers, and International Airlines." *Law and Society Review* 31: 505–29.

Gilroy, Paul. 1987. *"There Ain't No Black in the Union Jack": The Cultural Politics of Race and Nation*. London: Hutchinson.

———. 1993. *The Black Atlantic: Modernity and Double Consciousness*. London: Verso.

———. 2004. *After Empire: Melancholia or Convivial Culture?* London: Routledge.

Glenn, Evelyn Nakano. 2004. *Unequal Freedom: How Race and Gender Shaped American Citizenship and Labor*. Cambridge, MA: Harvard University Press.

Glissant, Édouard. 1997. *The Poetics of Relation*, trans. Betsy Wing. Ann Arbor: University of Michigan Press.

Godechot, Olivier. 2008. "'Hold-up' in Finance: The Conditions of Possibility for High Bonuses in the Financial Industry." *Revue Française de Sociologie* 49: 95–123.

Government of Canada. 2008. "Regulations Amending the Immigration and Refugee Protection Regulations (Canadian Experience Class)." *Canada Gazette*, September 4. Accessed April 16, 2012. http://gazette.gc.ca/rp-pr/p2/2008/2008–09–17/html/sor-dors254-eng.html.

Gramsci, Antonio. 1971. *Selections from the Prison Notebooks*, ed. and trans. Quintin Hoare and Geoffrey Nowell Smith. New York: International Publishers.

———. 1995. *Further Selections from the Prison Notebooks*, ed. and trans. D. Boothman. Minneapolis: University of Minnesota Press.

Grayson, John. 2012. "G4S Turns a Profit in 'Asylum Markets': Who's Speaking Out and Whose Lips Are Sealed." *Open Democracy*, February 28. Accessed March 18, 2012. http://www.opendemocracy.net.

Gregory, Derek. 1994. *Geographical Imaginations*. Oxford: Blackwell.

Greenspan, Anna. 2004. *India and the IT Revolution: Networks of Global Culture*. Hampshire, UK: Palgrave Macmillan.

Groh, Dieter. 1961. *Russland und das Selbstverständnis Europas. Ein Beitrag zur europäischen Geistesgeschichte*. Neuwied, Germany: Luchterhand.

Grotius, Hugo. 2005 [1625]. *The Rights of War and Peace*, ed. Richard Tuck. Indianapolis: Liberty Fund.

Guang-Zhen, Sun. 2005. "The Economics of Division of Labor from Xenophon to Hayek (1945): A Review of Selected Literature." In *Readings in the Economics of the Division of Labour: The Classical Tradition*, ed. Guang-Zhen Sun, 3–31. Singapore: World Scientific.

Guha, Ranajit. 1983. *Elementary Aspects of Peasant Insurgency in Colonial India*. New Delhi: Oxford University Press.

———. 2002. *History at the Limit of World-History*. New York: Columbia University Press.

Gurvitch, Georges. 1932. *L'idée du droit social: Notion et système du droit social*. Paris: Librairie de Recueil Sirey.

Gutiérrez, David, and Pierrette Hondagneu-Sotelo. 2008. "Introduction: Nation and Migration." *American Quarterly* 60 (3): 503–21.

Haass, Richard. 2008. "The Age of Nonpolarity: What Will Follow U.S. Dominance?" *Foreign Affairs* 87 (3): 44–56.

Habermas, Jürgen. 1989. *The New Conservatism and the Historians' Debate*, trans. Shierry Weber Nicholsen. Cambridge, MA: MIT Press.

Hage, Ghassan. 1998. *White Nation: Fantasies of White Supremacy in a Multicultural Society*. Sydney: Pluto Press.

Hall, Stuart. 1985. *Popular Culture as a Factor of Intercultural Understanding: The Case of Reggae*. Paris: UNESCO.

———. 1986a. "On Postmodernism and Articulation. An Interview with Lawrence Grossberg." *Journal of Communication Inquiry* 10: 45–60.

———. 1986b. "Gramsci's Relevance for the Study of Race and Ethnicity." *Journal of Communication Inquiry* 10: 5–27.

————. 1988. "The Toad in the Garden: Thatcherism among the Theorists." In *Marxism and the Interpretation of Culture*, ed. Lawrence Grossberg and Cary Nelson, 35–57. Urbana: University of Illinois Press.

————. 1990. "Cultural Identity and Diaspora." In *Identity: Community, Culture, Difference*, ed. Jonathan Rutherford, 222–37. London: Lawrence and Wishart.

————. 1992. "Cultural Studies and Its Theoretical Legacies." In *Cultural Studies*, ed. L. Grossberg and P. A. Treichler, 277–86. London: Routledge.

————. 2000. "Conclusion: The Multi-cultural Question." In *Un/Settled Multiculturalisms: Diasporas, Entanglements, Transruptions*, ed. Barnor Hesse, 209–41. New York: St. Martin's.

————. 2006. "Black Diaspora Artists in Britain: Three 'Moments' in Post-war History." *History Workshop Journal* 61 (1): 1–24.

Hamilton, Earl J. 1943. *World Regions in the Social Sciences*. New York: Social Science Research Council.

Hammar, Tomas. 1990. *Democracy and the Nation-State: Aliens, Denizens and Citizens in a World of International Migration*. Aldershot, UK: Avebury.

Hanssen, Beatrice. 2000. *Critique of Violence: Between Poststructuralism and Critical Theory*. London: Routledge.

Hardin, Garrett. 1968. "The Tragedy of the Commons." *Science* 162: 1243–48.

Hardt, Michael, and Antonio Negri. 1994. *Labor of Dionysus. A Critique of the State-Form*. Minneapolis: University of Minnesota Press.

————. 2000. *Empire*. Cambridge, MA: Harvard University Press.

————. 2004. *Multitude: War and Democracy in the Age of Empire*. New York: Penguin.

————. 2009. *Commonwealth*. Cambridge, MA: Harvard University Press.

Harris, Nigel. 2002. *Thinking the Unthinkable. The Immigration Myth Exposed*. London: I. B. Tauris.

Harvey, David. 1989. *The Condition of Postmodernity*. Oxford: Blackwell.

————. 2003. *The New Imperialism*. Oxford: Oxford University Press.

————. 2005. *A Brief History of Neoliberalism*. Oxford: Oxford University Press.

————. 2010. *A Companion to Marx's* Capital. London: Verso.

Hashmi, Sohail H., and David L. Miller, eds. 2001. *Boundaries and Justice: Diverse Ethical Perspectives*. Princeton, NJ: Princeton University Press.

Haug, Wolfgang Fritz. 1995. "Charaktermaske." In *Historisch-kritisches Wörterbuch des Marxismus*, vol. 2, ed. W. F. Haug, 435–51. Berlin: Argument.

Haviland, Keith. 2008. *Global Delivery: A Course to High Performance in a Multi-Polar World*. Dublin: Accenture.

Hawkins, Freda. 1991. *Critical Years in Immigration: Canada and Australia Compared*. Kingston, ONT: McGill-Queens University Press.

Hayter, Teresa. 2004. *Open Borders. The Case against Immigration Control*. London: Pluto.

Hegel, Georg Wilhelm Friedrich. 1991 [1821]. *Elements of the Philosophy of Right*. Cambridge: Cambridge University Press.

Heidegger, Martin. 2002 [1950]. *Off the Beaten Track*. Cambridge: Cambridge University Press.

Held, David. 1995. *Democracy and the Global Order: From the Modern State to Cosmopolitan Governance*. Stanford, CA: Stanford University Press.

Hess, Sabine. 2007. *Globalisierte Hausarbeit. Au-pair als Migrationsstrategie von Frauen aus Osteuropa*. Wiesbaden, Germany: VS Verlag für Sozialwissenschaften.

Hess, Sabine, and Bernd Kasparek, eds. 2010. *Grenzregime: Diskurse, Praktiken, Institutionen in Europa*. Berlin: Assoziation A.

Hess, Sabine, and Vassilis Tsianos. 2007. "Europeanizing Transnationalism! Provincializing Europe! Konturen eines neuen Grenzregimes." In *Turbulente Ränder. Neue Perspektiven auf Migration an den Grenzen Europas*, ed. Transit Migration Forschungsgruppe, 23–29. Bielefeld, Germany: Transcript Verlag.

Hilferding, Rudolf. 1981 [1910]. *Finance Capital: A Study of the Latest Phase of Capitalist Development*. London: Routledge and Kegan Paul.

Hilger, Marie-Elisabeth, and Lucian Hölscher. 1972. "Kapital, Kapitalist, Kapitalismus." In *Geschichtliche Grundbegriffe*, vol. 3, ed. Otto Brunner, Werner Conze, and Reinhardt Koselleck, 399–454. Stuttgart: Klett.

Hindess, Barry. 2004. "Liberalism—What's in a Name?" In *Global Governmentality: Governing International Spaces*, ed. Wendy Larner and William Walters, 23–29. London: Routledge.

Ho, Karen. 2009. *Liquidated: An Ethnography of Wall Street*. Durham, NC: Duke University Press.

Hobbes, Thomas. 1981 [1651]. *Leviathan*, ed. C. B. Macpherson. Harmondsworth, UK: Penguin.

Hochschild, Arlie. 1983. *The Managed Heart: Commercialization of Human Feeling*. Berkeley: University of California Press.

——. 2000. "Global Care Chains and Emotional Surplus Value." In *On The Edge: Living with Global Capitalism*, ed. Will Hutton and Anthony Giddens, 130–46. London: Jonathan Cape.

Holmes, Brian. 2005. "Continental Drift, or, the Other Side of Neoliberal Globalization." *Interactivist Info Exchange*, September 27. Accessed January 17, 2012. http://interactivist.autonomedia.org/node/4689.

——. 2011. "Do Containers Dream of Electric People? The Social Form of Just-in-time Production." *Open* 21: 30–44.

Honig, Bonnie. 2001. *Democracy and the Foreigner*. Princeton, NJ: Princeton University Press.

Hopkins, Terence K., and Immanuel Wallerstein. 1986. "Commodity Chains in the World Economy Prior to 1800." *Review* 10 (1): 157–70.

Horstmann, Alexander. 2007. "Violence, Subversion and Creativity in the Thai-Malaysian Borderland." In *Borderscapes: Hidden Geographies and Politics at Territory's Edge*, ed. Prem Kumar Rajaram and Carl Grundy-Warr, 137–60. Minneapolis: University of Minnesota Press.

Hugo, Graeme. 2002. "Australian Immigration Policy: The Significance of the Events of September 11." *International Migration Review* 36 (1): 37–40.

Hume, David. 1994. *Political Writings*, ed. S. D. Warner and D. W. Livingston. Indianapolis: Hackett.

Huntington, Samuel P. 1996. *The Clash of Civilizations and the Remaking of World Order*. New York: Simon and Schuster.

Huysmans, Jef. 2006. *The Politics of Insecurity: Fear, Migration and Asylum in the EU*. London: Routledge.

ICOC. 2012. "Draft Charter of the Oversight Mechanism for the International Code of

Conduct for Private Security Service Providers." International Code of Conduct for Private Security Service Providers. Accessed March 19, 2012. http://www.icoc-psp .org/uploads/Draft_Charter.pdf.

International Labour Organization. 2010. *International Labor Migration: A Rights-Based Approach*. Geneva: International Labour Organization. Accessed January 23, 2012. http://www.ilo.org/public/english/protection/migrant/download/rights _based_approach.pdf.

Isin, Engin F. 2002. *Being Political: Genealogies of Citizenship*. Minneapolis: University of Minnesota Press.

———. 2008. "Theorizing Acts of Citizenship." In *Acts of Citizenship*, ed. Engin F. Isin and Greg M. Nielsen, 15–43. London: Zed Books.

———. 2009. "Citizenship in Flux: The Figure of the Activist Citizen." *Subjectivity* 29: 367–88.

Isin, Engin, and Bryan S. Turner. 2008. "Investigating Citizenship: An Agenda for Citizenship Studies." In *Citizenship between Past and Present*, ed. E. F. Isin, P. Nyers, and B. S. Turner, 5–17. London: Routledge.

Iveković, Rada. 2010. "The Watershed of Modernity: Translation and the Epistemological Revolution." *Inter-Asia Cultural Studies* 11 (1): 45–63.

Ives, Peter. 2004. *Language and Hegemony in Gramsci*. London: Pluto Press.

Jameson, Fredric. 2011. *Representing Capital: A Reading of Volume One*. London: Verso.

Janicki, Jill Jana, and Thomas Böwing. 2010. "Europäische Migrationskontrolle im Sahel. Das CICEM in Mali." In *Grenzregime: Diskurse, Praktiken, Institutionen in Europa*, ed. Sabine Hess and Bernd Kasparek, 127–43. Berlin: Assoziation A.

Jenkins, Rob. 2007. "The Politics of India's Special Economic Zones." Center for the Advanced Study of India, University of Pennsylvania. Accessed January 6, 2011. http:// casi.ssc.upenn.edu/system/files/Rob+Jenkins.pdf.

Joerges, Christian. 2008. "Integration durch Entrechtlichung. Ein Zwischenruf." *European Journal of Legal Studies* 1 (3): 1–37.

———. 2011. "The Idea of a Three-dimensional Conflicts Law as Constitutional Form." In *Constitutionalism, Multilevel Trade Governance and Social Regulation*, 2nd ed., ed. Christian Joerges and Ernst-Ulrich Petersmann, 413–56. Oxford: Hart.

Jones, Andrew M. 2008. "Staff Shortages and Immigration in the Financial Services Sector." In *A Need for Migrant Labour?*, report prepared by COMPAS. London: Home Office.

Joseph, Miranda. 2002. *Against the Romance of Community*. Minneapolis: University of Minnesota Press.

Joxe, Alain. 2002. *Empire of Disorder*, trans. Ames Hodges. New York: Semiotext(e).

Kant, Immanuel. 2010 [1795]. *Perpetual Peace: A Philosophical Essay*, trans. Mary Campbell Smith. New York: Cosimo Classics.

Kaplan, Amy. 2002. *The Anarchy of Empire in the Making of U.S. Culture*. Cambridge, MA: Harvard University Press.

Karakayali, Serhat and Vassilis Tsianos. 2010. "Transnational Migration and the Emergence of the European Border Regime: An Ethnographic Analysis." *European Journal of Social Theory* 13(3): 373–87.

Karatani, Kôjin. 2005. *Transcritique: On Kant and Marx*, trans. Sabu Kosho. Cambridge, MA: MIT Press.

Kasparek, Bernd. 2010. "Laboratorium, Think Tank, Doing Border: Die Grenzschutzagentur Frontex." In *Grenzregime. Diskurse, Praktiken, Institutionen in Europa*, ed. Sabine Hess and Bernd Kasparek, 111–26. Berlin: Assoziation A.

Kaufman, Bruce E. 2004. *The Global Evolution of Industrial Relations: Events, Ideas and the IIRA*. Geneva: International Labour Organization.

Kern, Horst, and Michael Schumann. 1984. *Das Ende der Arbeitsteilung?: Rationalisierung in der industriellen Produktion: Bestandsaufnahme, Trendbestimmung*. Munich: C. H. Beck.

Kerr, Clark, John T. Dunlop, Frederick Harbison, and Charles A. Myers. 1960. *Industrialism and Industrial Man: Problems of Labor and Management in Economic Growth*. Cambridge, MA: Harvard University Press.

Klein, Naomi. 2008. *The Shock Doctrine: The Rise of Disaster Capitalism*. New York: Metropolitan Books.

Kofman, Eleonore, Annie Phizacklea, and Parvati Raghuram. 2000. *Gender and International Migration in Europe: Employment, Welfare, and Politics*. London: Routledge.

Kolossov, Vladimir. 2005. "Border Studies: Changing Perspectives and Theoretical Approaches." *Geopolitics* 10: 606–32.

Kotkin, Stephen. 1995. *Magnetic Mountain: Stalinism as a Civilization*. Berkeley: University of California Press.

Krahl, Hans-Jürgen. 1971. *Konstitution und Klassenkampf: Zur Historischen Dialektik von Bürgerlicher Emanzipation und Proletarischer Revolution*. Frankfurt: Verlag Neue Kritik.

Krishna, Sankaran. 1994. "Cartographic Anxiety: Mapping the Body Politic in India." *Alternatives* 19 (4): 507–21.

Kron, Stefanie. 2010. "Orderly Migration: Der 'Puebla Prozeß' und die Transnationalisierung der Migrationspolitik in Mittelamerika." In *Grenzregime. Diskurse, Praktiken, Institutionen in Europa*, ed. Sabine Hess and Bernd Kasparek, 73–86. Berlin: Assoziation A.

Kuczynski, Thomas. 2009. "Was wird auf dem Arbeitsmarkt verkauft?" In *Über Marx Hinaus: Arbeitsgeschichte und Arbeitsbegriff in der Konfrontation mit den globalen Arbeitsverhältnissen des 21. Jahrhunderts*, ed. Marcel van der Linden and Karl-Heinz Roth, 363–79. Berlin: Assoziation A.

Kumar, M. Satish, and David Vumlallian Zou. 2011. "Mapping a Colonial Borderland: Objectifying the Geo-body of India's Northeast." *Journal of Asian Studies* 70 (1): 141–70.

Laclau, Ernesto. 1977. *Politics and Ideology in Marxist Theory: Capitalism, Fascism, Populism*. London: New Left Books.

——. 1996. *Emancipation(s)*. London: Verso.

——. 1997. "The Death and Resurrection of the Theory of Ideology." *Modern Language Notes* 112 (3): 297–321.

——. 2005. *On Populist Reason*. London: Verso.

Laclau, Ernesto, and Chantal Mouffe. 2001 [1985]. *Hegemony and Socialist Strategy: Towards a Radical Democratic Politics*. London: Routledge.

Lacoste, Yves. 1976. *La Géographie, ça sert, d'abord, à faire la guerre*. Paris: F. Maspero.

Lahav, Gallya. 1998. "Immigration and the State: The Devolution and Privatization of Immigration Control in the EU." *Journal of Ethnic and Migration Studies* 24 (4): 675–94.

Laitinen, Ilkka. 2011. "Keeping Up with Schengen." *publicservice.co.uk*. Accessed April 24, 2012. http://www.publicservice.co.uk/feature_story.asp?id=17487.

Lash, Scott, and John Urry. 1987. *The End of Organized Capitalism*. Cambridge: Polity Press.

Latham, Robert. 2000. "Social Sovereignty." *Theory, Culture and Society* 17 (4): 1–18.

Latour, Bruno. 2005. *Reassembling the Social: An Introduction to Actor-Network Theory*. Oxford: Oxford University Press.

Law, John. 2004. *After Method: Mess in Social Science Research*. London: Routledge.

Lazzarato, Maurizio. 1996. "Immaterial Labor." In *Radical Thought in Italy: A Potential Politics*, ed. Michael Hardt and Paolo Virno, 133–47. Minneapolis: University of Minnesota Press.

———. 2012. *The Making of the Indebted Man: Essay on the Neoliberal Condition*, trans. Joshua David Jordan. Los Angeles: Semiotext(e).

Leander, Anna. 2012. "What Do Codes of Conduct Do? Hybrid Constitutionalization and Militarization in Military Markets." *Global Constitutionalism* 1 (1): 91–119.

Le Cour Grandmaison, Olivier. 2010. *De l'indigénat. Anatomie d'un "mostre" juridique: le droit colonial en Algérie et dans l'Empire français*. Paris: La Découverte.

Lee, Ching Kwan. 2007. *Against the Law: Labor Protests in China's Rustbelt and Sunbelt*. Berkeley: University of California Press.

Leidner, Robin. 1999. "Emotional Labor in Service Work." *Annals AAPSS* 561: 81–95.

Lemont, Michèle, and Virág Molnár. 2002. "The Study of Boundaries in Social Sciences." *Annual Review of Sociology* 28: 167–95.

Lenin, Vladimir Ilich. 1965 [1922]. "Five Years of the Russian Revolution and the Prospects of the World Revolution." In *Collected Works*, 2nd ed., vol. 33, 415–32. Moscow: Progress Publishers.

———. 1975 [1916]. *Imperialism, The Highest Stage of Capitalism: A Popular Outline*. Peking: Foreign Language Press.

Lentin, Alana, and Gavan Titley. 2011. *The Crises of Multiculturalism: Racism in a Neoliberal Age*. London: Zed Books.

Leonelli, Rudy M. 2010. "L'arma del sapere: Storia e potere tra Foucault e Marx." In *Foucault-Marx: Paralleli e paradossi*, ed. Rudy M. Leonelli, 113–42. Rome: Bulzoni Editore.

Lessig, Lawrence. 2004. *Free Culture: How Big Media Uses Technology and the Law to Lock Down Culture and Control Creativity*. New York: Penguin Press.

Lestringant, Frank. 1991. *L'atelier du cosmographe ou l'image du monde à la Renaissance*. Paris: Albin Michel.

Lewchuk, Wayne A. 1993. "Men and Monotony: Fraternalism as a Managerial Strategy at the Ford Motor Company." *Journal of Economic History* 53 (4): 824–56.

Lewis, Martin W., and Kären E. Wigen. 1997. *The Myth of Continents: A Critique of Metageography*. Berkeley: University of California Press.

Libreria delle donne di Milano. 1987. *Non credere di avere dei diritti*. Turin: Rosenberg and Sellier.

Light, Ivan, and Edna Bonacich. 1988. *Immigrant Entrepreneurs in America, Koreans in Los Angeles, 1965–1982*. Berkeley: University of California Press.

Linebaugh, Peter. 2008. *The Magna Carta Manifesto: Liberties and Commons for All*. Berkeley: University of California Press.

Linebaugh, Peter, and Marcus Rediker. 2000. *The Many-Headed Hydra: Sailors, Slaves, Commoners, and the Hidden History of the Revolutionary Atlantic*. London: Verso.

Linera, Álvaro García. 2008, *La potencia plebeya. Acción colectiva e identidades indí-genas, obreras y populares en Bolivia*, ed. Pablo Stefanoni. Buenos Aires: Prometeo.

Lipietz, Alain. 1986. *Mirages and Miracles: The Crisis in Global Fordism*, trans. David Macey. London: Verso.

———. 1992. *Towards a New Economic Order: Post-Fordism, Ecology and Democracy*. Oxford: Oxford University Press.

Locke, John. 1988. [1690]. *Two Treatises of Government*, ed. P. Laslett. Cambridge: Cambridge University Press.

Lonzi, Carla. 2010 [1970]. *Sputiamo su Hegel e altri scritti*. Milan: Et al.

Lo Piparo, Franco. 1979. *Lingua, intellettuali, egemonia in Gramsci*. Rome: Laterza.

Lorde, Audre. 2009. *I Am Your Sister: Collected and Unpublished Writings*, ed. R. P. Byrd, J. B. Cole, and B. Guy-Sheftall. Oxford: Oxford University Press.

Lowe, Lisa. 1996. *Immigrant Acts: On Asian American Cultural Politics*. Durham, NC: Duke University Press.

Lucassen, Jan, ed. 2006. *Global Labour History: A State of the Art*. Bern: Peter Lang.

Luhmann, Niklas. 1971. "Die Weltgesellschaft." *Archiv für Rechts- und Sozialphilosophie* 57: 1–35.

Luxemburg, Rosa. 2003 [1913]. *The Accumulation of Capital*, trans. Agnes Schwarzschild. New York: Routledge.

MacKenzie, Donald. 2004. "Social Connectivities in Global Financial Markets." *Environment and Planning D: Society and Space* 22: 83–101.

Macpherson, Crawford B. 1962. *The Political Theory of Possessive Individualism: Hobbes to Locke*. Oxford: Clarendon Press.

Maier, Charles. 1991. *The Marshall Plan and Germany: West German Development within the Framework of the European Recovery Program*. New York: St. Martin's.

Mandel, Ernest. 1975. *Late Capitalism*, trans. Joris De Bres. London: Humanities Press.

Mannheim, Karl. 1952 [1928]. "The Problem of Generations." In *Collected Works of Karl Mannheim*, vol. 5, 276–320. London: Routledge.

Marazzi, Christian. 2005. "Capitalismo digitale e modello antropogenetico del lavoro: L'ammortamento del corpo macchina." In *Reinventare il lavoro*, ed. Jean Louis Laville, Christian Marazzi, Michele La Rosa, and Federico Chicchi, 107–26. Rome: Sapere 2000.

———. 2008. *Capital and Language: From the New Economy to the War Economy*, trans. Gregory Conti. Los Angeles: Semiotext(e).

———. 2010. *The Violence of Financial Capitalism*, trans. Kristina Lebedeva. New York: Semiotext(e).

———. 2011. *Capital and Affects: The Politics of the Language Economy*, trans. Giuseppina Mecchia. Los Angeles: Semiotext(e).

Marchetti, Chiara. 2006. *Un mondo di rifugiati: Migrazioni forzate e campi profughi*. Bologna: EMI.

Marcus, George. 2008. "The End(s) of Ethnography: Social/cultural Anthropology's Signature Form of Producing Knowledge in Transition." *Cultural Anthropology* 23(1): 1–14.

Marella, Maria Rosaria, ed. 2012. *Oltre il pubblico e il privato: Per un diritto dei beni comuni*. Verona: Ombre corte.

Marshall, Thomas Humphrey. 1950. *Citizenship and Social Class, and Other Essays*. Cambridge: Cambridge University Press.

———. 1964. *Class, Citizenship, and Social Development: Essays*. Garden City, NY: Doubleday.

Martí, José. 1892. "Nuestra America." Accessed May 19, 2011. http://www.historyofcuba .com/history/marti/America.htm.

Martin, Randy. 2002. *Financialization of Daily Life*. Philadelphia: Temple University Press.

———. 2009. "Whose Crisis Is That? Thinking Finance Otherwise." *Ephemera* 9 (4): 344–49.

Marx, Karl. 1971. *Theories of Surplus Value*, vol. 3. Moscow: Progress Publishers.

———. 1973. *Grundrisse: Foundations of the Critique of Political Economy*, trans. Martin Nicolaus. Harmondsworth, UK: Penguin.

———. 1977. *Capital*, vol. 1, trans. Ben Fowkes. New York: Vintage Books.

———. 1978. *Capital*, vol. 2, trans. David Fernbach. London: Penguin.

———. 1981. *Capital*, vol. 3, trans. David Fernbach. London: Penguin.

———. 1988. *Economic and Philosophic Manuscripts and the Communist Manifesto*. Amherst, MA: Prometheus Books.

———. 2008. *The Poverty of Philosophy*, trans. Harry Quelch. New York: Cosimo.

Marx, Karl, and Friedrich Engels. 2002. *The Communist Manifesto*, ed. G. Stedman Jones. London: Penguin.

Massey, Doreen. 1984. *Spatial Divisions of Labour: Social Structures and the Geography of Production*. London: Macmillan.

Mathew, Biju. 2005. *Taxi! Cabs and Capitalism in New York City*. New York: New Press.

Mattei, Ugo. 2011. *Beni comuni. Un manifesto*. Rome: Laterza.

Mattei, Ugo, and Laura Nader. 2009. *Plunder: When the Rule of Law Is Illegal*. Oxford: Blackwell.

Mauss, Marcel. 1985. "A Category of the Human Mind: The Notion of Person; the Notion of Self," trans. W. D. Halls. In *The Category of the Person: Anthropology, Philosophy, History*, ed. M. Carrtihers, A. Collins, and S. Lukes, 1–25. Cambridge: Cambridge University Press.

May, Martha. 1982. "Historical Problems of the Family Wage: The Ford Motor Company and the Five Dollar Day." *Feminist Studies* 8: 395–424.

Mbembe, Achille. 2003. "Necropolitics." *Public Culture* 15 (1): 11–40.

———. 2009. "The Republic and Its Beast: On the Riots in the French Banlieues," trans. Jane Marie Todd. In *Frenchness and the African Diaspora: Identity and Uprising in Contemporary France*, ed. Charles Tshimanga, C. Didier Gondola, and Peter J. Bloom, 47–55. Bloomington: Indiana University Press.

McCall, Leslie. 2005. "The Complexity of Intersectionality." *Signs* 3: 1771–800.

McCormick, Ted. 2009. *William Petty and the Ambitions of Political Arithmetic*. Oxford: Oxford University Press.

McNevin, Anne. 2006. "Political Belonging in a Neoliberal Era: The Struggle of the Sans-Papiers." *Citizenship Studies* 10 (2): 135–51.

———. 2011. *Contesting Citizenship: Irregular Migrants and New Frontiers of the Political*. New York: Columbia University Press.

Menz, George. 2009. "The Neoliberalized State and Migration Control: The Rise of Private Actors in the Enforcement and Design of Migration Policy." *Debatte: Journal of Contemporary Central and Eastern Europe* 17 (3): 315–32.

Mercator, Gerardus. 1595. *Atlas sive Cosmographicae Meditationes de Fabrica Mundi et Fabricati Figura*. Duisburg, Germany: Rumold Mercator.

Mezzadra, Sandro. 1999. *La costituzione del sociale: Il pensiero politico e giuridico di Hugo Preuss*. Bologna: Il Mulino.

———. 2002. "Diritti di cittadinanza e Welfare State: Citizenship and Social Class di Tom Marshall cinquant'anni dopo." In T. H. Marshall, *Cittadinanza e classe sociale*, v–xxxiv. Rome: Laterza.

———, ed. 2004. *Cittadinanza: Soggetti, ordine, diritto*. Bologna: Clueb.

———. 2006. "Citizen and Subject: A Postcolonial Constitution for the European Union?" *Situations* 1 (2): 31–42.

———. 2011a. "The Topicality of Prehistory: A New Reading of Marx's Analysis of 'So-called Primitive Accumulation.'" *Rethinking Marxism* 23 (3): 302–21.

———. 2011b. "Bringing Capital Back In: A Materialist Turn in Postcolonial Studies?" *Inter-Asia Cultural Studies* 12 (1): 154–64.

———. 2011c. "How Many Histories of Labour? Towards a Theory of Postcolonial Capitalism." *Postcolonial Studies* 14 (2): 151–70.

———. 2011d. "The Gaze of Autonomy: Capitalism, Migration, and Social Struggles." In *The Contested Politics of Mobility: Borderzones and Irregularity*, ed. Vicki Squire, 121–42. London: Routledge.

———. 2011e. "En voyage: Michel Foucault et la critique post-coloniale." In *Cahier Foucault*, ed. P. Artières, J-F. Bert, F. Gros, and J. Revel, 352–57. Paris: Herne.

Mezzadra, Sandro, and Brett Neilson. 2003. "*Né qui, né altrove*—Migration, Detention, Desertion: A Dialogue." *Borderlands E-journal* 2 (1). Accessed October 23, 2010. http://www.borderlands.net.au/issues/vo12no1.html.

———. 2012. "Borderscapes of Differential Inclusion: Subjectivity and Struggles on the Threshold of Justice's Excess." In *The Borders of Justice*, ed. Étienne Balibar, Sandro Mezzadra, and Ranabir Samaddar, 181–203. Philadelphia: Temple University Press.

Midnight Notes Collective. 1990. "The New Enclosures." No. 10. Accessed January 2, 2012. http://www.midnightnotes.org/newenclos.html.

Mies, Maria. 1998. *Patriarchy and Accumulation on a World Scale: Women in the International Division of Labour*. London: Zed Books.

Mignolo, Walter D. 1995. *The Darker Side of the Renaissance: Literacy, Territoriality, and Colonization*. Ann Arbor: University of Michigan Press.

———. 2000. "La colonialidad a lo largo y a lo ancho: El hemisferio occidental en el horizonte colonial de la modernidad." In *La colonialidad del saber: Eurocentrismo y ciencias socials: Perspectivas latinoamericanas*, ed. E. Lander, 55–85. Buenos Aires: Clacso.

Mignolo, Walter, and Madina V. Tlostanova. 2006. "Theorizing from the Borders: Shifting to Geo- and Body-politics of Knowledge." *European Journal of Social Theory* 9: 205–21.

Miller, Toby, Nitin Govil, John McMurria, and Richard Maxwell. 2001. *Global Hollywood*. London: British Film Institute.

Mintz, Sidney W. 1985. *Sweetness and Power: The Place of Sugar in Modern History*. New York: Penguin.

Mirowski, Philip, and Dieter Plehwe, eds. 2009. *The Road from Mont Pèlerin: The Making of the Neoliberal Thought Collective*. Cambridge, MA: Harvard University Press.

Mitchell, Timothy. 2004. "The Middle East in the Past and the Future of Social Science." In *The Politics of Knowledge: Area Studies and the Disciplines*, ed. David Szanton, 74–118. Berkeley: University of California Press.

Mitropoulos, Angela. 2006. "Under the Beach, the Barbed Wire." *Mute Magazine—Culture and Politics After the Net*. Accessed January 4, 2012. http://www.metamute.org/en/Under-the-Beach-the-Barbed-Wire.

Model, Suzanne. 1985. "A Comparative Perspective on the Ethnic Enclave: Blacks, Italians, and Jews in New York City." *International Migration Review* 19 (1): 64–81.

Mohanty, Chandra Talpade. 2003. *Feminism without Borders: Decolonizing Theory, Practicing Solidarity*. Durham, NC: Duke University Press.

Mometti, Felice, and Maurizio Ricciardi. 2011. *La normale eccezione. Lotte migranti in Italia*. Rome: Edizioni Alegre.

Mommsen, Wolfgang J. 1984. *Max Weber and German Politics, 1890–1920*, trans. M. S. Steinberg. Chicago: University of Chicago Press.

Montgomery, David. 1993. *Citizen Worker*. Oxford: Oxford University Press.

Morini, Cristina. 2010. *Per amore o per forza. Femminilizzazione del lavoro e biopolitiche del corpo*. Verona: Ombre Corte.

Morokvasic, Mirjana. 1984. "The Overview: Birds of Passage Are Also Women." *International Migration Review* 68 (18): 886–907.

———. 1993. "In and Out the Labor Market." *New Community* 19 (3): 459–83.

Morris-Suzuki, Tessa. 2010. *Borderline Japan: Foreigners and Frontier Controls in the Postwar Era*. Cambridge: Cambridge University Press.

Mostov, Julie. 2008. *Soft Borders: Rethinking Sovereignty and Democracy*. New York: Palgrave Macmillan.

Mouffe, Chantal. 2005. *On the Political*. London: Verso.

Moulier Boutang, Yann. 1998. *De l'esclavage au salariat: Économie historique du salariat bridé*. Paris: PUF.

———. 2011. *Cognitive Capitalism*, trans. E. Emery. Cambridge: Polity Press.

Muraro, Luisa. 2004. *Maglia o uncinetto: Racconto linguistico-politico sulla inimicizia tra metafora e metonimia*, ed. Ida Dominijanni. Rome: Manifestolibri.

Nancy, Jean-Luc. 1991. *The Inoperative Community*, ed. Peter Condor. Minneapolis: University of Minnesota Press.

Neal, Andrew W. 2009. "Securitization and Risk at the EU Border: The Origins of Frontex." *Journal of Common Market Studies* 47 (2): 333–356.

Negri, Antonio. 1991. *The Savage Anomaly: The Power of Spinoza's Metaphysics and Politics*, trans. M. Hardt. Minneapolis: University of Minnesota Press.

———. 1999. *Insurgencies: Constituent Power and the Modern State*, trans. Maurizia Boscaglia. Minneapolis: University of Minnesota Press.

———. 2007a. *Political Descartes: Reason, Ideology and the Bourgeois Project*, trans. Matteo Mandarini and Alberto Toscano. London: Verso.

———. 2007b. *Dall' operaio massa all'operaio sociale: Intervista sull'operaismo*. Verona: Ombre Corte.

Negri, Antonio, and Maurizio Lazzarato. 1991. "Travail immatériel et subjectivité." *Futur Antérieur* 6: 86–99.

Neilson, Brett. 1996. "Threshold Procedures: 'Boat People' in South Florida and Western Australia." *Critical Arts* 10 (2): 21–40.

———. 2009. "The World Seen from a Taxi: Students-Migrants-Workers in the Global Multiplication of Labour." *Subjectivity* 29: 425–44.

———. 2012. "Five Theses on Understanding Logistics as Power." *Distinktion: Scandinavian Journal of Social Theory* 13 (3): 323–40.

Neilson, Brett, and Ned Rossiter. 2008. "Precarity as a Political Concept, or, Fordism as Exception." *Theory, Culture and Society* 25 (7–8): 51–72.

———. 2011. "Still Waiting, Still Moving: On Labour, Logistics and Maritime Industries." In *Stillness in a Mobile World*, ed. David Bissell and Gillian Fuller, 51–68. London: Routledge.

Ness, Immanuel. 2005. *Immigrants, Unions, and the New U.S. Labor Market.* Philadelphia: Temple University Press.

Neumayer, Eric. 2005. "Bogus Refugees? The Determinants of Asylum Migration to Western Europe." *International Studies Quarterly* 49: 389–409.

Newman, David. 2006. "The Lines That Continue to Separate Us: Borders in Our 'Borderless' World." *Progress in Human Geography* 30 (2): 143–61.

Newman, David, and Anssi Paasi. 1998. "Fences and Neighbors in the Postmodern World: Boundary Narratives in Political Geography." *Progress in Human Geography* 22 (2): 186–207.

Nickel, Rainer, ed. 2009. *Conflict of Laws and Laws of Conflict in Europe and Beyond: Patterns of Supranational and Transnational Juridification.* Oslo: ARENA.

Nugent, David. 2007. *Military Intelligence and Social Science Knowledge: Global Conflict, Territorial Control, and the Birth of Area Studies during WW II.* New York: Social Science Research Council.

———. 2010. "Knowledge and Empire: The Social Sciences and United States Imperial Expansion." *Identities* 17 (1): 2–44.

Nyers, Peter. 2006. *Rethinking Refugees: Beyond States of Emergency.* New York: Routledge.

Oberlechner, Thomas. 2004. "Perceptions of Successful Traders by Foreign Exchange Professionals." *Journal of Behavioral Finance* 5 (1): 23–31.

Observatorio Metropolitano. 2011. *Crisis y revolucion en Europa. People of Europe Rise Up!* Madrid: Traficantes de sueños.

Office of the Comptroller of the Currency (OCC). 2011. *OCC's Quarterly Report on Bank Trading and Derivatives Activities First Quarter 2011.* Washington, DC: U.S. Department of the Treasury. Accessed January 17, 2012. http://www.occ.treas.gov/topics/capital-markets/financial-markets/trading/derivatives/dq111.pdf.

Ōmae, Kenichi. 1990. *The Borderless World: Power and Strategy in the Interlinked Economy.* New York: Harper Business.

Ong, Aihwa. 1999. *Flexible Citizenship: The Cultural Logics of Transnationality.* Durham, NC: Duke University Press.

———. 2003. *Buddha Is Hiding: Refugees, Citizenship, the New America.* Berkeley: University of California Press.

———. 2006. *Neoliberalism as Exception: Mutations in Citizenship and Sovereignty.* Durham, NC: Duke University Press.

———. 2009. "Global Assemblages vs. Universalism." In *Toward a Global Autonomous University*, ed. Edu-factory Collective, 39–71. New York: Autonomedia Books.

Orléan, André. 1999. *Le pouvoir de la finance.* Rome: Éditions Odile Jacob.

Ostrom, Elinor. 1990. *Governing the Commons: The Evolution of Institutions for Collective Action.* Cambridge: Cambridge University Press.

Ó Tuathail, Gearóid. 1996. *Critical Geopolitics: The Politics of Writing Global Space.* London: Routledge.

Paasi, Anssi. 1999. "Boundaries as Social Practice and Discourse: The Finnish Russian Border." *Regional Studies* 33: 669–80.

Painter, Joe. 2008. "Cartographic Anxiety and the Search for Regionality." *Environment and Planning A* 40 (2): 342–61.

Panagiotidis, Efthimia, and Vassilis Tsianos. 2007. "Denaturalizing 'Camps': Überwachen und Entschleunigen in der Schengener Ägäis-Zone." In *Turbulente Ränder. Neue Perspektiven auf Migration an den Grenzen Europas*, ed. Transit Migration Forschungsgruppe, 57–85. Bielefeld, Germany: Transcript Verlag.

Papadopoulos, Dimitris, and Vassilis Tsianos. 2007. "How to Do Sovereignty without People? The Subjectless Condition of Postliberal Power." *Boundary 2* 34 (1): 135–72.

Papadopoulos, Dimitris, Niamh Stephenson, and Vassilis Tsianos. 2008. *Escape Routes: Control and Subversion in the Twenty-First Century.* London: Pluto Press.

Papastergiadis, Nikos. 2000. *The Turbulence of Migration: Globalization, Deterritorialization, Hybridity.* Cambridge: Polity.

Parreñas, Rhacel Salazar. 2001. *Servants of Globalization: Women, Migration, and Domestic Work.* Stanford, CA: Stanford University Press.

Pashukanis, Evgen Bronislavovich. 2002 [1924]. *The General Theory of Law and Marxism*, ed. Dragan Milovanovic. New Brunswick, NJ: Transaction.

Pasquinelli, Matteo. 2008. *Animal Spirits. A Bestiary of the Commons.* Rotterdam: NAi.

Pateman, Carole. 1988. *The Sexual Contract.* Cambridge: Polity.

Peña, Devon Gerardo. 1980. "Las Maquiladoras: Mexican Women and Class Struggle in the Border Industries." *Aztlán* 11 (2): 160–229.

——. 1997. *The Terror of the Machine. Technology, Work and Ecology on the U.S.-Mexico Border.* Austin, TX: CMAS books.

Perera, Suvendrini. 2002. "What Is a Camp . . . ?" *Borderlands* 1 (1). Accessed December 10, 2011. http://www.borderlandsejournal.adelaide.edu.au/vo11no1_2002/perera_camp.html.

——. 2007. "A Pacific Zone? (In)security, Sovereignty, and Stories of the Pacific Borderscape." In *Borderscapes: Hidden Geographies and Politics at Territory's Edge*, ed. Prem Kumar Rajaram and Carl Grundy-Warr, 201–27. Minneapolis: University of Minnesota Press.

——. 2009. *Australia and the Insular Imagination: Beaches, Borders, Boats, and Bodies.* New York: Palgrave Macmillan.

Petti, Alessandro. 2007. *Arcipelaghi e enclave: Architettura dell'ordinamento spaziale contemporaneo.* Milan: Bruno Mondadori.

Petty, William. 1690. *Political Arithmetick.* London: Robert Clavel and Hen. Mortlock.

Pickles, John. 2004. *A History of Spaces: Cartographic Reason, Mapping, and the Geo-Coded World.* New York: Routledge.

Pieper, Tobias. 2008. *Die Gegenwart der Lager: Zur Mikrophysik der Herrschaft in der deutschen Flüchtlingspolitik.* Münster: Westfälisches Dampfboot.

Piven, Frances Fox, and Richard A. Cloward. 1997. *The Breaking of the American Social Compact.* New York: New Press.

Poliakov, Léon. 1974. *The Aryan Myth*. New York: Basic Books.

Portes, Alejandro, and Leif Jensen. 1989. "The Enclave and the Entrants: Patterns of Ethnic Enterprise in Miami before and after *Mariel*." *American Sociological Review* 54: 929–49.

Portes, Alejandro, and Rubén G. Rumbaut. 1996. *Immigrant American: A Portrait*, 2nd ed. Berkeley: University of California Press.

———. 2001. *Legacies: The Story of the Immigrant Second Generation*. Berkeley: University of California Press.

Portes, Alejandro, and Min Zhou. 1993. "The New Second Generation: Segmented Assimilation and Its Variants." *Annals of the American Academy of Political and Social Science* 530 (1): 74–96.

Pratt, Andy C. 2008. "Cultural Commodity Chains, Cultural Clusters, or Cultural Production Chains?" *Growth and Change* 39 (1): 95–103.

Pratt, Mary Louise. 2008. *Imperial Eyes: Travel, Writing and Transculturation*, 2nd ed. London: Routledge.

Prescott, John Robert Victor. 1987. *Political Frontiers and Boundaries*. London: Allen and Unwin.

Prescott, John Robert Victor, and Clive Schofield. 2005. *The Maritime Political Boundaries of the World*, 2nd ed. Leiden: M. Nijhoff.

Prescott, John Robert Victor, and Gillian D. Triggs. 2008. *International Frontiers and Boundaries, Law, Politics and Geography*. The Hague: Martinus Nijhoff.

Pun Ngai. 2005. *Made in China: Women Factory Workers in a Global Workplace*. Durham, NC: Duke University Press.

———. 2008. "Reorganized Moralism: The Politics of Transnational Labor Codes." In *Privatizing China: Socialism from Afar*, ed. Li Zhang and Aihwa Ong, 87–102. Ithaca, NY: Cornell University Press.

———. 2009. "Chinese Migrant Women Workers in a Dormitory Labor System." *Asia Portal—Infofocus*. Accessed January 10, 2012. http://infocus.asiaportal.info.

Pun Ngai, and Lu Huilin. 2010. "Unfinished Proletarianization: Self, Anger, and Class Action among the Second Generation of Peasant-Workers in Present-day China." *Modern China* 36 (5): 493–519.

Pun Ngai, Chris King Chi Chan, and Jenny Chan. 2010. "The Role of the State, Labour Policy and Migrant Workers' Struggles in Globalized China." *Global Labour Journal* 1 (1): 132–51.

Quijano, Aníbal. 1997. "Colonialidad del poder, cultura y conocimiento en América Latina." *Anuario Mariateguiano* 9 (9): 113–21.

———. 2008. "Coloniality of Power, Eurocentrism, and Social Classification." In *Coloniality at Large: Latin America and the Postcolonial Debate*, ed. Mabel Moraña, Enrique Dussell, and Carlos A. Jáuregui, 181–224. Durham, NC: Duke University Press.

Rabinow, Paul, and Nikolas Rose. 2006. "Biopower Today." *BioSocieties* 1: 195–217.

Rahola, Federico. 2003. *Zone Definitivamente Temporanee: I Luoghi dell'Umanità in Eccesso*. Verona: Ombre Corte.

———. 2010. "The Space of Camps: Towards a Genealogy of Spaces of Internment in the Present." In *Conflict, Security, and the Reshaping of Society: The Civilization of War*, ed. Alessandro dal Lago and Salvatore Palidda, 185–99. London: Routledge.

Raikes, Philip, Michael Friis Jensen, and Stefano Ponte. 2000. "Global Commodity

Chain Analysis and the French Filière Approach: Comparison and Critique." *Economy and Society* 29 (3): 390–417.

Raimondi, Fabio. 1999. *Il sigillo della vicissitudine: Giordano Bruno e la liberazione della potenza*. Padua: Unipress.

Rajan, Kaushik Sunder. 2006. *Biocapital: The Constitution of Postgenomic Life*. Durham, NC: Duke University Press.

Rancière, Jacques. 1998. *Dis-Agreement: Politics and Philosophy*, trans. J. Rose. Minneapolis: University of Minnesota Press.

———. 2009. *Moments politiques. Interventions 1977–2009*. Paris: La Fabrique.

Ratfisch, Philipp, and Stephan Scheel. 2010. "Migrationskontrolle durch Flüchtlingschutz? Die Rolle des UNHCR in der Externalisierung des EU-Migrationsregimes." In *Grenzregime. Diskurse, Praktiken, Institutionen in Europa*, ed. Sabine Hess and Bernd Kasparek, 89–110. Berlin: Assoziation A.

Ratzel, Friedrich. 1899 [1891]. *Anthropogeographie, Erster Teil: Grundzüge der Anwendung der Erdkunde auf die Geschichte*, 2. Aufl. Stuttgart: Verlag von J. Engelhorn.

———. 1923 [1897]. *Politische Geographie*, 3. Aufl., durchgesehen und ergänzt von E. Oberhummer. Munich: Oldenbourg.

Read, Jason. 2003. *The Micro-Politics of Capital: Marx and the Prehistory of the Present*. Albany: SUNY Press.

Rediker, Marcus. 2007. *The Slave Ship: A Human History*. New York: Viking.

Reich, Robert B. 1991. *The Work of Nations: Preparing Ourselves for 21st-Century Capitalism*. London: Simon and Schuster.

Remesh, Babu P. 2004. "Cyber Coolies in BPO: Insecurities and Vulnerabilities of Nonstandard Work." *Economic and Political Weekly* 39 (5): 492–97.

Renault, Matthieu. 2011. *Frantz Fanon: De l'anticolonialisme à la critique postcoloniale*. Paris: Editions Amsterdam.

Reno, William. 1999. *Warlord Politics and African States*. Boulder, CO: Lynne Rienner.

Reuveny, Rafael, and William R. Thompson. 2010. *Limits to Globalization: North-South Divergence*. London: Routledge.

Revel, Judith. 2008. *Qui a peur de la banlieue?* Paris: Bayard Jeunesse.

———. 2010. *Foucault, une pensée du discontinu*. Paris: Mille et une nuits.

Reyneri, Emilio. 1979. *La catena migratoria*. Bologna: Il Mulino.

Ricardo, David. 1821 [1817]. *On the Principles of Political Economy and Taxation*. London: John Murray.

Ricciardi, Maurizio. 2010. *La società come ordine. Storia e teoria politica dei concetti sociali*. Macerata, Italy: EUM.

Rigo, Enrica. 2007. *Europa di confine: Trasformazioni della cittadinanza nell'Unione allargata*. Rome: Meltemi.

Rigouste, Mathieu. 2009. *L'ennemi intérieur: La généalogie coloniale et militaire de l'ordre sècuritaire dans la France contemporaine*. Paris: La Découverte.

Ritter, Carl. 1864. *Comparative Geography*, trans. William L. Gage. New York: American Book Company.

Robinson, Cedric J. 2000. *Black Marxism: The Making of the Black Radical Tradition*. Chapel Hill: University of North Carolina Press.

Rocca, Jean-Louis. 2006. *La condition chinoise: La mise au travaile capitaliste à l'âge des réformes (1978–2004)*. Paris: Karthala.

Rodríguez, Nestor. 1996. "The Battle for the Border: Notes on Autonomous Migration, Transnational Communities and the State." *Social Justice* 23: 21–39.

Roggero, Gigi. 2011. *The Production of Living Knowledge: The Crisis of the University and the Transformation of Labor in Europe and North America*, trans. Enda Brophy. Philadelphia: Temple University Press.

Romano, Santi. 1969. *Lo Stato moderno e la sua crisi*. Milan: Giuffrè.

Rose, Nikolas. 2007. *The Politics of Life Itself: Biomedicine, Power, and Subjectivity in the Twenty-First Century*. Princeton, NJ: Princeton University Press.

Rosen, George. 1985. *Western Economists and Eastern Societies: Agents of Change in South Asia, 1950–1970*. Baltimore: Johns Hopkins University Press.

Ross, Andrew. 2009. *Nice Work if You Can Get It: Life and Labor in Precarious Times*. New York: New York University Press.

Rossi, Pietro. 1975. *Storia universale e geografia in Hegel*. Florence: Sansoni.

Rossi, Ugo, and Alberto Vanolo. 2012. *Urban Political Geographies: A Global Perspective*. London: Sage.

Rostow, Walt Whitman. 1960. *The Stages of Economic Growth: A Non-Communist Manifesto*. Cambridge: Cambridge University Press.

Rouse, Roger. 1991. "Mexican Migration and the Social Space of Postmodernism." *Diaspora: A Journal of Transnational Studies* 1 (1): 8–23.

Rousseau, Jean-Jacques. 1997. *The* Discourses *and Other Early Political Writings*, ed. and trans. Victor Gourevitch. Cambridge: Cambridge University Press.

Roy, Ananya. 2011. "The Blockade of the World-class City: Dialectical Images of Indian Urbanism." In *Worlding Cities: Asian Experiments and the Art of Being Global*, ed. Ananya Roy and Aihwa Ong, 259–78. Oxford: Wiley-Blackwell.

Ruccio, David. 2011. "Cooperatives, Surplus, and the Social." *Rethinking Marxism* 23 (3): 334–40.

Ruggie, John Gerard. 1998. "What Makes the World Hang Together? Neo-Utilitarianism and the Social Constructivist Challenge." *International Organization* 52: 855–85.

Rygiel, Kim. 2010. *Globalizing Citizenship*. Vancouver: University of British Columbia Press.

Sakai, Naoki. 1997. *Translation and Subjectivity: On "Japan" and Cultural Nationalism*. Minneapolis: University of Minnesota Press.

———. 2000. "'You Asians': On the Historical Role of the West and Asia Binary." *South Atlantic Quarterly* 99 (4): 789–817.

———. 2011. "Theory and the West." *Transeuropéennes*. Accessed January 2, 2012. http://www.transeuropeennes.eu/en/articles/316/Theory_and_the_West.

Sakai, Naoki, and Jon Solomon. 2006. "Introduction: Addressing the Multitude of Foreigners, Echoing Foucault." In *Translation, Biopolitics, Colonial Difference*, ed. Naoki Sakai and Jon Solomon, 1–35. Hong Kong: Hong Kong University Press.

Saldívar, José David. 2012. *Trans-Americanity: Subaltern Modernities, Global Coloniality, and the Cultures of Greater Mexico*. Durham, NC: Duke University Press.

Salento, Franco Angeli. 2003. *Postfordismo e ideologie giuridiche: Nuove forme d'impresa e crisi del diritto del lavoro*. Milan: Angeli.

Samaddar, Ranabir. 1994. *Workers and Automation: The Impact of New Technology in the Newspaper Industry*. New Delhi: Sage.

———. 1999. *The Marginal Nation: Transborder Migration from Bangladesh to India*. New Delhi: Sage.

———. 2007a. *The Materiality of Politics*, vol. 1. London: Anthem Press.

———. 2007b. *The Materiality of Politics*, vol. 2. London: Anthem Press.

———. 2009. "Primitive Accumulation and Some Aspects of Life and Work in India." *Economic and Political Weekly* 44 (18): 33–42.

———. 2010. *The Emergence of the Political Subject*. New Delhi: Sage.

———. 2012. "What is Postcolonial Predicament?" *Economic and Political Weekly* 47 (9): 41–50.

Sanyal, Kalyan K. 2007. *Rethinking Capitalist Development: Primitive Accumulation, Governmentality and the Post-Colonial Capitalism*. London: Routledge.

Sassen, Saskia. 1991. *The Global City: New York, London, Tokyo*. Princeton, NJ: Princeton University Press.

———. 1996. *Losing Control? Sovereignty in an Age of Globalization*. New York: Columbia University Press.

———. 2006. *Territory, Authority, Rights: From Medieval to Global Assemblages*. Princeton, NJ: Princeton University Press.

———. 2007. *A Sociology of Globalization*. New York: W. W. Norton.

———. 2010. "A Savage Sorting of Winners and Losers: Contemporary Versions of Primitive Accumulation." *Globalizations* 7 (1–2): 23–50.

Sayad, Abdelmalek. 1980. "Le foyer des sans-famille." *Actes de la recherche en sciences sociales* 32–33: 89–104.

———. 2004. *The Suffering of the Immigrant*. Cambridge: Polity Press.

Schecter, Anna, Rhonda Schwartz, and Brian Ross. 2009. "CEOs, Bankers Used Corporate Credit Cards for Sex, Says New York Madam." ABC News, February 6. Accessed November 13, 2011. http://abcnews.go.com.

Scheel, Stephan. 2011. "What Is 'Illegality'? A Response to Iker Barbero." *Oecumene*. Accessed January 4 2012. http://www.oecumene.eu/blog/what-is-illegality-a-response-to-iker-barbero.

Scherer, Heinrich. 1703. *Geographia naturalis, sive, Fabrica mundi sublvnaris ab artifice et avthore saturæ inventa et elaborata*. Monachii, sumptibus Joannis Caspari Bencard, typis Mariæ Magdalenæ Rauchin.

Schiavone, Aldo. 2005. *Ius: L'invenzione del diritto in Occidente*. Turin: Einaudi.

Schiera, Pierangelo. 1987. *Il laboratorio borghese: Scienza e politica nella Germania dell'Ottocento*. Bologna: Il Mulino.

Schmitt, Carl. 1997 [1942]. *Land and Sea*, trans. Simona Draghici. Washington, DC: Plutarch Press.

———. 2003 [1950]. *The Nomos of the Earth in the International Law of the Jus Publicum Europaeum*, trans. Gary L. Ulmen. New York: Telos Press.

Scholten, Sophie, and Paul Minderhoud. 2008. "Regulating Immigration Control: Carrier Sanctions in the Netherlands." *European Journal of Migration and Law* 10 (2): 123–47.

Schumpeter, Joseph A. 1986 [1954]. *History of Economic Analysis*, ed. E. B. Schumpeter. London: Routledge.

Sciortino, Giuseppe. 2004. "Between Phantoms and Necessary Evils: Some Critical Points in the Study of Irregular Migration in Western Europe." *IMIS-Beiträge* 24: 17–44.

Scott, James C. 1998. *Seeing Like a State: How Certain Schemes to Improve the Human Condition Have Failed*. New Haven, CT: Yale University Press.

seasia. 2005/6. *Stowaways: Repatriation Corridors from Asia and the Far East.* Singapore: seasia p&i Services.

Sen, Sunanda, and Byasdeb Dasgupta. 2009. *Unfreedom and Waged Work: Labour in India's Manufacturing Industry.* New Delhi: Sage.

Seo, Myeong-Gu, and Lisa Feldman Barrett. 2007. "Being Emotional During Decision Making—Good or Bad? An Empirical Investigation." *Academy of Management Journal* 50 (4): 923–40.

Serafini, Alessandro, ed. 1974. *L'operaio multinazionale in Europa.* Milan: Feltrinelli.

Shachar, Ayelet. 2006. "The Race for Talent: Highly Skilled Migrants and Competitive Immigration Regimes." *New York University Law Review* 81: 148–206.

———. 2009. *The Birthright Lottery: Citizenship and Global Inequality.* Cambridge, MA: Harvard University Press.

Shaffer, Gregory C., and Mark A. Pollack. 2010. "Hard vs. Soft Law: Alternatives, Complements, and Antagonists in International Governance." *Minnesota Law Review* 94 (3): 706–99.

Shapiro, Martin. 2001. "Administrative Law Unbounded: Reflections on Government and Governance." *Indiana Journal of Global Legal Studies* 8 (2): 369–77.

Sharma, N. K. 2009. "Special Economic Zones: Socio-Economic Implications." *Economic and Political Weekly* 44 (20): 18–21.

Sidaway, James D. 2007. "Spaces of Postdevelopment." *Progress in Human Geography* 31 (3): 345–61.

Siegelbaum, Lewis H. 1990. *Stakhanovism and the Politics of Productivity in the USSR, 1935–1941.* Cambridge: Cambridge University Press.

Silver, Beverly. 2003. *Forces of Labor: Workers' Movements and Globalization since 1870.* New York: Cambridge University Press.

Simmel, Georg. 2009 [1908]. *Sociology: Inquiries into the Construction of Social Forms.* Leiden: Brill.

Sklair, Leslie. 1994. "Development in Global Perspective." In *Capitalism and Development,* ed. Leslie Sklair, 165–85. London: Routledge.

Slaughter, Anne-Marie. 2009. "America's Edge: Power in the Networked Century." *Foreign Affairs* 88 (1): 94–113.

Smith, Adam. 1976 [1776]. *An Inquiry into the Nature and Causes of the Wealth of Nations.* Oxford: Clarendon Press.

Smith, Dorothy E. 1987. *The Everyday World as Problematic: A Feminist Sociology.* Boston: Northeastern University Press.

Smith, Michael P. 2001. *Transnational Urbanism: Locating Globalization.* Oxford: Blackwell.

Smith, Neil. 2003. "After the American *Lebensraum*: 'Empire,' Empire, and Globalization." *Interventions* 5 (2): 249–70.

———. 2007. *Abysmal Ignorance: The Pre-life of Area Studies, 1917–1958.* New York: Social Science Research Council.

Snell-Hornby, Mary. 1988. *Translation Studies: An Integrated Approach.* Amsterdam: Benjamins.

Société Réaliste. 2011. *Empire, State, Building.* Paris: Éditions Amsterdam.

Soederberg, Susanne. 2009. *Corporate Power and Ownership in Contemporary Capitalism: The Politics of Resistance and Domination.* London: Routledge.

Sohn-Rethel, Alfred. 1978. *Intellectual and Manual Labour: A Critique of Epistemology.* London: Macmillan.

Soja, Edward. 1989. *Postmodern Geographies: The Reassertion of Space in Critical Social Theory.* London: Verso.

Spivak, Gayatri Chakravorty. 2008. *Other Asias.* Oxford: Blackwell.

Squire, Vicki, ed. 2011. *The Contested Politics of Mobility: Borderzones and Irregularity.* London: Routledge.

Standing, Guy. 2011. *The Precariat: The New Dangerous Class.* London: Bloomsbury Academic.

Steinfeld, Robert J. 1991. *The Invention of Free Labor.* Chapel Hill: University of North Carolina Press.

——. 2001. *Coercion, Contract, and Free Labor in the Nineteenth Century.* Cambridge: Cambridge University Press.

Stevens, Andrew, and Vincent Mosco. 2010. "Prospects for Trade Unions and Labour Organizations in India's IT and ITES Industries." *Work Organization, Labour and Globalization* 4 (2): 39–59.

Stoker, Gerry. 1998. "Governance as Theory: Five Propositions." *International Social Science Journal* 50 (155): 17–28.

Stoler, Ann Laura. 1995. *Race and the Education of Desire: Foucault's History of Sexuality and the Colonial Order of Things.* Durham, NC: Duke University Press.

——. 2006. "On Degrees of Imperial Sovereignty." *Public Culture* 18 (1): 125–46.

Streeck, Wolfgang. 2009. *Re-Forming Capitalism: Institutional Change in the German Political Economy.* New York: Oxford University Press.

Suárez-Navaz, Liliana. 2007. "Introducción. La lucha de los sin papeles: Anomalías democráticas y la (imparable) extensión de la ciudadanía." In *Las luchas de los sin papeles y la extensión de la ciudadanía. Perspectivas críticas desde Europa y Estados Unidos*, ed. Liliana Suárez-Navaz, Raquel Macià Pareja, and Ángela Moreno García, 15–33. Madrid: Traficantes de Sueños.

Supiot, Alain. 1994. *Critique du droit du travail.* Paris: PUF.

——. 2001. *Beyond Employment: Changes in Work and the Future of Labour Law in Europe.* New York: Oxford University Press.

Szanton, David. 2004. "Introduction: The Origin, Nature and Challenge of Area Studies in the United States." In *The Politics of Knowledge: Area Studies and the Disciplines*, ed. David Szanton, 1–33. Berkeley: University of California Press.

Taylor, Marcus. 2008. "Power, Conflict and the Production of the Global Economy." In *Global Economy Contested: Power and Conflict across the International Division of Labour*, ed. Marcus Taylor, 11–31. London: Routledge.

Teubner, Gunther. 1997. "Global Bukowina: Legal Pluralism in the World Society." In *Global Law without a State*, ed. Gunther Teubner, 3–28. Aldershot, UK: Dartmouth Gower.

——. 2004. "Societal Constitutionalism: Alternatives to State-centred Constitutional Theory." In *Transnational Governance and Constitutionalism*, ed. Christian Jeorges, Inger-Johanne Sand, and Gunther Teubner, 2–28. Oxford: Hart Publishing.

——. 2009. "The Corporate Codes of Multinationals: Company Constitutions beyond Corporate Governance and Co-determination." In *Conflict of Laws and Laws of Conflict in Europe and Beyond: Patterns of Supranational and Transnational Juridification*, ed. Rainer Nickel, 261–76. Oslo: ARENA.

———. 2010. "Fragmented Foundations: Societal Constitutionalism beyond the Nation-state." In *The Twilight of Constitutionalism?*, ed. Petra Dobner and Martin Loughlin, 327–41. Oxford: Oxford University Press.

Thomas, William I., and Florian Znaniecki. 1918–20. *The Polish Peasant in Europe and America: Monograph of an Immigrant Group*. Chicago: University of Chicago Press.

Thompson, Edward Palmer. 1963. *The Making of the English Working Class*. London: Victor Gollancz.

———. 1967. "Time, Work-discipline and Industrial Capitalism." *Past and Present* 38: 56–97.

Thompson, Liz, and Benjamin Rosenzweig. 2009. "Permanent Residency Not Sold Separately, Education Not Included." *Overland* 197: 197–202.

Thrift, Nigel. 1996. *Spatial Formations*. London: Sage.

Torpey, John. 2000. *The Invention of the Passport: Surveillance, Citizenship and the State*. Cambridge: Cambridge University Press.

Touraine, Alain. 2001. *Beyond Neoliberalism*, trans. David Macey. Cambridge: Polity Press.

Transit Migration Forschungsgruppe, ed. 2007. *Turbulente Ränder. Neue Perspektiven auf Migration an den Grenzen Europas*. Bielefeld, Germany: Transcript Verlag.

Traven, Bruno. 1934. *The Death Ship: The Story of an American Sailor*. New York: Knopf.

Tribe, Keith. 1983. "Prussian Agriculture—German Politics: Max Weber 1892–7." *Economy and Society* 12 (2): 181–226.

Tripathy, S. N. 2008. "SEZS and Labour Administration." *Labour File* 6 (4–5): 31–32.

Tronti, Mario. 1966. *Operai e capitale*. Turin: Einaudi.

Tsing, Anna. 2000. "The Global Situation." *Cultural Anthropology* 15 (3): 327–60.

———. 2005. *Friction: An Ethnography of Global Connection*. Princeton, NJ: Princeton University Press.

———. 2009. "Supply Chains and the Human Condition." *Rethinking Marxism* 21 (2): 148–76.

Turner, Bryan S. 2001. "The Erosion of Citizenship." *British Journal of Sociology* 52 (2): 189–209.

Turner, Frederick Jackson. 1920. *The Frontier in American History*. New York: Holt.

Upadhyay, C., and A. R. Vasavi. 2008. *In an Outpost of the Global Economy: Work and Workers in India's Information Technology Industry*. New Delhi: Routledge.

Van der Linden, Marcel. 2008. *Workers of the World: Essays toward a Global Labor History*. Leiden: Brill.

Vattel, Emerich de. 1916 [1758]. *Le droit de gens, ou principes de la loi naturelle appliqués à la conduite et aux affaires des Nations et de Souverains*. Washington, DC: Carnegie Institution.

Vaughan-Williams, Nick. 2009. *Border Politics: The Limits of Sovereign Power*. Edinburgh: Edinburgh University Press.

Vercellone, Carlo. 2006. "Mutazione del concetto di lavoro produttivo e nuove forme di distribuzione." In *Capitalismo cognitivo. Conoscenza e finanza nell'epoca postfordista*, ed. Carlo Vercellone, 189–208. Rome: Manifestolibri.

Vertova, Giovanna, ed. 2006. *The Changing Economic Geography of Globalization: Reinventing Space*. London: Routledge.

Vianello, Francesca A. 2009. *Migrando sole: Legami transnazionali tra Ucraina e Italia*. Milan: Angeli.

Vico, Giambattista. 1984. *The New Science of Giambattista Vico*. Unabridged Translation of the Third Edition (1744) with the addition of "Practic of the New Science," trans. Thomas Goddard Bergin and Max Harold Fisch. Ithaca, NY: Cornell University Press.

Vidal-Kopmann, Sonia. 2007. "La expansión de la periferia metropolitana de Buenos Aires. 'Villas miseria' y 'countries': De la ghettización a la integración de actores en el desarrollo local urbano." *Scripta nova. Revista electrónica de geografía y ciencias sociales* 11(245). Accessed January 16, 2012. http://www.ub.edu/geocrit/sn/sn-24542.htm.

Vila, Pablo. 2000. *Crossing Borders, Reinforcing Borders: Social Categories, Metaphors, and Narrative Identities on the U.S.–Mexico Frontier*. Austin: University of Texas Press.

Villacañas Berlanga, José Luis. 2010. "The Liberal Roots of Populism: A Critique of Laclau." *CR: The New Centennial Review* 10 (2): 151–82.

Viner, Jacob. 1965 [1937]. *Studies in the Theory of International Trade*. New York: Harper and Brothers.

Virno, Paolo. 2003. *A Grammar of the Multitude: For an Analysis of Contemporary Forms of Life*, trans. I. Bertoletti, J. Cascaito, and A. Casson. Cambridge: Semiotext(e).

———. 2010. *E così via, all'infinito: Logica e antropologia*. Turin: Bollati Boringhieri.

Von Eschen, Penny M. 1997. *Race against Empire: Black Americans and Anticolonialism, 1937–1957*. Ithaca, NY: Cornell University Press.

Walker, Gavin. 2011. "Primitive Accumulation and the Formation of Difference: On Marx and Schmitt." *Rethinking Marxism* 23 (3): 384–404.

Wallerstein, Immanuel. 1974. *The Modern World-System: Capitalist Agriculture and the Origins of the European World-Economy in the Sixteenth Century*. New York: Academic Press.

———. 1985. *Il capitalismo storico*. Turin: Einaudi.

———. 1991. "The Ideological Tensions of Capitalism: Universalism versus Racism and Sexism." In *Race, Nation, Class: Ambiguous Identities*, ed. Étienne Balibar and Immanuel Wallerstein, 29–36. London: Verso.

Walters, William. 2002. "De-naturalisng the Border: The Politics of Schengenland." *Environment and Planning D: Society and Space* 20 (5): 561–80.

———. 2008. "Bordering the Sea: Shipping Industries and the Policing of Stowaways." *Borderlands e-journal* 7(3). Accessed January 9, 2012. http://www.borderlands.net.au/vo17no3_2008/walters_bordering.htm.

———. 2009. "Foucault and Frontiers: Notes on the Birth of the Humanitarian Border." In *Governmentality: Current Issues and Future Challenges*, ed. Ulrich Bröckling, Susanne Krasmann, and Thomas Lemke, 138–64. London: Routledge.

Wang Hui. 2003. *China's New Order: Society, Politics and Economy in Transition*. Cambridge, MA: Harvard University Press.

———. 2009. *The End of the Revolution: China and the Limits of Modernity*. London: Verso.

———. 2011a. "Trans-systemic Society and Regional Perspective in Chinese Studies." *Boundary 2* 38 (1): 165–201.

———. 2011b. *The Politics of Imagining Asia*, ed. T. Huters. Cambridge, MA: Harvard University Press.

Weeks, Kathi. 2007. "Life within and against Work: Affective Labor, Feminist Critique, and Post-Fordist Politics." *Ephemera: Theory & Politics in Organization* 7 (1): 233–49.

——. 2011. *The Problem with Work: Feminism, Marxism, Antiwork Politics, and Post-work Imaginaries.* Durham, NC: Duke University Press.

Weizman, Eyal. 2007. *Hollow Land: Israel's Architecture of Occupation.* London: Verso.

Werbner, Pnina. 1990. "Renewing an Industrial Past: British Pakistani Entrepreneurship in Manchester." *Migration* 8: 7–41.

Whyte, Jessica. 2012. "Human Rights: Confronting Governments? Michel Foucault and the Right to Intervene." In *New Critical Legal Thinking: Law and the Political,* ed. Matthew Stone, Illan rua Wall, and Costas Douzinas, 11–31. London: Routledge.

Wihtol de Wenden, Catherine. 1988. *Citoyenneté, nationalité, et immigration.* Paris: Arcantere.

Winichakul, Thongchai. 1994. *Siam Mapped: A History of the Geo-Body of a Nation.* Honolulu: University of Hawaii Press.

Wright, Steve. 2002. *Storming Heaven: Class Composition and Struggle in Italian Autonomist Marxism.* London: Pluto Press.

——. 2005. "Reality Check: Are We Living in an Immaterial World?" In *Underneath the Knowledge Commons,* ed. Josephine Berry Slater, 34–45. London: Mute.

Xiang Biao. 2005. *Transcending Boundaries. Zhejiangcun: The Story of a Migrant Village in Beijing.* Leiden: Brill.

——. 2006. *Global "Body Shopping": An Indian Labor Regime in the Information Technology Industry.* Princeton, NJ: Princeton University Press.

——. 2008. "Transplanting Labor in East Asia." In *Transnational Migration in East Asia: Japan in a Comparative Focus* (Senri Ethnological Reports 77), ed. Yamashita Shinji, Makito Minami, David Haines, and Jeremy Edes, 175–86. Osaka: National Museum of Ethnology.

Yeates, Nicola. 2004. "Global Care Chains: Critical Reflections and Lines of Enquiry." *International Feminist Journal of Politics* 6 (3): 369–91.

Young, Robert J. C. 2001. *Postcolonialism: An Historical Introduction.* Oxford: Blackwell.

Yu Zhou. 2008. *The Inside Story of China's High Tech Industry: Making Silicon Valley in Beijing.* Lanham, MD: Rowman and Littlefield.

Yue-man Yeung, Joanna Lee, and Gordon Kee. 2009. "China's Special Economic Zones at 30." *Eurasian Geography and Economics* 50 (2): 222–40.

Zagor, Matthew. 2009. "The Oceanic Viking and Australia's Refugee Dilemma." *East Asia Forum,* December 26. Accessed September 4, 2010. http://www.eastasiaforum .org/2009/12/26/the-oceanic-viking-and-australias-refugee-dilemma/.

Zaloom, Caitlin. 2006. *Out of the Pits: Traders and Technology from Chicago to London.* Chicago: University of Chicago Press.

Zanini, Adelino. 2008. *Economic Philosophy: Economic Foundations and Political Categories,* trans. Cosma E. Orsi. Oxford: Lang.

Zanini, Piero. 1997. *Significati del confine: I limiti naturali, storici, mentali.* Milan: Bruno Mondadori.

Žižek, Slavoj. 1997. "Multiculturalism, or, the Cultural Logic of Multinational Capitalism." *New Left Review* 225: 28–51.

———. 1999. *The Ticklish Subject: The Absent Center of Political Ontology.* London: Verso.

———. 2006. *The Parallax View.* Cambridge, MA: MIT Press.

Zolberg, Aristide R., Sergio Aguayo, and Astri Suhrke. 1989. *Escape from Violence: Conflict and the Refugee Crisis in the Developing World.* Oxford: Oxford University Press.

Zwick, Detlev, and Nikhilesh Dholakia. 2006. "Bringing the Market to Life: Screen Aesthetics and the Epistemic Consumption Object." *Marketing Theory* 6 (1): 41–62.

INDEX

abstract labor, 88, 97, 118, 137, 272; finan-cialization of, 96, 111; and living labor relation, 92–93, 110, 121, 129, 134, 157, 310

accumulation by dispossession, 71, 233, 235, 244–46

accumulation of capital. *See* capitalist accumulation

activism: anticolonial, 57, 73; antiracist, 10–11; border, 62, 265, 266–70; migrant, 11–12, 142, 270; political movements, 308–10

Adkins, Lisa, 262

Africa, 34, 42, 55, 57, 211; debt crisis, 295; migrants/migration, 142, 172, 265; revolutions in, 308–9; transit camps, 168, 171; as a warren, 33–34

Agamben, Giorgio, 215, 301; analysis of the camp and bare life, 24, 147–48, 189; on sovereign exception, 132, 149, 189

Agnew, John, 29, 189

Akalyn, Ayşe, 109, 115

Anderson, Bridget, 108–9, 141, 267–68

Andrijasevic, Rutvica, 149

anti-imperialist struggles, 71, 73

Anzaldúa, Gloria, 6

Appadurai, Arjun, 62

appropriation: of the common, 292; of land, 291, 306; of space, 35; of surplus value, 245

Apter, Emily, 272

area form, 47–49, 54

area studies: continentalist schema of, 51–53; dominance of, 47; Ford Foundation's role in, 43–46, 50; knowledge geography of, 45; and myth of U.S. universalism, 57–58; patterns of the world and, 38, 46, 51; regionalism and, 53–54; rise of, 28, 42–43

Arendt, Hannah, 40, 147

Argentina, 241, 285, 299–300

Arnold, Dennis, 236–37

Aronowitz, Stanley, 98

Arrighi, Giovanni, 73, 81, 221

Artaker, Anna, 32–33

articulation(s): of borders, 3, 14, 66, 280; of capital/capitalism, 5, 213, 242, 251, 280, 307; of colonial expansion, 4; between dispossession and exploitation, 244–45; of labor, 223, 225, 248; of migration politics, 11; moment of, 255; notion or concept, 283–87; political or politics of, 122, 286, 288, 290; of social relations, 285–86; of space, 209, 211, 236; of technologies of power, 193, 197; translation as a form of, 289; of universalism and particularism, 25, 289

Asian Development Bank, 236

"Asian values" debate, 53

assemblages of power, 24, 148, 190, 196–97; and territory, 85, 195, 205, 207

assimilation, segmented, 156, 162–63

asylum seekers, 137, 145, 165, 186–87; and economic migrant distinction, 132, 143–44; offshore processing of, 168, 172

Atlas sive Cosmographicae Meditationes de Fabrica Mundi et Fabricati Figura (Mercator), 30–31

Australia: asylum seekers in, 12, 167–69; border policing, 175; detention camps/centers, 11–12, 24, 148; Indian migration to, 156–57, 270; migration scheme, 136–37, 140

Badiou, Alain, 255, 283

Balibar, Étienne, 154, 191, 254, 284, 305; on *banlieues*, 152; on borders, 4, 14, 16, 29, 62, 280; on citizenship and subjectivity, 258; on modern politics, 257, 259; on the universal, 290–91

Banerjee-Guha, Swapna, 233

banlieues/banlieusards, 132–33, 151–55, 258, 265

Barber, Brad M., 112

bare life, 22, 24, 148, 150, 189

Barth, Fredrik, 14

Bauder, Harald, 101

Beck, Ulrich, 52, 304

Becker, Gary, 196

Belnap, Jeffrey, 55

Bengali borderland, 48, 50–51

Benjamin, Walter, 36, 134, 158, 189

Bensaâd, Ali, 172

Benton, Lauren, 207

Berger, John, 103

Bernardot, Marc, 148

Best, Stephen, 262

Bharucha, Rustom, 56

Bigo, Didier, 187

biocapital, 86–87

biopolitics, 197, 261; borders and, 173, 175; Foucault on, 173, 192, 194

Blackstone, William, 292

Blair-Loy, Mary, 112

Bloch, Ernst, 232

Bloch, Marc, 70

body shopping system, 24, 133, 135–37; practice of benching, 136, 150, 158, 165

Bolivia, 32, 277, 306; migrants/migration, 55, 239–41

Boltanski, Luc, 128

border as method approach, 9–10, 16–19, 268, 304; to area studies, 47; border struggles and, 53, 57–58, 130, 280; to capital, 79–80, 203, 266; and critical regionalism, 58–59; mapping and, 36, 48; and production of subjectivity, 83, 311; and proliferation of borders, 27, 62–63, 96

border control: actors and agencies involved in, 53, 181–82, 184–86; as an exclusionary device, 7, 269; discrimination and selection, 114; displacement of, 171–72; EU practices, 11, 53, 172, 180–81; humanitarian intervention in, 24, 175–76; human rights and, 187; illegal migration and, 145; of international borders, 138; and mobility, 49, 93, 183, 270; Pacific Solution, 12, 168, 171; role in labor markets, 143, 266; securitization, 187, 195; sovereignty and, 180, 201; toughness and humaneness approaches to, 175–76. *See also* deportation; detention

borderless world, 13–14, 61–62, 268

border policing, 23, 53, 62, 175

border regimes, 21, 164, 176; conflicts, 185–88; European, 11, 172, 181, 305; governance/governmentalization of, 176, 179–83, 201, 237; race and ethnicity and, 173; technologies, 133; transformations in, 198

borders: biopolitical, 173, 175; of community, 301; concepts and definitions of, 3, 14, 16, 280; connecting/disconnecting capacities, 284; crossing of, 9, 133–34, 150, 175; and domestic care work, 108, 121, 130; dual natures of, 3–4, 38; effect on labor markets, 19, 103, 266; as an epistemological viewpoint, 18; exclusionary and inclusionary functions of, 7, 13, 148, 159, 301; and frontier distinction, 8; functions and kinds of, 4–6, 27–28; globalizing processes of, 61–62; and justice relations, 269; as laboratories, 61–62, 65; management of, 165, 174–75, 202; mapping or tracing of, 4, 28–30, 32, 35; material aspects of, 51; multiple locations for, 198; multiplication of, 85, 203, 239, 261;

politics, 30, 137, 183, 186, 267–69; power dynamics of, 2, 195–96; of private property, 292–93, 296; and production of labor power, 19–20, 96; as sites of violence and confrontation, 7, 27, 183, 186, 202; softening and hardening of, 175, 237, 279; symbolic dimensions of, 14; time and money relations of, 135; traditional images of, 3; urban, 1, 296; as walls, 6–8. *See also* cognitive and geographical borders; internal borders; proliferation of borders; temporal borders

borderscape, 9, 15–16, 132, 197; to Australia, 167, 175; concept, 12–13; sovereignty and governance of, 183, 195; struggles, 169, 270, 280; world's, 142, 159, 174

border struggles: actors involved in, 266; and capital, 280–81; for the common, 283, 306–8, 311; and law, 186–87, 189; as life and death matters, 18, 202, 312; materiality of, 19; mobility and, 269–70; movements and activism, 62, 265, 266–70; and political subjectivity, 13–14, 23–24, 66; power and, 195; and production of subjectivity, 20, 183, 188, 264–67, 311; temporalizing effects of, 133–34; translation and, 244, 281, 307–8

border studies, 9–10, 13; focus on Western contexts, 15–16

border technologies, 15, 101, 133, 138, 173, 211; multiple and heterogeneous, 225, 235, 238

border thinking, 18

borderzones, 12, 235–36, 241, 305

boundaries: disputes, 29–30; drawing or mapping of, 30, 33–35, 222; establishment of new, 78, 91, 97; of ethics and power, 174; between free and unfree labor, 100, 138, 262; and graduated sovereignty, 238; between inclusion and exclusion, 154, 164, 251; of intellectual and manual labor, 126; internal, 55, 100, 225, 257; between legal and illegal, 140, 236; linear, 4; linguistic, 274; multiple/multiplicity, 108, 209, 227, 237, 241, 266; national, 50, 79, 237; proliferation of, 85, 123; between public and private, 177, 294,

296; sexual and racial, 76, 84, 249; shifting, 103–4; sovereign state, 15, 30. *See also* borders

Bowman, Isaiah, 41, 71

Braudel, Fernand, 75

Braverman, Harry, 126

Brotton, Jerry, 34

Brown, Wendy, 8, 253

Bruno, Giordano, 30–31, 311

Bryan, Dick, 90

Buck-Morss, Susan, 247

Buenos Aires, 55, 152; *La Salada,* 12, 239–41

Bukowina, 199

Calcutta. *See* Kolkata

Caliban (from *The Tempest*), 55–56

Calichman, Richard, 57

Calico Act, The (1721), 77

Canadian migration policy, 140

Cap Anamur, 170–71

capital: alternative/community economies and, 299–300, 302, 306; axiomatic of, 23, 59, 81, 86, 88, 92, 302; cartography and, 23, 33; chains of, 119, 122; circuits/circulation of, 33, 216, 298; communitarian, 240; expansion of, 52, 66, 68, 132–33, 244; fixed, 90–91, 116; flows of, 237; gap in, 85; geographical movement of, 72–73; global dominance of, 59; individual, 68–69; and labor relations, 79, 84–85, 93, 100–103, 233, 266; Lenin's observations of, 80; Marx's formula for, 117; mobility of, 72, 84–85; postdevelopmental, 209; social relations of, 99, 119, 279–82, 302, 310; and society, 124; sovereignty and, 12, 202–3; and state legal framework, 101; and state relations, 5–6, 73, 77, 219, 310; struggles against, 280–81, 307, 310–11; time and space of, 116, 132–33, 203, 225; transformations or transitions of, 8, 88, 148, 212, 236; translation and, 273–74, 276; transnational, 217–18; unity of, 23, 123, 129, 302. *See also* finance; financialization; frontiers of capital; primitive accumulation

Capital (Marx), 68–69, 98, 117, 245, 263; commodities, 259; intensification of

Capital (Marx) (*cont.*)

labor, 88–89; primitive accumulation, 33, 85, 293; references to power(s), 192

capitalism: "advanced," 70; as an assemblage, 126; Atlantic, 100; cartography of, 5, 23, 86; cognitive, 137–40, 165, 224, 233; concepts and debates, 69–70; and consumer goods, 86; deterritorialization/reterritorialization of, 302; "disorganized," 52, 80; division of labor and rise of, 76–79; economic space of, 66; and exploitation, 243; and "free" wage labor, 56, 85; global, 4, 20, 53, 97, 121, 225, 302; history of, 56, 100–102, 213, 221, 224; industrial, 82, 101–2, 117; isomorphy and heterogeneity of, 86; labor relations and, 84–85, 104, 110; manual labor and, 126; modern or contemporary, 5, 21, 56, 66, 86, 148, 150, 292; monopoly, 127; neoliberal, 239; opposition to, 310; organization of labor under, 24; "outside" of, 71–72; postcolonial, 2, 232–33; spatial hierarchies of, 73; terms to describe, 80–81; and territorialism relation, 40, 70–71; transitions and transformations of, 23, 74, 81–82, 84, 123, 196

capitalist accumulation, 35, 58, 74, 178, 204, 241; and accumulation by dispossession, 244; global circuits of, 51, 64, 108, 236, 238; imperialism and, 71–72; primitive accumulation and, 245; role of women in, 83

capitalist development, 56, 72, 78, 262; concept, 234; exploitation for, 42, 243–44; in India, 233; and limits of space and time, 132–33

capitalist production, 50, 75, 79, 234, 241; and concept of articulation, 284; geography of, 203; organization of, 65–66, 284; socialization of, 68–69; of space, 68; subjection/subjectivity of, 252, 263; of surplus value, 67, 72, 88–89, 245; uneven transformations of, 5; and the world market, 67–68, 72

care workers. *See* domestic and care workers

cartographic anxiety or crisis, 6, 28–30, 49, 55

cartography: birth of modern, 31–33, 66; of capitalism, 5, 23, 86; and colonialism, 34;

early cartographers, 30–31; ontological moment in, 35–36; primitive accumulation of, 32–36, 66, 132. *See also* maps and mapping

Casarino, Cesare, 297

Castel, Robert, 154

Castells, Manuel, 135, 210–11

Castles, Stephen, 96, 161–62, 164

chains: of capital, 122; global care, 105, 108, 119–21; as a metaphor, 95, 119; supply, 228, 236; that bind workers, 95, 116, 121–22. *See also* commodity chains

Chakrabarty, Dipesh, 42, 110

Chalcraft, John, 300

Chang, Leslie, 224

Chatterjee, Partha, 151, 158, 234–35

Chen, Kuan-Hsing, 59

Chiapello, Eve, 128

China: economic development, 221, 223, 231; history, 222–23; *hukou* system, 220, 225–26; Japanese occupation of, 57; labor regimes, 223–25, 274; migrant workers, 220, 226–27; production and industrial zones, 12, 218, 227–28; SEZs, 9, 217, 224–26, 229–30; territory and borders, 24, 222–23

Chow, Rey, 42

CIGEM (Centre d'Information et de Gestion des Migrations), 172

citizenship: ambiguity of concept, 256; and borders, 151, 237, 249, 257; differential inclusion of, 249, 251; European, 181; French, 153–54; hierarchies of, 258; labor and, 247–51; Marshallian, 249–50; permanent residency and, 113, 139; political concept of, 239; production of subjectivity and, 250, 258–59; rights, 170, 230, 249, 261, 267; sovereignty and, 141, 173, 215; spaces of, 7, 155, 256; studies, 256–57; transformations of, 21

citizen-worker: disarticulation of, 24, 244, 247, 250, 256; dyadic structure of, 250–51; Soviet Stakhanovite worker, 247–48; U.S., 248–49

civil society, 35, 70, 151, 217, 288

class: capitalists as a, 84; concepts, 98–99, 130; consciousness, 99; contradictions, 285; differentials of, 66; in India, 157, 234;

operaista notion of, 99; relations, 272, 295; struggles, 5, 62, 196, 243, 257, 284, 311. *See also* working class

classical liberalism, 213, 253

Clinton, Bill, 11, 199

cognition and abstraction relation, 126–27

cognitive and geographical borders, 16–17, 28, 34–38, 58

cognitive expectations, 201

Cohen, Robin, 84

Cole, Philip, 268

Collier, Stephen, 195

colonial conquest, 35, 291–92; European expansion, 4, 32–33, 39; frontiers, 15, 39, 71, 78

"colonial difference," 18, 74

colonial experience, 195

commodity: the common as a, 298; consumption, 65, 86; double character of, 259; exchange, 126, 128; fetishism, 36, 259; of labor power, 19–21, 93, 95–96, 102, 105, 110, 261–63; production, 83, 126

commodity chains, 86, 92, 131; global, 83, 119–22, 129–30

commodity form: intellectual and manual labor and, 126–27; of labor power, 19, 263; law and, 293; Marx's analysis of, 259–61; sovereignty of the, 36; translation and, 272, 282

common, the: appropriation of, 35; borders and, 267, 279, 291–92, 296; circulation of, 297–98; and commons difference, 278; concept, 277–78; corruption and conflict of, 299, 302; creation and expansion of, 275, 298–300; destruction/tragedy of, 296; intellectual/creative movement surrounding, 297; management of, 297, 299, 301; politics of, 23, 281, 304–5; private/public property and, 292–96; production of, 25, 298–300, 310; spaces of, 283, 299–300, 305; struggles for, 267, 277–78, 306–11; translation of, 17, 275, 278, 283, 290–91, 301, 309; and the universal, 289–90

communism, 283, 300–301; primitive, 291

Communist Manifesto (Marx and Engels), 66–67

community economies, 299–302

comparative advantages theory, 66, 78–79

comparative literature, 16, 37, 42

continental blocs, 52–53, 55, 209

continental drift, 38, 55, 57–59; seminar series, 52

continentalist thinking, 55–56

Cooper, Frederick, 211

cooperatives, 298–300

core and periphery concepts, 18, 51, 73–74, 222; as world divisions (binaries), 64, 79, 83, 85–86, 303

corporate codes, 91, 217–18, 227–28

cosmopolitanism, 279, 303–5

creation, 31

Crenshaw, Kimberlé, 249

Cross, Jamie, 235

Curzon, Lord George, 39–40

Dalla Costa, Mariarosa, 160

d'Anania, Giovanni Lorenzo, 31

Das Potosí-Prinzip, 32

Davis, Mike, 92, 151

Death Ship, The (Traven), 275–76

debt, 118, 295

de Certeau, Michel, 133

decolonization, 46–47

De Genova, Nicholas, 22, 145–46

De Graffenreid v. General Motors, 249

Deleuze, Gilles, 81, 86, 195, 302

democracy, 303–4

denationalization, 5, 63, 70

Denning, Michael, 51, 97

dependency theory, 51, 73, 83. *See also* world system theory

De Peuter, Greig, 298

depoliticization, 41, 221

deportation, 76, 175, 265, 273; systems and regimes, 138, 146–49, 184, 206

Derrida, Jacques, 35, 269

Descartes, René, 31, 35

detention: administration and governance, 168–71, 181–82, 184; Agamben's analysis of, 24, 147–48, 189; camps and centers, 11–12, 24, 58, 148–50, 167–68, 172; growth of, 132; practices and systems, 138, 143–48, 175; temporal dimension of, 149–50 deterritorialization, 52, 173, 302

differential inclusion, 24, 73, 132, 289; of citizenship, 181, 249, 251; concept, 23, 159, 163–6; and differential exclusion concept, 161–62, 164, 215; feminist thought on, 159–60; and struggles, 269, 279; technologies of, 131, 195

differential incorporation, 161

Dis-Agreement (Rancière), 152, 254

displacement, 56, 120, 258, 312; of border control, 171–72; eternally displaced concept, 154; of Europe, 18, 42; of peasants in India, 122, 131, 230–33; of politics, 253

dispossession: accumulation by, 71, 233, 235, 244–46; exploitation and, 24, 242, 244–47, 263–64, 274, 311; in India, 230, 232–35; of peasants, 234, 240, 244

division of labor: ancient and historical accounts of, 75–78; in finance capital, 80, 82; gender/sexual, 83–84, 90, 104–5, 112, 121, 160; global, 92; and market expansion, 75–76; multiplication of labor and, 21–22, 87–88, 92; between skilled and unskilled, 22–23; social dimensions of, 91, 124. *See also* international division of labor; multiplication of labor

Djouder, Ahmed, 155, 159

Documenta exhibition (Kassel), 62

domestic and care workers, 96, 102, 111, 121; employer relations and labor contract, 108–10; Filipina, 106, 111, 112; and financial traders connection, 112, 115, 118; and image of the chain, 122; responsibilities and tasks, 105–6; transnational spaces of, 107–8

Dubet, François, 153

Du Bois, W. E. B., 41, 55–58, 71, 99

Durkheim, Émile, 69, 91, 129

Dyer-Witheford, Nick, 297–98, 306

Easterling, Keller, 230

East–West divide, 34–35, 54, 63

economic crisis (2007–8), 5, 97, 114–15, 203

economic division, 80, 85

economy: alternative/community, 300–302; global, 111, 136, 185; informal, 235, 240; knowledge, 137, 295; market, 62, 107,

300; national, 114; proletarian, 240–41; subsistence, 92, 108. *See also* political economy

Ehrenreich, Barbara, 106–7

Ehrlich, Eugen, 199

Elazar, Daniel J., 52

Elden, Stuart, 196

Elliot, William Yandell, 198

emotional labor, 104, 106, 109, 111, 125

empires, 40, 207–8, 222

enclosure, 241, 278–79, 297; Marx's analysis of, 32–33, 277, 292–93; "new," 295–96

Engels, Friedrich, 66–67, 95, 121, 123, 291

England, 75, 78

epistemology, 18

equivalences, 255–56, 286, 288–90

ergasterion, 32

Escobar, Arturo, 46, 239

Esposito, Roberto, 261

ethnographic practice, 9–10; studies, 113, 135

Europe: border regimes, 11, 172, 181, 305; borders and border control, 4, 32, 34, 38–40, 71, 77, 165, 180; depictions of the Orient, 34; displacement of, 18, 42; integration, 304–5; law, 200; maps/mapping of, 5, 32, 39–40, 42; migrant domestic workers from, 103, 107–8; modernity, 209

European Union, 52–53; external borders/frontiers, 9, 24, 165, 171–72, 180–81; member states, 172; migration flows, 144; migration regime, 155, 171

exception: concept of, 215; neoliberalism as, 235; sovereign, 132, 148–49, 189, 215–16; spaces of, 236; state of, 147, 183

exclusion. *See* inclusion and exclusion

exploitation: accumulation by, 235, 245; for capitalist development, 42, 243–44; and dispossession, 24, 242, 244–47, 263–64, 274, 311; labor, 111, 141, 212, 233, 246; power and, 252; shifting regimes of, 239

externalization, 11, 146, 168, 172

fabrica mundi, 23, 36, 280, 310; ontological dimension of, 52, 65; origins and meanings, 30–32

Farinelli, Franco, 30, 36

feminist thought, 159–60; critiques and debates, 106, 109

feminization of labor, 23, 83–84, 104–5

Ferguson, James, 211

Fernández, Raul, 55

finance: capital/capitalism, 79–80, 89, 117, 203, 279; expansion of, 81, 111, 118, 121

financialization, 5, 81, 118; of abstract labor, 96; of capital/capitalism, 23, 84, 88–89, 111, 253, 294, 302; of the economy, 138; and household, 90; mimetic rationality of, 117, 129

financial markets, 82; global/globalization of, 92, 111–12, 128–29, 244, 295; trading, 116–17

financial traders, 23, 96, 111–18; and image of the chain, 119–20, 122

Fischer-Lescano, Andreas, 185, 200–201

fixes, partial, 285–86

flow: of capital, 237; metaphor of, 209–11; migration, 138, 144, 172, 183; production, 126–27; space of, 210–11, 303

forced labor, 32–33, 263

Forcellini, Egidio, 32

Ford Foundation, 43–46, 50

Fordism, 43–44, 87, 294; crisis of, 87, 124–25, 152, 213; "peripheral," 83

foreign markets, 68

foreign trade, 75, 78

Fortress Europe, 7, 165

Foucault, Michel, 35, 169–70; biopolitics, 173, 192, 194; concept of population, 194; critique of sovereignty, 190–91, 197; on governmentality, 174, 176–77, 190, 256; on human capital, 128, 196; on migration and mobility, 196, 204; *The Order of Things*, 31–32; on power, 193–94, 204, 243; references to Marx, 191–92

France, 102, 152–55, 270. See also *banlieues/banlieusards*

free trade, 77, 207, 225, 236

free wage labor, 56, 81, 83, 85, 110; slavery connection, 262

Frontex, 53, 180–82

frontiers: and border distinction, 15–16; of China, 222; colonial, 15, 39, 71; establishment of new, 211; of the EU, 9, 24, 165, 171–72, 180–81; of Palestinian territories, 8

frontiers of capital: expansion, 5, 66, 70, 72–74, 80, 241; multiple borders and, 209, 266; political borders and, 66–67, 70–71, 76, 78, 93; territorial borders and, 121–22, 242, 251, 261, 303; world market and, 67–68, 85, 92

G4S, 184

Gago, Veronica, 239–40

Galli, Carol, 52, 65

García Canclini, Néstor, 61–62, 65

Gardner, Andrew M., 274

Geiger, Martin, 182

gender: composition of migration, 104–5, 107, 258; division in labor, 83–84, 90, 112–13; oppression, 226

general crisis (1970s), 88

General Motors, 82, 248–49

generation, concept of the, 155–56

geopolitical borders, 3, 30, 237

geopolitics, 40–41

Germany, 70, 144, 170–71

Ghosh, Amitav, 27–28, 37–38, 49, 52

Ghosh, Bimal, 179

Gibson-Graham, J. K., 300–302, 306

Gilroy, Paul, 55, 163

Glenn, Evelyn Nakano, 248

Glissant, Édouard, 275–76

global care chains, 105, 108, 119–21

global connections, 12, 210–11, 232, 238

globalization, 2–4, 10, 65, 237, 251; borders and, 52, 61–62; capitalist, 6, 30, 189, 197, 203, 250, 266; of democracy, 304; of financial markets, 92, 111–12, 128–29, 244, 295; and flow metaphor, 209–11; legal, 199–200; private governance regimes under, 217; spatiality of, 211, 238; state processes of, 197–98

global labor, 96–97, 128; history and historians of, 56, 85, 99, 110, 245

global space, 4, 62–66, 69; of flows, 210–11; heterogeneity/heterogenization of, 2, 6, 22–23, 52, 65, 84, 95; smooth, 133, 203, 210

Godechot, Olivier, 115–16

governance: border/migration regimes and,

governance (*cont.*)

176, 179–83, 201, 237; corporate, 177,
184; debates and theories, 177–78, 224;
global, 8, 304; humanitarian, 171, 187–
88; migration, 148–49, 165, 171, 174,
202; neoliberal, 288; private, 217; role of
epistemic communities in, 178; sovereignty and, 8, 118, 141, 169, 183, 190,
227; of the "third world," 47

governmentality: assemblages of, 221, 236;
border/migration regimes and, 179–80,
201; concepts and theories, 174, 176–77,
190, 256; human rights and, 176; liberal,
174; market, 215; neoliberal, 163, 177,
180, 213, 216; of society, 173; sovereign
machine of, 24, 175, 204, 206, 216–17,
238–39, 242; and sovereignty, 188–90,
202–4, 212–17

Gramsci, Antonio, 161, 278, 284; Fordism,
43–44; references to Lenin, 270–71; on
translatability of languages, 9, 270–72,
307

Grande, Edgar, 304

Great Mekong Subregion (GMS), 236–37

Gregory, Derek, 28

Grenze, 16, 67

Grotius, Hugo, 291–92

Grundrisse (Marx), 67–68, 88, 110, 271–72

Guatemalan-Honduras boundary, 29–30

Guattari, Félix, 81, 86, 92, 195, 302

Guha, Ranajit, 37

Haas, Richard, 64

Hage, Ghassan, 163

Hall, Stuart, 161, 163, 243, 286–87

Hanssen, Beatrice, 191

Hardin, Garrett, 296

Hardt, Michael, 71, 125, 203, 290, 294, 307

Harvey, David, 72, 74, 133; accumulation by
dispossession, 233, 243–46

Haushofer, Karl, 41

Hegel, Georg Wilhelm Friedrich, 37, 39, 70,
160

hegemony, 76–77, 91, 285, 289; European,
42; immaterial labor's, 125; U.S., 5, 199;
Western and capitalist, 46

Hegemony and Socialist Strategy (Laclau
and Mouffe), 255, 283, 285

Heidegger, Martin, 32, 42

Held, David, 303–4

Hess, Sabine, 108

heterogeneity/heterogenization: of borders,
3–4, 18, 166, 239, 265, 269, 302; of capital, 161; of discipline and biopolitics, 194;
of global space, 2, 23, 65, 84, 97, 277; isomorphy and, 2, 86; of labor and living
labor, 21, 85, 91–92, 110, 125, 128; and
multiplication similarity, 251; of population and workforces, 21, 96, 100, 104; of
the social, 255, 285; of space/spatial, 86,
129, 210, 223, 225, 303; of translation, 282

hierarchies: border, 7, 16; of capitalism, 73;
citizenship, 257; gendered, 104–5; labor,
21–22, 266, 274; mobility, 149; space/
spatial, 37, 64, 66, 86, 125, 225

Hobbes, Thomas, 191, 252, 287–88;
Leviathan, 260, 271

Hochschild, Arlie, 104–7

hospitality, 279, 292

households, 90, 105–6

human capital, 92, 128, 174, 196, 251

humanitarianism: intervention and activism, 24, 169–71, 187–88; practices of,
176, 183–84

human–nonhuman difference, 283–84

human potentiality, 20

human rights, 189, 261; activism, 267, 269;
of asylum seekers, 144, 187; and migration management, 175–76; protocols and
laws, 169, 175, 181–82, 184, 187

Hume, David, 87, 91

Huntington, Samuel, 53

hyperbolical moment, 35

Ibn Khaldûn, 75

illegalization, 122, 142–45; inclusion
through, 145–46, 165

"illegal" migrants, 8, 50, 144–45, 254, 257,
270; deportation and detention of, 11,
146–150, 273; emergence of, 142–43;
labels for, 142, 266; and skill level
assumptions, 137

imperialism, 77, 79–80, 203, 222; debate on,
71–72; European, 23, 40–41, 80; Japanese, 57; U.S., 208

inclusion and exclusion, 148, 158, 162, 215,

labor markets (*cont.*)
　traders, 113, 116; and migration/migratory movements, 101–3, 137–41, 143, 150, 156, 161–62; national, 22, 101–3, 113, 134, 244, 249–50; needs, 139, 172; and practices of manipulation, 115, 141; reorganization of, 103, 132, 143; role of borders in, 7, 19, 21, 96, 103, 135, 266
labor mobility, 1, 96–97; borders and, 2, 55; control of, 52, 93, 100, 237; differential inclusion and, 23–24. *See also* migration; mobility
labor movements, 44–45, 198, 246–47, 253; nationalization of, 101; slave revolts, 56; unity concept in, 123
labor power: commodity of, 19–21, 93, 95–96, 102, 105, 110, 261–63; concept of legal person and, 262–63, 270; and credit commitments, 90; of domestic care workers, 102, 108; in India, 50; and living body of the worker, 89–90, 102, 109–10, 194, 263; Marx's conception of, 19–20, 110, 169, 190, 193–94, 204; money and, 20, 116, 193, 260–61, 268; (re)production of, 20, 99, 107–8, 116, 120, 150, 310; and role of temporal borders, 138
labor regimes, 52, 88, 238; in China, 223–25, 274; continuities and gaps in, 65; slavery or indenture, 56
labor struggles, 45, 47, 54, 56, 84–85; in China, 226–27; against dispossession, 246–247; as social conflicts, 59; and unity concept, 123
Laclau, Ernesto, 166, 255, 288, 306; class theory, 284–85; notion of articulation, 283–86; on universalism and particularism, 287, 289–90
La Haine (Kassovitz), 151
la partage de la raison, 17
Lapeyronnie, Didier, 153
La Salada, 12, 239–41
Laski, Harold, 198
Last Train Home (Lixin Fan), 220
Latham, Robert, 189, 202
Latin America, 74, 213, 239
law: civil, 278, 292–93; conflicts, 200; global, 91, 185, 199–202; international, 181, 184–87, 198–200; living, 199–200; and

Marxism, 260; private/public property, 292–94; Roman, 292–93; ships and, 207; slave, 222, 262; social, 297; State apparatuses and, 193; translation and, 271; U.S. immigration, 145
Lebensraum, 40–41
legal orders, 199–200
Lenin, Vladimir Ilich, 79–80, 85, 119; Russian Revolution speech (1922), 270–73, 307
Lentin, Alana, 164
Lessig, Lawrence, 297
Lestringant, Frank, 33
Lewis, Martin W., 27
linear borders, 3, 5, 14–15, 68; of Europe, 32, 39–40, 71, 77; of India and Pakistan, 28, 37–38
Linebaugh, Peter, 100, 295
Linera, Álvaro García, 240
linguistic barriers, 274. *See also* translation
living body of the worker, 89–90, 102, 109–10, 194, 263
living labor, 19, 122, 266, 273; and abstract labor relations, 92–93, 110, 121, 129, 134, 157, 310; borders and boundaries of, 91, 100, 123, 130, 251; of carers and traders, 96, 103, 111, 121; in China, 227; division of, 253; heterogeneity of, 23, 85; multiplication of labor and, 21–23. *See also* domestic and care workers; financial traders
Locke, John, 20, 262
Lonzi, Carla, 160
Lorde, Audre, 273
Luhmann, Niklas, 199–201
Luxemburg, Rosa, 71–72, 241

Machete (Rodriguez), 264–65, 270
Macpherson, Crawford B., 295
Maghreb, 172
Making of the English Working Class, The (Thompson), 98, 100
Malta, 170
Managed Heart, The (Hochschild), 104
Mandeville, Bernard, 76
Mannheim, Karl, 155
maps and mapping: appropriation of space in, 35; for capitalist development, 5, 23,

42; of cognitive borders, 35–37; and colonialism, 15, 27, 33–34; practices, 28–30; of primitive accumulation, 32–34, 36; of social class, 98; of sovereign territory, 3, 15, 141; used in boundary disputes, 29–30. *See also* cartographic anxiety or crisis; cartography

Marazzi, Christian, 82, 88, 90–91, 117

Marcus, George, 10

maritime routes, 12, 206

market expansion, 75–76

Marshall, T. H., 249–50

Martí, José, 41, 55–56

Martin, Randy, 90

Marx, Karl, 97, 291, 298; *Charaktermaske* usage, 260; commodity form analysis, 259–61; definition of the state, 85; *dramatis personae* usage, 193, 260; enclosure analysis, 32–33, 277, 292–93; exploitation critique, 192; formula for capital, 117; Foucault's references to, 191–92; on the hidden abode of production, 193, 196; on human potentiality, 20; on intensification of labor, 88–89; international division of labor concept, 78–79; labor power theory, 19–20, 110, 169, 190, 193–94, 204; on large-scale industry, 87, 91; political economy critique, 56, 66–67, 258; on primitive accumulation, 32–34, 85, 241, 245; quote on the chains of workers, 95, 121, 123; references to power(s) in *Capital*, 192; on slavery, 263; on social classes, 98; on subjectivity, 252, 259; on surplus value, 67, 72, 88–89, 245; on translation and money, 271–72; world market analysis, 67–69, 71, 77, 88, 132, 280

Mathew, Biju, 1–2, 19

Mattei, Ugo, 293, 297, 306

Mbembe, Achille, 154, 174

Mercator, Gerardus, 30–31, 34, 36

metageography, 27, 34, 37–39, 41, 55

Mexico–U.S. border, 3, 6–7, 236; control and policing, 53, 145, 147

Mezzadra, Sandro, 10–11

Midnight Notes Collective, 295

Mies, Maria, 83–84

Mignolo, Walter, 18, 34, 74

migrant workers: Chinese, 220; choice limitations of, 102; competition for, 140; iconic representations of, 103; labor power of, 102; NYC taxi drivers, 1–2; remittances, 106, 118; skilled and unskilled, 22–23, 132, 137–39, 141; from South Asia, 1–2; temporary, 140, 162, 220. *See also* domestic and care workers; financial traders; information technology (IT)

migration: activism, 11–12, 62, 142, 270; African, 142, 172, 265; Bolivian, 55, 239–41; and differential exclusion, 161–62; feminization of, 104–5; flows, 138, 144, 172, 183; forced, 143; generational differences in, 155–57; global woman in, 106; governance, 148–49, 165, 171, 174, 202; Indian, 49–50, 156–57, 270, 274; and labor markets, 101–3, 137–41, 143, 150, 156, 161–62; management, 53, 168, 171–76, 179, 182–83, 197; policies, 138–42, 154, 172–73, 182; politics, 11, 148, 181–82, 189; schemes, 102–3, 114, 132, 138–42, 164–65; skilled and unskilled, 132, 137–39, 141; struggles, 49–50, 142–43, 148–49, 227, 270; studies, 23, 105, 141, 155, 161–62; systems, 136, 156, 172–73, 178, 274; temporality of, 134, 143, 158. *See also* deportation; detention; "illegal" migrants; mobility

migration control, 3, 53, 101, 144, 174, 182

migration regimes, 2, 24, 164, 169, 174; concept, 178–79; European, 155, 165, 172, 181; governance and, 179–80; U.S., 264. *See also* border regimes

migratory movements, 105, 138, 142, 148, 269; continental drift and, 53–54; generational pattern of, 156–57; global scope of, 96; and labor power, 103; role of geography in, 54–55; selection and filtering methods in, 114, 149, 165

militarization of thinking, 42

Miller, Mark, 96

Miller, Toby, 82

Mitropoulos, Angela, 266

mobility: and border control, 49, 93, 183, 270; of capital, 72, 84–85; of care workers, 96, 107–8, 121, 130; of European borders, 165; of financial traders,

mobility (*cont.*)
   96, 113–14; Foucault on, 196, 204; global, 66; of Indian IT workers, 24, 135–37, 150; and internal borders, 151; labor, 55, 84, 93, 100, 103, 212, 237; patterns, 6, 215; of point system scheme, 139–40; practices of, 54, 209–10, 225, 239; of skilled and unskilled workers, 141; social, 153, 223. *See also* migratory movements
modernity: alternative, 56, 58, 209; baroque, 240–41; biopolitical paradigm of, 147; capitalism and, 59, 127; in China, 222; colonial, 18, 158; political, 160; postcolonial, 209; slavery and, 275; transformative dynamic of, 281
modern state, 15, 252, 255, 303
Mohanty, Chandra, 13, 106
Mohr, Jean, 103
money, 88, 135, 300; as capital, 117, 124; and cartography connection, 33, 36; and labor power, 20, 116, 193, 260–61, 268; market, 68–69; translation and, 271–72, 282; universality of, 259, 261
Montgomery, David, 248
Morris-Suzuki, Tessa, 58
Mouffe, Chantal, 166, 255, 288, 306; notion of articulation, 283–86; on universalism and particularism, 287, 289–90
Moulier Boutang, Yann, 100
multiculturalism, 2, 163–64
multiplication of labor, 90, 97, 103, 122; in Argentina, 241; of Chinese labor regimes, 223–24; concept, 21–23, 87–88, 123, 251; elements of division in, 92, 119; global, 65, 112, 113; and proliferation of borders, 125, 253. *See also* division of labor; living labor
multiplicity, 161, 199, 275, 285, 310; of borders, 4, 14, 108, 214, 308; of boundaries, 237, 266; of citizenship statuses, 256; of links, 124–25; of living labor, 110, 121, 129, 266; of migratory regimes, 179, 183; of the nation-state, 165–66; unity in, 124, 275, 311
multitude, concept of, 21, 252–53

NAFTA, 52–53, 55
Nancy, Jean-Luc, 283, 301

national borders, 2, 49, 85, 265
nationalism, 40, 84, 134, 287; postcolonial, 48, 158; studies of, 47
nationalization, 36, 101; of state in Europe, 39–40
"national spirits" *(Volksgeiste)*, 39
nation form, 47–48
nation-state, 185, 195; borders and, 48, 101, 136, 181, 222, 266, 303; capital–labor relations and, 2, 79; European, 32, 41, 71; German, 70; globalization of, 5, 62–63; labor markets and, 22, 101–3; sovereign power of, 179, 216; time and spatial dimensions of, 157–59, 163, 165–66
Negri, Antonio, 125, 290, 294, 307; on imperialism, 71, 203
Neilson, Brett, 11
neoliberalism, 2, 239, 251; in Bolivia, 240–41; and capitalist transitions, 212–13; in China, 221; and classical liberalism, 213, 253; development in East Asia, 213, 215; development in Latin America, 213–14; and economic rationality, 202; as exception, 235; and governmentality, 163, 177, 180, 213, 216; policies, 105, 253
Neoliberalism as Exception (Ong), 215
network of relations, 124
No Border politics, 266–68
noncapitalist economy, 300–302
"No one is illegal" slogan, 62, 142
normativity, fragmentation of, 183
North–South divide, 21, 54, 63–64, 92, 101
Nugent, David, 43, 50
NYC taxi drivers, 1–2, 21

Oberlechner, Thomas, 114
Occupied Territories, 8, 12
Oceanic Viking, 167–70, 186
Odean, Terrance, 112
OEMS (original equipment manufacturers), 227–28
Ōmae, Kenichi, 62
Ōmura Detention Center (Japan), 58
Ong, Aihwa, 162, 195, 210, 238, 291; latitudes concept, 214–15; on sovereign power, 216–17
operaismo, 99, 124
Ostrom, Elinor, 296

Pacific Solution, 12, 168, 171
Palestinian territories, 8, 12
Panagiotidis, Efthimia, 149
particularism, 57, 287–91
Pashukanis, Evgeny, 260, 293
Pasquinelli, Matteo, 299
Pateman, Carole, 160
patriarchy, 104, 107, 160, 226
peasants: displacement of, 122, 131, 230–33; dispossession of, 234, 240, 244; movements and resistance, 229, 234; struggles, 229, 277, 306
Pécoud, Antoine, 182
Perera, Suvendrini, 12–13
Peronism, 285
person, concept of, 260–63
Petty, William, 76–77
Pickles, John, 30, 236–37
planning, concept of, 46
Plato, 75
pluralism, legal, 198–200, 217–18, 294
point systems, 22, 138–41, 150
police regime, 254–55
Political Arithmetick (Petty), 76–77
political borders, 3, 49, 80, 292; frontiers of capital and, 66–67, 70–73, 76, 78
political economy: classical, 21, 35, 65, 70, 75, 78, 83; and division of labor, 59; Marx's critique of, 56, 66–67, 258
political geography, 5, 13, 39, 71
political organization, 98, 222, 253, 310; autonomous, 299, 302; of labor, 95; role of translation in, 270, 273, 308–9; of space, 15
political philosophy, 254, 256, 259, 268
political society, 151, 234
political subjectivity/subjects, 298; border struggles and, 13, 23–24, 66; of the citizen, 14, 21, 256–57; debate on, 252–54, 257; and struggles for the common, 25, 307, 311
population and people distinction, 173
populism, 285, 287
Portes, Alejandro, 162
ports, 205–7
Portugal, 78
possessive individualism, 295
postcolonialism: and capitalism, 2, 232–33;

critics and feminists of, 18, 106, 158, 275
postdevelopmental geographies, 15, 238–39, 242, 251
Potosí (Bolivia), 32–33, 56
power(s): of borders, 2, 195–96; China's economic, 220, 225, 227; Foucault on, 193–94, 204, 243; governmental, 168–69, 176–77, 188; individualizing, 194; knowledge and, 30, 43, 178–79, 195, 251; market, 215; Marx's references to, 192; pastoral, 195; political, 7, 77, 118, 188, 214, 221, 234; relations, 105, 159, 252, 288; soft, 209; technologies of, 193–94, 196–97; U.S. global, 41, 42, 219. *See also* assemblages of power; labor power; sovereign power
Prescott, John Robert Victor, 29
primitive accumulation, 37, 177, 192, 277; and accumulation of capital, 245; and capitalist expansion, 241–42, 244; by governmental reversal, 234–35; Harvey on, 246; in India, 229, 232, 234–35; Marx on, 32–34, 85, 241, 245; and modern cartography, 32–36, 66, 132; political spaces of, 208; slavery and, 56
Prison Notebooks (Gramsci), 44, 270–71
private property, 35; conversion of common land to, 295; Grotius's theory of, 291–92; and role of the state, 292–94
production: abstract elements of, 121; of the area form, 48; of the common, 25, 290, 298–300, 307, 310; cycle, 126–27; and exploitation, 213, 214; flow, 126–27; and Fordism, 43–44; global systems of, 96, 131; hidden abode of, 193, 196, 243; of illegality, 146, 150; industrial, 79, 82, 209, 223; of labor power, 20, 99, 107–8, 116, 120, 150, 310; mass, 103, 126; of new consumption, 67; noncapitalist modes of, 71, 302; ontological moment of, 35–36; shift or fragmentation of, 82–83; spatial and temporal dimensions of, 49, 54, 58, 68, 121, 229, 245; of the world, 42. *See also* capitalist production
production of subjectivity, 19, 44, 83, 154, 235, 253; from the articulation of class interests, 285; border struggles and, 20,

production of subjectivity (*cont.*)
183, 188, 264–67, 311; under capitalism, 252; and citizenship, 250, 258–59; division, 261; in emotional labor, 104, 109; and labor power, 110, 116, 193, 263, 270; and production of space, 54; role of boundaries in, 265; and technologies of power, 196; translation and, 272, 276, 278, 282
proletarianization, 220–21, 226
proletarian micro-economies, 240
proliferation of borders, 2–3, 6, 18, 27, 85, 123, 280; and border struggles, 265; elimination of, 268; of internal borders, 151, 225; multiplication of labor and, 125, 253; and organization of labor, 95; role of carers and financial traders in, 96; and social relations, 129
property: and personhood, 262; public, 294; rights, 294; of the self, 20. *See also* private property
Pun Ngai, 217, 228, 274; study on women factory workers, 84, 225–26

Quijano, Anibal, 74, 245

Rabinow, Paul, 174
racism, 53, 55, 249, 258; in France, 152–53; in labor markets, 73–74
Rafferty, Mike, 90
Rajan, Kaushik Sunder, 86–87
Rajarhat (India), 229, 231–35
Rancière, Jacques, 152, 255, 273; *Dis-Agreement*, 254
Ratzel, Friedrich, 39
Read, Jason, 252
Rediker, Marcus, 100, 274
reductionism, 286
refugees, 148, 174, 176, 189, 265; protection for, 143–44, 171; threat of illegalization of, 144–45
regime, concept of, 178–79. *See also* border regimes; labor regimes; migration regimes
regionalism: and area studies, 53–54; critical, 55–58; global, 23, 53, 219; new forms of, 96, 236
regional units, 53

Reich, Robert, 125
Renaissance thought, 31
repatriation, 146; corridors, 205–6
reterritorialization, 52, 302
Ricardo, David, 66, 78
riots: in France, 132, 153, 154; in Genoa, 10–11
Ritter, Carl, 38–39
Rocca, Jean-Louis, 223
Rodríguez, Nestor, 265
Rose, Nikolas, 174
Rostow, Walt Whitman, 46
Rousseau, Jean-Jacques, 35, 190
Ruccio, David, 300
Rudd, Kevin, 167
Ruggie, John Gerard, 178
Ruhs, Martin, 141
Rumbaut, Rubén G., 162

Sakai, Naoki, 36–37, 57, 284; homolingual and heterolingual concepts, 281–83; on translation, 272, 289–90, 308
Salazar Parreñas, Rhacel, 107
Samaddar, Ranabir, 47–51, 54
Sanyal, Kalyan, 46, 234
Sassen, Saskia, 3, 195, 256; on state sovereignty, 197–98, 202
Schily, Otto, 171
Schmitt, Carl, 70, 189, 198–99; *The Nomos of the Earth*, 4, 33
Schumann, Michael, 88
Sciortino, Giuseppe, 178–79
SEAsia, 205–6
sea trade, 77
semi-periphery concept, 18, 51, 64, 73–74
September 11, 2001, 7, 164
sexism, 73–74, 249
Shachar, Ayelet, 113, 140
Shadow Lines, The (Ghosh), 27–28, 37–38
Sharma, Nandita, 267–68
Shenzhen (Guangdong Province), 225–26
ships, 205, 207
Sidaway, James D., 238
Siegelbaum, Lewis H., 248
silver, 32–33
Silver, Beverly, 47, 72, 84, 86, 92
sisterhood, notions of, 106
16Beaver group, 52, 54

skilled and unskilled labor, 22–23, 136, 156; migration and mobility, 132, 137–39, 141

Slaughter, Anne-Marie, 219

slavery, 56–57; and concept of person, 262; language and translation in, 274–75; laws, 222, 262

Smith, Adam, 76, 78, 87

Smith, Neil, 43

social class, 98, 299

social relations: abstract, 10, 69, 121, 284; articulatory practice of, 285–86; borders and, 19, 265, 267, 279; of capital/capitalism, 70, 84, 99, 119, 279–82, 302, 310; and commodity form, 259; of community economies, 300; money as, 68; and power, 288; and sovereignty, 258; of translation, 281–83, 289, 308

social reproduction, 108, 117

social sciences, 14, 43, 133, 178, 201

"social synthesis," 124, 126–28

Société Réaliste, 36

societization, 125, 127, 129

sociology, 14, 98; classical, 69, 129; contributions to border concepts, 14

Sohn-Rethel, Alfred, 123–24, 126–29

solidarity, 91, 129, 248, 301; international, 96–97

Solomon, Jon, 36–37, 282

Songjiang Industrial Zone, 227–28

South Asia: area formation in, 48–49; geographical divisions, 38, 41; nationalism, 47–48

sovereign power, 150, 191, 215–16, 236; assemblage of power and, 195–96; exceptions, 148, 183; intervention, 169, 171; and law, 189; of SEZs, 218, 228; transformations of, 3, 190

sovereignty: Agamben's analysis of, 132, 189; and border control, 180, 201; and capital, 12, 202–3; and citizenship, 141, 173, 215; crisis of, 198; governmentality and, 188–90, 202–4, 212–17; gradating, 238; graduated, 24, 215–16, 238; imperial, 203, 208; intervention, 170–71; Israel's, 8; of money, 272; and private property, 293; of SEZs, 216, 218; state, 8, 52, 189, 197–98, 202, 293; and subjection, 258; theories and concepts, 188–89,

197; transformations of, 52, 189–90, 197–98, 201

space(s): ambiguous, 15, 208; articulations of, 209, 211, 236; borders as, 3–4, 133, 183, 188; bounded, 102, 129, 134, 159, 240; of citizenship, 7, 155, 256; of the common, 283, 299–300, 305; continental, 5, 304; domestic, 78; economic, 65–66, 73, 85–86, 234–35; European, 15–16, 34, 165, 181; of exception or exceptional, 220, 236; of flows, 210–11, 303; heterogeneous, 86, 129, 210, 223, 225, 236, 303; hierarchies of, 37, 64, 66, 86, 125, 225; of holding, 147; lateral, 126, 214–16, 232; mapping of, 33, 35–36, 38, 210; multiplication of, 238; of nation-states, 63, 163; political, 6, 52, 65, 208, 212, 303, 305–6; of power, 207; production of, 15, 49, 54, 58, 229; and scale, 244, 249, 308; of segregation, 151–52, 154; social, 13, 65, 96, 239, 255; temporal dimensions of, 131–33; transnational, 96, 107–8, 238, 240; of zones, 219, 241. See also global space; time and space relations

spatial fixes, 72

special economic zones (SEZs): in China, 9, 217, 224–26, 229–30; corporate involvement, 217–18; in India, 229–33; labor practices/regimes of, 24, 236; in Mae Sot–Myawaddy (near Thai border), 237–38; sovereignty of, 216, 218

Stakhanovites, 247–48

state, the: borders of, 5, 73, 211, 294; and capital relations, 5–6, 73, 77, 219, 310; citizen-worker and, 246–47; class influence on, 234; and the commons, 298–99; crisis of, 198; developmental, 46, 247; global democracy and, 304; Marx's definition of, 85; monopoly role of, 64, 197; nationalization of, 39–40; ontology of, 177; political philosophy and, 256; politics of, 189, 253; private property and, 292–94; time of, 225; transformations of, 197–98, 221, 256. See also nation-state; sovereignty

Steinfeld, Robert J., 101

Stoker, Gerry, 177

Stoler, Ann Laura, 194–95, 208

stowaways, 205–6

Strausz-Hupé, Robert, 41

student visas, 55, 140, 156–57

subjectivity, 84, 247, 258; bloc, 54; and borders, 267–68; of labor/workers, 84–85, 104, 110, 116, 121, 212; modern, 20; and power, 120, 204. *See also* political subjectivity/subjects; production of subjectivity

Sub-Saharan migrants, 170–71

supply chains, 228, 236

surplus, 298, 300; labor, 67, 244

surplus value, 243; absolute and relative, 67, 72, 88–89, 245

sweatshops, 214, 240–41

Tagore, Rabindranath, 41, 56

Tamil migrants, 167–68

Tampa incident (2001), 11–12

Taxi! Cabs and Capitalism in New York City (Mathew), 1

Taylorism, 87, 126

temporal borders: of *banlieues*, 152, 154; and citizenship, 155; concept, 133; detention and, 24, 148–50; of different generations, 156–57; and labor power, 138; of the nation-state, 157–59, 163, 165–66; and practices of benching, 136, 138; relation to territorial borders, 138–39; and skilled migration, 137

temporality: of migration, 132, 134, 143, 156–57, 188; of politics, 254; of space, 131–33

territorial division, 80, 85

territory, 196; delimiting or defining, 16, 238, 280; economic, 80; elasticity of, 8; empires and, 207–8; European, 181, 305; jurisdiction from, 91, 208, 263, 306; mapping of, 28–29; state, 195, 197, 292–93

Territory, Authority, Rights (Sassen), 197–98

Teubner, Gunther, 183–84, 187, 217–18; conflicts law, 200; global law theory, 185, 199–201

Thailand borders, 237–38

Thompson, E. P., 98, 100–101, 157

time and space relations, 101, 206, 278; of capital, 116, 132–33, 203, 225; compression, 233; heterogeneity of, 97, 223, 225;

of the nation-state, 158. *See also* space(s); temporality

Titley, Gavan, 164

trade unions, 97, 246–47

Transit Labor project, 212, 227–28, 231

translation: and border struggles, 21, 281, 307–8; and capital, 276, 281; of the common, 17, 275, 278, 283, 290–91, 301, 309; and creation of common language, 274–76; as a form of articulation, 289; homolingual and heterolingual modes of, 281–83, 298; labor of, 271, 273, 275–76, 310; and political organization, 270–71, 308–9; role of borders in, 272, 289; role of money in, 271–72; social practices of, 273–75; struggles, 17, 24–25, 271, 308–10; and subject in transit, 289; and translatability of languages, 9, 19, 270–72, 307

transnationalism, 52, 64, 107, 161

Traven, Bruno, 275–76

tricontinentalist scheme, 51

Triggs, Gillian D., 29

Tronti, Mario, 84–85, 127

Tsianos, Vassilis, 149, 178

Tsing, Anna, 120, 210–11, 228, 236

Turner, Bryan, 250

United Nations (UN), 11, 168, 175, 304; Foucault's address to, 169–70; High Commissioner of Refugees (UNHCR), 171, 182

United States: citizen-worker, 248–49; debt crisis, 295; as a global power, 41–42, 219; hegemony, 199; immigration law, 145; imperialism, 208; industrial production, 45, 247; Mexican migration, 145; occupation of Japan, 45; relationship with India, 86–87; slave laws, 262; universalism, 57–58; working class, 97

unity: of the border regime, 179, 181; of capital, 23, 123, 129, 302; concepts, 95, 123, 130; governmentality and, 188; multiplicity and, 124, 275, 311; of the multitude, 253; of the universal, 290–91; working-class, 128, 160

universalism, 58, 73; claim to unity, 290–91; and the common, 289–90; and particularism, 57, 287–89, 291

U.S.–Mexico border, 3, 6–7, 236; control and policing, 53, 145, 147

value: autonomization of, 69; exchange, 36, 261, 272, 281; of labor, 128, 134–36; production of, 127, 135, 228, 245. *See also* surplus value
van der Linden, Marcel, 85
Vercellone, Carlo, 137–39
Vico, Giambattista, 293
Vila, Pablo, 3, 175
Villacañas Berlanga, José Luis, 288
Viner, Jacob, 79
Virno, Paolo, 252, 290
virtual migration, 20, 131, 231, 233

wage labor, 46, 248, 262; "free," 56, 81, 85, 110
Walker, Gavin, 32, 33–34
Wallerstein, Immanuel, 73–74
Walters, William, 173, 187, 195, 197, 205
Wang Hui, 213, 221–22, 304
Weber, Max, 70
Weeks, Kathi, 104, 109
Weizman, Eyal, 8, 12
Westphalia, 6, 32, 133, 207; Treaty of, 77, 190
Wigen, Kären E., 27
Winichakul, Thongchai, 35, 37
working class, 44–45, 99, 255, 311; changing composition of, 252; industrial, 100–101; unity, 128, 160; U.S., 97

world, pattern of the, 38–43, 51, 59, 101
"World Flag Ant Farm" (Yanagi), 61–62
world history, 37, 39
world market, 85, 92, 132; abstract dimension of, 68–69, 72; emergence of, 75–76; Marx's analysis of, 67–69, 71, 77, 88, 132, 280
world regions, 41–43, 51; binary divisions, 63–64; continental blocs, 52–53, 55, 209. *See also* area studies
world system theory, 18, 51, 64, 70, 73–74, 81
Wright, Cynthia, 267–68

Xenophon, 75
Xiang Biao, 135–36, 139, 172–73

Yanagi, Yukinori, 61–63
"yellow Asia," 57
Yu Zhou, 223–24

Zaloom, Caitlin, 113, 117
Zhongguancun (Beijing), 223–24, 228
Zhou, Min, 162
Žižek, Slavoj, 254, 300
zones, 209, 225, 305; holding, 147–48, 207; production, 12, 212, 217–18, 227–28; proliferation of, 208; as spaces, 219, 236; temporal, 149–50. *See also* special economic zones (SEZs)
zoning technologies, 203, 210, 216–17